Jon E. Lewis is a writer and h
include *The Mammoth Book of*
An Anthology, *The Mammoth B*
Book of True War Stories, *The M*
New Rights of Man, *The Mammoth Book of Endurance and Adventure*, *The Mammoth Book of Polar Journeys* and *The Mammoth Book of How It Happened*.

Also available

The Mammoth Book of

ADVENTURES ON THE EDGE

Epic Accounts of Triumph and Tragedy
on the Mountains

Edited and with an Introduction by
JON E. LEWIS

ROBINSON

RUNNING PRESS
PHILADELPHIA · LONDON

Constable & Robinson Ltd
3 The Lanchesters
162 Fulham Palace Road
London W6 9ER
www.constablerobinson.com

First published in the UK as *The Mammoth Book of Climbing Adventures*, 2001 and
The Mammoth Book of The Edge,
by Constable & Robinson, 2003.
This revised and updated edition published by Robinson,
an imprint of Constable & Robinson, 2009

Copyright © Jon E. Lewis, 2009 (unless otherwise indicated)

The right of Jon E. Lewis to be identified as the author of this work has been
asserted by him in accordance with the Copyright, Designs & Patents Act 1988.

A copy of the British Library Cataloguing in Publication
Data is available from the British Library

UK ISBN 978-1-84529-924-8

1 3 5 7 9 10 8 6 4 2

First published in the United States in 2009 by
Running Press Book Publishers

US Library of Congress number: 2008940990
US ISBN 978-0-7624-3632-3

Running Press Book Publishers
2300 Chestnut Street
Philadelphia, PA 19103-4371
www.runningpress.com

Visit us on the web!

www.runningpress.com

Printed and bound in the EU

"Well, we knocked the bastard off"
                                Edmund Hillary, 1953

"Have we vanquished an enemy? None but ourselves"
                                George Mallory

Contents

Introduction

There is, of course, nothing new about climbing mountains. Humankind has probably scrambled up slopes and along ridges since they took to two legs way back in the African dawn. Doubtless these early ventures were prompted by needs of warfare, of hunting, of exploration and colonization, but it is tempting to think that some ancestral *homo sapiens sapiens* reached the top simply because the mountain "was there".

As an organized sport, however, mountaineering is an entirely modern phenomenon and owes much to de Saussure's reward, offered in 1760, to the first person to conquer Mont Blanc. This was not achieved until 1786, when Balmat and Paccard reached the top, followed by de Saussure himself a year later. Within a century, Mont Blanc and the Alps were crawling with advocates of the new sport of mountaineering, the Alpine Club had been formed, and Edward Whymper had become the pursuit's first bonafide star, a celestial ranking he ensured by his 1865 ascent of the Matterhorn. And like many a climber after him, Whymper was no mean hand with a pen as well as a piton. Mountaineering literature may not have begun with Whymper but his *Scrambles amongst the Alps*, 1871, defined and established the form like little else.

It was perhaps inevitable that climbers, having scaled the major peaks of the Alps, should turn their eyes ever higher, to the Andes, the Caucasus and most of all to the Himalayas, where taunted the giants, Kanchenjunga, Nanga Parbat,

Annapurna, K2 and greatest of all, Everest (88,48m/29,028 ft). The first serious attempt on Everest came in 1922 but it was the tragedy of Mallory and Irvine, who disappeared almost within grasp of the top, in 1934 that elevated that lofty peak into legend. Everest was finally summitted in 1953 by Edmund Hillary and Tenzing Norgay. Summitted but not beaten. Scores of climbers since have been thrown off Everest's white walls to their death. Nature is only subdued for the moment, never mastered. Which is part of the allure of mountaineering. If Nature wasn't dangerous, mountaineering wouldn't be exciting, neither for those that do it nor for those who like their dangers experienced vicariously from the safety of the armchair.

The world's biggest mountain may have been conquered in 1953, but mountaineering itself had far from peaked. There are always fresh challenges, new routes, even in some remote corners unclimbed summits. And new ways of doing things. Over the last half century, the fashion in mountaineering has been towards "alpine style" lightly equipped fast assaults, exemplified by Reinhold Messner's solo, oxygen-less assault on Everest in 1980. This singular achievement required athleticism of the highest order; there is little doubt that the late 20th century, early 21st century climber is pushing harder against the limits of the body than his or her predecessors. There is equally little doubt that mountaineering today takes what it has always taken: courage, the ability to endure. And the triumph of the mind.

It is a curious fact, I think, that the real beauty, drama and interest of mountaineering is not the mountains themselves, not even the physical aspect of their conquest but what goes on in the mind of the men and women who climb the far peaks.

No one sees further, clearer, deeper than those whose life is hanging by fingertips on the edge of the abyss.

Thus the selections on the following pages, eyewitness accounts of epic exploits by some of the world's greatest climbers, make up a book of high adventure and of philosophy too. It only helps that the more epic and dangerous the recounted exploit, the better the writing, the more nerve-wracking the read, the bigger the illumination of the human soul.

What more could you want?

Glossary

A
abseil   descent of rock face by sliding down a rope
arete   sharp rock or ridge

B
bergschrund   the gap between a glacier and upper face

C
col   a pass
cornice   protuding mass of snow
couloir   open gully
crevasse   crack or gap
cwm   valley or rounded hollow in valley formed by glacial action

J
jumar   friction device to aid climbers ascending fixed ropes

M
moraine   loose stone

N
neve   bed of frozen snow

S
serac   pinnacle of ice, usually unstable

Ladder Down the Sky

Robert Bates

Bates was a member of the 1953 American expedition to K2 (Trans-Himalaya), at 8,611 m (28,261 ft) the second highest mountain in the world. A ten day storm foiled the summit bid and when Art Gilkey developed thrombophlebitis his comrades determined to lower him down from Camp VIII on the Abruzzi Ridge. The weather notwithstanding.

We all knew now that some of us might never get down the mountain alive. Each had long recognized the near impossibility of evacuating an injured man from the upper ledges of K2. We had told one another that "if somebody broke a leg, you never could get him down the mountain," but now that we were faced with Gilkey's helplessness, we realized that we *had* to get him down. We didn't know how, but we knew that we had to do it.

Schoening in particular, and also Bob Craig and Dec Molenaar, had done a lot of mountain rescue work, and the rest of us placed great confidence in their faith that somehow we could get our casualty to Base Camp. Gilkey's high morale and his confidence in us was a great boost to our spirits and we faced the job ahead with strong determination. When on the morning of August 10th Charlie Houston thrust his shoulders through the tunnel entrance of the tent where Schoening, Streather and I, shoulder rubbing shoulder, had tossed during the long night hours, we spoke almost in unison: "How is he?"

"We've got to take him down," said the doctor. "His other leg has a clot now and he can't last long *here*."

The wind was hammering the tent fabric so hard that we had to yell at one another. Drifts of fine powder snow were sifting in through a strained seam in the tent vestibule, though we had done our best to keep the shelter airtight, and we could feel the whole tent vibrate as gusts stretched the fabric to the utmost.

"What? Move in this storm?" said someone.

"We've got to," said Houston. "He'll soon be dead if we don't get him down."

Nothing needed saying after that, for we knew what this decision meant. All of us had fought mountain storms before, but we had never seen anything like the duration and violence of this furious wind and snow that was still battering us. We all knew the story of the storm on Nanga Parbat in 1934, when nine members of a German expedition had died of exhaustion while battling the wind and snow. Willy Merkl, Uli Wieland and Willi Welzenback had been famous mountaineers, but a storm had exhausted them and killed them one by one. Here on K2 we had not only the storm to fight but the steepest part of the mountain, and we were trying to bring down these precipitous slopes a crippled companion as well!

We all realized that our adventure had now become grim, for the odds against getting Art down were obvious, and our own position was getting more critical all the time. While Houston and Schoening were easing Art out of his tent into the storm, the rest of us began packing light loads to take down. We would need one tent in case of emergency, and we took the Gerry tent, our lightest one. We also might need a stove and pot, and some meat bars, chocolate, or quick-energy food that needed no cooking. Often the effects of altitude so weaken one's determination that doing nothing becomes a positive pleasure, but this was no time for lethargy, and as we moved purposefully out of the tents into the stinging blasts of snow, we knew that we had to move fast, while fingers and toes still had feeling. Little was spoken. Each of us realized that he was beginning the most dangerous day's work of his lifetime.

Gilkey seemed in no pain as we wrapped him in the smashed tent, put his feet in a rucksack, and tied nylon ropes to him in such a way that they cradled him. Four ropes, tied to this cradle, could be held by one man ahead, one man behind, and one on either side. We had already put on all our warm clothing – sweaters, wool jackets, down jackets and nylon parkas – and stripped our packs to the minimum. As we worked, the disabled man watched the preparations silently. He was an experienced mountaineer and realized what all of us were up against. But he knew also that we would never leave him, and that we would bring him down safely if it were humanly possible. Art's cap was pulled down over his face, which looked drawn and bluish-grey, but he gave a wan smile whenever someone asked, "How is it going?"

"Just fine," he would say. "Just fine." And his mouth would smile. He never showed a moment's fear or the slightest lack of confidence, but he realized of course that he had been stricken by something that was likely to be fatal, that his condition was getting worse, and that he was 9,000ft above Base Camp in a terrible monsoon storm. The nearest tent, at Camp VI, was 2,000 ft below. He knew that we could not carry him down the tricky route we had come up, and that we must go only where we could lower him. Even in perfect weather with all men in top physical condition, the task might prove impossible – yet Art Gilkey could smile, and his smile gave us strength.

While we were adjusting the tow ropes, Schoening and Molenaar strapped on their crampons and disappeared into the storm. They were to find the best route past the dangerous avalanche slope that had blocked us a few days before, and to go over to the Camp VII cache to get a climbing rope that was strung on the ice slope just above. It would be useful in the descent. After their departure Houston called Base Camp on the walkie-talkie and told Ata-Ullah our plans. "It's pretty desperate, Ata," he said grimly, "but we can't wait. We're starting down now. We'll call you at three o'clock."

Each man took his place on a rope tied to Gilkey and for a couple of hundred yards we lunged hard at the tow ropes to pull Art through the knee-deep drifts of powder snow; then gravity took over and we had to hold back just as strongly to keep our helpless 185-pound load from plunging into the abyss. The steep slope we were on disappeared below us into nothingness. Was there a cliff there, a jumping-off place? We strained our eyes peering into the storm, but we could not wait for clearing weather. Instead we had to depend on Schoening and Molenaar, who had gone ahead to scout out the way. As we descended, Craig and Bell pulled the front ropes, one on each side, and Houston directed operations from a point immediately behind Gilkey, while Streather and I anchored the rope higher up. Gradually we worked our way to a rock ridge, climbed down alongside it, and then began to lower Gilkey down a steep snow slope leading to a snow chute and an ice gully below. This route was not the one we would have taken had Gilkey been able to walk, but now we had no choice: we could go only where we could lower our companion, and we had faith that the two men ahead would find a route down. Once we were well started, return to Camp VIII would be impossible for any of us.

The wind and cold seeped insidiously through our layers of warm clothing so that by the end of the third hour none of us had feeling in his toes any longer, and grotesque icicles hung from our eyebrows, beards and moustaches. Goggles froze over and we continually raised them on our foreheads in order to see how to handle the rope. Moving the sick man was frightfully slow. We had to belay one another as well as Gilkey, and our numb fingers would not move quickly. Somehow, when we got to the steepest pitch, however, someone managed to tie two 120-foot nylon ropes together and we started to lower Gilkey down, down in the only direction the slope would permit. Houston and I, braced on the storm-swept ridge, backs to the wind, could feel the terrible gusts trying to hurl us off the rocks. We could not see where we were lowering Art, but we could hear faint shouts from Schoening and Molenaar, who were out of sight below. As we slowly paid out the coils of rope, thankful that they were of nylon and would not freeze in kinks, Bob Craig unroped from us and climbed down alongside the injured man to direct the descent. Soon he was completely obscured, too, but Streather climbed down to where he could see Craig's arm signals, yet still see us, and so we belayers had communication with Craig and Gilkey and knew whether to lower or to hold the rope. Alternatively we anchored and paid out line until we were nearly frozen, and our arms were strained when Tony Streather, whom we could barely see, turned and shouted, "Hold tight! They're being carried down in an avalanche!"

We held. Our anchorage was good and the rope stretched taut. For a moment snow flurries blotted out everything, and then we could hear a muffled shout from Streather. "They're still there!" The rope had broken loose a wind-slab avalanche of powder snow that had roared down over both men, blotting them from sight. Craig clung to the rope to Gilkey, and held on to it for his life. The pull of the hissing particles must have been terrible, but the avalanche was of unconsolidated snow. The falling powder slithered out of sight and down off the side of the mountain, where it must have kept falling long after we could hear it. When it was gone, Craig still clung to the rope, grey and very chilled. Both men were safe. The grim descent continued.

Schoening and Molenaar, who were not far from Camp VII, soon were able to reach Gilkey, but it seemed like hours to the four of us on the icy rocks of the wind-swept ridge before they shouted up that they had him strongly belayed "on the edge of a cliff," and we could climb down. Stiffly we shifted from our frozen positions, and climbed clumsily down the steep, crumbly rocks to the snow chute above the ice gully. Houston and I were on one rope, Bell and Streather on the other. All were so cold, so near exhaustion, that moving down over dangerous, snow covered ice stretched us to the limit. Through the murk of blowing snow we saw Schoening standing in front of a large, rounded rock that had become frozen on to a narrow ledge. His ice-axe was thrust deep into the snow above the rock and the rope with which he held Art Gilkey was looped tightly around the shaft of the axe. The sick man was at the edge of a 20-foot cliff, beneath which we could glimpse the ice gully dropping off steeply into the storm toward the Godwin-Austen Glacier nearly two miles below.

Schoening looked like a man from another world. So much frost had formed on our beards that faces were unrecognizable, and we knew that we were fast reaching the breaking point. We could not continue much longer without shelter from the driving storm and food to renew our energy. Some 150 yards below us to the east was the tiny shelf, at 24,500 ft, nicked into the ice slope, where Schoening and Gilkey had spent the night of July 30th during their reconnaissance above Camp VI. We had called it Camp VII or Camp VII cache. None of us had expected anyone to spend another night there, but Bob Craig, whose struggle against the avalanche had so completely exhausted him temporarily that he could hardly tie a crampon strap, had been belayed over to this site to rest and clear some of the avalanche snow that had seeped under his parka. We yelled to him to try to enlarge the ledge. Meanwhile, with Schoening anchoring the rope, we lowered Gilkey slowly over the short rock cliff until he was resting against the forty-five degree ice slope. Streather, who was roped to Bell, climbed down to Gilkey. Schoening held Gilkey's rope firmly while Houston belayed me across a delicate pitch of steep, hard ice and then Houston climbed down to a point opposite the man suspended against the slope. The problem now was not to get Gilkey down, but to swing him across the steep ice slope to the ice shelf at Camp VII. Our plan was to get a firm anchorage and then pendulum him across, but unfortunately the ice near him was too hard for axes to be driven in and the slope was relentlessly steep.

Even during the best weather conditions the manoeuvre would have been dangerous, and our position at that moment I shall never forget. Schoening was belaying Gilkey, who hung 60 feet below him, suspended against the sharply angled ice. On the same level as Gilkey, and forty feet across from him, five of us, facing into the stinging, drifting snow, were searching for a place where we could stand and anchor the rope to Gilkey as we pulled him across the ice in the direction of Craig on the ice shelf. With our spiked crampons biting the hard ice, Streather, Houston, Molenaar and I stood close together. Bell and Streather were roped together, Houston and I were on a rope together – and Molenaar had just "tied in" to a loose rope to Gilkey. He had done this when Craig had unroped and gone over to the ice shelf to rest, and it was Molenaar's precaution that saved us all, for George Bell, who was some 60 feet above us, began to descend a delicate stretch of hard ice in order to help with Gilkey's ropes. At that moment, what we had all been dreading occurred. Something threw Bell off balance and he fell.

I never saw Bell fall, but to my horror I saw Streather being dragged off the slope and making desperate efforts to jam the pick of his axe into the ice and stop. Streather had been standing above the rope from Houston to me. In almost the same instant I saw Houston swept off, and though I turned and lunged at the hard ice with the point of my axe, a terrible jerk ripped me from my hold and threw me backward headfirst down the slope. *This is it!* I thought as I landed heavily on my pack. There was nothing I could do now. We had done our best, but our best wasn't good enough. This was the end. Since nobody was on the rope with Houston and me, there was no one else to hold us, and I knew that nothing could stop us now. On the slope below, no rock jutted on which the rope between us could catch. Only thousands of feet of empty space separated us from the glacier below. It was like falling off a slanting Empire State Building six times as high as the real one.

Thrown violently backward, with the hood of my down jacket jammed over my eyes, I had a feeling of unreality, of detachment. The future was beyond my control. All I knew was that I landed on my pack with great force, bouncing faster and faster, bumping over rocks in great thumps. The next bound I expected to take me over a cliff in a terrible drop that would finish it all, when, by a miracle, I stopped sliding.

I was on my back with my hood over my eyes and my head a yard below my feet. My arms, stretched over my head, were so completely tangled with the taut rope that I could not loosen them. I was helpless, and when I tried to move, I realized that I was balanced on the crest of some rocks and that a change of position might throw me off the edge. The rope had apparently snagged on a projection – though how and where I couldn't imagine – but it might not be securely caught. Whether it was firmly held, whether anyone else was alive, I did not know, but I didn't need to wait. Almost immediately I heard a groan coming from nearly on top of me. "Get me loose," I called, and immediately I felt the pressure of a leg braced against my shoulder and the rope was pulled off my arms.

Grabbing a rock, I swung my head around. Dee Molenaar and I were clinging to a rocky outcrop at the side of a steep ice slope, studded with rocks, about 150 to 200 ft below the place

where we had been working on the ropes to Gilkey. Blood from
Dee's nose trickled across his moustache and beard, and he
looked badly shaken. My rope was tight to someone or something above, and I heard a distant yell, "Get your weight off
that rope!" Fifty feet higher, through a mist of blowing snow, I
could see Tony Streather staggering to his feet, a tangle of ropes
still tight about his waist. Below me I heard a cry, "My hands
are freezing!" and, looking down, to my amazement, I saw
George Bell, who seconds before had been sixty feet above me.
Now about sixty feet *below*, he was climbing up over the edge of
nothingness. He wore neither pack nor glasses and was staggering up over the steep rocks, obviously dazed, with his hands
held out grotesquely in front of him. His mittens had been
ripped off in the fall, and already the colour of his hands had
turned an ugly fish-belly white. If his hands were badly frozen,
of course, we might never be able to get him down off the
mountain.

Turning to Molenaar, I thrust my pack into his arms. Most of
the lashing had ripped loose and the walkie-talkie radio, which
had been on rope, was gone; my sleeping bag was half off, held
by a single twist of line. Without sleeping bags we were unlikely
to survive the night, no matter how we tried! Since Molenaar
wore no pack, I imagined that his sleeping bag also had been
torn off in the fall. Whether or not the tent someone had been
carrying had survived the fall, I didn't know. "For God's sake,
hold this," I yelled above the wind, placing my load in Molenaar's arms. (For all I knew, mine was the only sleeping bag to
survive the fall and we must not lose it now.) The loose pack was
awkward to hold securely while we were standing on such steep
rock, but Molenaar grasped it and I unroped and started to
climb shakily down to meet Bell. As I climbed down, I wondered about the ropes that had saved us. They were snagged to
something up above, but the driving snow kept us from seeing
what was holding them. Luckily I had a spare pair of dry,
loosely woven Indian mitts in the pouch pocket of my parka,
and when I reached Bell, whose face was grey and haggard, I
helped him to put them on. Already his fingers were so stiff with
cold that he couldn't move them, but balancing on projections
of rock on the steep slope, we struggled to save his hands and

finally forced the big white mittens past his stiff thumbs and down over his wrists.

Bell's fall had ended with him suspended over the edge of a ledge, below which the slope dropped away precipitously for thousands of feet. The weight of his pack pulled his head down, and he had lost it while trying to get right side up and back over the ledge. While Bell crouched down, working desperately to warm his hands under his parka, I left him, for Molenaar and I had seen a crumpled figure lying below a 30-foot cliff on a narrow shelf that seemed projecting over utter blankness below. It was Houston. Somehow a rope to him was snagged high above us, too. Climbing unsteadily but cautiously, for I was not roped and felt shaken by the fall, I worked my way down the steep rocks and across to the ledge. Houston was unconscious, but his eyes opened as I touched his shoulder. When he staggered to his feet, I felt relief it is impossible to describe.

"Where are we?" he asked. "What are we doing here?"

He was obviously hurt. His eyes did not focus and he appeared to be suffering from a concussion. Again and again I tried to persuade him to climb up the cliff, while Molenaar anchored the rope still attached to him from above. He didn't understand. "Where are we?" he kept saying, for my replies did not convey any meaning to him in his confused state.

The wind and blowing snow were searing our faces. We were all near exhaustion and in danger of crippling frost-bite. If we were to survive, we had to get shelter at once, or we would be so numbed by exposure that we could not protect ourselves. What had happened in the Nanga Parbat storm which had taken so many men was a grim reminder. All of us working together did not now have strength enough to pull or carry Houston up the steep rock and snow to the ice ledge, 150 ft above, which we had called Camp VII.

"Charlie," I said with the greatest intensity, remembering the names of his wife and daughter, and looking directly into his eyes, "if you ever want to see Dorcas and Penny again, climb up there *right now*!"

Somehow this demand penetrated to his brain, for with a frightened look and without a word, he turned and, belayed by Molenaar, fairly swarmed up the snowy rocks of the cliff.

Instinct and years of climbing helped him now in his confused condition, for he climbed brilliantly up to Molenaar. I followed more slowly because, being fully conscious, I had a good deal of respect for this steep rock wall, and with great care I pulled myself up over the snow covered slabs. When I reached Molenaar, he was looking puzzled and very unhappy as he tried to answer Houston's repeated question, "What are we doing here?"

When I reached Molenaar, I still did not know what had caused the near disaster or how all five of us who fell had been saved. Up above, through the murk of blinding snow, I caught glimpses of Art Gilkey, anchored where he had been before the fall, but now Bob Craig was near him. Tony Streather, in a direct line above me, seemed to be untangling himself from a confused snarl of nylon climbing ropes, one of which led down to me.

Much later I learned the sequence of events that had put us in this position and marvelled even more at our escape. When Bell fell, he pulled off Streather, who was hurled into the rope between Houston and me and became entangled with it. We were in turn knocked off by the impact, and all three of us – Streather, Houston and I – began tumbling in a blind, uncontrolled whirl toward the glacier far below. Nothing we could do could stop us now. But our time had not come. For Molenaar was standing below us on the slope, farther away from the sick man, and he had just tied one of the loose ropes from Art Gilkey about his waist. That circumstance saved us, for our wild fall sent us all into and across the rope from Gilkey to Molenaar, and somehow Streather fouled on to this rope too. But our impact had thrown Molenaar head-first down the slope, and we all bounded on unchecked until stopped by the tightening of the rope from Gilkey to Molenaar – a rope in which Streather was now completely tangled. Gilkey was not pulled loose, for he was anchored by Schoening, who stood on a rock ledge 60 feet above him, and the whole strain of the five falling men, plus Gilkey, was transmitted to Schoening, the youngest member of the party. Fortunately for us all, Schoening is an expert belayer, and his skill and quick thinking saved our lives. Later he told us how he did it.

By the time I returned to Molenaar and Houston, it was clear that through some miracle every climber was still able to move under his own power, but our exposure to the wind-driven snow was chilling us dangerously; we had to move fast to take shelter before we became too numb to set up a tent or became so crippled by frost-bite that we would never be able to continue the descent. Since Molenaar's leg hurt and he didn't feel like moving much, I took Charlie Houston's rope and began climbing slowly up toward the ice ledge at Camp VII. I couldn't hurry to save my life. Houston was obviously confused, but by instinct he climbed well and did what was asked. I hadn't climbed far when Tony Streather threw me a rope-end, and then Bob Craig returned from anchoring Art Gilkey and he and Streather took over the task of escorting Houston to the ledge. Craig had not seen the fall, but had looked up suddenly and been horrified to see the slope bare except for Schoening and Gilkey and a solitary ice-axe with its pick end jabbed into the ice. At that moment a cloud of snow had blown across the ice, blotting out everything. When it cleared, Schoening, whose tight grip on the rope was freezing his hands, called to Craig to help him to anchor Gilkey. The sick man had not fallen, and he lay suspended against the ice as he had been at the time of the accident. He was probably the warmest of us all, but we could not continue to move him until the injured were cared for and we had more manpower to help get him across the slope.

When Craig reached him, Art handed over his ice-axe, which he had retained for use in the descent. To make a secure anchorage was not easy, and Craig, still exhausted from his struggle against the avalanche, was not secured by anyone while he did it, but he skilfully found firm snow and drove in Art's ice-axe right up to the head. He told the sick man that we would return for him as soon as we had a tent up. Gilkey understood. Not until then, when Craig had an ice-axe firmly embedded, could Pete Schoening release his grip – which had held six men! – and begin to warm his freezing hands. Craig had not been involved in the accident, but all the rest of us owed our lives to Schoening's skill, courage and technique.

Fortunately the tent had not been in one of the lost packs, but as I started to unroll it, the wind threatened to sweep it off the mountain. Craig and I were trying to wrestle the corners of the tent into position when Streather, who had now anchored Gilkey with a second ice-axe, joined us to help pin the flapping edges under loose rocks till we could get anchorage for the guy ropes. The slope was so steep that the outer third of the tent was off the ledge and overhanging, so that it was impossible to keep the wind from sucking under the tent and trying to tear it away.

We were fortunate that this was our smallest two-man tent, for it held the ledge better than a wider one. Actually, in Exeter before the expedition, we had thought it too small for two men and had almost failed to bring it. Pitching the tent was frustrating, for each time we would secure one corner, another corner would shudder loose. Finally we tied the front guy rope to a rock piton and lashed the inside corners as well as we could to projecting rocks. When Bob Craig later pounded in a Bernays ice-piton, we felt somewhat safer, though the nylon shroud line attached to it didn't look too strong and the outer section of the tent bulged out over the slope. If someone inside forgot how precariously the tent was poised and leaned against the outer wall, we knew that the fabric would probably tear or the whole tent pull loose from the little ledge, and with everyone in it roll down the mountain into space.

The moment the tent was up, we moved Bell and Houston inside, where they would be under shelter and their weight would be useful in anchoring the tent. Molenaar at this point joined them to help take care of Houston, for Dee by now had lashed my loose pack together and carried it to the ledge. His left thigh hurt and he had a cracked rib.

While these men were trying to warm themselves in the tent, the rest of us began to hack out another platform in the ice for Schoening's bivouac tent, which had previously been cached on the ledge as a safeguard for Streather and me on the day when we climbed from Camp VI to Camp VIII. This tent was meant for one person or in any emergency two, but if we could get it up, we meant to use it for three men to huddle inside.

At this moment Peter Schoening climbed down to us and declared laconically, "My hands are freezing." He too crawled into the tent to try to save his hands. All of us were still too busy to find out how Schoening had held us, for it seemed as if we would never get a platform flat enough or wide enough to pitch the bivouac tent. All our strength and energy went into chipping out an ice platform, for we had to get shelter from the bitter blast for everyone; but when we did get an uneven floor carved out, the wind whipped the fabric violently. It was like working in the slipstream behind an airplane as it taxied across the snow, spraying stinging particles behind. Finally Pete crawled out to help us insert the poles and we fastened the tent insecurely to rócks and pitons near the shelf of ice. It, too, overhung in an alarming manner.

The moment the bivouac tent was up, three of us prepared to go back for Art Gilkey. He was only 150 ft away, but a low rib of rock hid from sight the ice gully where we had left him suspended from the two widely separated ice-axes, each firmly thrust into the snow. Gilkey had called to us a couple of times while we were desperately hacking at the slope to make a platform for the bivouac tents, but the severity of the storm and the position of the gully made it impossible to distinguish words. Gilkey sounded as if he were shouting encouragement, but the wind blurred his words, as it must have muffled our answering shouts to him. He knew that we were making a shelter and would come for him as soon as we could.

About ten minutes after Gilkey's last shout, Streather, Craig and I roped up and began to cross the slope to reach the injured man and move him somehow to the ice ledge where we now had two small tents. We knew that moving him even this short distance would take every bit of strength we had left, and we roped together carefully and braced ourselves for the effort.

Schoening would have come with us, but as he emerged from the tent, he began a fit of coughing so long and painful that it doubled him up and made us urge him to crawl back into the tent. Pete had gulped in deep draughts of frigid air while climbing up to collect the fixed rope above Camp VII earlier in the day, and apparently the cold had somehow temporarily affected his lungs. He coughed until he seemed exhausted. At the moment we were particularly dismayed by Schoening's near collapse, because he had always been strong and we were counting heavily on him to help in moving Gilkey and in getting the party down the mountain. We didn't know at the moment what his trouble was or how serious it might be, and in great distress we started out into the wind to traverse the slope to Art Gilkey. Streather and I had had our snow glasses off most of the day, because snow had frozen over the lenses, turning them almost to blinders. Apparently we had developed a touch of snow blindness, because we now seemed to be seeing everything through a very light mist. This mist was hard to distinguish from blowing snow, and we seemed to be moving in a dream. Fortunately, the wind had dropped as we reached the rock rib and looked into the gully where Art had been left suspended. What we saw there I shall never forget. The whole slope was bare of life. Art Gilkey had gone!

Our sick comrade, who had called to us a few minutes before, had disappeared. Even the two ice-axes used to anchor him safely had been torn loose. The white, wind-swept ice against which he had been resting showed no sign that anyone had ever been there. It was as if the hand of God had swept him away.

The shock stunned us. Blowing snow stung our faces as we silently stared and stared, but the slope remained empty. Something about it had changed, however, for there seemed to be a groove on the lower part of the slope that had not been there before. A snow or ice avalanche must have swept the sick man away scant minutes before we came to get him. As Craig and I belayed Streather out on to the centre of the gully, he looked down past his cramponed feet to where the slope disappeared into the storm below. We called and shouted, but all of us knew that there would be no answer. Nobody could slide off that slope out of sight and remain alive. Dazed and incredulous, we turned and plodded back to the tents.

Triumph and Tragedy on the Matterhorn

Edward Whymper

A London wood-engraver, Whymper first went to the Alps as an illustrator for the publisher W. Longman. Once there, however, he determined to become a climber (he had no previous climbing experience) and ambitiously concentrated on untrodden Alpine peaks. The most prestigious of these was the Matterhorn at 4,477 m (14,782 ft) and from 1861 onwards Whymper made no less than seven attempts on the mountain until it finally succumbed to him in 1865 from the Swiss side.

Accompanying Whymper was Lord Francis Douglas and the guide Young Peter Taugwalder. Through chance meetings, the party had grown to include the guides Old Peter Taugwalder and Michel-Auguste Croz, together with the mountaineer Charles Hudson and his inexperienced companion Hadow. Whymper's account of the climb, and its tragic denouement, begins with the party at 3,352 m (11,000 ft), preparing to make their summit bid.

We assembled together outside the tent before dawn on the morning of July 14th, and started directly it was light enough to move. Young Peter came on with us as a guide, and his brother returned to Zermatt. We followed the route which had been taken on the previous day, and in a few minutes turned the rib which had intercepted the view of the eastern face from our tent platform. The whole of this great slope was now revealed, rising for 3,000 ft like a huge natural staircase. Some parts were more, and others were less, easy; but we were not once brought to a halt by any serious impediment, for when an obstruction was met in front it could always be turned to the right or to the left. For the greater part of the way there was, indeed, no occasion for the rope, and sometimes Hudson led, sometimes myself. At 6.20 we had attained a height of 12,800 ft, and halted for half an hour; we then continued the ascent without a break until 9.55, when we stopped for fifty minutes, at a height of 14,000 ft. Twice we struck the NE ridge, and followed it for some little distance – to no advantage, for it was usually more rotten and steep, and always more difficult, than the face. Still, we kept near to it, lest stones perchance might fall.

We had now arrived at the foot of that part which, from the Riffelberg or from Zermatt, seems perpendicular or overhanging, and could no longer continue upon the eastern side. For a little distance we ascended by snow upon the arete – that is, the ridge – descending towards Zermatt, and then, by common consent, turned over to the right, or to the northern side. Before doing so, we made a change in the order of ascent. Croz went first, I followed, Hudson came third; Hadow and old Peter were last. "Now," said Croz, as he led off, "now for something altogether different." The work became difficult, and required caution. In some places there was little to hold, and it was desirable that those should be in front who were least likely to slip. The general slope of the mountain at this part was *less* than forty degrees, and snow had accumulated in, and had filled up, the interstices of the rock-face, leaving only occasional fragments projecting here and there. These were at times covered with a thin film of ice, produced from the melting and refreezing of the snow. It was the counterpart, on a small scale, of the upper 700 ft of the Pointe des Ecrins – only there was this material difference; the face of the Ecrins was about, or exceeded, an angle of fifty degrees, and the Matterhorn face was less than forty degrees. It was a place over which any fair mountaineer might pass in safety, and Mr Hudson ascended this part, and, as far as I know, the entire mountain, without having the slightest assistance rendered to him upon any occasion. Sometimes, after I had taken a hand from Croz, or received a pull, I turned to offer the same to Hudson; but he invariably declined, saying it was not necessary. Mr Hadow, however, was not accustomed to this kind of work, and required continual assistance. It is only fair to say that the difficulty which he found at this part arose simply and entirely from want of experience.

This solitary difficult part was of no great extent. We bore away over it at first, nearly horizontally, for a distance of about 400 ft; then ascended directly towards the summit for about 60 ft; and then doubled back to the ridge which descends towards Zermatt. A long stride round a rather awkward corner brought us to snow once more. The last doubt vanished! The Matterhorn was ours! Nothing but 200 ft of easy snow remained to be surmounted!

You must now carry your thoughts back to the seven Italians who started from Breil on the 11th of July. Four days had passed since their departure, and we were tormented with anxiety lest they should arrive on the top before us. All the way up we had talked of them, and many false alarms of "men on the summit" had been raised. The higher we rose, the more intense became the excitement. What if we should be beaten at the last moment? The slope eased off, at length we could be detached, and Croz and I, dashing away, ran a neck-and-neck race, which ended in a dead heat. At 1.40 p.m. the world was at our feet, and the Matterhorn was conquered. Hurrah! Not a footstep could be seen.

It was not yet certain that we had not been beaten. The summit of the Matterhorn was formed of a rudely level ridge, about 350 ft long, and the Italians might have been at its farther extremity. I hastened to the southern end, scanning the snow right and left eagerly. Hurrah! again; it was untrodden. "Where were the men?" I peered over the cliff, half doubting, half expectant. I saw them immediately – mere dots on the ridge, at an immense distance below. Up went my arms and my hat. "Croz! Croz! come here!" "Where are they, Monsieur?" "There, don't you see them, down there?" "Ah! the *coquins*, they are low down." "Croz, we must make those fellows hear

us." We yelled until we were hoarse. The Italians seemed to
regard us – we could not be certain. "Croz, we *must* make them
hear us; they *shall* hear us!" I seized a block of rock and hurled it
down, and called upon my companion, in the name of friendship, to do the same. We drove our sticks in, and prised away the
crags, and soon a torrent of stones poured down the cliffs.
There was no mistake about it this time. The Italians turned
and fled.

Still, I would that the leader of that party could have stood
with us at that moment, for our victorious shouts conveyed to
him the disappointment of the ambition of a lifetime. He was
the man, of all those who attempted the ascent of the Matterhorn, who most deserved to be the first upon its summit. He
was the first to doubt its inaccessibility, and he was the only
man who persisted in believing that its ascent would be
accomplished. It was the aim of his life to make the ascent
from the side of Italy, for the honour of his native valley. For a
time he had the game in his hands: he played it as he thought
best; but he made a false move, and he lost it. Times have
changed with Carrel. His supremacy is questioned in the Val
Tournanche; new men have arisen; and he is no longer
recognized as *the* chasseur above all others: though so long
as he remains the man that he is today, it will not be easy to
find his superior.

The others had arrived, so we went back to the northern
end of the ridge. Croz now took the tent-pole, and planted it
in the highest snow. "Yes," we said, "there is the flag-staff,
but where is the flag?" "Here it is," he answered, pulling off
his blouse and fixing it to the stick. It made a poor flag, and
there was no wind to float it out, yet it was seen all around.
They saw it at Zermatt – at the Riffel – in the Val Tournanche. At Breil, the watchers cried, "Victory is ours!" They
raised "bravos" for Carrel, and "vivas" for Italy, and hastened
to put themselves *en fête*. On the morrow they were unde-
ceived. "All was changed; the explorers returned sad – cast
down – disheartened – confounded – gloomy." "It is true,"
said the men. "We saw them ourselves – they hurled stones at
us! The old traditions *are* true – there are spirits on the top of
the Matterhorn!"

We returned to the southern end of the ridge to build a cairn, and then paid homage to the view. The day was one of those superlatively calm and clear ones which usually precede bad weather. The atmosphere was perfectly still, and free from all clouds or vapours. Mountains fifty – nay a hundred – miles off looked sharp and near. All their details – ridge and crag, snow and glacier – stood out with faultless definition. Pleasant thoughts of happy days in bygone years came up unbidden, as we recognized the old, familiar forms. All were revealed – not one of the principal peaks of the Alps was hidden. I see them clearly now – the great inner circles of giants, backed by the ranges, chains and *massifs*. First came the Dent Blanche, hoary and grand; the Gabelhorn and pointed Rothhorn; and then the peerless Weisshorn: the towering Mischalbelhörner, flanked by the Allalcinhorn, Strahlhorn and Rimpfischhorn; then Monte Rosa – with its many Spitzes – the Lyskamm and the Breithorn. Behind was the Bernese Oberland governed by the Finsteraarhorn, and then the Simplon and St Gothard groups; the Disgrazia and the Orteler. Towards the south we looked down to Chivasso on the plain of Piedmont, and far beyond. The Viso – one hundred miles away – seemed close upon us; the Maritime Alps – one hundred and thirty miles distant – were free from haze. Then came my first love – the Pelvoux; the Ecrins and the Meije; the clusters of the Graians; and lastly, in the west, gorgeous in the full sunlight, rose the monarch of all – Mont Blanc. Ten thousand feet beneath us were the green fields of Zermatt, dotted with chalets, from which blue smoke rose lazily. Eight thousand feet below, on the other side, were the pastures of Breil. There were black and gloomy forests, bright and cheerful meadows; bounding waterfalls and tranquil lakes; fertile lands and savage wastes; sunny plains and frigid plateaux. There were the most rugged forms, and the most graceful outlines – bold, perpendicular cliffs, and gentle, undulating slopes; rocky mountains and snowy mountains, sombre and solemn, or glittering and white, with walls – turrets – pinnacles – pyramids – domes – cones – and spires! There was every combination that the world can give, and every contrast that the heart could desire.

We remained on the summit for one hour:

"One crowded hour of glorious life."

It passed away too quickly, and we began to prepare for the descent.

Hudson and I again consulted as to the best and safest arrangement of the party. We agreed that it would be best for Croz to go first, and Hadow second; Hudson, who was almost equal to a guide in sureness of foot, wished to be third; Lord F. Douglas was placed next, and old Peter, the strongest of the remainder, after him. I suggested to Hudson that we should attach a rope to the rocks on our arrival at the difficult bit, and hold it as we descended, as an additional protection. He approved the idea, but it was not definitely settled that it should be done. The party was being arranged in the above order whilst I was sketching the summit, and they had finished, and were waiting for me to be tied in line, when someone remembered that our names had not been left in a bottle. They requested me to write them down, and moved off while it was being done.

A few minutes afterwards I tied myself to young Peter, ran down after the others, and caught them just as they were commencing the descent of the difficult part. Great care was being taken. Only one man was moving at a time; when he was firmly planted the next advanced, and so on. They had not, however, attached the additional rope to rocks, and nothing was said about it. The suggestion was not made for my own sake, and I am not sure that it even occurred to me again. For some little distance we two followed the others, detached from them, and should have continued so had not Lord F. Douglas asked me, about 3 p.m., to tie on to old Peter, as he feared, he said, that Taugwalder would not be able to hold his ground if a slip occurred.

A few minutes later, a sharp-eyed lad ran into the Monte Rosa hotel, to Seiler, saying that he had seen an avalanche fall from the summit of the Matterhorn on to the Matterhorngletscher. The boy was reproved for telling idle stories; he was right, nevertheless, and this was what he saw.

Michel Croz had laid aside his axe, and in order to give Mr

Hadow greater security, was absolutely taking hold of his legs, and putting his feet, one by one, into their proper positions. As far as I know, no one was actually descending. I cannot speak with certainty, because the two leading men were partially hidden from my sight by an intervening mass of rock, but it is my belief, from the movements of their shoulders, that Croz, having done as I have said, was in the act of turning round to go down a step or two himself; at this moment Mr Hadow slipped, fell against him, and knocked him over. I heard one startled exclamation from Croz, then saw him and Mr Hadow flying downwards; in another moment Hudson was dragged from his steps, and Lord F. Douglas immediately after him. All this was the work of a moment. Immediately we heard Croz's exclamation, old Peter and I planted ourselves as firmly as the rocks would permit: the rope was taut between us, and the jerk came on us both as on one man. We held; but the rope broke midway between Taugwalder and Lord Francis Douglas. For a few seconds we saw our unfortunate companions sliding downwards on their backs, and spreading out their hands, endeavouring to save themselves. They passed from our sight uninjured, disappeared one by one, and fell from precipice to precipice on to the Matterhorngletscher below, a distance of nearly 4,000 ft in height. From the moment the rope broke it was impossible to help them.

So perished our comrades! For the space of half an hour we remained on the spot without moving a single step. The two men, paralyzed by terror, cried like infants, and trembled in such a manner as to threaten us with the fate of the others. Old Peter rent the air with exclamations of "Chamounix! Oh, what will Chamounix say?" He meant, Who would believe that Croz could fall? The young man did nothing but scream or sob, "We are lost! we are lost!" Fixed between the two, I could neither move up nor down. I begged young Peter to descend, but he dared not. Unless he did, we could not advance. Old Peter became alive to the danger, and swelled the cry, "We are lost! we are lost!" The father's fear was natural – he trembled for his son; the young man's fear was cowardly – he thought of self alone. At last old Peter summoned up courage, and changed his position to a rock to which he could fix the rope; the young man then descended, and we all stood together. Immediately we did so, I asked for the rope which had given way, and found, to my surprise – indeed, to my horror – that it was the weakest of the three ropes. It was not brought, and should not have been employed, for the purpose for which it was used. It was old rope, and, compared with the others, was feeble. It was intended as a reserve, in case we had to leave much rope behind, attached to rocks. I saw at once that a serious question was involved, and made him give me the end. It had broken in mid-air, and it did not appear to have sustained previous injury.

For more than two hours afterwards I thought almost every moment that the next would be my last; for the Taugwalders, utterly unnerved, were not only incapable of giving assistance, but were in such a state that a slip might have been expected from them at any moment. After a time we were able to do that which should have been done at first, and fixed ropes to firm rocks, in addition to being tied together. These ropes were cut from time to time, and were left behind. Even with this assurance the men were sometimes afraid to proceed, and several times old Peter turned with ashy face and faltering limbs, and said, with terrible emphasis, "*I cannot!*"

About 6 p.m. we arrived at the snow upon the ridge descending towards Zermatt, and all peril was over.

The Storm

Herbert Tichy

Tichy led the successful 1954 Austrian assault on Cho Oyu, an 8201 m (26,913 ft) peak in East Nepal. Success was preceded by near disaster, however, when Tichy was forced down the mountain by a hurricane.

I t was not a comfortable evening, but you could not expect better at that altitude. No cause for worry. Once I was inside the tent I could not bring myself to creep out again and photograph Camp IV. Tomorrow, I decided, on our return from the summit. Then the two tents would be seen from above standing out like dark pearls against the white snow; the Nangpa La glacier, the grey mountain-ranges of Tibet and the evening sky would form the background.

Sleeplessness, the great problem at these heights, is a cause of bodily and nervous fatigue. If you take sleeping-pills there is the danger of falling asleep in the early morning just when you need all your energy. Lowe, the New Zealander, had that experience on Everest.

I was lucky. As I lay in my sleeping bag side by side with Pasang I felt the fatigue of the day overcoming me and had scarcely time to notice how at this altitude breathing is not automatic but a conscious effort. On many a night much lower down I had got up with a feeling of suffocation and fought for breath because I had forgotten in my sleep to breathe consciously as one does for a medical examination. I heard Pasang breathing regularly; probably he was already asleep.

I felt protected and safe in spite of the utter solitude of our bivouac and although I was perhaps sleeping at a point higher and more remote from the world than any other man alive. I had Pasang with me, and Adjiba, and Ang Nyima. I tried to explain to myself the intimacy and warmth of my feeling for them, but weariness carried my thoughts away as the current of a river floats the drift-wood away from its banks. The day was over; I fell asleep.

I did not dream that night, but waking was a nightmare and I clung to the hope that it was actually a bad dream. The sound of Pasang groaning convinced me that it was real. The side of the tent was being pressed down on my face by some invisible force, preventing me from breathing, and an uproar of rattling, whistling and screaming filled the air. It took me half a minute to realize what had occurred.

The wind had become a hurricane and had torn our tents from their moorings; the tent pegs had snapped. I put out my hand and felt for Pasang, who was groaning, in his sleep perhaps, or perhaps from a presentiment of disaster to come. Stare as I might, no chink of light was to be seen. It was still night.

There was no actual cause for anxiety. We two and our rucksacks were heavy enough to hold the tent down. We should not be blown away. I edged over to the outer side to deprive the wind of purchase, and after making a free space for my mouth fell into a doze. No, there was no cause for anxiety. Often a storm at night was followed by a clear, still day.

By the time daylight glimmered through the canvas, the wind had increased in violence. I can't say whether I had slept in the interval or lain awake, but it was now day and I had to come to some decision. I couldn't lie on in a twilight state between sleeping and waking, between life and death; that would be too easy.

The sun penetrated the yellow fabric. It seemed to promise life and warmth, in strange contrast to the icy hurricane which threatened to hurl us down the mountainside.

I nudged Pasang again.

"Wait? Go down?" he asked.

I didn't know which. I didn't even know whether it was morning or evening, whether we had passed a long day in our wretched tents, or whether the sun had just risen and we still had the day to endure.

"We'll see," I added.

We crept out from under the tent. It was not easy, for the wind kept the canvas tight down on us like a fisherman's net and hugged us. As soon as I was out I was surprised to see the sun in the east, and about two hours up. So the day was not behind us and we could not indulge in any illusion that the time for decision had passed by. If we had had the night in front of us we could have settled down to wait in resignation.

There was not a cloud in the sky. But we could not always see the sky; it was hidden by thick flurries of snow. A hurricane of a force I had never experienced scourged the snow-covered mountainside, and Helmut, who took observations from lower down with his instruments, estimated its speed at about eighty miles an hour. The temperature was thirty to thirty-five degrees below zero. The most horrible part of it was the cloudless blue sky.

I crouched down beside Pasang in the snow. We could not stand up. The wind would have thrown us down or lifted us from the ground.

The other tent was also wrecked. The huddled bodies of Ang Nyima and Adjiba were moulded by the flattened canvas. We gave them a prod. They were still alive and crept out to join us.

The four of us cowered together beside the flattened tents and stared into the vortex. We could only speak in shouts.

"Never known a storm like this," Pasang shouted. "All die." He repeated it again and again.

I agreed with him. We should all die.

Adjiba and Ang Nyima said nothing. They sat huddled and dumb, their faces a bluish grey, marked by death – no, dead already. Their dark eyes were fixed on mine, asking no questions, hinting no reproach. They were gates to another world, at whose frontier we had now arrived.

I experienced a strange split in my ego.

Like Pasang and Adjiba and Ang Nyima, I was a poor wretch,

tortured by cold and the fear of death, whose only comfort in face of the final and utter solitude was derived from the presence of my three companions. And at the same time the other part of me looked down without the least emotion, almost with irony, on the four of us. My fate was not at all terrible to this second me. "You've always played fast and loose a bit with this possibility; you can't complain if it has come true. But how can you answer to yourself for the death-stricken faces of these three Sherpas?"

This split personality persisted throughout the events that followed; one part acted instinctively and suffered in the flesh, and the other followed events without feeling or pity, merely as a critical observer, coldly making his own comments upon them.

We were still huddling together, overwhelmed by the violence of nature and incapable of coming to any decision, when suddenly the wind lifted the other tent and threatened to blow it right away. I threw myself on it without thinking and held it down, my body on the tent, my hands in the snow. I had had my mittens stripped off in creeping out of our own tent, but that did not matter very much as I had put my hands in my warm trouser pockets inside an outer windproof smock. While we sat cowering together, I never thought of my hands; they were well off compared with the rest of my shuddering body.

Now they were in contact with the snow, and in the next two or three minutes this is what happened:

The tent was rescued. The Sherpas salvaged it. But I felt a burning sensation in my hands. The pain got worse and throbbed through my whole body.

Probably their warmth melted the snow when they first touched it. The icy hurricane seized on and sucked at the moisture, a hurricane of eighty miles an hour at a temperature of thirty-five degrees below zero, and the circulation of the blood at that altitude is sluggish.

The pain got worse and worse. I chafed my hands, and beat them against my sides; it did not stop the pain. I thought of creeping into my tent, but it lay like a sail, flat on the snow. I got into a panic, as if I had been on fire – and actually the injuries caused by frost and fire are similar – and started shouting.

The Sherpas, who had been busy so far salvaging the tent, rushed up, and as soon as they realised my disaster, Pasang and Ang Nyima undid their trousers and my hands felt a little warmth between their thighs. It was the only place in our half-frozen bodies where any warmth lingered. Pasang knew that. Meanwhile, Adjiba was hunting under my tent for my mittens.

My watching, critical self showed up again. I saw it all before my eyes as a picture, Pasang and Ang Nyima with their backs pressed against the wind, and myself kneeling crucified between them, my hands outstretched and hidden within the remnants of warmth which might still be my salvation. My animal self relished these few seconds of warmth and shelter, but that other self thought: "What a subject for Kubin to paint! 'The Crucifixion' or 'Journey's End'."

I tried to think of a good title for this macabre scene, then went on inconsequently to wonder where Kubin lived now. Was he still at Linz, among those misty, sombre Danube landscapes which inspired his paintings?

Then my animal, life-loving self returned. Adjiba brought my mittens; I seized them. My hands were white and swollen. I felt they were done for, but *we* were not done for yet.

Panic returned.

"If we mean to live," I yelled, "we must go down, not sit here."

The Sherpas' grey death-masks did not come alive, but the three men acted promptly.

Values had altered. A wrap was worth more than a Rolleiflex. We snatched up any aid to warmth among the equipment and left everything else behind. The tents stayed where they were. The storm might destroy them completely or perhaps we might be able to recover them later, but now our lives were all we thought of.

I don't mean to suggest that it was my panic-stricken initiative that got us down. Our retreat was not the reward of my efforts or my fright, but the work of the three Sherpas. All the same, I feel that my will played the decisive part.

The Sherpas, owing perhaps to their religious faith or to their almost animal links with the earth, do not, as we do, regard death as the dark gateway to unknown dread. They die more simply and more harmoniously, and if I had said to Pasang, "There's no way down. We must die where we are," we should have stayed in Camp IV – for ever.

Yet it was nothing I did; it was just that un-asiatic tincture in my blood which made me shout: "We must get down unless we mean to die here."

The Sherpas took the brunt of the journey down. Their resource and energy returned as soon as the decision was made. We anchored the tents and left them where they were. It was not a retreat, but a rout.

My hands were useless. Pasang had to strap on my crampons for me, then we roped up and began the descent. I recall very little of the strenuous hours which ended in Camp III. I can only remember the violence of the storm, which drove us on over the snow, and the sight of the Sherpas throwing themselves down and creeping like cats when a sudden gust caught us. I could feel the throbbing agony in my hands and the wind cutting my face like a knife. I could see the clouds of driven snow, which showed us how vain our hopes and efforts were. It was hard going.

But I also remember the feeling of security and friendship. We were four on a rope, and I felt sure that all or none would get down. It was not conceivable that the strongest of us would unrope and leave the rest to their fate; it was equally inconceivable that we should abandon the weakest because he hindered the rest. Anything of the sort would have made nonsense of the life we led.

Perhaps memory idealises, but I doubt it. The rope was not just a rope to be tied and untied as desired. It was too strong a bond to be severed lightly.

As we got down the storm abated, but by now the Sherpas too had their finger-tips frost-bitten. When we reached the perpendicular step in the ice-fall we let each other down on the rope to Camp III, where we found Sepp.

He had got back his form and climbed up to Camp III, from where he had tried for several hours to come to our rescue, but he was blown again and again off the steps of the ice-fall. Once the wind carried him a hundred and seventy feet through the air and he landed in soft snow not far from a sheer drop.

He looked ghastly. His face was aged and furrowed, and ice and snow clung to his beard.

Later I asked him, when we were looking over our photographs, why he had not taken some shots of us then. He could have got some striking pictures.

"I didn't like to," he said. "You looked so frightful. Pasang was crying and talking about dying all the time."

I remember nothing of all that. I only remember how glad I was to see Sepp, and how it dawned on me for the first time that we had failed.

I showed him my hands. They were like tuberous growths by now.

"They're finished and the summit's finished."

The flight was resumed, Camp III vacated. The rope was no longer needed, we were at home on the ridge now, and at this height the storm was endurable. We had given death the slip. But the pain in my hands pulsated through my whole body. I knew my life was saved; I was sure my hands were done for.

Down to Camp II. I tottered down the ridge which we had ascended a few days before feeling so confident of success. Glorious, no doubt, to have been on such terms with death. But sad to be a cripple, I thought, as I tottered on.

Camp II. Late afternoon by now. Helmut was there. Although not yet well and although it was his job to organize the "lift", he had come up through the storm with the presentiment that we might need his help. He was not a doctor of medicine, but he was able to give me the first injection to stimulate my circulation.

Tents were not yet put up. I sat among the rocks in the wind and bared my arm. Pasang held me in his arms with motherly solicitude while Helmut gave the injection.

Flight was still our one thought. We wanted to get away from the mountain which had handled us so cruelly, down to Camp I, where we should be less exposed to the storm, but I was too weak and could go no farther. I was afraid of the long screes. I was tired and only wanted to forget.

Two tents were set up and four of us stayed there for the night, Sepp and I in one, Gyalsen and Da Nurbu in the other. All the rest went on down.

I was lying down when Pasang came to say goodbye. He was going to take my hand when he saw my hands, so he bent over me instead and kissed my cheek. I felt like a corpse to whom he was bidding farewell.

Never could I have dared to believe that we should kiss each other again two weeks later, again with tears in our eyes, tears not of pain this time but of happiness because we stood together on the summit.

But that night at Camp II I had no hope whatever. All I had was the ever-recurrent certainty that my hands were done for and the peak lost.

I was as helpless as a babe and Sepp looked after me with tender care. The same thoughts went round and round in my head like a never-resting wheel; again I asked the question mankind has always asked: Why had it to be? Why could the weather not have held up one day longer? Why had the wind to blow with that destructive fury? Where and when had I committed the crowning mistake? But no, the assault had been properly organized and there had not been any mistake. Where then was the hidden blight? Was it that arrogant self-confidence of the evening before? Or could we be so cruelly punished for no reason?

Despite the frost-bite injury to his fingers, Tichy summitted Cho Oyu just two weeks later. He was accompanied by J. Jochter and Pasang Dawa Lama.

The Death Zone

Walter Bonatti

Walter Bonatti was an Italian alpinist, and his 1955 solo ascent of the South-West Pillar of Petit Dru was one of the outstanding achievements of European postwar climbing. Five years later, on the Central Pillar of Mont Blanc, Bonatti was involved in one of its greatest tragedies . . .

We climbed quickly and reached the base of the last pinnacle about noon instead of two o'clock as we had expected. We had noticed mist trailing overhead, but it had not worried us overmuch considering the altitude we had now reached; we hoped to be able to reach the summit before any brewing storm should break. However the storm caught us just as Mazeaud and Kohlman were beginning to climb the last pinnacle. We had only about 150 ft of overhanging monolith to climb to complete our climb on the Pillar and to reach the ridge which led to the summit of Mont Blanc.

We all gathered together on the few ledges there were. The snowstorm was now raging furiously; it was thundering and the lightning flashed around us. The air was saturated with electricity and the gusts of wind blew powdered snow into our faces, blinding us. We were at a height of nearly 15,000 ft on the Pillar, the lightning-conductor of Mont Blanc. We three Italians were squatting on a little ledge; the Frenchmen were in two groups. Then, without warning, Kohlman's face was grazed by a flash of lightning. He was blinded by the flash but Mazeaud with a leap caught hold of him and managed to support him. For some minutes Kohlman was almost paralyzed. We looked for the coramine and Mazeaud made him gulp some down. At last the Frenchman recovered and we were able to settle down.

At this moment, with the storm raging, we were as follows: I was on one narrow ledge, with Oggioni and Gallieni; Vielle, Mazeaud and Guillaume were on another ledge beside us while Kohlman was by himself on a third and slightly larger one farther down to give him a chance of stretching out. It was perhaps here that his psychological tragedy began, though we did not know it at the time.

The summit of Mont Blanc was not more than twelve hours' climb away from us. Beyond the summit, after we had conquered the Pillar, the Vallot hut was waiting, a sure shelter; after that, it was an easy descent to Chamonix. A break in the clouds for half a day would have been enough for us to achieve this, but in fact we never reached the summit.

It began to grow darker. The storm was more and more violent. We shut ourselves into our little tent and could judge the strength of the storm only by the intensity of the thunderclaps. Sometimes our spirits rose when we thought them to be very far off, sometimes we lost heart when we thought them close to us. The lightning flashes blinded us even through the opaque tent. We were there, alive, yet unable to do anything against the furious outpouring of the elements. Around us, secured to the same pitons that supported us in space, hung all our equipment for the climb: pitons, crampons and ice-axes; better bait for the lightning could not be imagined. We would have liked to throw them away, but how could we either ascend or descend without them? No one spoke; everyone was wrapped up in his own thoughts.

Just as we were thinking for the nth time that we were at the mercy of fate, we felt as if some force wanted to tear off our legs. We had all been grazed by the lightning. We yelled wildly. But we were alive, though now we knew that the storm could reduce us all to ashes at any time it chose. We called to one another to find out if everyone was still all right. Then there was a terrifying lull, which we knew heralded a last concentration of electricity which would inevitably break loose around us.

A few moments later a shock, similar to the one we had already experienced, but even more violent, nearly threw us off the face. Amid the commotion and shouts I could hear one voice clearly. I heard: "We must get away!" I don't know if it was Oggioni or Gallieni. The words were born of despair and mirrored our state of mind. I thought that we were lost and I believe that we all thought the same. I relived my whole life and in my mind's eye saw all those dear faces and places which I should certainly never see again. Though by now resigned to my fate, I felt sorry that during my life I had not been able to do all the things I had intended. These are sensations which last only for seconds, yet they are clear and seem incredibly long.

Miraculously, however, the storm seemed to be dying away in the distance. Now we could only hear the drumming of the frozen snow on the rubberised cloth which covered us. We remained inert and apathetic; we did not even look outside the tent, for outside it was already dark. No one spoke. We did not eat. We were indifferent to everything. The snow which was falling though it was a very serious matter for us, almost gave us a sense of relief. We had been saved from the lightning and were still alive. I had never before been on such a face in such a storm: there was no skill and no technique which could have saved us.

Our complete immobility and the long stay in the tent had stifled us. We tore away a piece of the cloth and breathed avidly. Our tent was now buried in the snow, and the warmth of our bodies had created inside it watery drops which were transformed, by the sudden changes in temperature, now into water and now into ice crystals. I did not want to look at my watch, so as not to be disappointed by the slow passage of time. We did not speak to one another. All that could be heard were moans due sometimes to the discomfort of our positions, sometimes to the cold and sometimes to the feeling of suffocation which tortured us. We knew nothing about the Frenchmen, but we could often hear similar noises from them.

The night passed and a milky radiance heralded Wednesday's dawn. Only then did we emerge from the tent and were amazed

at the amount of snow which had fallen during the night. The
Frenchmen beside us were quite buried in it. Kohlman, on the
wider ledge, was already standing up and looked like a dark
blotch against the incandescent horizon, which seemed to
announce a splendid day. We were overcome by a feeling of
joy; the enormous quantity of fallen snow and the terrible frost
were harbingers of good weather. Soon all of us were out of the
tent, ready to begin the last stretch. I took a few snaps and we
dismantled the little tent. But just as we were packing it up we
found ourselves – I still do not know where those mists could
have come from – again enveloped in the snowstorm. The very
strong wind made the fresh snow whirl around us; we could not
tell if it were snowing or whether this was the work of the wind.

We once more took refuge in our tent and the Frenchmen did
the same. This time we went farther down, to Kohlman's ledge,
which was larger and where the three of us – Oggioni, Gallieni
and myself – could be a little more comfortable. Kohlman
climbed up a few feet to where we had passed the night. He
took his own bivouac equipment with him, a down sleeping-bag
covered with plastic cloth, which wrapped him like a mummy.
We belayed ourselves to pitons and settled down to wait.

During a short break a little earlier I had noticed that the
snow had fallen even at a low altitude. We could scarcely believe
that after snowing so long, the storm could come back once
more. The Frenchmen asked me what I intended to do. I
replied that we would wait, always in the hope of being able
to get to the summit, the shortest way to safety. We were not
short of provisions or equipment and could stay where we were.
At this time of year the bad weather could not last very much
longer and the idea of so dangerous and complicated a descent
in the midst of a snowstorm terrified us, since we could reach
the summit in less than half a day.

Mazeaud and his companions were belayed to a piton about
twenty feet above me. Kohlman was alongside them. Mazeaud,
who had a certain leadership over his companions, exchanged a
few words with me and proposed that we two should set out
together as soon as a break in the weather made it possible. Our
job would be to fix pitons and ropes up the last 250 ft of
overhang, so that our five companions could come up after

us. We agreed on this, but the break never came. We ate a little ham, some roast meat and jam, but we could not drink anything because the storm made it impossible to light a fire to make tea with melted snow.

It went on snowing, hour after monotonous hour. Amid the thoughts which jostled one another in my mind, I tried to remember other occasions, similar to this, when I had been trapped in the mountains by bad weather. I remembered that snowstorms had never lasted more than a day or two. So I said to myself: "One day has gone already. The snowstorm cannot last more than another twenty-four hours. It is only a question of lasting out one day longer and then we shall be able to start."

To remain in this very uncomfortable position squashed one against the other in a space which could hardly hold a single person, became more and more intolerable. We could not turn our heads, we could not lie on our sides and the constant slope made it seem that our spines would crack. In such conditions it is easy to fall prey to irritability. There were moments when we would have liked to tear off our covering, but woe to us had we done so! Oggioni, Gallieni and I talked; we talked of everything; memories, plans, hopes, friendships, happy and unhappy reminiscences, just to kill time and to keep ourselves occupied.

Oggioni said to me: "Do you remember when we said in Peru: Will the day ever come when we shall be together on the Pillar?" He said it sarcastically, since at that time we thought that everything on our home mountains would be easier. Yet now we were in conditions similar to those we had found on the Rondoy, when we had had to master that peak in the midst of a snowstorm and had been without shelter for two days and two nights. Gallieni was our vitamin man; he gave us pills, especially of vitamins C and A, to make up for our lack of food. He gave them to the Frenchmen by a primitive sort of pulley which we had made out of ropes and added some of our provisions. The Frenchmen were a little short of food.

The problem of passing water then arose. It was not possible to go out of the tent. I suggested to Gallieni that he should sacrifice his plastic cap and we each used it in turn. It was a terrifying experience; we had to make all sorts of contortions and hold fast to one another not to fall over. The whole operation took half an hour; our legs were hanging in space and our clothes hampered us.

It was now Wednesday evening. It was snowing harder than ever. I asked Gallieni, who was near the edge: "Where's the wind blowing from?" "Still from the west," he said. That meant a snowstorm. Mazeaud, full of vitality and initiative, shouted to me: "As soon as it gets better, you and I ought to go. If you think it would be better to start towards the left, then we will certainly go that way." Oggioni, who did not know French, asked me what Mazeaud had been saying and I explained. He agreed but asked: "Do you think it possible to get out by way of the summit even in this weather?" He knew that I could find the way down from the summit whatever the weather, as I had already done it several times before. I said: yes, but that we should have to stay where we were another night, since in my heart I felt almost certain that the snowstorm would end next day.

Our breath in the tent was transformed into watery vapour and we were wet through. I thought with terror about what might happen when the hard frost which always precedes good weather came and hoped I would be able to bear it. We would have to spend an hour or so warming ourselves in the sun before making the last assault. We could not sleep. Night came upon us almost unawares. We were all on edge. Gallieni began to speak of his young children. My thoughts were ten thousand feet farther down, with my loved ones, in the intimacy of my home. Oggioni talked of Portofino. He had never been there and said: "We mountaineers are really unlucky . . . with all the lovely things there are in the world, we get caught up in this sort of thing . . ." Gallieni said: "And to think that I have a cosy home in Milano Marittima and such a nice beach: you can jump into the warm water and don't even have to take the trouble to swim, it's so shallow . . . You can walk for miles and miles . . ." Oggioni hid his apprehension with jokes. To look at, he was the calmest of the lot of us. I was sure that he, other than myself, was the only one to be fully aware that our plight was desperate.

The night between Wednesday and Thursday passed. In the fore-noon Mazeaud came into our tent, because the plastic cloth over the Frenchmen's sleeping-bags had split under the gusts of wind. We managed to arrange ourselves after a thousand contortions and so passed the day. We tried to keep up our spirits, telling ourselves that the next day – Friday – would be fine, but we were not greatly convinced. In my inmost self I was already considering which would be the safest manner of retreating down the way we had come; in my opinion it was now impossible to reach the summit of the Pillar. I did not mention this to my companions so as not to discourage them.

Mazeaud told me about the south-west pillar of the Petit Dru which he had made the previous week. We spoke of our pleasure at getting to know one another and in sharing this adventure. We promised to meet again one day at Courmayeur or Chamonix and to talk over today's experiences. Our thirst was intense and we had to quench it by eating snow. We made pellets of snow and kept gnawing at them. We thought longingly of a tap at home which would give us all the water we wanted at a turn. It was paradoxical that in the midst of so much snow we should have a burning thirst. The frozen snow made our mouths burn and very sore.

Thursday passed and night came. During the long hours of darkness Oggioni and I, who were farthest from the edge, suffered particularly from lack of air. To him alone I confided my intention of descending at all costs. He agreed, but was terrified at the idea. Thursday night also passed. We had to set the alarm for half-past three. When I heard it ringing I shouted to everyone: "We must go down at all costs. We cannot stay here any longer, otherwise it will be too late and we will not have the strength."

When dawn began to break on the Friday morning the storm had been ranging incessantly for more than sixty hours. Mist and snow merged into an impenetrable curtain. We dismantled everything and left a certain amount of our equipment behind. I was without an ice-axe which one of my companions had let fall by mistake on the first day. We began the descent by double rope. We had decided that I must lead, preparing the rappels. Behind me came all the others: Mazeaud, whose task was to help anyone who needed it, then the others and finally Oggioni who, strong in his experience, would be last man and recover the ropes.

At exactly six I lowered myself into the grey and stormy void almost blindly, without knowing where I was going. I felt as if I were in a stormy sea. The snow flurries gave me a feeling of dizziness. I had to watch every detail and try to recognize every fold of the rock to find out where I was. The manoeuvre took a long time and waiting for the ropes and pitons to come down from above in order to make the next rappel took even longer. Sometimes we were all bunched together, belayed to a piton, four or five of us hanging in space. About half-way down the Pillar I was unable to find a place to stop when the double rope came to an end. With some difficulty because of the snow flurries I managed to make myself understood. I needed another rope to attach to the one I was holding on to. There were no holds; the snow had packed tight even under the overhangs. I tied the two ropes together with my bare hands and continued my descent into space. There was now a 400-ft rope down which I was sliding like a spider.

It was now no longer possible to talk with any of the others. I was completely suspended, looking for a hold which I could not find. I was worried, partly because I did not know where I could halt in my descent, partly because an enormous overhang cut off all possibility of communicating with my companions who, higher up, were waiting for my signal. At last, after some acrobatic swings in space, I managed to land on an outcrop of rock. I shouted repeatedly through the storm, hoping that my companions would understand that they could begin their descent. At one moment I saw the rope ascending and thought that one of them was on it and had begun to descend. Then, suddenly, the rope slipped away from me and disappeared from sight. I was left there, on an outcrop, secured by a cord to a piton, in the heart of the Pillar, without any means of continuing my descent and wondering if my companions would be able to find me or would descend in some other direction. I went on shouting at the top of my voice, hoping to be heard, so that, if nothing else, they could tell me where they were. Several moments of anxiety passed. At last a dark patch appeared near me; it was Mazeaud who had realised where I was and had come to join me.

Our rappels continued with the same rhythm. We were

getting closer to the foot of the Pillar. We were frozen and soaked through. Then, hearing the dull thuds of some snow-falls, I realized that we had reached the base of the Pillar. But by now it was late in the afternoon and all we could do that night was to prepare a camp on the Col de Peuterey, which forms the base of the Pillar. We set foot on the level but the snow was extraordinarily deep; sometimes we sank into it up to our chests. I made Mazeaud take the lead for a bit, followed by all the others. I stayed where I was to give the direction. At one time the group seemed to have foundered in a very deep snowdrift. I joined them and then took the lead again, setting out by instinct towards the spot I thought suitable for a camp. Though I could not see it, it was imprinted on my mind. Behind me was Oggioni with whom I discussed whether it would be better to chance the protection which a crevasse could give us rather than build an igloo, since the snow was unstable. This was not so important for us who had our tent as for the four Frenchmen who hadn't one. We decided on the crevasse and told the Frenchmen, who accepted our advice.

We made arrangements for our camp before the night between Friday and Saturday fell. We had been making rappels for twelve hours. Kohlman seemed the most exhausted of all of us. We put him in our tent. With what was left of a butane gas cylinder Guillaume prepared some hot tea and gave it to him. The cold was atrocious. The wind was blowing continually and made the snow whirl around us. That was the worst night of all. We divided what was left of the provisions; prunes, chocolate, sugar and a little meat, now frozen. Oggioni refused the meat, preferring the sweetstuffs. All the others, however, nibbled at it. Kohlman showed me his fingers; they were livid. I thought it a good idea to massage them with cooking alcohol, of which we still had plenty. I passed him the alcohol flask, but he put it to his mouth and began to gulp it down. It was a most ill-advised action, but I thought he must have mistaken it for drinking alcohol. I took the flask away from him, but not before he had swallowed a couple of gulps. Were we already on the brink of madness?

It was pitch dark. We were in an inferno. Everyone was moaning and shivering with cold. The wind howled and the snow fell more and more heavily. Every now and then we would shake the snow off the tent, otherwise it would have smothered us. I tried to light the spirit-stove but had to give up for lack of air and, as in the last few days, we had to eat snow to quench our thirst. We were desperate, but no one said a word. Finally Oggioni said to me: "Let's make a vow: if we get out of this safely, let us forget that the Pillar even exists." I said, "Yes."

The night passed slowly and despairingly. At the same time as on the day before, at half-past three, at the sound of my little alarm, we rose from our uncomfortable resting-place. We wanted to save time and to get out of that terrifying situation which seemed as if it would never come to an end. The night had added another eighteen inches of snow to what had been there before. We set out in the midst of the storm. We all seemed to have endured that terrible camp well enough. Now I no longer had to take counsel with my companions; they left everything to me and I felt the heavy responsibility of a guide who must bring everyone back safely by the only possible route, the very dangerous Roches Gruber. We had to get to the Gamba before evening, otherwise it would be all over for all of us.

Before starting, Robert Guillaume gave Kohlman a coramine injection. Meanwhile, I, followed by Oggioni and Gallieni, began to clear a burrow through the very deep snow in the direction of the route chosen for our descent. We were now on a single rope in this order: Bonatti, Oggioni, Gallieni, Mazeaud, Kohlman, Vielle and Guillaume. The face which precedes the Roches Gruber was heavily laden with fresh snow which might avalanche at any moment. I told my companions to hurry up and join me and to get into shelter so that I could hold on to a rope if an avalanche should catch me while I was cutting the channel which would lead us to the Roches Gruber. I managed to do so and called to the others to pass, one by one, but when it came to Vielle's turn he could not do it. He kept falling and rising again, with every sign of exhaustion. Guillaume was beside him and encouraged him. He took Vielle's rucksack which he had thrown away on the slope, but Vielle seemed deaf to all our appeals which became rougher and rougher.

Meanwhile I went on to prepare the first of a very long series of rappels down the Roches Gruber. The sky had cleared for a moment, but the fine spell only lasted a short time. I could hear my companions inciting Vielle who had still not got across the couloir. I shouted to them to hurry up and begin the descent if we didn't want to die up there. I was the farthest down and was waiting for Kohlman who had followed me. Half an hour passed. Not understanding the delay, I again went up the rope for a few feet to see what was happening. Gallieni told me that Vielle was exhausted, that he was unable to cross the couloir by himself. He asked me if it would be possible to slide him along the snow to lighten the fatigue of walking. I agreed and told him to act quickly, adding that at this pace not only would we not get to the Gamba hut, but we would not even get down the Roches Gruber.

I went down again and rejoined Kohlman. I gathered from the excited voices of my companions that they were putting their plan into effect. I went on waiting for one of them to lower himself to me. Another half hour passed and not only did no one come down to join me, but their voices began little by little to die away. I didn't know what to do. Must every rappel take as long as this? Once again I shinned up the rope a few feet, far enough to be able to see my companions. I asked them: "Why don't you come down?" A voice, possibly Gallieni's, followed by that of Mazeaud, told me: "Vielle is dying!" I was petrified. I could see before me the little group of friends gathered around Vielle's body, which looked like a dark, inert bundle on the white snow. He was belayed to the rock and wrapped in our tent-cover to prevent the crows from getting at him.

I went back to Kohlman without telling him anything. Several more minutes, perhaps twenty, passed; now I knew it was all over with Vielle. There were no more voices to be heard, only the sound of the wind. It had begun to snow again. This agony unbroken by any human word was terrible. I went up the rope again and saw my companions busy securing to a piton Vielle's body and Gallieni's rucksack, full of superfluous things. There were no laments. It was then ten o'clock. I went back again to Kohlman and told him to hold fast. Then Mazeaud arrived, who told him in broken phrases what had happened. Kohlman was deeply affected, and wept.

We continued the rappel. Taking advantage of a moment

when all six of us were hanging on the same piton, I advised the greatest possible speed if we did not want to share Vielle's fate. Oggioni, as always, was my right-hand man and took the rear. Like Mazeaud, Guillaume and myself, he was carrying a full rucksack. Mazeaud, the strongest and the acknowledged leader of the Frenchmen, had the job of keeping the others up to the mark.

Not quite an hour had passed when we heard voices. I was the farthest down the rope at the time and I thought they must be the voices of my companions above me. Soon, however, I was convinced that someone was searching for us on the glacier below. I shouted back and asked my companions to shout all together, so that they could hear us. From the cries which came from below I understood that they wanted to tell me something, but the gusts of wind prevented me from understanding. For my part, I was quite certain that down there they would not be able to understand what I was shouting, which was: where were they and could they hear us. We went on in better spirits. When we reached the end of the Roches Gruber; about half-past three, I calculated that from the morning before, when we had begun the descent, we had made at least fifty rappels.

A brief break in the storm allowed us to see the whole surface of the chaotic Freney glacier. What a lot of snow had fallen! There were no furrows in the snow, which meant that no rescue party had passed that way. Where had the voices come from? We could see no one and fell into a mood of the blackest despair. Perhaps it was all over for all of us. We had been sure that the voices had come from the foot of the Roches Gruber and that had given us strength to overcome the terrible difficulties and dangers of that exceedingly difficult passage. We were, however, alone at the foot of the rocks and we still had before us many unforeseeable dangers on our way to the Gamba hut.

The slow and exhausting descent of the glacier began. We refused to accept our bad luck. The snow was still very deep. Not even in winter climbs could I recall having met with so much. We left behind us not a trail but a burrow. Fortunately the mists were beginning to rise and visibility gradually improved. That made it possible for us to enter safely the labyrinth of crevasses which led to the Col de l'Innominata, the last serious difficulty on our way to safety. But the deep snow so slowed down our advances, that we despaired of being able to reach the base of the col while there was still daylight.

I felt faint with fatigue, physical suffering and cold, but refused to give up.

Our file grew longer. Oggioni was stumbling every few steps, at the end of his tether. He was without a rucksack, which he had handed over to Gallieni. Sometimes he was last man, sometimes last but one. We groped our way on to the glacier in complete disorder, drunk with fatigue. We were roped together, but each went his own way without heeding anything. I realized that in such conditions it would be very hard for us to reach the foot of the Col de l'Innominata in daylight. Gallieni, behind me, seemed the least exhausted. I decided to unrope myself and him in order to go ahead as quickly as we could and prepare the couloir of the Innominata, otherwise our companions would no longer be able to climb it. This task would have to be completed by nightfall.

Our companions followed in our tracks. Meanwhile I attacked the terrible ice which had encrusted the Col de l'Innominata. Guillaume had remained behind. Within half an hour it would be dark and we were still struggling to reach the col. Now we were again all roped together; myself, Gallieni, Oggioni, Mazeaud and Kohlman. Our only hope was to reach the rescue parties while we still had a little strength left. They alone might be able to save those left behind. It was pitch dark when I reached the Col de l'Innominata. It was Saturday evening, after nine o'clock, and we had been out for six days. The powdery snow driven by the wind had begun again and in the west we could see the flashes of an approaching thunderstorm. There was nowhere to fix a piton to anchor the rope which supported my four companions and I had to hold it on my shoulders. I urged them to hurry. But the operation was very long and desperate. Orders mingled with cries of pain and desperation. Behind Gallieni, Oggioni seemed unable to grip the rock. Gallieni tried to help him in every way he could, supported in his turn by the rope which I held on my shoulders. The two Frenchmen down at the end of the rope were shouting and raving.

It was chaos. Three hours passed and we were still at the same point. I could not move. Every so often there were tugs at the rope which nearly pulled me into space. The pain of the rope and the cold made me feel faint. But if I collapsed it meant the end for everyone. In all those three hours Oggioni had not been able to move. All encouragement was in vain. Now and then he would reply with a wail; he seemed to be in a sort of trance. He was attached by a karabiner to a piton, and would have to free himself from it to give us a chance of hauling him up. But he hadn't the strength and he was so exhausted that perhaps he was incapable of thinking. I would have liked to go down to him but that was impossible since I had to keep the rope, which was holding him as well as Gallieni, firmly on my shoulders. At last, not being able to do anything else, Gallieni made sure that Oggioni was firmly fixed to the piton, undid the rope that bound him to Oggioni and the Frenchmen and came up to join me and was thus able to carry on rapidly towards the rescue parties. Oggioni remained roped to the strong Mazeaud, to whom I shouted to wait and look after the others who would soon be rescued.

While we were doing this we saw Kohlman fumbling his way along the rope in the darkness on the ice-covered face. He was unroped. He came towards us and passed Mazeaud, Oggioni and Gallieni with an energy born of desperation which bordered on madness. Gallieni, guessing his state, managed to grasp him and tie him to the rope. Soon all three of us reached the col. Kohlman told us he was hungry and thirsty and then went on: "Where is the Gamba hut?" He was completely out of his senses, but we could not abandon him.

We roped him between us. Gallieni was the first to begin the descent, followed by Kohlman who seemed to have forgotten all the rules of prudence. The slope was very difficult, steep and covered with ice. For the first 150 ft we let ourselves slide along a fixed rope evidently left there by the rescue parties searching for two Swiss on the Pointe Gugliermina. Then we went on as best we could. But Kohlman became more and more dangerous. He let himself slide on his back, hanging on to the rope and without using his crampons. At the end of the rope he continued to hang there and I had to support him, which made it impossible for me to catch up with him. When at last the rope became lighter, after he had found some sort of foothold, an unexpected tug told me he had again broken away and exposed us all to the risk of falling.

Neither threats nor encouragements moved him. He shouted disconnected phrases, gesticulated, raved. We thought we should have managed to get down in an hour; with Kohlman, now delirious, that hour became three.

With God's help, we reached the bottom. We still had an hour before us to reach the Gamba hut over snowdrifts which presented neither dangers nor difficulties save for their depth. We began to recover our spirits and our only thought was how to reach the hut quickly when an unexpected incident delayed us. Gallieni had dropped one of his gloves. He bent down to recover it and tried to keep his hand warm by thrusting it into his jacket. Kohlman, who interpreted this movement as an attempt to draw a pistol, spread his arms and rushed on Gallieni, clasping him tightly and making him roll down the slope. Gallieni managed to break free and I tried to check their movements with the rope. Kohlman then hurled himself at me. I dodged and he fell and began to roll, writhing in delirium. He had completely lost his senses. Then he rose again and tried to rush at us. By pulling both ends of the rope, we managed to keep him at a distance. We were all three roped together and one of us could break free. We could not drag him with us and it was essential not to lose a minute.

To untie ourselves from him, we had first to undo the iced-up knots. We had no knife, yet we had to get away from our poor crazed companion. He was watching every movement, ready to launch himself at us. One at a time, keeping the rope taut with our teeth, we lowered our breeches so as to be able to slip the noose of rope about our waists over our hips. We succeeded in this without Kohlman realizing what we were doing. Then I shouted to Gallieni: "Let go and run!" and we rushed off, rolling on the snow. There was ony one thing to do: we must get to the hut in time to tell the rescue squads. Kohlman, up there, was in no danger of falling. But, as it happened, the first squad only arrived in time to see him draw his last breath.

In this way we covered the last 1,200 ft which still divided us from the Gamba hut. It was pitch dark. We only managed to find it because I knew this area as well as my own house. Gallieni followed me unhurt. We circled the hut, hammering on the windows with our fists. We had just reached the door when we heard heavy steps inside and a hand raised the latch. The door burst open; we saw the interior of the hut dimly lit by a small lamp. It was full of sleeping men. We stepped over several bodies without recognizing anyone. Then suddenly one of the men leapt to his feet and shouted: "Walter, is that you?" and there was a rush of people and we were suffocated by embraces.

"Be quick!" I shouted. "There's one man still out there! The others are on the Innominata! Be quick!" It was three o'clock on Sunday morning. The storm was still raging. We stretched out on the table in the middle of the hut and the others took the frozen crampons from our feet, undressed us and gave us dry clothes and warm drinks. I fell into a heavy stupor. When I awoke about three hours had gone by. The bodies of my companions had been found, except Vielle. They told me that Oggioni was dead and I was filled with uncontrollable grief. Dear Mazeaud, the only one of them to be found alive, embraced me and wept with me.

Mirror, Mirror

Ed Drummond

In 1972 the American Ed Drummond made the first ascent of Arch Wall on the North Face of Trollrygen in Norway. The climb took twenty days.

We reached Oslo in two days, nudging in under the shrouds of cloud spreading a thin fine rain upon toast-faced Norwegians and palefaces alike. It was the first rain for a month. Burning up to Romsdal on the bike, I found my cagoule was promiscuous in the rain, but Lindy, at the back of me, kept dry and fed me on chocolate and made me hum with her big hugs. I couldn't lean on her as I could my cold companion of other years who pulled on my neck: my rain-slimed haul bag, my meticulous Humpty Dumpty. She was continually delighted at new waterfalls; she flew oohs to my ears and near the end of the journey, my goggles crying with rain, I raised a soggy arm at the alp of cloud shearing up a white mile. "That's the wall," I roared. She gripped her hand on my arm, and yelled about the coming bend.

Where am I? I'm cold. Thin mists shift past, touching me. Where is she? She must have got out of the bag. I shake my head out, struggling to look. There is another near me, raw-red in the white air. Hugh! A dream. I'm not on the Romsdalhorn. That was a week ago. Lindy isn't here. This is the wall.

So. Three nights. Almost 1,000 ft. Our second ledge, Luckys.

Seven pitches and a paper-dry cag. Hugh's still in the bag, sleeping the sleep of the just, sound as a foetus, on his first wall. During the past three years I had, in three summers and a spring, snailed the mile-long approach scree twenty-three times and twenty times I came back. Not this time. "The Northern European Wall"; "The Mourning Wall"; "The Rurt Wall" (Realised Ultimate Reality Troll); "The Lord of the Walls"; "The Drummond Route" (if we said nothing they'd call it this); "The Royal Wall", naw, what has Robbins ever done for you? You'll never level with him.

On our first cralk up to the wall – the scree is so steep that it's like trying to ski uphill – we had climbed the first slabs, 200 ft or so, gritty, nasty, wobbling to extreme. There had been the snow pitch, cricket size, and the jokes about forgetting the ice-axes, using skyhooks and etriers as we had no crampons and the ice was marble. Then the 'schrund and my little leap; it was all fun. After three trips we'd brimmed the hauls and I'd climbed the third, a squirrelly free up a great crooked slab, funnelling to an upside-down squeeze chimney that made me squeak. Then we went down, Lindy, who'd come up to watch, and I, slowly, like two old people, while Hugh flew off to the river where he swam among the salmon; the fishermen had all gone home. We just promised us a swim when it was all over.

Returning, two days later, Hugh went first and the hauls went after, quite a while after. His first haul; his first artyfishyl; first hamouac; first air jumar (barring one from a tree in Mexico). Hugh was, slowly, going up the wall. So it was noon when I set out on the fourth pitch.

And it was seven in the evening when Hugh's jumars gritted their teeth to follow. What passed in those seven hours is unforgettable: my mouth, sock-hot; my larynx strangling for spit; a fine trembling as of a thin wind trembling through me. It began with a layback of twenty feet, wonderful but for the iron stone around my neck – it was a struggle, favourite uncle, was it not? Then the footholds faded away and I muttered on nuts under this thin roof until the only way up was up.

There was a crack, not a crack crack, but a line, a cra . . .; the start of a crack say. At any rate the bolts were in the haul bag and this was the third pitch of the N.A. Wall as far as I was concerned. My rurps curled up when I banged their heads and refused to sit still. After five fingernail knifeblades I got out my hook and sat on that, about as secure as the last angel to make it on to that pin head. Then I struck dirt. Now dirt is okay if you can get dug in. I began and ended with a knifeblade which dangled sillily from my waist, and I was glad that it was not me that was holding the rope, for after four hours and forty feet I might have been caught napping. But Hugh wasn't and as it was I only went fifteen feet for the hook stuck and though it trembled it snapped not, O Dolt.

So then I had to free that bit, but after that it eased some. Nuts hammered in the dirt and at long last a ding dong bong. Hotheaded I'd reached a ledge, feeling a bit sorry for myself. "No Ledges" we called it and it all hung out. There we had a pantomime in hammocks by headtorch which was really not in the least bit funny. Hugh, as chattery as a parrot, floated above me in his one-point. He even said he was comfortable and had the cheek to take a shit. By a battery *son-et-lumiere* I watched his anus line an angry eye; no voyeur but it might look my way. However, he missed me, my arms full of ropes like some deeply confused spider.

"Ed! Come on, it's light."

Oh, God, awake already.

"Look at the sun."

Why don't you go back to sleep?

"Unh uh."

There and then I decided that if he was unable to lead the next pitch, then that was it. I'd led every pitch so far (didn't you want to?) and it was unthinkable that I'd lead all of them. Not bloody likely. I'd make that clear. I tortoised out. What are you smiling at? Rather him than me. I've had about bloody five minutes bloody sleep. "Right, coming."

It was strange to be there, sitting up in the hammock, feet stirring in the air over the side, opening the haul, fingers weaseling in the cold stuff bags, tramp-thankful for food in the hand. Eating quietly we heard the whipcrack of breaking ice in the gloomy cwm below and I'd yell "hello" with a dervish fervour (wake up, Drummond, grow up, you can't go back). The echoes yodelled and I'd say to Hugh, "He's there."

"Who?" he'd ask.

"That bloke," I'd tell him. "Listen." And I'd do it again and we'd both cackle like kids with a home-made phone.

By 7 a.m. I was ready to belay him. I wasn't laughing now. One more pitch and there would be no retreat. I moled into the cold rope bag, my arms up to my elbows, fingers fiddling for the iron sling. I had a krab, empty, ready on the belay to receive it. My fingers curled in the sling; I moved my arm gracefully, slowly (I was cold), to clip it into the krab before passing it up to him. If I drop the iron sling we'll have to go back down. From the end of my arm my little family of fingers waved at me. And it went, there, no, once, twice, there, oh, down, out, there, and under and into the heart of the icefield, clinking like lost money.

I couldn't believe it. Hugh was silent. I kept saying I was sorry. I didn't mean it. Not this time (How do you know?). I couldn't believe it. Hugh said nothing.

"I've done it now."

Instantly, "How long will it take you to get back up?"

He's got you now.

I got back by noon, gasping. I'd come down to earth. A 600 ft abseil, my figure-of-eight sizzling my spits at it, and then a free jumar all the way back. I was furious. "Right, belay on."

His pitch was perfect after a bit. Dirty at first, then a cool, clean fist-lock crack. Iron out in the air like a bunch of weapons, he groped at the sky like something falling. All around a sea-sheer swell of wall, untouchable. Him the one sign of life.

Then the rain came. A dot in the eye. I heave for my cagoule, one eye on Hugh, an invisible drizzle blackening the rock. New noises fizz in. Twitters of water and Hugh is yelling for his cagoule, but I point out the time and that he's leaking already. Well, for a couple of hours I kept pushing boiled sweets in my mouth and Hugh kept on moaning and kept on. After 150 ft he had to stop and pin himself to the wall.

Early evening. There he hung, wringing himself like fresh washing. Thank God he had no cagoule, or we would both have been up there for the night, him perched above, if not on, my head like a great wet heron. The waterfalls would weep all night. "Why wait for Godot?" I yelled up. He said, "Eh?" so I said, "Come on down, let's piss off."

We stripped the ropes off the hauls, tied the lot together and down we went, happy as nuns in a car. A slalom down the scree and back before dark. Back in the camp hut we listened with Lindy, gladly, to the rain hissing outside while we kissed at a smug mug of tea and drooled on the food to come. That night I slept like a child.

Eight days later, well picked, we humped up the boulder-fields in epileptic sunshowers, snagged at by cold-cutting winds. The days were getting shorter.

The bergschrund had rotted back and we had to go down inside the mouth. Our ropes were twenty feet up the slabs, strung taut to a peg. I manteled up on this mica jug, massaging off the dust, feeling sick with this white pit under me, thirty feet deep, rocks in its dark, lurking.

When I had the end of the rope I dangled a bong on and looped it to him. Three times I threw and three times I missed; each time the bong tolled dolefully. "Hey, our funeral knell," I yelled, but he wasn't impressed.

Two and half jumehours later Hugh brooded on the haul eggs, sucking the sacred sweet, as I botched up the freeasy and awkwaid of the next pitch. When I warbled down about the ledge I'd found, he said he'd kiss me, but on arrival he didn't hold me to the treat. In fact, the first thing that he said was that the next pitch looked a bit steep for him and ordered me to do it. But since it was dark I could wait until tomorrow. Under the tube-tent, scarfed in cigar smoke, we crept to sleep like refugees.

Pitch 7 took me all the next day. It is 156 ft long; our ropes were 150 ft long, at a stretch. That last six feet to the belay cracks saw me lying flat on my face on the ledge, hammering like front-crawling. Hugh climbed up from his end, pulling the haul bags (one at a time, and there were three, each weighing over 50 lb) on to his shoulder and then weightlifting them up so that I could get them through the pulley. Hugh studied Law at university.

So. Three nights. Almost 1,000 ft. Lucky's Ledge is no longer important. A stab of butter, a jab of honey; the pumpernickel crumbling among your fingers, a steamy censer of tea, packing your bags, hurrying as a jostle of cumulus smudges out the sun and the stove starts to fizz the drizzle.

As I remember we made three pitches that day in a rain as insidious as gas. For two or three seconds, suddenly the valley would come like an answer, and we would stumble into conversation, then numb up, sullen with wet clothes and cold, clubbed feet. In the downpouring darkness I jumed up to Hugh, squatting on blocks, owl aloof. While he belayed me I hand-traversed down to a ledge on his left, where I backheeled and rubbled away for over half an hour, making the bed. We couldn't find pin placements for the tube tent, so we hung our bivi bags from the rope and crept into their red, wet dark.

Sneaking out the next day at noon like shell-less tortoises, I realized as we both emptied a gallon of fresh water from our bags, that it might be better to have the opening at the front rather than at the top of the bag. A point that had escaped me as I tried out the bag on the floor in front of the fire at home. Sneer not. Wasn't the first Whillans Box a plastic mac and a pram? The Drummond Cot would have its night in time. Well, we strung the tube tent as an awning, lit the stove, and wrung our pulpy feet out, sitting in the cloud, machine-gunned by water drops from the great roofs that crashed out over 200 ft wide, a thousand feet above our heads. We wriggled a little in the tent, slowly gulping lumpy salami, a bit stunned, stuttering with cold.

At about four we took the hood off our heads and saw the valley for the first time in twenty hours: the curve of the railway line, the thin black line of the road, pastures of grass, the glitter of the river, the big stacks of corn like yellow firs. The red tractor a slow blood drop. Then we heard yells, names, my name, and saw a spot of orange jump at the toe of the scree. It was Lindy calling, calling, and I called for my favourite team: "LindyLindy LindyLindy," and the wall called with me. Hugh even asked if I was going out that night.

Morning. The fifth day. Cornflower blue skies, fiord-cold in the shade, and above us brooded a huge wing of white granite, its edge a thin black slab about as long and steep as the spire of Salisbury Cathedral. I had seen this from the scree. We go that way.

Two skyhooks raised me off the rubble, and dash, wobbling, for ten feet without protection – a necessary enema after the 30-hour sit-in. Then I'm staring at a poor flare where I belt a nut. Little chains of sweat trickle down my back. I'm struggling to free climb and Hugh's not even looking. Jerkily I straggle to a ledge, not a word of wonder escaping his lips as I braille for holds and shake on to this ledge with a flurry of boots. With time against us I was doing all the leading. Hugh sat still on his stone throne while I squirmed about, greasing my palms with myself. Still, a cat may look, and he was the one rock, the one unshakeable, all the way there and back.

Abseiling down in the dying day, the bergschrund breaking its wave beneath my feet 1,500 ft below in the cold ammonia air, the tube tent was a rush of bright flesh, raw on the ledge, and Hugh, his back bent, peering, was a black bird feeding at it. After a soup supper, watched by the smouldery eye of Hugh's cigar, I blew my harmonica, and brought tears of laughter to our eyes. We were doing okay. Hugh even said he liked to hear me play.

Two days later we were barely 300 ft higher, and what I could see was not pretty. It looked as though, during the night, someone had pumped Hugh's foot up. His skin transparent as tracing paper, the foot was a mallet of flesh, the toes tiny buds; thalidomide. I didn't want to say too much. Perhaps the strain of his jumaring had done it, or the rotting wet when we were at Lucky's taking the waters. It was early yet; we had a long way to go. He said he just needed to rest it.

The ledge was lovely and I was glad to linger there. We spread ourselves around, Hugh blowing gently on his foot while I had a bath. A snip of cotton for a flannel, line for a towel, and a nip of antiseptic to give my spit a bit of bite. With behindsight I don't recommend the antiseptic neat, my dears. Let me tell you it wasn't a red face I had. The funny thing was it didn't hurt at the time I dabbed it, lovingly, my back turned while I blinked over the drop; but the day after, well, as they say, there hangs a tale.

A week later, his feet out like two heady cheeses in the dim pink light of the tent, Hugh has the mirror. He's checking on the stranger – the first time in twelve days, squeezing his pimples, humming some Neil Young song. For four days we've been in and out of this womb tube, harassed each time we go outside by the web of stuff bags breeding at the hole end. They are our other stomachs. We feel in them for our pots, our pottage, and our porter (although the porter is water since we've finished the orange). Cosmetics ended, we turn to draughts, drawing a board on the white insulating pad and inventing a set of signs for pieces and moves. So we pass an hour; doze, shift, fidget, sleep, talk, warn, fart, groan or cackle, plan, doze, and watch the light dissolve like a dye in the darkness. Snuggled together we are pre-eminently grateful that there is another here at the end of the day. We don't talk about failing and I hardly think about it now – we've been here so long it's a way of life. The pendulum's done now and the only sign I'm waiting for is a weather one. The valley in my mind is out of sight.

In raggy mists we moved quickly, leaving our hauls on the bivouac ledge. Hugh, some deflated astronaut, swam slowly up on jumars as though someone had taken the gravity away. Breezes whiffed up my cuffs and my icy cagoule etherised the back of my neck. After those two pitches, I frog-legged left, my numb hands bungling on the flat holds, to reach a little ledge from where I would go down to pendulum. After each pitch I was getting a bit desperate with the cold and I'd can-can to keep warm. Hugh, only forty feet away, was a white ghastly shadow.

Below us, Norway was at war. A volcanic pit of bursting water; the cwm boomed, a vat of slashed air. Stones howled around us and avalanching crashes trembled the wall. And I. Nothing could be seen in the gassing mist. No pendulum today.

Going back to our home, Hugh passed out into the cloud first, using the haul lines as a back rope to the bivouac ledge, which would otherwise have been impossible to return to because of the overhanging wall. When I got down he'd a brew ready which lit a fire, briefly, inside me. My thanks that it wasn't snowing just about made it.

During the night it snowed.

In the morning it was still falling, so we rolled over; better sleep on it. In the fitful sleep of that day I had my dream! The editor of *Mountain* had arrived at the foot of the scree and, with a foghorn or some kind of voice, had managed to wake me, telling me that he had come all the way from England to let me know what a great job I was doing for British rock-climbing (he never mentioned Hugh), and also how we were contributing to better Anglo-Norwegian political relations.

By the time I awoke he was gone but Hugh hadn't; he was just vanishing down the hole at the other end. My watch told 4 a.m., the night had gone. I oozed out of my pit to find lard-pale Hugh with the blue black foot, sitting stinking in a skinful of sun. For half an hour we wallowed, exposing ourselves to the warm air. New creatures we were, able, if not to fly, at least to jumar, up there. And up there, today, I had to swing for it.

I try, flying, at thirty feet below Hugh, then fifty feet, then eighty feet, then at over a hundred feet and I'm a bit too low so I jume up to about ninety-five. "Ed Leadlegs," I tell him but only the wind hears me. I'm getting a bit tired; Hugh has given up asking me how I'm doing and he is just hanging, staring, his pipe alight – the wind brings a tang of it to me. No doubt he's thinking of his girl in Mexico.

The white wall is so steep here that I can barely keep hold of it when I crab myself right for the big swing. But my first swings wing me out into space away from the wall and I have to pirouette to miss smashing my back. This is ridiculous. Like a spider at puberty I toil but spin not. It's after 2 p.m. Lindy will be here soon.

When I've fingernailed back as far right as I can (and this time I manage about four feet more) I'm nearly eighty feet away from the groove that I'm trying to reach.

I'm off, the white rushing past; out, out, away from the wall, way past the groove, out – I tread air, the valley at my feet. Hugh moons down, he's yelling something – can't hear a word he's saying – rushing, coming back, crashing in, wall falling on top of me, I kick, jab, bounce my boot, bounce out, floating, an easy trapeze. Then the unknown groove is running into my open arms and I strike at a flake and stick. Fingers leeching its crack.

I hung a nut in (my jumars attaching me to the rope are pulling me up), then I get an et. and stand in it. The nut stays put. Jumars down. Now put a knife under that block. The press of the block keeps it in as I weigh in on it. Out flips the nut. Whoops. I know I'm going to get there. I can't see Hugh but I know he's there. A tiny nut like a coin in a slot. Watch me. The knifeblade tinkles out. Thank you. The nut gleams a gold tooth at me. There you go. To climb is to know the universe is All Right. Then I clink a good pin in at a stretch. Can't get the nut now (it's still there). And then I'm in the groove, appalled at the sheer, clean walls around and below me, baying for breath, my heart chopping through my chest.

We have lost 100 ft, but gained a narrow track of cracks that will, I believe, lead to the "Arch Roof", the huge, square-cut overhang that from the valley looks like an old press photo of the Loch Ness Monster. I saw a crack in 1970 through binoculars going out through the top of his head. "Loch Ness Monster sighted on Troll Wall." I'd out-yeti Whillans yet. Just before dark Hugh lands and goes on ahead to order dinner; we're eating out at the Traveller's Tube tonight, a farewell meal. The pendulum being done, our time was going and so must we.

But it snowed for two days.

On the thirteenth day the sun rubbed shoulders with us again, and Hugh jumared up at a snail sprint. He found that the yellow perlon he was on had rubbed through to half its core, so he tied that out with an overhand before I came up at a slow rush. Halfway up I worked loose a huge detached flake which had hung 100 ft above our tent; it took me five minutes so we had no need to worry. We watch it bounce, bomb-bursting down to the cwm, and the walls applaud.

The crack above the pendulum's end was a nice smile for standard angles except where a ladder of loose flakes is propped. Bloody visions slump at the belay below me. Silence. Care. The hauls zoom out well clear.

The next two pitches, up a bulging, near-blind groove, were ecstasy. I had to free climb. The hooks were only for luck, and I was quick in the blue fields. Above, suddenly, two swifts flashed past, thuds of white. "That's us," I yelled to myself. Lindy may not have been here, but there she was. I could hear her, naming my name, and I flew slowly up. Four fine patches of ledgeless pleasure that day. In the dark Hugh jumared up to the Arch, me guiding his feet with my head torch.

But that night the sky shone no stars. Packs of black cloud massed. Not enough food to eat. A sweet or two. No cigar. And too late to fish for hammocks. All night, four hours, I squirmed in my seat sling. I speculated on recommending to the makers that they rename it the Iron Maiden, but it was too suitable an epitaph to laugh about. My hip is still numb from damaged nerves.

Came the morning I was thrashed. The sun did not exist. The roof over my head was a weight on my mind. Suddenly, over Vengetind the weather mountain, clouds boiled, whipping and exploding in avalanching chaos. Over Lillejfel, a low shoulder on the other side of the valley cauldron, a dinosaur mass of white cloud was rat-arrowing toward us. We could hardly run away; we were so cold and hungry we could hardly move.

I was scared as I moved out under the Arch, a clown without props, all these things were real, there were no nets here, only dear patient Hugh blowing on his fingers.

No man walks on air was all my thought as I melted out of sight, upside down for forty feet, my haul line dissolving in the mist. I couldn't feel that I was connected to anything solid. Fly sized, I mimed away under three giant inverted steps, lips. Not a single foothold, not a toehold in a hundred feet. Just over the final lip, in a single strand of crack, I pinned myself to a wall of water and started to land the hauls.

They must have seen me coming. I couldn't believe it. Raindrops ripped into me, making me wince. The cold rose an octave, catapulting hail into my face. The wind thrummed a hundred longbow cords. I could hardly see through my chinese eyes. Only while I hauled could I stop shaking. My fingers, cut deeply at the tips, were almost helpless. People at upstairs windows watching a road accident in the street below. My feet were dying. My silent white hands.

Hugh came up for air, grinning. He'd had no idea down there. Up here he had the thing itself. Murdering, washing out more than ears. I led off, hardly knowing where, except that we couldn't stay there. I could only just open my karabiners with two hands. Sleet had settled thickly on the bunches of tie-offs.

Both of us were really worried. Hugh cried up after an hour that he was getting frostbite. What could I say? I had to find a place for the night.

If you ever go there and have it the way we did, you'll know why we called it "The Altar". I remember the rush in the drowning dark to hang the tent, the moss churning to slush beneath our feet. Back to back, our backs to the wall, we slumped on three feet of ledge for three days. We had nothing to drink for the first two of those days; our haul bags were jammed below us and we were diseased with fatigue. Lice trickles of wet get everywhere.

I remember Hugh drinking the brown water that had collected in his boots, instantly vomiting it out, and me silently mouthing the gluey water from my helmet. You didn't miss much. Hugh. He shared his food with me, some cheese and dates and a bag of sweets; rare fruits. After a day he had to piss and used quadrupled poly bags which I politely declined to use; I had no need. A day later my proud bladder was bursting. But sitting, propped in a wet bed of underwear, I was impotent. For over two hours I strained and grunted in scholastic passion. Hugh said it was trench penis. A sort of success went to my head, however, or rather on to and into my sleeping bag. After that I felt like some great baby, trapped in his wet cot, the air sickly with urine, and sleep would not come.

To get more room, both of us, we later confessed when there were witnesses present, developed strategies of delay while we shuffled the status quo. "Could you sit forward a minute?" Or, "Would you hold this for me?" At times I'd get Hugh to tuck my insulating pads around me to bluff off the cold stone. It was deeply satisfying to have someone do that. Grizzly, bristly Hugh: what a mother.

We wondered if this could continue for more than a week. But we didn't wonder what would happen if it did. We never talked about not finishing. (We were just over 1,000 ft below the summit.) It was no longer a new route to us. It was not possible to consider anything else as real. There were no echoes from the valley. There was no valley. There was no one to call your name. No wall now; unhappy little solipsists, all we had was each other.

We began to get ratty, like children locked in a bedroom. An elbow scuffled against a back once or twice as we humped back to stop the slow slide off the ledge. A ton of silence rested on us like a public monument, for hours on end. I felt that this was all sterile. I ate food, wore out my clothes, used up my warmth, but earned nothing, made nothing. The art was chrysalising into artifice. A grubby routine. Trying not to die. Millions have the disease and know it not. My sleep a continual dream of hammering: banging in pins, clipping in, moving up, then back down, banging, banging, taking them out. A bit like having fleas. Searching for an ultimate belay. Unable to stop: the Holy Nail. My Dad, my dad, why hast thou forsaken me? At times I was pretty far gone.

But it wasn't all self-pity. We talked about the plight of the Trolls and could clearly see a long bony hairy arm poking under the tent, handing us a steaming pan of hot troll tea, and although nothing appeared in our anaesthetic dark, the idea lit a brief candle.

Three days later we were released.

Lindy yelled us out. A giant marigold sun beamed at us. Everywhere up here – and we could see hundreds of miles – was white, perfect, appalling. Across the river I could clearly make out scores of tourists, a distant litter of colour in one of the camping fields opposite the wall. Cars flashed their headlamps and horns bugled as we struggled into view and flagged them with our tent.

Then, quickly, the charging roar of an avalanche. I flattened to the wall. And then I spotted it, a helicopter, gunning in a stone's throw from the wall, a military green with yellow emblems. A gun poked from the window. "Hugh, they're going to shoot us," then, tearing his head up he saw it: an arm waving. We waved arms, heads, legs; danced, jigged, yelled, while they circled in and away like something from another world. Later we learned that it was Norwegian television, but we fluttered no blushes on the wall. The spell of our selves was broken.

Five hours later, after a long lovely 130 ft of aid, intricate and out in space, I was on the final summit walls, the last roofs wiped with light, 700 ft above me.

All that night, while a white moon sailed over our shoulders, we perched on our haul bags and cut off the blood to our already damaged feet, too exhausted to know. Sharing our last cigar while the nerves in our feet were suffocating to death, we shone in our hunger and smiled a while.

As soon as I put my weight on my foot in the new dawn I knew I'd had it. Hugh's foot was an unspeakable image, and I had to tell him when his heel was grounded inside his boot. He could hardly have his laces tied at all and I was terrified that one of his boots might drop off.

All that day the feeling was of having my boots being filled with boiling water that would trickle in between my toes and flood my soles. Then a sensation of shards of glass being wriggled into the balls of my feet. And upon each of my feet a dentist was at work, pulling my nails and slowly filing my toes. Then nothing but a rat-tatting heart when I stopped climbing. I would tremble like water in a faint breeze. I knew it was hypothermia. We had had no food for three days. Maybe it was two.

All the last day we called, a little hysterically I think, for someone on the summit; they were coming to meet us. Sitting fifteen feet below the top, with Hugh whimpering up on jumars I heard whispers . . . "Keep quiet . . . wait until he comes over the top".

There was no one there. Only, thank God, the sun. It seemed right in a way to meet only each other there. At the summit cairn Hugh sucked on his pipe while my tongue nippled at a crushed sweet that he had found in his pocket. We dozed warm as new cakes, in a high white world, above impenetrable clouds which had shut out the valley all day. We were terribly glad to be there. After midnight we collapsed into a coma of sleep, half a mile down in the boulder-field.

We met them the next morning, quite near the road; it must have been about half-past eight. They were coming up to meet us. Lindy flew up the hill to hug me forever. I was Odysseus, with a small o, I was Ed, come back for the first time. Hugh grinned in his pain when I told the Norwegian journalists that his real name was Peer Gynt, and that he was an artist like Van Gogh, but that he had given a foot for the wall, instead of an ear to his girl.

On our last hobble, he had, before we met the others, found himself dreaming of the walks he used to have with his Dad, as a child, into the park to feed the ducks, and of the delights of playing marbles (we were both pocketing stones and rare bits from the summit on down). When we arrived in Andalsnes with our friends, I saw the apples burning on the boughs, glowy drops of gold and red (the green gargoyle buds, the little knuckle apples had lit while we were gone); and the postbox in its red skirt shouted to me as we turned the corner into town. Bodil washed Hugh's feet, sent for her doctor, and everyone in our house was alive and well. Only the Troll Wall gave me black looks, over the hill and far away at last. Black iceberg under eye-blue skies.

Back in England my feet were as irrefutable as war wounds. I was on my back for a month, and I had the cuttings from the Norwegian press, as precious as visas. But nowhere to get to.

Thin Air

Greg Child

An Australian mountaineer, in 1986 he made, along with T. Macartney-Snape and T. Margis, the first ascent of Gasherbrum IV, 7,925 m (26,000 ft) in Trans-Himalaya via the North-West Ridge.

We continue up the ridge, Tim now in the lead. With every foot gained, the tempo of the wind increases. The slope steepens to 65 degrees. We follow Tim's footsteps, kicked into a frozen surface of perfect consistency. I marvel at the parking-lot size imprints his size 12 feet leave behind, but, as I stretch my shorter legs to match his lanky stride, I begin to hyperventilate from the effort.

The slope crests out on a narrow horizontal ridge at 24,500 ft. We catch the full force of the wind here, and crampon for 100 ft to shelter in a rocky outcrop at the ridge's end. We pause to examine the options. The continuation of the ridge above is steep, rocky, difficult. But to the left a band of ice curls toward another icefield. That is the way.

"Rope up?" I ask.

"No. Too slow. We can handle this," says Tim after a moment of consideration.

One by one we front-point across the traverse. Nothing holds us to the face but the inch-long steel fangs of our crampons and the tips of our ice tools. A slip and we'd be sliding down the

Northwest Face, toward the glacier 5,000 ft below. Exposure and exertion create a tingling feeling that runs up the back of my neck. I try to relax. A nervous, thumping heart is an inefficient mechanism up here. Around the corner of the rocks Tim begins to climb up a 300 ft prow of 65 degree ice. Tom and I linger behind. The unroped climbing is increasingly unnerving. Our calves ache from front-pointing. I see Geoff and Andy 100 ft below. Their faces read a mixture of unease and intense concentration. Geoff, front-pointing on a broken crampon, looks particularly concerned.

"I don't like the looks of where Tim is going," I say to Tom.

"Me neither. I'll try out left."

He traverses 80 ft to a more gentle slope but ends up in waist-deep snow. He shakes his head. The wind-polished ridge crest is the only safe path. We return to Tim's prow. At 10.00 a.m. we exit the ice field and huddle into a wind-carved niche bounded by a ridge wall of sun-warmed orange-brown marble. The altitude is 25,000 ft. In front of us, the final 40 degree ice slope to the headwall glints in the sun. But for the snow ramps I'd seen from Broad Peak, switchbacking up the wall, interspersed by vertical cliffs, few weaknesses break the smooth headwall. Somewhere left of our line is Voytek's line of descent. One look at the wall tells us that we won't be back at the tents tonight. In the niche we brew up and talk turns to tactics.

"It looks like hard going above," says Tim. "I reckon we dump everything here and go light. We should be able to make it to the summit and back to here by nightfall."

Geoff, fiddling with his broken crampon, listens on with reservations. If Tim reasoned by leaps of optimism, Geoff reasoned by clear-headed pessimism. We had ten hours to climb 1,000 vertical feet to the North Summit and traverse 1,500 ft horizontally to the true summit. Just by looking at the headwall it was obvious that there'd be climbing as hard as grade 5.9. We'd be pushing to do all that, and abseil down, in ten hours. Even with our light packs, we'd move slowly, yet without bivouac gear up there, we'd be committed to bivouac in the niche. If we were caught out on the headwall, it wouldn't be pretty.

The water in the pot heats up and we share a drink of hot chocolate.

"Well?" Tim asks.

"Okay, we go light," I say.

We stash the stove and bivouac gear in the niche and head to the base of the headwall with only climbing gear and headlamps. We each carry a partially full water bottle stuffed inside our down suits. Tim carries the cine camera, shooting film as he goes.

The icefield butts against the headwall. We arrive at a steep crack in a fifty foot cliff. Above this, the snowramps begin. It seems like the best place to start. Tom hammers in a belay piton and I tie in to lead. After a few easy feet I stand beneath a bulge. I hammer in a piton, strip my mittens down to my liner gloves, and begin jamming my fists and feet into the crack, hauling myself around an overhang. The marble is glass smooth. Crampons scrattle and slip as I inch up, gloves become sodden, hands cold and wooden. The amount of oxygen I need is more than I can suck out of the air. A heady lightness, like a glimpse of unconsciousness, washes over me in waves. Gasping desperately, I pause above the bulge, with one foot wedged into the crack, the other stemmed out onto a flake. It's a rest, of sorts. I will myself to breathe more slowly, and suck on my fingers to warm them. I find myself thinking of Voytek's letter. "Do not fear the headwall, it is nice surprise," he'd written. Some surprise.

As I creep up I hear a shout from Geoff: "I'm going down."

I know what he's thinking. That we're too slow and we'll never make it before dark, that the weather has been good for five days and can't last much longer, that to be caught in a storm without bivvy gear on this wall will be the end of us, that with his snapped crampon it's too risky. I try to shout to him that I'm nearly on the snow ramp, that it looks easier for a long way above, but only a croak exits my dry throat. I see him zigzagging down the slope, toward the niche, where he will bivouac and await us. Watching him descend is like losing a piece of my own body. He'd given his all to get us here but he knew where to draw the line. I hoped we'd be as clear-headed as the day wore on.

I continue up the crack for twenty feet, to a point where ice fills the cracks and the footing again becomes insubstantial. I try for ten minutes to rig protection but nothing works. Finally I take my ice hammer and swing it into the frozen crack. Half of the pick bites. I clip the hammer's wrist-loop to the rope and gasp and grasp onto a patch of snow ten feet above.

"I'm okay now," I shout, turning to crampon up the ramp.

"Well done. It looked hard," calls a voice over my shoulder.

I turn to see Andy, just a few feet away, wobbling onto the snow ramp after soloing up another crack.

"Jesus, Tuthill. Why didn't you tell me it was easier over there? I thought I was gonna die on this crack!"

"I thought I was gonna die on *this*."

I inspect the verglassed wall he'd just climbed. If anything, it looked more difficult than my crack. He just felt like moving, that's all. 150 ft later I reach a large block and secure the rope around it. Andy, followed by the others, jumars up. Tom is coughing wildly again, his lung infection back in full force.

Andy leads a second long pitch, then Tim takes over for two leads. The route alternates between steep ramps covered in snow and short vertical rock steps. Marble, limestone, and occasional lenses of diorite collide. Protection is minimal, the climbing tricky. We grow more and more tired, move slowly and slower. At 3.00 p.m. I join Tim on a ledge: 100 ft above us the headwall ends and the ridge to the smaller North Summit begins. I tie in to the lead end of the rope and begin to pull up over some blocks. After a few feet I return to the ledge and, gasping and weak, hand the task to Tim.

"You lead it. I'm exhausted. I need time to rest."

Tim disappears into a chimney. Thirty minutes later he reaches the ridge.

As the four of us jumar up and gather on the narrow crest at 25,850 ft, we consider our position. About 150 easy feet higher and some 700 horizontal feet east is the North Summit. From there, due south by 1,500 horizontal feet, we see the true summit, 40 ft higher than the North Summit. The time is 4.00 p.m., the skies are still clear but on the ridgecrest we are exposed to a wind that makes conversation almost impossible. No one needs to be told that we will not make the summit and get back to the foot of the headwall before dark.

Our bodies burn with fatigue. We stand there, watching dusk

gather over the Karakoram. The realization that we've blown it begins to sink in. If we descend, we'll never climb Gasherbrum IV, yet to press on seems like insanity. Everything seems about to turn to shit. Then the worm of unfinished ideas begins to twist in our heads. The crazy talk begins.

"I'm certain I can make it through the night without frostbite," says Tim, the words ripped out of his mouth by wind.

"Bivvy out?" I ask.

"Either that or go down."

We have nothing but the clothes on our backs. No water, food, or stove. I'd read long ago about Hermann Buhl sitting out a night just below the summit of Nanga Parbat. It seemed to me then something only a superman could endure or a madman conceive. I'd also heard the separate tales of Nazir Sabir and Jim Wickwire, both of whom had sat out nights near the summit of K2. Nazir had suffered memory loss for months. Jim's bivouac had cost him a piece of lung when fluid had frozen in his chest. And there was Bonatti and Mahdi on K2. Even with an oxygen cylinder, Mahdi had lost his feet. A bivouac here would be harsh, but at the same time I felt that our chances were good; the weather was clear, and we still had some strength left. Instinct condoned the idea, the ambition put words in my mouth.

"I'll risk it," I hear myself say.

Our own private epic begins to take shape.

Tom and Andy look with uncertainty about the clear horizon. That hacking cough is hammering Tom's ribs again. He's running on sheer determination. Andy, who'd frozen toes in years past, looks about the icescape, justly concerned.

"Don't be talked into this by us. It could be a bad night. Maybe frostbite. Think hard," I say.

They bat it about for a few moments, torn between the rationality of descent and the irrationality of success.

"I'm staying," says Tom.

"No, it's not worth it to me. I'm going down," says Andy, seeing the enormity of the gamble.

"Alone?" Descending the rock band unaccompanied seemed dangerous.

"You're worried about me? I'm more worried about you!

Anyway, tonight is the summer solstice, the shortest night of the year."

"Yeah? At least we've got that going for us."

Andy rips a 12 in by 24 in foam pad out of the back of his rucksack and hands it to us. We divide the hardware: he takes three slings, five pitons, a wired chock, and a rope. We give him the larger share of the gear in order that he should have enough to make five or six abseils. We hope that the next day we'll find his anchors, maybe Voytek's as well . . .

"Good luck." He turns and leaves to descend to Geoff at the niche.

Now we are three.

"Well, this is a grand idea but what do we do now?" I ask, as if reproaching myself.

"Gotta dig a hole. That's the only way to make it through the night," Tim replies.

We continue along the narrow ridge for another hour, looking for a suitable site to claw out a snowcave. Just below the North Summit, we find a cluster of snow drifts and cornices. We poke our axes about, to see if the drifts allow a snowcave to be dug into them. All are solid ice. Time creeps by. Despite our leg-heaviness our search for a place to endure the night becomes laced with a certain desperation. To sit out the night on the bare ice and rocks could be fatal if the wind didn't drop. I begin to chop into the ice at my feet. Even crouching in a pit would be better than nothing.

Tim crampons down the side of the ridge to a point where a steep spur joins the Northwest Ridge. It's the ridge the Italians had climbed. Somewhere on that ridge, at the site of the Italian Camp VI, at 24,770 ft, the climber Giuseppe de Francesch had left a statue of the Madonna of Lourdes, given him by his wife, to invoke a blessing for the mountain. Perhaps even after all these years, the Madonna was still there, propped against the rock. It occurs to me that we could use a little divine intervention right now. Then Tim shoves his ice axe into a triangular mound of snow perched on the narrow crest of the Italian Ridge and the shaft sinks deeply.

"Hey, we can get a cave down here."

Tom and I descend. Digging begins.

We scratch out little handfuls of snow with the adzes of our ice axes, digging for five minutes each, then kicking and clawing the snowy payload toward the entrance for the others to remove. The effort is almost more than we are capable of. As I take my turn at digging I think of the bridge we have burned, of what might happen, and what might not. Framed in the entrance to the cave is Broad Peak, where Pete had died and where he still lay. It is almost three years to the day since our struggle to get down the mountain. As oxygen starved as my thoughts are, the essence of my reason for returning to the Karakoram falls clearly into place, as never before. It seemed that finishing that idea I had shared with Pete, to climb G4, would close a circle, would somehow set a cruel score a little more even. Why had I taken so long to understand that this was the fundamental reason I'd come here? And what of my two companions? What drew them here? The beauty? To be able to say they had done it? Did they too have hidden compartments inside them full of thoughts pounding for resolve? Or was adventure enough reason? No time for thoughts. I return to digging.

"Greg, come out here. Look at the sky," Tim calls.

Sky? How can he stand there looking at the sky when night will be on us in a matter of minutes and the snowcave is only half dug?

I back out of the cave. The wind has dropped. Gasherbrums I, II, and III poke up like huge tusks, their snows pearly white, their rocks shining amber. The shadow of Gasherbrum IV is cast across them and the sky is indigo blue, fading into a deeply pink upper atmosphere. Stars penetrate the fading daylight, led by Venus, glinting in the north. Low on the horizon the rising full moon blasts a surreal glow across the Karakoram, from the monsoon thunderheads over Indian Kashmir, to Nanga Parbat in the west.

We stand looking, breathing. For a moment all our doubts vanish. We are quite certain we have chosen the right place to be. As we settle into the cave I feel like a stranded astronaut bedding down for the night on a hostile planet. But no, it's our own wild and beautiful earth.

Cold is the immediate sensation that overcomes us as we seal the entrance to the snowcave with Tim's pack. Height, length, and width, the cave measures four feet in each direction. As the day's last light filters through the thin walls we remove our crampons, then take stock of the few possessions we have. The foam pad from Andy's pack goes beneath us. Whoever is in the middle gets a full seat, while those on either end get one buttock on the pad, the other on snow. We decide to rotate positions during the night.

A mouthful of water remains in each of our bottles. We mix the water with snow to stretch it further and sip it down. The water soaks into our tongues, then is gone. We search the pack and the pockets of our down suits for scraps of food. A mangled energy bar comes up from the bottom of the pack, and from Tim's pocket a stale, crumbling lump of fruitcake. He breaks the cake into three portions. Tom and I sample it and gag: it has the consistency of sawdust.

"Can't eat this shit up here," I grumble.

"That's my mother's fruitcake you're talking about," counters Tim.

"I'm sure it's very nice at Base Camp, but up here it's shit."

Nothing is palatable at altitude. We have no appetites, only a great thirst. Tom and I store the cake in our pockets till we can find a use for it. We contemplate the energy bar.

"Save it for 'ron," I mutter.

"Who?" Tom asks.

Tim chuckles at a familiar Australian wordplay.

"Later-ron," I explain.

We continue the search for anything useful. Tim checks his cine camera. I notice the sheepskin insulation jacket surrounding the camera and suggest someone could sit on it, or we might take turns wearing it as a hat. Tim rejects the proposition, concerned that the motor in the camera might freeze. He is determined to film us on the summit, but if the temperature keeps dropping as fast as it was, we wouldn't see any summit. Teeth were already chattering. Tom was coughing at full force.

"What about the rope?" asks Tom. "We could sit on that."

"I anchored it in the rocks above us. I thought we'd want to be tied in," I reply, grabbing the strand that runs through the door. The snowcave was burrowed into a precarious mound of snow. Its walls were thin enough to knock down with a misplaced elbow. It didn't seem too remote a possibility that the entire cave might fall to bits during the night, emptying us out of it. With that thought, we keep our headlamps ready. We pull what slack is left in the rope into the cave, clip our harnesses into it, and put the rest behind our backs. Then, zipping our suits up and drawing our hoods and balaclavas tightly around our faces, we sit tight.

"What's the time?" Tom asks. His voice wakes me from a snatch of sleep. I notice that Tim is singing.

"Don't ask that, Tom," Tim begs.

I check my watch. Little more than an hour has passed since we entered the cave. I announce the discouraging fact. It seems as though we'd been there longer. Tim resumes his singing, louder, some school song by the sound of it. We begin to shiver violently. I rock my body back and forth, slapping my thighs to the beat of Tim's song, wriggling my toes at the same time. The movement produces a trancelike effect, takes the focus off the cold. I notice Tom moving to the same beat, see him rubbing his hands and banging his feet together, mumbling as he counts sets of a hundred wriggles, loses count, and starts over. My shivering gradually becomes a low wail that sounds very much like someone in constant pain. I begin to think about this pain, the pain we are feeling now, the pain of cold. What is it like, how to quantify it? Like having a tooth pulled without anaesthetic, all day.

"What's the worst bivvy you've ever had?" Tim asks, prompting me to think back on years of cold, wet bivouacs.

"This is," I reply without reservation.

Tom coughs again. Something like a pale green, blood-spattered tadpole flies out of his gullet, hits the wall, and freezes solid. He retreats into himself and takes on the countenance of a zombie. The luxury of conversation, even of the occasional caring "How are you feeling?" drops away. Suddenly I cannot feel my toes.

"My feet – they're going!"

I kick off my boots. Tim unzips his down suit. I put my socked and lifeless feet against his chest. We squirm and shift positions in the tiny hole, like a *ménage à trois* in deep freeze. All we need is a few more hours of windlessness to survive. As we sit shivering, a state, neither sleep nor wake but more like a sedative overdose, full of strange, restless dreams, carries us into our own worlds. All grasp of the flow of time falls away. The night fills with strange mumblings.

As 22 June dawns, sunlight creeps into the snowcave and onto our stiff, hurting bodies. A minuscule veil of frozen moisture momentarily clasps my eyelids together, then releases. We look at each other. Faces are puffed and bloated with mild edema. Capillaries bulge red and angry on our brows. Lips and noses look like peeling sausages. Icicles hang from beards and noses. I recognize none of this ugly crew. Still, the mountain has been kind to us. No one is frostbitten, our lungs breathe free, our heads are untroubled by pain. Outside, the daily wind is building, but the skies remain clear. We enter the daylight, clip crampons to boots, and plod like machines to the nearby North Summit.

Between the North Summit and the summit proper is a long ridge of wind-polished ice that on our right drops over the two mile high West Face, and on our left plunges to a snow plateau 4,000 ft below. The wind from China slams into the East Face and tumbles over the ridge like surf pounding a seawall. At the end of the ridge, somewhere amongst a series of steep-faced limestone towers, is the summit.

We traverse the ice ridge unroped, reaching the cluster of towers in an hour, sheltering from the wind beside the first rocks, where we break out the rope. I tie in and lead off, traversing a snowfield beneath the 80 ft towers, peering through my iced-over goggles, looking for the highest tower. But any one of five separate points above me could be the one. It's a puzzle my altitude-addled brain can barely cope with. I decide we have two choices to the summit: either climb a crack directly in front of me and straddle the jagged summit crest until we reach the highest point, or traverse across the foot of the towers, over verglassed slabs, until we see the summit, and then climb directly up to it.

For some reason I choose the crack. The limestone is solid, 80 degrees steep, the wall sheltered from the brunt of the wind. In

the half-hour the tower takes to climb I become so completely
involved with the task of pulling up on handjams and flakes that
I ignore the bigger picture I'm painting until I reach the
summit crest and see a long double-corniced knife-edge ahead
of me. I've climbed into a dead end.

"This is the wrong way!" I shout down to Tim and Tom.
Spindrift blowing over the ridge sprays them. Watching
through openings in their tightly drawn stormhoods, they've
been aware I was heading into a dead end for several minutes,
but, like me, have been too lost in their windy oxygen-starved
dream-world to be overly concerned.

Cursing my mistake I drape one of our precious slings around
a rock spike and abseil down. Tim takes over, heads toward the
low traverse, balances unroped across the 50 ft wide verglassed
slab beside us, toward a snowfield. His crampons creak shrilly
against the rock. One mittened hand pads over the holdless wall,
the other holds his ice axe, which he hooks into smears of ice.
Neither Tom nor I like the look of the traverse. We rope up.
Tom leads across, placing a piton for protection two-thirds of
the way across.

On the other side of the traverse, the wind is moderate.
There, we stand in a small snowy bowl, directly beneath the
true summit. Tim, ahead of us, is already at the end of the snow
slope, clambering up the summit rocks. Tom and I follow,
towing the rope behind us. Deep pockets in the rock form sure
holds for the final steep moves. Meanwhile Tim sits sheltered
from the wind by a boulder, the cine camera fast against his face,
filming our every move. He holds his breath, shoots a sequence,
then gasps wildly. A few steps to his right is a pointed crest of
snow encrusted onto the summit rocks. I look around, expecting
some final obstacle to surmount, but no, we are on the summit.
It is 10.00 a.m.

Tom, coughing at every step, moves a few steps behind.

"He's a determined bastard," Tim says in admiration.

Seeing the end of the climb, Tom's ashen face breaks into a
smile. The obscure object of desire is reached, the worm within
us is satisfied. Too exhausted for clever words we simply clasp
one mittened hand in another, shake, gaze about us, and turn to
our own thoughts. We'd gone beyond words two days ago,

forced by necessity into a state in which we functioned as a single being. Now on the summit, that being, drunk with euphoria, felt suddenly as if it had merged with sky and mountain as well to become a single, elemental entity, like some rare particle, formed in an atom smasher, existent for a millisecond in time.

The catenulate shapes of Broad Peak, K2, the Gasherbrums, and Chogolisa loom around us. The Trango Towers stand like distant castles at the head of the Baltoro. The sky is cloudless right up to Nanga Parbat. A few photographs later, we jam a stone in a crack on the summit rock-fin, sling it, loop the rope through this, and abseil off the summit. As I back down the rope I feel a moment of regret for not having left something up there in memory of Pete, for the summit we never reached. Instead, I leave a fond thought. It's the best thing I had to give.

It's still there.

The Devil's Thumb

Jon Krakauer

*Born in 1954, Krakauer is an American climber and journal-
ist famous for his account of the 1996 Everest disaster,* Into
Thin Air. *Here he recalls a 1977 solo ascent of* The Devil's
Thumb, *a peak on the Stikine Icecap in Alaska.*

I awoke early on 11 May to clear skies and the relatively warm
temperature of twenty degrees Fahrenheit. Startled by the
good weather, mentally unprepared to commence the actual
climb, I hurriedly packed up a rucksack nonetheless, and began
skiing toward the base of the Thumb. Two previous Alaskan
expeditions had taught me that, ready or not, you simply can't
afford to waste a day of perfect weather if you expect to get up
anything.

A small hanging glacier extends out from the lip of the icecap,
leading up and across the north face of the Thumb like a
catwalk. My plan was to follow this catwalk to a prominent
rock prow in the centre of the wall, and thereby execute an end
run around the ugly, avalanche-swept lower half of the face.

The catwalk turned out to be a series of fifty-degree ice fields
blanketed with knee-deep powder snow and riddled with crevasses. The depth of the snow made the going slow and
exhausting; by the time I front-pointed up the overhanging
wall of the uppermost *bergschrund*, some three or four hours
after leaving camp, I was whipped. And I hadn't even gotten to

the "real" climbing yet. That would begin immediately above, where the hanging glacier gave way to vertical rock.

The rock, exhibiting a dearth of holds and coated with six inches of crumbly rime, did not look promising, but just left of the main prow was an inside corner – what climbers call an open book – glazed with frozen melt water. This ribbon of ice led straight up for two or three hundred feet, and if the ice proved substantial enough to support the picks of my ice axes, the line might go. I hacked out a small platform in the snow slope, the last flat ground I expected to feel underfoot for some time, and stopped to eat a candy bar and collect my thoughts. Fifteen minutes later I shouldered my pack and inched over to the bottom of the corner. Gingerly, I swung my right axe into the two-inch-thick ice. It was solid, plastic – a little thinner than I would have liked but otherwise perfect. I was on my way.

The climbing was steep and spectacular, so exposed it made my head spin. Beneath my boot soles, the wall fell away for 3,000 ft to the dirty, avalanche-scarred cirque of the Witches Cauldron Glacier. Above, the prow soared with authority toward the summit ridge, a vertical half-mile above. Each time I planted one of my ice-axes, that distance shrank by another twenty inches.

The higher I climbed, the more comfortable I became. All that held me to the mountainside, all that held me to the world, were six thin spikes of chrome-molybdenum stuck half an inch into a smear of frozen water, yet I began to feel invincible, weightless, like those lizards that live on the ceilings of cheap Mexican hotels. Early on a difficult climb, especially a difficult solo climb, you're hyperaware of the abyss pulling at your back. You constantly feel its call, its immense hunger. To resist takes a tremendous conscious effort; you don't dare let your guard down for an instant. The siren song of the void puts you on edge, it makes your movements tentative, clumsy, herky-jerky. But as the climb goes on, you grow accustomed to the exposure, you get used to rubbing shoulders with doom, you come to believe in the reliability of your hands and feet and head. You learn to trust your self-control.

By and by, your attention becomes so intensely focused that you no longer notice the raw knuckles, the cramping thighs, the strain of maintaining nonstop concentration. A trance-like state settles over your efforts, the climb becomes a clear-eyed dream. Hours slide by like minutes. The accrued guilt and clutter of day-to-day existence – the lapses of conscience, the unpaid bills, the bungled opportunities, the dust under the couch, the festering familial sores, the inescapable prison of your genes – all of it is temporarily forgotten, crowded from your thoughts by an overpowering clarity of purpose, and by the seriousness of the task at hand.

At such moments, something like happiness actually stirs in your chest, but it isn't the sort of emotion you want to lean on very hard. In solo climbing, the whole enterprise is held together with little more than *chutzpa*, not the most reliable adhesive. Late in the day on the north face of the Thumb, I felt the glue disintegrate with a single swing of an ice-axe.

I'd gained nearly 700 ft of altitude since stepping off the hanging glacier, all of it on crampon front-points and the picks of my axes. The ribbon of frozen melt water had ended 300 ft up, and was followed by a crumbly armour of frost feathers. Though just barely substantial enough to support body weight, the rime was plastered over the rock to a thickness of two or three feet, so I kept plugging upward. The wall, however, had been growing imperceptibly steeper, and as it did so the frost feathers became thinner. I'd fallen into a slow, hypnotic rhythm – swing, swing; kick, kick; swing, swing; kick, kick – when my left ice-axe slammed into a slab of diorite a few inches beneath the rime.

I tried left, then right, but kept striking rock. The frost feathers holding me up, it became apparent, were maybe five inches thick and had the structural integrity of stale cornbread. Below was 3,700 ft of air, and I was balanced atop a house of cards. Waves of panic rose in my throat. My eyesight blurred, I began to hyperventilate, my calves started to vibrate. I shuffled a few feet farther to the right, hoping to find thicker ice, but managed only to bend an ice axe on the rock.

Awkwardly, stiff with fear, I started working my way back down. The rime gradually thickened, and after descending about eighty feet I got back on reasonably solid ground. I stopped for a long time to let my nerves settle, then leaned back from my tools and stared up at the face above, searching for a hint of solid ice, for some variation in the underlying rock strata, for anything that would allow passage over the frosted slabs. I looked until my neck ached, but nothing appeared. The climb was over. The only place to go was down.

Heavy snow and incessant winds kept me inside the tent for most of the next three days. The hours passed slowly. In the attempt to hurry them along I chain-smoked for as long as my supply of cigarettes held out, and read. I'd made a number of bad decisions on the trip, there was no getting around it, and one of them concerned the reading matter I'd chosen to pack along: three back issues of *The Village Voice*, and Joan Didion's latest novel, *A Book of Common Prayer*. The *Voice* was amusing enough – there on the icecap, the subject matter took on an edge, a certain sense of the absurd, from which the paper (through no fault of its own) benefited greatly – but in that tent, under those circumstances, Didion's necrotic take on the world hit a little too close to home.

Near the end of *Common Prayer*, one of Didion's characters says to another, "You don't get any real points for staying here, Charlotte." Charlotte replies, "I can't seem to tell what you do get real points for, so I guess I'll stick around here for awhile."

When I ran out of things to read, I was reduced to studying the ripstop pattern woven into the tent ceiling. This I did for hours on end, flat on my back, while engaging in an extended and very heated self-debate: Should I leave for the coast as soon as the weather broke, or stay put long enough to make another attempt on the mountain? In truth, my little escapade on the north face had left me badly shaken, and I didn't want to go up on the Thumb again at all. On the other hand, the thought of returning to Boulder in defeat – of parking the Pontiac behind the trailer, buckling on my tool belt, and going back to the same brain-dead drill I'd so triumphantly walked away from just a month before – that wasn't very appealing, either. Most of all, I couldn't stomach the thought of having to endure the smug expressions of condolence from all the chumps and nimrods who were certain I'd fail right from the get-go.

By the third afternoon of the storm I couldn't stand it any

longer: the lumps of frozen snow poking me in the back, the clammy nylon walls brushing against my face, the incredible smell drifting up from the depths of my sleeping bag. I pawed through the mess at my feet until I located a small green stuff sack, in which there was a metal film can containing the makings of what I'd hoped would be a sort of victory cigar. I'd intended to save it for my return from the summit, but what the hey, it wasn't looking like I'd be visiting the top any time soon. I poured most of the can's contents onto a leaf of cigarette paper, rolled it into a crooked, sorry looking joint, and promptly smoked it down to the roach.

The reefer, of course, only made the tent seem even more cramped, more suffocating, more impossible to bear. It also made me terribly hungry. I decided a little oatmeal would put things right. Making it, however, was a long, ridiculously involved process: a potful of snow had to be gathered outside in the tempest, the stove assembled and lit, the oatmeal and sugar located, the remnants of yesterday's dinner scraped from my bowl. I'd gotten the stove going and was melting the snow when I smelled something burning. A thorough check of the stove and its environs revealed nothing. Mystified, I was ready to chalk it up to my chemically enhanced imagination when I heard something crackle directly behind me.

I whirled around in time to see a bag of garbage, into which I'd tossed the match I'd used to light the stove, flare up into a conflagration. Beating on the fire with my hands, I had it out in a few seconds, but not before a large section of the tent's inner wall vaporized before my eyes. The tent's built-in rainfly escaped the flames, so the shelter was still more or less weatherproof; now, however, it was approximately thirty degrees cooler inside. My left palm began to sting. Examining it, I noticed the pink welt of a burn. What troubled me most, though, was that the tent wasn't even mine – I'd borrowed the shelter from my father. An expensive Early Winters Omnipo Tent, it had been brand new before my trip – the hang-tags were still attached – and had been loaned reluctantly. For several minutes I sat dumbstruck, staring at the wreckage of the shelter's once-graceful form amid the acrid scent of singed hair and melted nylon. You had to hand it to me, I thought: I had a real knack for living up to the old man's worst expectations.

The fire sent me into a funk that no drug known to man could have alleviated. By the time I'd finished cooking the oatmeal my mind was made up: the moment the storm was over, I was breaking camp and booking for Thomas Bay.

Twenty-four hours later, I was huddled inside a bivouac sack under the lip of the *bergschrund* on the Thumb's north face. The weather was as bad as I'd seen it. It was snowing hard, probably an inch every hour. Spindrift avalanches hissed down from the wall above and washed over me like surf, completely burying the sack every twenty minutes.

The day had begun well enough. When I emerged from the tent, clouds still clung to the ridge tops but the wind was down and the icecap was speckled with sunbreaks. A patch of sunlight, almost blinding in its brilliance, slid lazily over the camp. I put down a foam sleeping mat and sprawled on the glacier in my long johns. Wallowing in the radiant heat, I felt the gratitude of a prisoner whose sentence has just been commuted.

As I lay there, a narrow chimney that curved up the east half of the Thumb's north face, well to the left of the route I'd tried before the storm, caught my eye. I twisted a telephoto lens onto my camera. Through it I could make out a smear of shiny grey ice – solid, trustworthy, hard-frozen ice – plastered to the back of the cleft. The alignment of the chimney made it impossible to discern if the ice continued in an unbroken line from top to bottom. If it did, the chimney might well provide passage over the rime-covered slabs that had foiled my first attempt. Lying there in the sun, I began to think about how much I'd hate myself a month hence if I threw in the towel after a single try, if I scrapped the whole expedition on account of a little bad weather. Within the hour I had assembled my gear and was skiing toward the base of the wall.

The ice in the chimney did in fact prove to be continuous, but it was very, very thin – just a gossamer film of verglas. Additionally, the cleft was a natural funnel for any debris that happened to slough off the wall; as I scratched my way up the chimney I was hosed by a continuous stream of powder snow, ice chips, and small stones. One hundred twenty feet up the groove the last remnants of my composure flaked away like old plaster, and I turned around.

Instead of descending all the way to Base Camp, I decided to spend the night in the 'schrund beneath the chimney, on the off chance that my head would be more together the next morning. The fair skies that had ushered in the day, however, turned out to be but a momentary lull in a five-day gale. By mid-afternoon the storm was back in all its glory, and my bivouac site became a less than pleasant place to hang around. The ledge on which I crouched was continually swept by small spindrift avalanches. Five times my bivvy sack – a thin nylon envelope, shaped exactly like a Baggies brand sandwich bag, only bigger – was buried up to the level of the breathing slit. After digging myself out the fifth time, I decided I'd had enough. I threw all my gear in my pack and made a break for base camp.

The descent was terrifying. Between the clouds, the ground blizzard, and the flat, fading light, I couldn't tell snow from sky, nor whether a slope went up or down. I worried, with ample reason, that I might step blindly off the top of a serac and end up at the bottom of the Witches Cauldron, a half-mile below. When I finally arrived on the frozen plain of the icecap, I found that my tracks had long since drifted over. I didn't have a clue how to locate the tent on the featureless glacial plateau. I skied in circles for an hour or so, hoping I'd get lucky and stumble across camp, until I put a foot into a small crevasse and realized I was acting like an idiot – that I should hunker down right where I was and wait out the storm.

I dug a shallow hole, wrapped myself in the bivvy bag, and sat on my pack in the swirling snow. Drifts piled up around me. My feet became numb. A damp chill crept down my chest from the base of my neck, where spindrift had gotten inside my parka and soaked my shirt. If only I had a cigarette, I thought, a single cigarette, I could summon the strength of character to put a good face on this fucked-up situation, on the whole fucked-up trip. "If we had some ham, we could have ham and eggs, if we had some eggs." I remembered my friend Nate uttering that line in a similar storm, two years before, high on another Alaskan peak, the Mooses Tooth. It had struck me as hilarious at the time; I'd actually laughed out loud. Recalling the line now, it no longer seemed funny. I pulled the bivvy sack tighter around my shoulders. The wind ripped at my back. Beyond shame, I cradled my head in my arms and embarked on an orgy of self-pity.

I knew that people sometimes died climbing mountains. But at the age of 23 personal mortality – the idea of my own death – was still largely outside my conceptual grasp; it was as abstract a notion as non-Euclidian geometry or marriage. When I decamped from Boulder in April, 1977, my head swimming with visions of glory and redemption on the Devil's Thumb, it didn't occur to me that I might be bound by the same cause-effect relationships that governed the actions of others. I'd never heard of hubris. Because I wanted to climb the mountain so badly, because I had thought about the Thumb so intensely for so long, it seemed beyond the realm of possibility that some minor obstacle like the weather or crevasses or rime-covered rock might ultimately thwart my will.

At sunset the wind died and the ceiling lifted 150 ft off the glacier, enabling me to locate Base Camp. I made it back to the tent intact, but it was no longer possible to ignore the fact that the Thumb had made hash of my plans. I was forced to acknowledge that volition alone, however powerful, was not going to get me up the north wall. I saw, finally, that nothing was.

There still existed an opportunity for salvaging the expedition, however. A week earlier I'd skied over to the south-east side of the mountain to take a look at the route Fred Beckey had pioneered in 1946 – the route by which I'd intended to descend the peak after climbing the north wall. During that reconnaissance I'd noticed an obvious unclimbed line to the left of the Beckey route – a patchy network of ice angling across the south-east face – that struck me as a relatively easy way to achieve the summit. At the time, I'd considered this route unworthy of my attentions. Now, on the rebound from my calamitous entanglement with the nordwand, I was prepared to lower my sights.

On the afternoon of 15 May, when the blizzard finally petered out, I returned to the south-east face and climbed to the top of a slender ridge that abutted the upper peak like a flying buttress on a gothic cathedral. I decided to spend the night there, on the airy, knife-edged ridge crest, 1,600 ft below the summit. The evening sky was cold and cloudless. I could see all the way to tidewater and beyond. At dusk I watched, transfixed, as the house lights of Petersburg blinked on in the west. The closest thing I'd had to human contact since the airdrop, the distant lights set off a flood of emotion that caught me completely off guard. I imagined people watching the Red Sox on the tube, eating fried chicken in brightly lit kitchens, drinking beer, making love. When I lay down to sleep I was overcome by a soul-wrenching loneliness. I'd never felt so alone, ever.

That night I had troubled dreams, of cops and vampires and a gangland-style execution. I heard someone whisper, "He's in there. As soon as he comes out, waste him." I sat bolt upright and opened my eyes. The sun was about to rise. The entire sky was scarlet. It was still clear, but wisps of high cirrus were streaming in from the southwest, and a dark line was visible just above the horizon. I pulled on my boots and hurriedly strapped on my crampons. Five minutes after waking up, I was front-pointing away from the bivouac.

I carried no rope, no tent or bivouac gear, no hardware save my ice-axes. My plan was to go ultralight and ultrafast, to hit the summit and make it back down before the weather turned. Pushing myself, continually out of breath, I scurried up and to the left across small snowfields linked by narrow runnels of verglas and short rock bands. The climbing was almost fun – the rock was covered with large, in-cut holds, and the ice, though thin, never got steep enough to feel extreme – but I was anxious about the bands of clouds racing in from the Pacific, covering the sky.

In what seemed like no time (I didn't have a watch on the trip) I was on the distinctive final ice field. By now the sky was completely overcast. It looked easier to keep angling to the left, but quicker to go straight for the top. Paranoid about being caught by a storm high on the peak without any kind of shelter, I opted for the direct route. The ice steepened, then steepened some more, and as it did so it grew thin. I swung my left ice-axe and struck rock. I aimed for another spot, and once again it glanced off un-yielding diorite with a dull, sickening clank. And again, and again. It was a reprise of my first attempt on the north face. Looking between my legs, I stole a glance at the glacier, more than 2,000 ft below. My stomach churned. I felt my poise slipping away like smoke in the wind.

Forty-five feet above the wall eased back onto the sloping summit shoulder. Forty-five more feet, half the distance between third base and home plate, and the mountain would be mine. I clung stiffly to my axes, unmoving, paralyzed with fear and indecision. I looked down at the dizzying drop to the glacier again, then up, then scraped away the film of ice above my head. I hooked the pick of my left axe on a nickel-thin lip of rock, and weighted it. It held. I pulled my right axe from the ice, reached up, and twisted the pick into a crooked half-inch crack until it jammed. Barely breathing now, I moved my feet up, scrabbling my crampon points across the verglas. Reaching as high as I could with my left arm, I swung the axe gently at the shiny, opaque surface, not knowing what I'd hit beneath it. The pick went in with a heartening *THUNK*! A few minutes later I was standing on a broad, rounded ledge. The summit proper, a series of slender fins sprouting a grotesque meringue of atmospheric ice, stood twenty feet directly above.

The insubstantial frost feathers ensured that those last twenty feet remained hard, scary, onerous. But then, suddenly, there was no place higher to go. It wasn't possible, I couldn't believe it. I felt my cracked lips stretch into a huge, painful grin. I was on top of the Devil's Thumb.

Fittingly, the summit was a surreal, malevolent place, an improbably slender fan of rock and rime no wider than a filing cabinet. It did not encourage loitering. As I straddled the highest point, the north face fell away beneath my left boot for 6,000 ft beneath my right boot; the south face dropped off for twenty-five hundred. I took some pictures to prove I'd been there, and spent a few minutes trying to straighten a bent pick. Then I stood up, carefully turned around, and headed for home.

The Ascent of Nanda Devi

H. W. Tilman

*Bill Tilman made the first ascent of India's Nanda Devi –
7,817 m (25,655 ft) – in 1936, aged 38. After a lifetime of
mountaineering and adventuring, he disappeared in 1977
sailing a cutter from Rio de Janeiro to the Falkland Islands.*

O ur plan now was for two of us to occupy Camp II or the
Gite, as it was appropriately called, and on the following
day, while those two went up higher to look for a Camp III, two
Sherpas would join them at the Gite. We assumed that a site for
Camp III would be found on the snow saddle, and on the third
day the Sherpas would assist in establishing the two Sahibs
there while two more of us in turn occupied the Gite.

It was a fine morning on the 14th, but we did not get away
until 10 a.m. Graham Brown and Houston, who were going to
sleep at Camp II, had to pack up the bivouac tent and their own
gear and then someone dropped a mug down the *khud* and
Houston very sportingly went down after it. The task looked
hopeless in all the new snow, but he got it. Odell stayed in camp
to catch up with his geological notes, but six of us started with
Pasang and Nima.

At the roping-up place Carter went back as he had not yet
acclimatised, and from there we climbed on three ropes, Lloyd
and Nima, Pasang and myself, and Graham Brown, Houston,
and Loomis. As usual the steps had to be cleared of snow and in

places they were now not very reliable, but by cutting deep in they held sufficiently well. The passage round and up the projecting nose below the Gite roused so much misgiving that we talked of putting a fixed rope there. But it was an awkward place to fix anything and in the end familiarity bred sufficient contempt for us to do without. A rope of two can move quicker than one of three, so Lloyd and I got there well ahead of the others and Pasang and Nima began making a platform; it now looked as though there would just be room for the bivouac tent and a big one. When they had finished I took them down on my rope, Lloyd waiting for the others, who had not yet arrived. By six o'clock it was snowing again.

The journey to Camp II, though now a daily routine, was never boring however unpleasant it might be in other ways. The unstable rocks of the lower half still lay in wait to punish any carelessness, and on the upper section the daily snow-fall made it at least look like a new ascent.

The next day all started except Phuta and, when we reached the roping-up place, we descried what looked like two flies crawling up the steep snow arete above the Gite. These of course were Graham Brown and Houston, and we watched them anxiously, making ribald remarks about their rate of progress and their frequent halts. The fact that we were ourselves sitting down eating chocolate by no means lessened our enjoyment of this spectacle and certainly increased the flow of wit. We felt like dramatic critics eating their chocolates in the stalls, and sharpened the pencils of our wit accordingly.

It was a fine day for a change and the bright sun on the snow sapped our energy. We were up by 2 p.m. and having seen the tent pitched, for which there was just room enough, and Pasang and Nima safely established there, Lloyd and I went down, while Odell and Loomis waited to hear the news from above. An hour later Graham Brown and Houston got back to Camp II, and reported that there were a couple of hundred feet of difficult climbing before the snow arete was reached, that this was steep and long, but that a good site for a camp had been found where the arete merged into the broad saddle. They had felt the sun even more severely than we had.

We got down to Camp I at four o'clock and Phuta requested

that he might go to the Base Camp that evening. It was no use keeping him, so I gave him a chit to Emmons and sent him down. There were now five of us at Camp I, two Sahibs and two Sherpas at Camp II, and Emmons, Kalu, and three Sherpas at the Base Camp.

Next day, the 16th, two more Sahibs had to occupy Camp II, and at half-past nine we all started, Odell and I carrying our personal kit and some odds and ends. Some student of human nature has remarked that "no one can do an act that is not morally wrong for the last time without feelings of regret", but now I was doing the climb from Camp I to Camp II for the fifth and last time and can very positively refute that statement. Of course devout Hindus might say that in climbing Nanda Devi we *were* committing an immoral act and that would account satisfactorily for my absence of regret.

Before reaching the roping-up place, we were bothered by seeing two tents still standing at the Gite and it looked as though no move was in progress. Later we made out somebody on the arete but could see only two instead of the four we expected. We puzzled our heads over this and made many wild conjectures. If Graham Brown and Houston were not moving up to Camp III there would be some congestion at the Gite, but Odell and I were determined to sleep there, even if it meant four in a tent. We could not face yet another ascent from Camp I.

It was no use speculating, and as Odell was going slowly, and I was not unwilling to do the same, he and I went along together while the other three pushed on as fast as they could to find out what the matter was. We two continued in leisurely fashion, not arriving until three o'clock. Perhaps we were carrying heavier loads; Odell certainly was, for he was cluttered up with hypsometers, clinometers, and thermometers, and was so attached to certain favourite but unnecessary articles of clothing that his personal kit was a portentous affair – nor was Da Namgyal there to carry it as he should have been. I remember particularly a hideous yellow sweater, a relic of the War, which weighed more than the five Shetland woollies carried by us all; and at the highest camp he produced a hat which none of us had ever seen before and which, I suppose, had some attributes peculiarly fitting it for wear at 24,000 ft.

The mystery of the two tents was solved by a note and the presence of both Sherpas. Nima was sick and Pasang was completely snow-blind. The note told us that they had gone up with food and kit and asked us to bring on the tent and their sleeping bags. Loomis and Lloyd had already left with these when we arrived and halfway up the snow arete they were met by Houston and Graham Brown. For these four it was a hard day.

Houston's note went on to say that the necessary dope for alleviating snow-blindness had been unaccountably left at Camp I, and suggested that strong tea should be tried in the interim. Tea was at a premium, for we were carefully conserving our solitary ounce for higher up, but we brewed some and did what we could for Pasang, who was in considerable pain. He was lying on his face in the tent and quite unable to open his eyes, but by forcing the lids apart we managed to get some tea in. This treatment was continued until the medicine arrived two days later, but had little effect; nor had the medicine either for that matter, and, though we did not then suspect it, Pasang was now out of the hunt.

It was not easily understood how he had managed to get such a severe attack. Yesterday had been very bright and sunny but no one noticed him with his glasses off, nor were these any different from Nima's which were perfectly efficient. While he was preparing the platform here, I noticed he was working without glasses and it must have been then that his eyes were affected, although the platform was in shadow and there was more rock than snow. But a rarefied atmosphere makes the light more dangerous in this respect and we read that on Everest in 1924 Norton was snow-blind merely from the glare off rocks. In 1930 Shipton and I climbed Kilimanjaro (19,700 ft), and on snow near the summit we both took off our glasses to see where we were, for there was a thick mist and not a sign of the sun. Nevertheless that same night we both went snow-blind and suffered great pain, but in twenty-four hours it passed off without any treatment and this led me to think that Pasang's would do the same.

When Lloyd and Loomis returned, we agreed that they should please themselves whether they came up tomorrow with the little that was left at Camp I to bring. They would not be able to sleep here because Odell and I would still be in residence. Another tent, more food, and our own kits had to be carried to Camp III before we could move up, and for reasons of acclimatisation it was a sound plan to sleep two nights at a camp before going on to the next.

When they had gone, we took stock of our surroundings. These consisted of blank rock wall and thin air in equal proportions; there were about four feet of terra firma between the two tents and one could walk, without a rope, for about ten paces round the corner where the exit lay. All view of the ridge was cut off and only a little of it immediately below the Gite was visible, but to the east a wide field of vision included East Nanda Devi, "Longstaff's Col" now well below us, a great crescent of fluted ice wall on the rim to the south of it, and, beyond, the beautifully proportioned Nanda Kot. The height was about 20,400 ft.

Having brewed the tea for Pasang's eyes and drunk some ourselves, we tried to instil some life into Nima, who seemed very lugubrious and lethargic – in much the same frame of mind as a passenger in the last stages of sea-sickness, who having prayed long and earnestly for the ship to sink has almost abandoned hope that it will. I think they had not eaten since they got there, so we made him light his stove and cook some pemmican, which the Sherpas relish far more than we do. They were in the roomy 6 ft × 7 ft tent while we occupied the small bivouac tent vacated by Graham Brown and Houston, who had taken up one of the larger ones. We graciously allowed the Sherpas to remain in the enjoyment of their luxurious quarters, but this generosity will not be counted unto us for righteousness because the atmosphere in their tent was such that no tent at all would have been preferable.

I forget the exact dimensions of our tent, but it was very long and narrow and the two occupants lay, literally, cheek by jowl – that is if the human face has a jowl; or is it confined to pigs? It was admirably suited to Odell, who is also long and a bit narrow, and I think this was the first night that he was able to lie at full length since he had left Ranikhet. On this expedition we were experimenting with air beds as insulation when lying on snow, instead of the usual rubber mats, half an inch thick and 3 ft × 4 ft. The extra room they took up was very noticeable in a small tent and apart from that they were not altogether successful. Punctures were numerous and unless they amounted to bursts, as they sometimes did, they were not easy to locate; situated as we were, the method of plunging them into a bath and watching for bubbles was seldom practicable. If your bed did go flat, it was a serious matter because no protection at all was afforded, and the result was a cold and sleepless night. Again, if you blew them up too hard you rolled off, and if they were too soft you were in contact with the ground and therefore cold. The Sherpas used to blow them up as if they were blowing up a dying fire, with the result that one bounded about like a pea on a drum, and if two people sat on it when in that state the whole thing exploded. Pasang got a lot of amusement out of the operation of blowing up and deflating beds by making them produce discordant noises like ill-played bagpipes. Now that only two of the Sherpas were left, and those two incapable of raising even a zephyr, we had to blow our own up, and this process provided yet another example of the perfection of natural laws which can even legislate for the remote association of a mountaineer and an air bed; as we gained in altitude and lost breath, the beds required less air to fill them owing of course to the diminution of pressure.

There was a storm in the night but, packed as we were, it was easy to keep warm and difficult to keep cool. Pasang was still blind and very sorry for himself, but Nima was brighter and offered to come with us to Camp III. Odell and I took a tent and paraffin, and Nima 40 lb of sugar. Care was required on a short stretch above the camp and an upward traverse on rather shaky snow took us on to the ridge. We left it again where it suddenly stood on end and got into trouble on the rocks which would, when climbed, bring us out above this steep bit which had so frightened us. Odell led over a steep ice-glazed traverse which Nima and I resolved mentally to have nothing to do with, and when he was securely placed we had ourselves more or less pulled up in a direct line.

We were now at the foot of the steep snow arete which was such a prominent feature from below, and we settled down to kicking steps up it very slowly and methodically, the steps made by our forerunners having vanished. It was a narrow ridge, but we were able to stick to the crest, or slightly on the Rishi side, which was now less steep than the east side, though both fell away sharply, and the upward angle was 40 or 45 degrees; it will be remembered that from Camp I to Camp II the route lay always on the east flank and that the Rishi side was a precipice. As might be expected after the persistent falls of the last week, there was a lot of fresh snow to kick through before solid footing was obtained, and when we reached the tent at Camp III Graham Brown told us exactly how many of these steps we had kicked out, he having counted them. As far as I remember, the figure was disappointingly small for we felt that it must be something astronomical, but in sober fact there were only about 700 ft of snow ridge. Approaching the tent, the angle eased off and we found it pitched snugly under the shelter of a steep snow bank.

It was after midday, but Graham Brown and Houston were still in bed and evidently intended "lying at earth" after their efforts of yesterday. Going back we rattled down in an hour, and this time reversed our upwards procedure by descending the very steep snow patch in order to avoid the rocks. Nobody had come up from below, Pasang was still blind, we both had slight headaches, it was snowing again, and there was a big sun halo; but all this was forgotten in the warm glow of self-righteousness induced by our virtuous activity.

Having thus acquired enough merit for the time being by working while others slept, we sat about next morning until Graham Brown and Houston came down from Camp III for more loads. We found it such a pleasant occupation that we sat about some more until the other three came up from Camp I. As soon as the first man's head appeared round the corner of the bulge below us, a shout went up to know if they had found the tea. They had no tea, but they brought the zinc-sulphate medicine and we now hoped that Pasang's recovery would be speedy; at present his eyes were as firmly closed as ever. Nima too had relapsed into his former state of misery, but even yet we did not despair of getting some useful work out of these two. There was still a load to come up from Camp I, so it was arranged that Carter and Nima should go down tomorrow for this and as much more food as they could carry.

At three o'clock four of us started back for Camp III, Odell and Houston on one rope, Graham Brown and myself on the other. We had the advantage of the steps made by them on the way down and, in spite of heavy loads, were up in two hours. Our tent platform was ready for us, so the others had not been so idle yesterday as we thought, and it was pleasant to have some room again, room outside as well as in. I was sorry we had not got a cat to swing.

As Odell and I lay that night with our cheeks and our jowls at a reasonable distance apart, we wondered happily whether the three below were suffocating in the bivouac tent or succumbing to asphyxiation in the overripe atmosphere of the Sherpas.

We flattered ourselves that the height of this camp was about 21,500 ft but, if it was, it seemed highly improbable that from here we could put a bivouac within striking distance of the summit. It postulated a carry of 2,000 ft, at the very least, 2,500 would be better, and on the difficult going below we had not done a carry of more than 1,500. The climbing was likely to get harder rather than easier and, of course, the increasing altitude would slow us up progressively. Repeated trials with the hypsometer made things appear even more discouraging by giving Camp III a height of only 21,200 ft, and though we knew by now that this instrument was, to put it mildly, subject to error, we had perforce to accept the lower figure in making future plans.

The question of the height of our camps bothered us a lot and, quite early on, the hypsometer had earned for itself an opprobrious name of a like sound which may not be printed. For some reason or other we omitted to bring an aneroid barometer graduated for reading height; possibly our numerous scientists scorned an instrument which even the half-wits of the party could read. I remember in 1934 Shipton and I, having no scientific training, took with us an aneroid barometer out of an aeroplane. I think it cost ten shillings at one of those miscellaneous junk shops in Holborn. Our Sherpas conceived a great affection for it and called it "Shaitan", probably because we consulted it so frequently. It worked very well until we dropped it. But this hypsometer, or boiling-point thermometer, while not giving us any very precise information, afforded everyone a lot of fun and the scientists food for thought. The results it gave were always interesting, sometimes amusing, and seldom accurate. For example, after several hours of exhausting climbing in what we foolishly thought was an upward direction, it was startling to learn that we had in reality descended a hundred feet from where we started. The learned scientists explained with bland assurance that such vagaries were to be expected, and were accounted for quite simply by the presence of a "column of cold air"; the unlearned oafs on the contrary thought that it must be something to do with "hot air", and plenty of it.

But there is generally some use to be found for the most unlikely things, and so it was with the hypsometer. It had as part of its equipment a small bottle of methylated spirits, and when we ran out of solid methylated for priming the stoves, this came in very handy. Priming a stove with paraffin is both noisome and inefficient.

On the 19th Graham Brown and Houston went down again to Camp II for loads while Odell and I went to spy out the land higher up. At the point we had reached, our ridge had widened out into a great hog's-back, so wide that it was in reality the south face, though up the middle of this face a ridge was still discernible, and 1,000 ft higher up it again stood out prominently. We struck straight up the middle of the face over what we called the "snow saddle", avoiding the steep bank above the camp by a short traverse to the left. The snow was in good condition and the angle of slope about thirty degrees for the first 700 ft, after which it began to steepen. Above this was a sort of glacis of snow-covered rock lying at an angle of forty-five to fifty degrees. In the steep places outcrops of rock appeared through the snow. This broad glacis appeared to stretch upward for 1,000 ft until it narrowed again to a sharp ridge. On our immediate right was a forbidding gully, a trap for falling stones and ice, and beyond that the tremendous cirque which forms the connecting ridge between East Nanda Devi and Nanda Devi itself. Some two or three hundred yards to the left was a wide shallow depression, scarcely a gully, and on the far side of it the horizon was bounded by a very bold and steep ridge, probably the same which we had looked at from Pisgah.

We attacked the glacis in the centre and worked upwards and to the left, making for what looked like a slight ridge overlooking the shallow gully. As we mounted, the angle grew steeper and the climbing more difficult. At first a good covering of snow overlay the rocks, but presently this became thinner and the outcrops of rocks more numerous. For mountaineering as well as geological reasons we were keenly interested to reach the first of these outcrops, for the line we should take, and our progress, depended greatly upon its quality. We hoped that at this height it might have changed to something more honest than the treacherous rock of the lower ridge, and that the strata might lie in a more favourable direction. Technically it may have differed, but for a climber it was substantially the same crumbling yellow stuff upon which no reliance could be placed, and, though the dip of the strata was now more in our favour, little comfort was to be derived from that on rock of such rottenness.

When we had climbed about 500 ft from the foot of the glacis, it became apparent that the supposed ridge we were making for was no ridge at all. To go straight up was still possible, but with loads on it would be both difficult and dangerous, for nowhere was there enough snow for an anchorage with an axe, or any rock round which a rope could be belayed. We decided to traverse to the left and go for the shallow gully which appeared to offer a safe route on snow for at least 1,000 ft. But shortly after putting this resolve into practice, we contrived to get ourselves into such a mess on the ice-glazed face of a rock outcrop that all our attention was concentrated on getting out of it, and instead of continuing the traverse to the left we were compelled to embark upon a long and tricky traverse in the opposite direction. By sticking wherever possible to snow, and avoiding any rock like the plague, we worried a way back down the glacis until we rejoined our earlier track.

A lower route was obviously the best line for the gully, but it was now too late for any more and we hurried back to camp, where we arrived in time to avoid the start of a blizzard. Two days had elapsed since the warning of the sun halo.

Lloyd and Loomis had come up here to sleep after only one night at Camp II in defiance of our self-imposed rule of two at each camp. No one, however, with experience of the Gite would doubt their wisdom in making that camp an exception to the rule.

The results of our reconnaissance were mainly negative but not without value. It was clear that a route directly up the glacis should only be tried as a last desperate resource, and also that whichever way we went it was going to be a painfully long carry before a place where a tent could be pitched would be found. The conclusions were that further reconnaissance was needed, that the most promising line was the broad gully, and that in any case it would be advantageous to move the present camp to a new site at the foot of the glacis.

The night was cold and windy and no one turned out until nine o'clock. Lloyd and Loomis started out to have a look at the way to the gully, and the rest of us went down to Camp II for loads. All the tracks down had to be remade after the blizzard and we had long ceased to expect any tracks to last for twenty-four hours. To anticipate, they did not last so long to-day, and when we returned in the afternoon all were once more obliterated.

We found Pasang still blind and Nima not well, and it was pretty clear that neither would be any use. Nima's single journey to Camp III, the highest reached by any of the porters, was but a dying kick. The almost total failure of the Sherpas is easily explained, for, as I have pointed out, we had to take the leavings of several other expeditions. The only two I expected to go high were Pasang and Kitar. Of the others three were past their best and one was too young and inexperienced. Pasang of course was unlucky to be struck down with snow-blindness, but it cannot be said that it was not his own fault. Kitar was a victim to disease.

The medicine seemed to be having little effect on Pasang's eyes, and Nima's cheery grin was a thing of the past. That they should both go down was now the best course, but this was not possible until Pasang could see something. Apart from their rather miserable mode of existence at the Gite, I was anxious to have them safely down at the Base Camp before we lost touch with them entirely by going higher up the mountain. We left them there, alone now, in the big tent, having told them that two of us would come down again tomorrow, and we started back, Carter with us, taking the small bivouac tent. Carter had a note which he had found at Camp I telling us that Emmons had moved the Base Camp down to the foot of the scree slope and that he was busy with the plane table, but only Kalu was able to help him by carrying loads.

It was cold and windy when we reached Camp III in a flurry of snow. There was a halo round the sun and two mock suns, and I have seldom seen a more ominous-looking sky. The report of the reconnoitring party was more cheering than the weather. Taking a line below and to the left of ours, they had reached a point from where they could see into and up the gully. They had not got into it, but they reported that it could be reached by a route which lay almost entirely on snow, and that the going up the near side of it looked straightforward enough. Like us, they had seen no promise of a camp site higher up, and it was agreed to move this camp to the top of the snow saddle and to press the attack by the gully.

It was a quiet night in spite of all the signs of approaching storm, but the morning of the 21st dawned dull, misty, and snowy. We had a late breakfast and spent the morning in one tent discussing ways and means. Now that the thing was to be put to the test, it was clear that some difficult decisions would have to be made, and the upshot of our talk was that the responsibility for these decisions was put upon the writer. The too frequent use of the word "I" in this narrative will not have escaped the notice of the reader. The reason for this is that up to now I may have had most to say in our affairs; but that was merely through the accident of my being the only one who knew the country or the porters. We had no official leader, and managed very well without, until at this crisis the need was felt for some kind of figure-head.

After a cup of cocoa additional to our lunch which, by the way, was usually a slab of chocolate and nothing else, Lloyd, Carter, and I went down again to Camp II for more loads, and the others took a first instalment of loads up to what would presently be Camp IV.

Pasang and Nima still appeared to be immovable, but I told them that two of us would come down again tomorrow and see them safely over the worst of the route to Camp I. Until they were down they were merely a source of anxiety, and, after tomorrow, we expected to be out of reach. We climbed up again in one and a quarter hours and it was satisfactory to see that our time on the snow arete became faster, indicating that we were still acclimatising and not deteriorating. The other party had found a good camp site on the snow saddle near the foot of the glacis, and had dug out one tent platform.

The sunset was again threatening, with greasy-looking cigar-shaped clouds hanging low over East Nanda Devi, a greenish watery haze to the west, and, to the south, black banks of cumulus tinged with copper.

We woke to find the tent shaking and banging to the blasts of a fierce blizzard. The wind was coming out of the south-east, some snow was falling, but it was impossible to tell what was new snow and what was drift, for outside was nothing but a whirling cloud of driving snow. The three tents were close together and guyed to each other for mutual support. Six of us occupied the two big ones and Carter was by himself (a doubtful privilege under these conditions) in the small bivouac tent, pitched on the weather side. Odell, Lloyd, and I held the baby in the shape of the Primus stove, but it was conceivable that the inconvenience of fetching ice and breathing paraffin fumes was outweighed by the advantage of getting the food hot without having to fetch it. Going from the comparative warmth of the sleeping bag and the tent out into the blizzard was a breath-taking experience. Breathing was almost impossible facing the wind and nothing could be handled without mittens, while the act of leaving or entering the tent by the small sleeve entrance required the quick co-operation of all, unless the inside was to be covered with a layer of snow.

There was nothing to be done but lie in our bags, with one eye on a book and the other on the furiously flapping fabric and the quivering tent pole. The pole was of very light aluminium and we were rather nervous about it, but it stood the strain well, as did the tents, for which we forgave them all our past discomforts. At five o'clock, when we cooked our evening pemmican, conditions were unchanged. The wind still maintained a steady roar with occasional gusts of gale force, and we discussed the advisability of sleeping with windproofs on in case the tent went in the night. However, we pinned our faith to the fabric and did not resort to these extreme measures.

Morning brought no change in these unpleasant conditions; and we wondered whether it was blowing as hard at the Gite and how the Sherpas were faring. Anyhow, with the direction of the wind as it was, the rock wall would stop them being blown off their ledge.

The snow was being blown away as soon as it fell, and round our tent it had not accumulated to any great depth. The other big tent had not fared so well and there was a high bank of snow around it by morning. The pressure of this snow had reduced the space inside by half, so that the unfortunate residents were sleeping almost on top of each other. They had the consolation of knowing that their tent was now securely anchored. Carter too, in the bivouac, was experiencing trouble in keeping the snow-laden walls off his face.

Another weary day of inactivity and torpor passed, but towards evening the wind began to moderate and we were able to get outside, clear the accumulated snow away from the doors, and attend to the guys. Snow was still falling lightly and a leaden pall hid everything but the snow at our feet and three forlorn-looking tents.

Followed another cold and stormy night, but the morning of Monday the 24th dawned fine, calm and sunny. Had it been black as night, we would not have complained, for stillness was all we asked for after the battering of the last two days. The loss of this valuable time was disturbing, and though it may seem strange that two days in bed could be anything but beneficial, there was no doubt that the strain and the inaction had done us harm physically. Nor could we tell what effect the blizzard might have had on the snow of the upper slopes. It was imperative now to push on with all speed, and surely after such a snorter we might expect several days of fine weather.

These blizzards which we experienced, three of them lasting for thirty-six, twelve, and forty-eight hours respectively, all came from between east and south-east. Monsoon weather in the hills generally comes from between south and west, but these storms may have been deflected by the mountain. Such blizzards are more to be expected prior to the break of the monsoon, and during two previous monsoon periods in the Himalaya, one in Garhwal and one in the Everest region, I do not recollect one of any severity. This year the monsoon broke early and ended late, and was exceptionally severe in the United Provinces and Garhwal.

At nine o'clock Lloyd and I started out for Camp II in accordance with our promise to the Sherpas, the fulfilment of which the blizzard had compelled us to postpone. We left to the others the cold work of breaking out the tents from their frozen covering and digging out the buried stores, preparatory to carrying one big tent and the bivouac to the new Camp IV site. Five of us were to sleep up there tonight in readiness for carrying up a bivouac for the first summit party next day.

The presence of a lot of powder snow made conditions on the arete bad, and we both felt weak and got progressively weaker as we descended. Arrived at the Gite, we were surprised to find it empty; evidently the Sherpas had tired of waiting for us and left early. It was comforting to know that the tent had weathered the storm, that Pasang's eyes must be better, and that we ourselves had not to descend any farther. Indeed, we were now in such a state of languor that our chief concern was how on earth we were going to get up again. We lolled about on the ledge, assailed by a violent thirst, feeling complete moral and physical wrecks; and it was evident that two days and nights in our sleeping bags had taken more out of us than a really hard day's work.

The Sherpas had taken the stove and cooking pot with them, but there was some food here and we opened a tin with an ice-axe – not for the sake of the food but for the tin, in which to catch the elusive drips from the rock wall. We had to sleep at the higher camp that night, so at midday we summoned up all our resolution and, taking with us all the food that was left here, we crawled weakly away from the Gite.

I should be ashamed to say how long it took us to get back to Camp III, but by the time we arrived we were feeling better and our strength was beginning to return. Graham Brown and

Carter, who were spending the night here, came down from Camp IV just as we arrived and informed us that up there it was perishing cold. Carter thought his toes were slightly touched with frost-bite.

Adding some more food to our loads, Lloyd and I went off once more and an hour of steady plodding brought us to the new camp. They had evidently started late that morning owing to the frozen tents, and, when we got up, the second tent was just being pitched. There was a bitter wind blowing and Loomis was inside attending to his feet, which also had been slightly affected by cold.

In spite of the cold, it was difficult to turn away from the astonishing picture painted by the fast-sinking sun. Nanda Kot still shone with dazzling purity like an opal, and beyond to the east was range upon range of the snow peaks of Nepal, looking like rollers breaking in white foam on a sunny sea. From the snow slope falling away out of sight at our feet, the eye swept across a great void till arrested by the castellated ivory wall of the Sanctuary, dominated by Trisul, up which the shadows were already stealing. And to the west was the dark chasm of the Rishi gorge, the clear-cut outline of the "Curtain", and the blue-green swell of the foothills.

The height of Camp IV we estimated to be 21,800 ft, and with five of us here and food for nearly a fortnight we were in a strong position. If we could push a bivouac up another 2,000 ft, the summit would be within reach, and, big "if" though this was, the time had come to make the attempt. Of the five now at this camp, it was not difficult to decide which two should have the privilege of first shot. Odell was going very well and his experience, combined with Houston's energy, would make a strong pair. Assuming that we could place the bivouac high enough tomorrow, they were to have two days in which to make their attempt, and on the third day a second pair would take their place, whether they had been successful or not. The form shown tomorrow would indicate which two would have the second chance, and, provided the weather held, it might be possible to send up a third pair.

The 25th broke fine, but it was ten o'clock before we had made up our loads of 15 lb each, which included food for two men for six days. During the blizzard, not very much snow had actually settled, and since then sufficient time had elapsed for this new snow to consolidate. We found it in good condition. After gaining some height by kicking steps, we approached the gully by a long traverse where steps had to be cut and great care exercised. The snow covering grew thinner and we came to an uncomfortable halt on the steep lip of a minor hollow, cutting us off from the main gully. This was the farthest point reached by Lloyd and Loomis, and they had seen that this difficult little gully could be avoided by working round the head of it, 200 ft higher.

We sat here for a little, but it was no place for a long sojourn without prehensile trousers. There was not enough snow to afford a step, much less a seat, and the angle of the rock was such that mere friction was of no avail – boots, hands, and ice-axe were all needed to prevent the beginning of a long slither which would only end on the glacier 6,000 ft below. Turning up the slope, the next few feet were of the same precarious nature that Odell and I had experienced on the glacis, but this was as yet the only part of the route where we had to forsake the security of the snow for the uncertainty of the rock. Once over this, we settled down to a long steady grind, kicking and cutting our way up very steep snow, and having rounded the head of this minor hollow, we took a line up the true left bank of the broad gully.

We were climbing on two ropes, so by changing the leading rope and also the leading end of each rope, the work was divided among four. It was a beautiful day, but in our perverse way we were not content, and were captious enough to wish the sun obscured so that we could climb in more comfort. Nanda Kot, 22,500 ft, sank below us and we began to cast jealous eyes on Trisul, which still looked down upon us majestically from its height of 23,400 ft. Meantime we began to search the snow above us for the slightest break in the relentless angle of the slope which might afford a site for a tent. We were tempted momentarily by the broken outline of the skyline ridge away across the gully, but we decided it was too far off and the approach to it too steep.

As we gained height, the curve of the face to our right grew rounder and narrower and the central ridge was beginning to stand out again like the bridge of a Roman nose. We edged over towards it, thinking that the rocks might provide easier going than the snow, and aiming for the foot of a rock tower where there might be a platform. Knowing by now the sort of rock we might expect, it was curious that we should so think, but such was the distorting effect on our minds of five hours of laborious step-kicking. The change of course was for the worse and we had some awkward moments before we dragged ourselves to the foot of the tower, to find it sloping away as steeply as the rest of the mountain.

The time was now three o'clock and our height something over 23,000 ft, practically level with Trisul. Loomis had an attack of cramp, but when he had recovered we turned our attention to the rock tower at our backs, on top of which we hoped to find better things. Lloyd did a grand lead up a steep rock chimney with his load on and was able to give the rest of us some much needed moral and, in my case, physical encouragement with the rope. This took some time and it was four o'clock before we were all on top of the tower, where there was barely room for five of us to stand, much less pitch a tent. Looking up the ridge, it was impossible to say where such a place would be found, but it was sufficiently broken to offer considerable hope. Meantime three of us had to get back to Camp IV and at this time of the afternoon of a bright sunny day the snow would be at its worst. With the assent of all, it was decided to dump our loads here leaving Houston and Odell to shift for themselves. It seemed a selfish decision at the time and it seems so now; no doubt we could have cut it a bit finer and yet got down before dark, but it was likely that they would not have to go far before finding a bivouac, and, in any case, with sleeping bags and warm clothing they could not come to much harm.

We learnt afterwards that they had an uncommonly busy evening. They had to climb another 150 ft before even the most imaginative could discern the makings of a platform, and then they had to make two journeys up and down with the loads. It was dark before they were finally settled.

Oblivious of this activity and the curses which were being bestowed, rather unjustly, on us for our premature desertion, we climbed hastily but cautiously down, reaching the camp at sundown. There was no sign of Graham Brown and Carter, so we assumed they were having a day off at Camp III.

Discussing the results of this day's work, we decided the bivouac was about 23,500 ft, probably too low for an attempt on the summit, but as high as we could push it in the day. We thought they would probably move it higher tomorrow and make their bid on the following day. The closer view of the upper part of the mountain which we had obtained had not made it look any easier, and it was a puzzle to make out where exactly the peak lay. I began to fear we had not allowed them enough time, but now it was too late to alter plans.

Next day was fine, but mist shrouded the upper mountain from our anxious gaze. We felt slack, and took the morning off before going down to Camp III to give Graham Brown and Carter a hand with their loads. As their tent was the one which had been half-buried by the blizzard, it took them a long time to dig it out, so we returned before them and prepared a platform.

The 27th was to be for us at Camp IV another day of idleness. That at least was the plan, but the event was different, and for some of us it was a day of the greatest mental and physical stress that we had yet encountered.

I had been worrying all night over the waste of this day, trying to devise some scheme whereby the second pair could go up at once to the bivouac. The trouble was that a second tent was essential, and having seen something of the extraordinary difficulty of finding a site even for the small tent, to go up there on the slim chance of finding a site for the big one as well was incurring the risk of exhausting the party to no purpose. While we were having breakfast, debating this knotty point and wondering how far the summit party had got, Loomis disclosed the fact that all was not well with his feet, the toes being slightly frost-bitten, and that henceforward we should have to count him out. This loss of carrying power knocked the scheme for a second tent on the head and a few moments later we had something else to think about.

We had just decided they must be well on the way to the top when we were startled to hear Odell's familiar yodel, rather like the braying of an ass. It sounded so close that I thought they must be on the way down, having got the peak the previous day, but it suddenly dawned on us that he was trying to send an S.O.S. Carter, who had the loudest voice, went outside to try and open communication, and a few minutes later came back to the tent to announce that "Charlie is killed" – Charlie being Houston. It was impossible to see anyone on the mountain, but he was certain he had heard correctly. As soon as we had pulled ourselves together, I stuffed some clothes and a bandage into a rucksack and Lloyd and I started off as fast as we could manage, to be followed later by Graham Brown and Carter with a hypodermic syringe.

It was a climb not easily forgotten – trying to go fast and realizing that at this height it was impossible to hurry, wondering what we should find, and above all what we could do. The natural assumption was that there had been a fall, and that since they were sure to be roped, Odell was also hurt, and the chance of getting a helpless man down the mountain was too remote to bear thinking about. As if to confirm this assumption, we could get no answer to repeated calls on the way up.

Remembering our struggles yesterday on the ridge and in the chimney, we took a different line and tackled a band of steep rock directly above us, in between the gully and the ridge. It proved to be much worse than it looked and, when we had hauled ourselves panting on to the snow above, we vowed that the next time we would stick to the gully, which here narrowed and passed through a sort of cleft in the rock band.

The time was now about two o'clock, and traversing up and to the right over snow in the direction of the ridge, the little tent came in sight not thirty yards away. Instinctively we tried almost to break into a run, but it was no use, and we advanced step by step, at a maddening pace, not knowing what we should find in the tent, if indeed anything at all. The sight of an ice-axe was a tremendous relief; evidently Odell had managed to crawl back. But when another was seen, conjecture was at a loss. Then voices were heard talking quietly and next moment we were greeted with, "Hullo, you blokes, have some tea." "Charlie is ill" was the message Odell had tried to convey!

Lloyd and I experienced a curious gamut of emotions; firstly and naturally, of profound relief, then, and I think not unnaturally, disgust at having suffered such unnecessary mental torture, and, of course, deep concern for Houston. While we swallowed tea, tea that reeked of pemmican but which I still remember with thankfulness, we heard what they had done and discussed what we were to do.

They had devoted yesterday to a reconnaissance. Following the ridge up they found, at a height of about 500 ft above the bivouac, a flat snow platform capable of holding two tents comfortably. Beyond that the climbing became interesting and difficult, but they had reached the foot of a long and easy snow slope leading up to the final rock wall. Here they turned back, having decided to move the bivouac next day to the higher site. Both were going strongly, but early that night Houston became violently ill, and in the cramped quarters of the tent, perched insecurely on an inadequate platform above a steep slope, both had spent a sleepless and miserable night. Houston attributed his trouble to the bully beef which both had eaten; Odell was unaffected, but it is possible that a small portion was tainted and certainly the symptoms pointed to poisoning of some kind.

Houston was still very ill and very weak, but it was he who suggested what should be done, and showed us how evil might be turned to good. It was only possible for two people to stay up here, and his plan was that he should go down that afternoon and that I should stay up with Odell, and thus no time would have been lost. We demurred to this on the ground that he was not fit to move, but he was so insistent on the importance of not losing a day and so confident of being able to get down that we at last consented.

We all four roped up, with Houston in the middle, and started slowly down, taking frequent rests. We struck half-right across the snow and joined the gully above the rock band according to our earlier resolution, and there the two rear men anchored the party while Lloyd cut steps down the narrow cleft, which was very icy. Houston was steady enough in spite of his helpless state of weakness, and having safely negotiated this awkward bit, we kicked slowly down to the left and found our up-going tracks. Presently Graham Brown and Carter hove in sight, and I imagine their amazement at seeing four people coming down was as great as ours had been at the sight of the two ice-axes.

When we met, Lloyd and Houston tied on to their rope and continued the descent, while Odell and I climbed slowly back to the bivouac.

This illness of Houston's was a miserable turn of fortune for him, robbing him as it did of the summit. Bad as he was, his generous determination to go down was of a piece with the rest of his actions.

Scenically the position of the bivouac was very fine but residentially it was damnable. It was backed on two sides by rock, but on the others the snow slope fell away steeply, and the platform which had been scraped out in the snow was so narrow that the outer edge of the tent overhung for almost a foot, thus reducing considerably both the living space and any feeling one yet had of security. Necessity makes a man bold, and I concluded that necessity had pressed very hard that night when they lit on this spot for their bivouac. Odell, who had had no sleep the previous night, could have slept on a church spire, and, as I had Houston's sleeping bag and the extra clothing I had fortunately brought up, we both had a fair night. Odell, who was the oldest inhabitant and in the position of host, generously conceded to me the outer berth, overhanging space.

The weather on the 28th still held and without regret we packed up our belongings and made the first trip to the upper bivouac. The snow slope was steeper than any we had yet met but, at the early hour we started, the snow was good and in an hour we reached the spacious snow shelf which they had marked down. It was about 20 ft × 20 ft, so that there was room to move about, but on either side of the ridge on which it stood the slope was precipitous. After a brief rest the increasing heat of the sun warned us to be on the move again and we hurried down for the remaining loads. The snow was softening rapidly under a hot sun nor was this deterioration confined only to the snow. We already knew, and it was to be impressed on us again, that at these altitudes a hot sun is a handicap not to be lightly assessed.

Guessing the height of this camp, aided by the absence of the hypsometer, we put it at about 24,000 ft. Trisul was well below us and even the top of East Nanda Devi (24,379 ft) began to look less remote. The condition of the wide belt of snow which had to be crossed, the difficulties of the final wall, and the weather were so many large question marks, but we turned in that night full of hope, and determined to give ourselves every chance by an early start.

We were up at five o'clock to begin the grim business of cooking and the more revolting tasks of eating breakfast and getting dressed. That we were up is an exaggeration, we were merely awake, for all these fatigues are carried out from inside one's sleeping bag until it is no longer possible to defer the putting on of boots. One advantage a narrow tent has, that at lower altitudes is overlooked, is that the two sleeping bags are in such close proximity that boots which are rammed into the non-existent space between them generally survive the night without being frozen stiff. It worked admirably on this occasion so that we were spared the pangs of wrestling with frozen boots with cold fingers. Frozen boots are a serious matter and may cause much delay, and in order to mitigate this trouble we had, since the start, carefully refrained from oiling our boots. This notion might work well enough on Everest in pre-monsoon conditions where the snow is dry, but we fell between two stools, rejoicing in wet feet down below and frozen boots higher up.

By six o'clock we were ready, and shortly after we crawled outside, roped up, and started. It was bitterly cold, for the sun had not yet risen over the shoulder of East Nanda Devi and there was a thin wind from the west. What mugs we were to be fooling about on this infernal ridge at that hour of the morning! And what was the use of this ridiculous coil of rope, as stiff as a wire hawser, tying me for better or for worse to that dirty-looking ruffian in front! Such, in truth, were the reflections of at least one of us as we topped a snow boss behind the tent, and the tenuous nature of the ridge in front became glaringly obvious in the chill light of dawn. It was comforting to reflect that my companion in misery had already passed this way, and presently as the demands of the climbing became more insistent, grievances seemed less real, and that life was still worth living was a proposition that might conceivably be entertained.

This difficult ridge was about 300 yards long, and though the general angle appeared slight it rose in a series of abrupt rock and snow steps. On the left was an almost vertical descent to a big ravine, bounded on the far side by terrific grey cliffs that supported the broad snow shelf for which we were making. The right side also fell away steeply, being part of the great rock cirque running round to East Nanda Devi. The narrow ridge we were on formed a sort of causeway between the lower south face and the upper snow shelf.

One very important factor which, more than anything, tended to promote a happier frame of mind was that the soft crumbly rock had at last yielded to a hard rough schistose-quartzite which was a joy to handle; a change which could not fail to please us as mountaineers and, no doubt, to interest my companion as a geologist. That vile rock, schist is, I believe, the technical term, had endangered our heads and failed to support our feet from the foot of the scree to the last bivouac. It was a wonder our burning anathemas had not caused it to undergo a geological change under our very eyes – metamorphosed it, say, into plutonic rocks. But, as has been said – by others, there is good in everything, and, on reflection, this very sameness was not without some saving grace because it meant that we were spared an accumulation of rock samples at every camp. A bag of assorted stones had already been left at the Glacier Camp, and I tremble to think what burdens we might have had to carry down the mountain had the rock been as variegated as our geologist, and indeed any right-minded geologist, would naturally desire.

Thanks to the earlier reconnaissance by him and Houston, Odell led over this ridge at a good pace and in an hour and a half we had reached the snow mound which marked the farthest point they had reached. It was a ridge on which we moved one at a time.

In front was a snow slope set at an angle of about 30 degrees and running right up to the foot of the rock wall, perhaps 600 or 700 ft above us. To the west this wide snow terrace extended for nearly a quarter of a mile until it ended beneath that same skyline ridge, which below had formed the western boundary of the broad gully. On our right the shelf quickly steepened and merged into the steep rock face of the ridge between East Nanda Devi and our mountain. We were too close under the summit to see where it lay, but there was little doubt about the line we should take, because from a rapid survey there seemed to be only one place where a lodgement could be effected on the final wall. This was well to the west of our present position, where a snow rib crossed the terrace at right angles and, abutting against the wall, formed as it were a ramp.

We began the long snow trudge at eight o'clock and even at that early hour and after a cold night the snow was not good and soon became execrable. The sun was now well up. After it had been at work for a bit we were going in over our knees at every step, and in places where the slope was steeper it was not easy to make any upward progress at all. One foot would be lifted and driven hard into the snow and then, on attempting to rise on it, one simply sank down through the snow to the previous level. It was like trying to climb up cotton wool, and a good deal more exhausting, I imagine, than the treadmill. But, like the man on a walking tour in Ireland, who throughout a long day received the same reply of "20 miles" to his repeated inquiries as to the distance he was from his destination, we could at any rate say, "Thank God, we were holding our own."

The exertion was great and every step made good cost six to eight deep breaths. Our hopes of the summit grew faint, but there was no way but to plug on and see how far we could get. This we did, thinking only of the next step, taking our time, and resting frequently. It was at least some comfort that the track we were ploughing might assist a second party. On top of the hard work and the effect of altitude was the languor induced by a sun which beat down relentlessly on the dazzling snow, searing our lips and sapping the energy of mind and body. As an example of how far this mind-sapping process had gone, I need only mention that it was seriously suggested that we should seek the shade of a convenient rock which we were then near, lie up there until evening, and finish the climb in the dark!

It is noteworthy that whilst we were enjoying, or more correctly enduring, this remarkable spell of sunshine, the foot-hills south and west of the Basin experienced disastrous floods. As related in the first chapter, it was on this day that the Pindar river overflowed sweeping away some houses in the village of Tharali, while on the same day nineteen inches of rain fell at the hill station of Mussoorie west of Ranikhet.

We derived some encouragement from seeing East Nanda Devi sink below us and at one o'clock, rather to our surprise, we found ourselves on top of the snow rib moving at a snail's pace towards the foot of the rocks. There we had a long rest and tried to force some chocolate down our parched throats by eating snow at the same time. Though neither of us said so, I think both felt that now it would take a lot to stop us. There was a difficult piece of rock to climb; Odell led this and appeared to find it stimulating, but it provoked me to exclaim loudly upon its "thinness". Once over that, we were landed fairly on the final slope with the summit ridge a bare 300 ft above us.

Presently we were confronted with the choice of a short but very steep snow gully and a longer but less drastic route to the left. We took the first and found the snow reasonably hard owing to the very steep angle at which it lay. After a severe struggle I drew myself out of it on to a long and gently sloping corridor, just below and parallel to the summit ridge. I sat down and drove the axe in deep to hold Odell as he finished the gully. He moved up to join me and I had just suggested the corridor as a promising line to take when there was a sudden hiss and, quicker than thought, a slab of snow, about forty yards long, slid off the corridor and disappeared down the gully, peeling off a foot of snow as it went. At the lower limit of the avalanche, which was where we were sitting, it actually broke away for a depth of a foot all round my axe to which I was holding. At its upper limit, forty yards up the corridor, it broke away to a depth of three or four feet.

The corridor route had somehow lost its attractiveness, so we finished the climb by the ridge without further adventure, reaching the top at three o'clock.

The summit is not the exiguous and precarious spot that usually graces the top of so many Himalayan peaks, but a solid snow ridge nearly 200 yards long and 20 yards broad. It is seldom that conditions on top of a high peak allow the climber the time or the opportunity to savour the immediate fruits of victory. Too often, when having first carefully probed the snow to make sure he is not standing on a cornice, the climber straightens up preparatory to savouring the situation to the full, he is met by a perishing wind and the interesting view of a cloud at close quarters, and with a muttered imprecation turns in his tracks and begins the descent. Far otherwise was it now. There were no cornices to worry about and room to unrope and walk about. The air was still, the sun shone, and the view was good if not so extensive as we had hoped.

Odell had brought a thermometer, and no doubt sighed for the hypsometer. From it we found that the air temperature was 20 degrees F, but in the absence of wind we could bask gratefully in the friendly rays of our late enemy the sun. It was difficult to realize that we were actually standing on top of the same peak which we had viewed two months ago from Ranikhet, and which had then appeared incredibly remote and inaccessible, and it gave us a curious feeling of exaltation to know that we were above every peak within hundreds of miles on either hand. Dhaulagiri, 1,000 ft higher, and 200 miles away in Nepal, was our nearest rival. I believe we so far forgot ourselves as to shake hands on it.

After the first joy in victory came a feeling of sadness that the mountain had succumbed, that the proud head of the goddess was bowed.

At this late hour of the day there was too much cloud about for any distant views. The Nepal peaks were hidden and all the peaks on the rim, excepting only Trisul, whose majesty even our loftier view-point could not diminish. Far to the north through a vista of white cloud the sun was colouring to a warm brown the bare and bleak Tibetan plateau.

After three-quarters of an hour on that superb summit, a brief forty-five minutes into which was crowded the worth of many hours of glorious life, we dragged ourselves reluctantly away, taking with us a memory that can never fade and leaving behind "thoughts beyond the reaches of our souls".

If our thoughts were still treading on air, the short steep gully, swept by the avalanche bare of steps, soon brought us to earth. We kicked slowly down it, facing inwards and plunging an arm deep into the snow for support. Followed another exhausting drag across the snow, hindered rather than helped by the deep holes we had made coming up, and then a cold hour was spent moving cautiously, one at a time, down the ice and the benumbing rocks of the long ridge above the bivouac. We paused to watch a bird, a snow pigeon, cross our ridge and fly swiftly across the grey cliffs of the ravine beneath the snow terrace, like the spirit of Nanda Devi herself, forsaking the fastness which was no longer her own.

At six o'clock we reached the tent and brewed the first of many jorums of tea. After such a day nothing could have tasted better and our appreciation was enhanced by our long enforced abstinence. There was but a pinch left and we squandered it all recklessly, saving the leaves for the morning. Food was not even mentioned.

We paid for this debauch with a sleepless night to which no doubt exhaustion and a still-excited imagination contributed. Each little incident of the climb was gone over again and again, and I remember, in the small hours when the spark of life burns lowest, the feeling which predominated over all was one of remorse at the fall of a giant. It is the same sort of contrition that one feels at the shooting of an elephant, for however thrilling and arduous the chase, however great has been the call upon skill, perseverance, and endurance, and however gratifying the weight of the ivory, when the great bulk crashes to the ground achievement seems to have been bought at the too high cost of sacrilege.

It was very cold next morning when we packed up and started down. Near the bottom of the gully we were met by Lloyd and Loomis, who were coming up to help us down and who were overjoyed when they heard that success had crowned the efforts of the whole party. Houston and Graham Brown had already gone down and we decided to stop the night at Camp IV. There were still three or four days' food left in hand but Loomis and Carter were both troubled with their feet, which must have been touched with frost the day Camp IV was occupied. Lloyd was going stronger than ever and it was much to be regretted that we could not make up a second party.

The weather, which during this crucial period had been so kind, now broke up and on the morning of the 31st it was blowing half a gale out of a clear sky. Lloyd, Loomis, and I started some time before the other two, all carrying heavy loads because we left nothing but the two big tents, some snow-shoes, and two pairs of crampons or ice-claws. The snow-shoes had been lugged up to assist us on soft snow and the crampons for use on hard snow, but the slopes were, of course, all too steep for snow-shoes, and the only time we might have used the crampons was now when they had been abandoned.

It was bitterly cold, and the snow on the arete was hard and dangerous – the mountain had not finished with us yet. We started to descend in the usual way, plunging the heel in at each step with a stiff leg. When one or two "voluntaries" had been cut, we should have taken warning that the snow was not right for such tactics, but we were all pretty tired and in a hurry to get down, and it is in such circumstances that care is relaxed and the party comes to grief. Fortunately before this happened we had another warning which could not well be ignored. The leader's heels went from under him and he slid down the slope pulling the second man after him until checked by the rope belayed round the end man's axe, which fortunately held firm. We all felt rather ashamed of ourselves after this exhibition and abandoned that method in favour of the slower but safer one of cutting steps and moving one at a time, which should have been adopted at the start.

There was another slip, quickly checked, when one of the snow steps above the Gite gave way, and we reached this camp in a chastened frame of mind and hoping that the mountain had now exhausted its spite. After a brief rest we pushed on, unroped gladly when we were off the snow, and picked our way with great caution down the unstable rocks to Camp I. On the way we noticed with concern that Odell and Carter were still high up on the arete and moving very slowly.

We found here Graham Brown and Pasang. The former's leg was troubling him, so he had spent the night here where there were still two tents, and Pasang had come up from below to take his load. We heard that Graham Brown and Houston too had narrowly escaped disaster on the previous day by the breaking of a step above the Gite. Pasang had completely recovered his sight, but he was not yet his former bright self, for I think he felt keenly the disability which prevented him from helping his Sahibs at grips with the mountain.

It was now midday and after a drink of cocoa, which served only to bring home to us the loss we had suffered, we continued the descent. The cocoa so wrought upon Lloyd that, with a desperation born of thirst, he turned aside to prosecute a last and unsuccessful search for the tea. On the Coxcomb ridge I met Phuta going up to help Pasang and was shocked to hear that Kitar had died in the night. We got down to the new Base Camp at the foot of the scree at two o'clock and but for the melancholy news of Kitar's death there was nothing to mar our contentment. Twenty-one days had elapsed since we left.

Annapurna, Mon Amour

Maurice Herzog

Born in France in 1919, Herzog led the 1950 conquest of Annapurna, 8,075 m (26,493 ft) in Nepal, the first 8,000-metre peak to be scaled. Unfortunately for the French team, the descent turned into a disaster when the monsoon broke around them.

A fierce and savage wind tore at us.

We were on top of Annapurna! 8,075 metres, 26,493 feet.

Our hearts overflowed with an unspeakable happiness.

"If only the others could know . . ."

If only everyone could know!

The summit was a corniced crest of ice, and the precipices on the far side, which plunged vertically down beneath us, were terrifying, unfathomable. There could be few other mountains in the world like this. Clouds floated half way down, concealing the gentle, fertile valley of Pokhara, 23,000 ft below. Above us there was nothing!

Our mission was accomplished. But at the same time we had accomplished something infinitely greater. How wonderful life would now become! What an inconceivable experience it is to attain one's ideal and, at the very same moment, to fulfil oneself. I was stirred to the depths of my being. Never had I felt happiness like this – so intense and yet so pure. That brown rock, the highest of them all, that ridge of ice – were these the goals of a lifetime? Or were they, rather, the limits of man's pride?

"Well, what about going down?"

Lachenal shook me. What were his own feelings? Did he simply think he had finished another climb, as in the Alps? Did he think one could just go down again like that, with nothing more to it?

"One minute, I must take some photographs."

"Hurry up!"

I fumbled feverishly in my sack, pulled out the camera, took out the little French flag which was right at the bottom, and the pennants. Useless gestures, no doubt, but something more than symbols – eloquent tokens of affection and goodwill. I tied the strips of material – stained by sweat and by the food in the sacks – to the shaft of my ice-axe, the only flag-staff at hand. Then I focused my camera on Lachenal.

"Now, will you take me?"

"Hand it over – hurry up!" said Lachenal.

He took several pictures and then handed me back the camera. I loaded a colour-film and we repeated the process to be certain of bringing back records to be cherished in the future.

"Are you mad?" asked Lachenal. "We haven't a minute to lose: we must go down at once."

And in fact a glance round showed me that the weather was no longer gloriously fine as it had been in the morning. Lachenal was becoming impatient.

"We must go down!"

He was right. His was the reaction of the mountaineer who knows his own domain. But I just could not accustom myself to the idea that we had won our victory. It seemed inconceivable that we should have trodden those summit snows.

It was impossible to build a cairn; there were no stones, and everything was frozen. Lachenal stamped his feet; he felt them freezing. I felt mine freezing too, but paid little attention. The highest mountain to be climbed by man lay under our feet! The names of our predecessors on these heights chased each other through my mind: Mummery, Mallory and Irvine, Bauer,

Welzenbach, Tilman, Shipton. How many of them were dead –
how many had found on these mountains what, to them, was the
finest end of all.

My joy was touched with humility. It was not just one party
that had climbed Annapurna today, but a whole expedition. I
thought of all the others in the camps perched on the slopes at
our feet, and I knew it was because of their efforts and their
sacrifices that we had succeeded today. There are times when
the most complex actions are suddenly summed up, distilled,
and strike you with illuminating clarity: so it was with this
irresistible upward surge which had landed us two here.

Pictures passed through my mind – the Chamonix valley,
where I had spent the most marvellous moments of my childhood. Mont Blanc, which so tremendously impressed me! I was
a child when I first saw "the Mont Blanc people" coming home,
and to me there was a queer look about them; a strange light
shone in their eyes.

"Come on, straight down," called Lachenal.

He had already done up his sack and started going down. I
took out my pocket aneroid: 8,500 metres. I smiled. I swallowed
a little condensed milk and left the tube behind – the only trace
of our passage. I did up my sack, put on my gloves and my
glasses, seized my ice-axe; one look round and I, too, hurried
down the slope. Before disappearing into the couloir I gave one
last look at the summit which would henceforth be all our joy
and all our consolation.

Lachenal was already far below; he had reached the foot of the
couloir. I hurried down in his tracks. I went as fast as I could,
but it was dangerous going. At every step one had to take care
that the snow did not break away beneath one's weight. Lachenal, going faster than I thought he was capable of, was now on
the long traverse. It was my turn to cross the area of mixed rock
and snow. At last I reached the foot of the rock-band. I had
hurried and I was out of breath. I undid my sack. What had I
been going to do? I could not say.

"My gloves!"

Before I had time to bend over, I saw them slide and roll.
They went further and further straight down the slope. I
remained where I was, quite stunned. I watched them rolling

down slowly, with no appearance of stopping. The movement of those gloves was engraved in my sight as something ineluctable, irremediable, against which I was powerless. The consequences might be most serious. What was I to do?

"Quickly, down to Camp V."

Rebuffat and Terray should be there. My concern dissolved like magic. I now had a fixed objective again: to reach the camp. Never for a minute did it occur to me to use as gloves the socks which I always carry in reserve for just such a mishap as this.

On I went, trying to catch up with Lachenal. It had been two o'clock when we reached the summit; we had started out at six in the morning; but I had to admit that I had lost all sense of time. I felt as if I were running, whereas in actual fact I was walking normally, perhaps rather slowly, and I had to keep stopping to get my breath. The sky was now covered with clouds, everything had become grey and dirty-looking. An icy wind sprang up, boding no good. We must push on! But where was Lachenal? I spotted him a couple of hundred yards away, looking as if he was never going to stop. And I had thought he was in indifferent form!

The clouds grew thicker and came right down over us; the wind blew stronger, but I did not suffer from the cold. Perhaps the descent had restored my circulation. Should I be able to find the tents in the mist? I watched the rib ending in the beak-like point which overlooked the camp. It was gradually swallowed up by the clouds, but I was able to make out the spearhead rib lower down. If the mist should thicken I would make straight for that rib and follow it down, and in this way I should be bound to come upon the tent.

Lachenal disappeared from time to time, and then the mist was so thick that I lost sight of him altogether. I kept going at the same speed, as fast as my breathing would allow.

The slope was now steeper; a few patches of bare ice followed the smooth stretches of snow. A good sign – I was nearing the camp. How difficult to find one's way in thick mist! I kept the course which I had set by the steepest angle of the slope. The ground was broken; with my crampons I went straight down walls of bare ice. There were some patches ahead – a few more steps. It was the camp all right, but there were *two* tents.

So Rebuffat and Terray had come up. What a mercy! I should be able to tell them that we had been successful, that we were returning from the top. How thrilled they would be!

I got there, dropping down from above. The platform had been extended, and the two tents were facing each other. I tripped over one of the guy-ropes of the first tent; there was movement inside – they had heard me. Rebuffat and Terray put their heads out.

"We've made it. We're back from Annapurna!"

Rebuffat and Terray received the great news with excitement and delight.

"But what about Biscante?" asked Terray anxiously.

"He won't be long. He was just in front of me! What a day – started out at six this morning – didn't stop . . . got up at last."

Words failed me. I had so much to say. The sight of familiar – faces dispelled the strange feeling that I had experienced since morning, and I became, once more, just a mountaineer.

Terray, who was speechless with delight, wrung my hands. Then the smile vanished from his face: "Maurice – your hands!" There was an uneasy silence. I had forgotten that I had lost my gloves: my fingers were violet and white, and hard as wood. The other two stared at them in dismay – they realized the full seriousness of the injury. But, still blissfully floating on a sea of joy remote from reality, I leant over towards Terray and said confidentially, "You're in such splendid form, and you've done so marvellously, it's absolutely tragic you didn't come up there with us!"

"What I did was for the Expedition, my dear Maurice, and anyway you've got up, and that's a victory for the whole lot of us."

I nearly burst with happiness. How could I tell him all that his answer meant to me? The rapture I had felt on the summit, which might have seemed a purely personal, egotistical emotion, had been transformed by his words into a complete and perfect joy with no shadow upon it. His answer proved that this victory was not just one man's achievement, a matter for personal pride; no – and Terray was the first to understand this – it was a victory for us all, a victory for mankind itself.

"Hi! Help! Help!"

"Biscante!" exclaimed the others.

Still half intoxicated and remote from reality, I had heard nothing. Terray felt a chill at his heart, and his thoughts flew to his partner on so many unforgettable climbs; together they had so often skirted death, and won so many splendid victories. Putting his head out, and seeing Lachenal clinging to the slope a hundred yards lower down, he dressed in frantic haste.

Out he went. But the slope was bare now; Lachenal had disappeared. Terray was horribly startled, and could only utter unintelligible cries. It was a ghastly moment for him. A violent wind sent the mist tearing by. Under the stress of emotion Terray had not realized how it falsified distances.

"Biscante! Biscante!"

He had spotted him, through a rift in the mist, lying on the slope much lower down than he had thought. Terray set his teeth, and glissaded down like a madman. How would he stop? How would he be able to brake, without crampons, on the wind-hardened snow? But Terray was a first-class skier, and with a jump turn he stopped beside Lachenal, who was concussed after his tremendous fall. In a state of collapse, with no ice-axe, balaclava, or gloves, and only one crampon, he gazed vacantly round him.

"My feet are frost-bitten. Take me down . . . take me down, so that Oudot can see to me."

"It can't be done," explained Terray regretfully. "Can't you see we're in the middle of a storm . . . It'll be dark soon."

But Lachenal was obsessed by the fear of amputation. With a gesture of despair he tore the axe out of Terray's hands and tried to force his way down, but soon saw the futility of his action, and resolved to climb up to the camp. While Terray cut steps without stopping, Lachenal, ravaged and exhausted as he was, dragged himself along on all fours.

Meanwhile I had gone into Rebuffat's tent. He was appalled at the sight of my hands and, as rather incoherently I told him what we had done, he took a piece of rope and began flicking my fingers. Then he took off my boots, with great difficulty, for my feet were swollen, and beat my feet and rubbed me. We soon heard Terray giving Lachenal the same treatment in the other tent.

For our comrades it was a tragic moment: Annapurna was
conquered, and the first "eight-thousander" had been climbed.
Every one of us had been ready to sacrifice everything for this.
Yet, as they looked at our feet and hands, what can Terray and
Rebuffat have felt?

Outside the storm howled and the snow was still falling. The
mist grew thicker and darkness came. As on the previous night
we had to cling to the poles to prevent the tents being carried
away by the wind. The only two air-mattresses were given to
Lachenal and myself while Terray and Rebuffat both sat on
ropes, rucksacks and provisions to keep themselves well off the
snow. They rubbed, slapped and beat us with a rope; sometimes
the blows fell on the living flesh, and howls arose from both
tents. Rebuffat persevered; it was essential to continue, painful
as it was. Gradually life returned to my feet as well as to my
hands, and circulation started again. It was the same with
Lachenal.

Now Terray summoned up the energy to prepare some hot
drinks. He called to Rebuffat that he would pass him a mug, so
two hands stretched out towards each other between the two
tents and were instantly covered with snow. The liquid was
boiling though at scarcely more than 60° Centigrade (140°
Fahrenheit). I swallowed it greedily and felt infinitely better.

The night was absolute hell. Frightful onslaughts of wind
battered us incessantly, while the never-ceasing snow piled up
on the tents.

Now and again I heard voices from next door – it was Terray
massaging Lachenal with admirable perseverance, only stopping to ply him with hot drinks. In our tent Rebuffat was quite
worn out, but satisfied that warmth was returning to my limbs.

Lying half-unconscious I was scarcely aware of the passage of
time. There were moments when I was able to see our situation
in its true dramatic light, but the rest of the time I was plunged
in an inexplicable stupor with no thought for the consequences
of our victory.

As the night wore on the snow lay heavier on the tent, and
once again I had the frightful feeling of being slowly and silently
asphyxiated. Occasionally in an access of revolt I tried, with all
the strength of which I was capable, to push off with both

forearms the mass that was crushing me. These fearful exertions left me gasping for breath and I fell back into the same state as before. It was much worse than the previous night.

"Hi! Gaston! Gaston!"

I recognized Terray's voice.

"Time to be off!"

I heard the sounds without grasping their meaning. Was it light already? I was not in the least surprised that the other two had given up all thought of going to the top, and I did not at all grasp the measure of their sacrifice.

Outside the storm redoubled in violence. The tent shook and the fabric flapped alarmingly. It had usually been fine in the mornings: did this mean the monsoon was upon us? We knew it was not far off – could this be its first onslaught?

"Gaston! Are you ready?" Terray asked again.

"One minute," answered Rebuffat. He did not have an easy job: he had to put my boots on and do everything to get me ready: I let myself be handled like a baby. In the other tent Terray finished dressing Lachenal, whose feet were still swollen and would not fit into his boots. So Terray gave him his own, which were bigger. To get Lachenal's on to his own feet he had to make some slits in them. As a precaution he put a sleeping bag and some food into his sack and shouted to us to do the same. Were his words lost in the storm? Or were we too intent on leaving this hellish place to listen to his instructions?

Lachenal and Terray were already outside.

"We're going down!" they shouted.

Then Rebuffat tied me on to the rope, and we went out. There were only two ice-axes for the four of us, so Rebuffat and Terray took them as a matter of course. For a moment, as we left the two tents of Camp V, I felt childishly ashamed at abandoning all our good equipment.

Already the first rope seemed a long way down below us. We were blinded by the squalls of snow and we could not hear each other a yard away. We had both put on our cagoules, for it was very cold. The snow was apt to slide and the rope often came in useful.

Ahead of us the other two were losing no time. Lachenal went first and, safeguarded by Terray, he forced the pace in his anxiety to get down. There were no tracks to show us the way, but it was engraved on all our minds – straight down the slope for 400 yards then traverse to the left for 150 to 200 yards to get to Camp IV. The snow was thinning and the wind less violent. Was it going to clear? We hardly dared to hope so. A wall of seracs brought us up short.

"It's to the left," I said, "I remember perfectly."

Somebody else thought it was to the right. We started going down again. The wind had dropped completely, but the snow fell in big flakes. The mist was thick, and, not to lose each other, we walked in line: I was third and I could barely see Lachenal, who was first. It was impossible to recognize any of the pitches. We were all experienced enough mountaineers to know that even on familiar ground it is easy to make mistakes in such weather – distances are deceptive, one cannot tell whether one is going up or down. We kept colliding with hummocks which we had taken for hollows. The mist, the falling snowflakes, the carpet of snow, all merged into the same whitish tone and confused our vision. The towering outlines of the seracs took on fantastic shapes and seemed to move slowly round us.

Our situation was not desperate, we were certainly not lost. We would have to go lower down: the traverse must begin further on – I remembered the serac which served as a milestone. The snow stuck to our cagoules, and turned us into white phantoms noiselessly flitting against a background equally white. We began to sink in dreadfully, and there is nothing worse for bodies already on the verge of exhaustion.

Were we too high or too low? No one could tell. Perhaps we had better try slanting over to the left! The snow was in a bad state, but we did not seem to realize the danger. We were forced to admit that we were not on the right route, so we retraced our steps and climbed up above the serac which overhung us – no doubt, we reflected, we should be on the right level now. With Rebuffat leading, we went back over the way which had cost us such an effort. I followed him jerkily, saying nothing, and determined to go on to the end. If Rebuffat had fallen I could never have held him.

We went doggedly on from one serac to another. Each time we thought we had recognized the right route, and each time there was a fresh disappointment. If only the mist would lift, if only the snow would stop for a second! On the slope it seemed to be growing deeper every minute. Only Terray and Rebuffat were capable of breaking the trail and they relieved each other at regular intervals, without a word and without a second's hesitation.

I admired this determination of Rebuffat's for which he is so justly famed. He did not intend to die! With the strength of desperation and at the price of superhuman effort he forged ahead. The slowness of his progress would have dismayed even the most obstinate climber, but he would not give up, and in the end the mountain yielded in face of his perseverence.

Terray, when his turn came, charged madly ahead. He was like a force of nature: at all costs he would break down these prison walls that penned us in. His physical strength was exceptional, his will-power no less remarkable. Lachenal gave him considerable trouble. Perhaps he was not quite in his right mind. He said it was no use going on; we must dig a hole in the snow and wait for fine weather. He swore at Terray and called him a madman. Nobody but Terray would have been capable of dealing with him – he just tugged sharply on the rope and Lachenal was forced to follow.

We were well and truly lost.

The weather did not seem likely to improve. A minute ago we had still had ideas about which way to go – now we had none. This way or that . . . We went on at random to allow for the chance of a miracle which appeared increasingly unlikely. The instinct of self-preservation in the two fit members of the party alternated with a hopelessness which made them completely irresponsible. Each in turn did the silliest things: Terray traversed the steep and avalanchy slopes with one crampon badly adjusted. He and Rebuffat performed incredible feats of balance without the least slip.

Camp IV was certainly on the left, on the edge of the Sickle. On that point we were all agreed. But it was very hard to find. The wall of ice that gave it such magnificent protection was now our enemy, for it hid the tents from us. In mist like this we should have to be right on top of them before we spotted them.

Perhaps if we called, someone would hear us? Lachenal gave

the signal, but snow absorbs sound, and his shout seemed to carry only a few yards. All four of us called out together: "One . . . two . . . three . . . Help!"

We got the impression that our united shout carried a long way, so we began again: "One . . . two . . . three . . . Help!" Not a sound in reply!

Now and again Terray took off his boots and rubbed his feet; the sight of our frost-bitten limbs had made him aware of the danger and he had the strength of mind to do something about it. Like Lachenal, he was haunted by the idea of amputation. For me, it was too late: my feet and hands, already affected from yesterday, were beginning to freeze up again.

We had eaten nothing since the day before, and we had been on the go the whole time, but man's resources of energy in face of death are inexhaustible. When the end seems imminent, there still remain reserves, though it needs tremendous will-power to call them up.

Time passed, but we had no idea of it. Night was approaching, and we were terrified, though none of us uttered a complaint. Rebuffat and I found a way we thought we remembered, but were brought to a halt by the extreme steepness of the slope – the mist turned it into a vertical wall. We were to find, next day, that at that moment we had been almost on top of the camp, and that the wall was the very one that sheltered the tents which would have been our salvation.

"We must find a crevasse."

"We can't stay here all night!"

"A hole – it's the only thing."

"We'll all die in it."

Night had suddenly fallen and it was essential to come to a decision without wasting another minute; if we remained on the slope, we should be dead before morning. We should have to bivouac. What the conditions would be like, we could guess, for we all knew what it meant to bivouac above 23,000 ft.

With his axe Terray began to dig a hole. Lachenal went over to a snow-filled crevasse a few yards further on, then suddenly let out a yell and disappeared before our eyes. We stood helpless: would we, or rather would Terray and Rebuffat, have enough strength for all the manoeuvres with the rope that would be needed to get him out? The crevasse was completely blocked up save for the one little hole where Lachenal had fallen through.

"Hi! Lachenal!" called Terray.

A voice, muffled by many thicknesses of ice and snow, came up to us. It was impossible to make out what it was saying.

"Hi! Lachenal!"

Terray jerked the rope violently; this time we could hear.

"I'm here!"

"Anything broken?"

"No! It'll do for the night! Come along."

This shelter was heaven-sent. None of us would have had the strength to dig a hole big enough to protect the lot of us from the wind. Without hesitation Terray let himself drop into the crevasse, and a loud "Come on!" told us he had arrived safely. In my turn I let myself go: it was a proper toboggan-slide. I shot down a sort of twisting tunnel, very steep, and about thirty feet long. I came out at great speed into the opening beyond and was literally hurled to the bottom of the crevasse. We let Rebuffat know he could come by giving a tug on the rope.

The intense cold of this minute grotto shrivelled us up, the enclosing walls of ice were damp and the floor a carpet of fresh snow; by huddling together there was just room for the four of us. Icicles hung from the ceiling and we broke some of them off to make more head room and kept little bits to suck – it was a long time since we had had anything to drink.

That was our shelter for the night. At least we should be protected from the wind, and the temperature would remain fairly even, though the damp was extremely unpleasant. We settled ourselves in the dark as best we could. As always in a bivouac, we took off our boots; without this precaution the constriction would cause immediate frost-bite. Terray unrolled the sleeping-bag which he had had the foresight to bring, and settled himself in relative comfort. We put on everything warm that we had, and to avoid contact with the snow I sat on the cine-camera. We huddled close up to each other, in our search for a hypothetical position in which the warmth of all bodies could be combined without loss, but we could not keep still for a second.

We did not open our mouths – signs were less of an effort than words. Every man withdrew into himself and took refuge in his own inner world. Terray massaged Lachenal's feet; Rebuffat felt his feet freezing, too, but he had sufficient strength to rub them himself. I remained motionless, unseeing. My feet and hands went on freezing, but what could be done? I attempted to forget suffering, to forget the passing of time, trying not to feel the devouring and numbing cold which insidiously gained upon us.

Terray shared his sleeping-bag with Lachenal, putting his feet and hands inside the precious eiderdown. At the same time he went on rubbing.

"Anyhow the frost-bite won't spread further," he was thinking.

None of us could make a movement without upsetting the others, and the positions we had taken up with such care were continually being altered so that we had to start all over again. This kept us busy. Rebuffat persevered with his rubbing and complained of his feet; like Terray he was thinking: "We mustn't look beyond tomorrow – afterwards we'll see." But he was not blind to the fact that "afterwards" was one big question mark.

Terray generously tried to give me part of his sleeping-bag. He had understood the seriousness of my condition, and knew why it was that I said nothing and remained quite passive; he realized that I had abandoned all hope for myself. He massaged me for nearly two hours: his feet, too, might have frozen, but he did not appear to give the matter a thought. I found new courage simply in contemplating his unselfishness; he was doing so much to help me that it would have been ungrateful of me not to go on struggling to live. Though my heart was like a lump of ice itself, I was astonished to feel no pain. Everything material about me seemed to have dropped away. I seemed to be quite clear in my thoughts and yet I floated in a kind of peaceful happiness. There was still a breath of life in me, but it dwindled steadily as the hours went by. Terray's massage no longer had any effect upon me. All was over, I thought. Was not this cavern the most beautiful grave I could hope for? Death caused me no grief, no regret – I smiled at the thought.

After hours of torpor, a voice mumbled, "Daylight!" This made some impression on the others. I only felt surprised – I had not thought that daylight would penetrate so far down.

"Too early to start," said Rebuffat.

A ghastly light spread through our grotto and we could just vaguely make out the shapes of each other's heads. A queer noise from a long way off came down to us – a sort of prolonged hiss. The noise increased. Suddenly I was buried, blinded, smothered beneath an avalanche of new snow. The icy snow spread over the cavern, finding its way through every gap in our clothing. I ducked my head between my knees and covered myself with both arms. The snow flowed on and on. There was a silence. We were not completely buried, but there was snow everywhere. We got up, taking care not to bang our heads against the ceiling of ice, and tried to shake ourselves. We were all in our stockinged feet in the snow. The first thing to do was to find our boots.

Rebuffat and Terray began to search, and realized at once that they were blind. Yesterday they had taken off their glasses to lead us down, and now they were paying for it. Lachenal was the first to lay hands upon a pair of boots. He tried to put them on, but they were Rebuffat's. Rebuffat attempted to climb up the shoot down which we had come yesterday, and which the avalanche had followed in its turn.

"Hi, Gaston! What's the weather like?" called up Terray.

"Can't see a thing. It's blowing hard."

We were still groping for our things. Terray found his boots and put them on awkwardly, unable to see what he was doing. Lachenal helped him, but he was all on edge and fearfully impatient, in striking contrast to my immobility. Terray then went up the icy channel, puffing and blowing, and at last reached the outer world. He was met by terrible gusts of wind that cut right through him and lashed his face.

"Bad weather," he said to himself, "this time it's the end. We're lost . . . we'll never come through."

At the bottom of the crevasse there were still two of us looking for our boots. Lachenal poked fiercely with an ice-axe. I was calmer and tried to proceed more rationally. We extracted crampons and an axe in turn from the snow, but still no boots.

Well – so this cavern was to be our last resting-place! There was very little room – we were bent double and got in each other's way. Lachenal decided to go out without his boots. He called out frantically, hauled himself up on the rope, trying to get a hold or to wriggle his way up, digging his toes into the snow walls. Terray from outside pulled as hard as he could: I watched him go; he gathered speed and disappeared.

When he emerged from the opening he saw the sky was clear and blue, and he began to run like a madman, shrieking, "It's fine, it's fine!"

I set to work again to search the cave. The boots *had* to be found, or Lachenal and I were done for. On all fours, with nothing on my hands or feet, I raked the snow, stirring it round this way and that, hoping every second to come upon something hard. I was no longer capable of thinking – I reacted like an animal fighting for its life.

I found one boot! The other was tied to it – a pair! Having ransacked the whole cave I at last found the other pair. But in spite of all my efforts I could not find the camera, and gave up in despair. There was no question of putting my boots on – my hands were like lumps of wood and I could hold nothing in my fingers; my feet were very swollen – I should never be able to get boots on them. I twisted the rope round the boots as well as I could and called up the shoot:

"Lionel . . . boots!"

There was no answer, but he must have heard, for with a jerk the precious boots shot up. Soon after the rope came down again. My turn. I wound the rope round me; I could not pull it tight so I made a whole series of little knots. Their combined strength, I hoped, would be enough to hold me. I had no strength to shout again; I gave a great tug on the rope, and Terray understood.

At the first step I had to kick a niche in the hard snow for my toes. Further on I expected to be able to get up more easily by wedging myself across the runnel. I wriggled up a few yards like this and then I tried to dig my hands and my feet into the wall. My hands were stiff and hard right up to the wrists and my feet had no feeling up to the ankles; the joints were inflexible and this hampered me greatly.

Somehow or other I succeeded in working my way up, while Terray pulled so hard he nearly choked me. I began to see more distinctly and so knew that I must be nearing the opening. Often I fell back, but I clung on and wedged myself in again as best I could. My heart was bursting, and I was forced to rest. A fresh wave of energy enabled me to crawl to the top. I pulled myself out by clutching Terray's legs; *he* was just about all in and I was in the last stages of exhaustion. Terray was close to me and I whispered:

"Lionel . . . I'm dying!"

He supported me and helped me away from the crevasse. Lachenal and Rebuffat were sitting in the snow a few yards away. The instant Lionel let go of me I sank down and dragged myself along on all fours.

The weather was perfect. Quantities of snow had fallen the day before and the mountains were resplendent. Never had I seen them look so beautiful – our last day would be magnificent.

Rebuffat and Terray were completely blind; as he came along with me Terray knocked into things and I had to direct him. Rebuffat, too, could not move a step without guidance. It was terrifying to be blind when there was danger all round. Lachenal's frozen feet affected his nervous system. His behaviour was disquieting – he was possessed by the most fantastic ideas:

"I tell you we must go down . . . down there . . ."

"You've nothing on your feet!"

"Don't worry about that."

"You're off your head. The way is not there . . . it's to the left!"

He was already standing up; he wanted to go straight down to the bottom of the glacier. Terray held him back, made him sit down, and though he couldn't see, helped put his boots on.

Behind them I was living in my own private dream. I knew the end was near, but it was the end that all mountaineers wish for – an end in keeping with their ruling passion. I was consciously grateful to the mountains for being so beautiful for me that day, and as awed by their silence as if I had been in church. I was in no pain, and had no worry. My utter calmness was alarming. Terray came staggering towards me, and I told him:

"It's all over for me. Go on . . . you have a chance . . . you must take it . . . over to the left . . . that's the way."

I felt better after telling him that. But Terray would have none of it: "We'll help you. If we get away, so will you."

At this moment Lachenal shouted: "Help! Help!"

Obviously he didn't know what he was doing . . . Or did he? He was the only one of the four of us who could see Camp II down below. Perhaps his calls would be heard. They were shouts of despair, reminding me tragically of some climbers lost in the Mont Blanc massif whom I had endeavoured to save. Now it was our turn. The impression was vivid: we were lost.

I joined in with the others: "One . . . two . . . three . . . *Help!* One . . . two . . . three . . . *Help!*" We tried to shout all together, but without much success; our voices could not have carried more than ten feet. The noise I made was more of a whisper than a shout. Terray insisted that I should put my boots on, but my hands were dead. Neither Rebuffat nor Terray, who were unable to see, could help much, so I said to Lachenal: "Come and help me put my boots on."

"Don't be silly, we must go down!"

And off he went once again in the wrong direction, straight down. I was not in the least angry with him: he had been sorely tried by the altitude and by everything he had gone through.

Terray resolutely got out his knife, and with fumbling hands slit the uppers of my boots back and front. Split in two like this I could get them on, but it was not easy and I had to make several attempts. I lost heart – what was the use of it all anyway since I was going to stay where I was? But Terray pulled violently and finally he succeeded. He laced up my now gigantic boots, missing out half the hooks. I was ready now. But how was I going to walk with my stiff joints?

"To the left, Lionel!"

"You're crazy, Maurice," said Lachenal, "it's to the right, straight down."

Terray did not know what to think of these conflicting views. He had not given up, like me: he was going to fight; but what, at the moment, could he do? The three of them discussed which way to go.

I remained sitting in the snow. Gradually my mind lost grip –

why should I struggle? I would just let myself drift. I saw pictures of shady slopes, peaceful paths, there was a scent of resin. It was pleasant – I was going to die in my own mountains. My body had no feeling – everything was frozen.

"Aah . . . aah!"

Was it a groan or a call? I gathered my strength for one cry: "They're coming!" The others heard me and shouted for joy. What a miraculous apparition! "Schatz . . . It's Schatz!"

Barely 200 yards away Marcel Schatz, waist-deep in snow, was coming slowly towards us like a boat over the surface of the slope. I found this vision of a strong and invincible deliverer inexpressibly moving. I expected everything of him. The shock was violent, and quite shattered me. Death clutched at me and I gave myself up.

When I came to again the wish to live returned and I experienced a violent revulsion of feeling. All was not lost! As Schatz came nearer my eyes never left him for a second – twenty yards – ten yards – he came straight towards me. Why? Without a word he leant over me, held me close, hugged me, and his warm breath revived me.

I could not make the slightest movement – I was like marble. My heart was overwhelmed by such tremendous feelings and yet my eyes remained dry.

"Well done, Maurice. It's marvellous!"

I was clear-headed and delirious by turns, and had the queer feeling that my eyes were glazed. Schatz looked after me like a mother, and while the others were shouting with joy, he put his rope round me. The sky was blue – the deep blue of extreme altitude, so dark that one can almost see the stars – and we were bathed in the warm rays of the sun. Schatz spoke gently:

"We'll be moving now, Maurice, old man."

I could not help obeying him with a good grace, and with his assistance I succeeded in getting up and standing in balance. He moved on gradually, pulling me after him. I seemed to make contact with the snow by means of two strange stilt-like objects – my legs. I could no longer see the others; I did not dare to turn round for fear of losing my balance, and I was dazzled by the reflection of the sun's rays.

Having walked about a couple of hundred yards, and skirted round an ice wall, without any sort of warning, we came upon a tent. We had bivouacked 200 yards from the camp. Couzy got up as I appeared, and without speaking held me close and embraced me. Terray threw himself down in the tent and took off his boots. His feet, too, were frost-bitten; he massaged them and beat them unmercifully.

The will to live stirred again in me. I tried to take in the situation: there was not much that we could do – but we should have to do whatever was possible. Our only hope lay in Oudot; only he could save our feet and hands by the proper treatment. I heartily agreed to Schatz's suggestion that we should go down immediately to the lower Camp IV which the Sherpas had re-established. Terray wanted to remain in the tent, and as he flailed his feet with the energy of despair he cried out:

"Come and fetch me tomorrow if necessary. I want to be whole, or dead!"

Rebuffat's feet were affected, too, but he preferred to go down to Oudot immediately. He started the descent with Lachenal and Couzy, while Schatz continued to look after me, for which I was deeply grateful. He took the rope and propelled me gently along the track. The slope suddenly became very steep, and the thin layer of snow adhering to the surface of the ice gave no foothold; I slipped several times, but Schatz, holding me on a tight rope, was able to check me.

Below there was a broad track: no doubt the others had let themselves slide straight down towards the lower Camp IV, but they had started an avalanche which had swept the slope clear of snow, and this hardly made things easier for me. As soon as we drew in sight of the camp the Sherpas came up to meet us. In their eyes I read such kindliness and such pity that I began to realize my dreadful plight. They were busy clearing the tents which the avalanche had covered with snow. Lachenal was in a corner massaging his feet; from time to time Pansy comforted him, saying that the Doctor Sahib would cure him.

I hurried everyone up; we must get down – that was our first objective. As for the equipment, well it could not be helped; we simply must be off the mountain before the next onslaught of the monsoon. For those of us with frost-bitten limbs it was a matter of hours. I chose Aila and Sarki to escort Rebuffat, Lachenal and myself. I tried to make the two Sherpas understand that they must watch me very closely and hold me on a short rope. For some unknown reason, neither Lachenal nor Rebuffat wished to rope.

While we started down, Schatz, with Angtharkay and Pansy, went up to fetch Terray who had remained on the glacier above. Schatz was master of the situation – none of the others were capable of taking the slightest initiative. After a hard struggle, he found Terray:

"You can get ready in a minute," he said.

"I'm beginning to feel my feet again" replied Terray, now more amenable to reason.

"I'm going to have a look in the crevasse. Maurice couldn't find the camera and it's got all the shots he took high up."

Terray made no reply; he had not really understood, and it was only several days later that we fully realized Schatz's heroism. He spent a long time searching the snow at the bottom of the cavern, while Terray began to get anxious; at last he returned triumphantly carrying the camera which contained the views taken from the summit. He also found my ice-axe and various other things, but no cine-camera, so our last film shots would stop at 23,000 feet.

Then the descent began. Angtharkay was magnificent, going first and cutting comfortable steps for Terray. Schatz, coming down last, carefully safeguarded the whole party.

Our first group was advancing slowly. The snow was soft and we sank in up to our knees. Lachenal grew worse: he frequently stopped and moaned about his feet. Rebuffat was a few yards behind me.

I was concerned at the abnormal heat, and feared that bad weather would put an end here and now to the epic of Annapurna. It is said that mountaineers have a sixth sense that warns them of danger – suddenly I became aware of danger through every pore of my body. There was a feeling in the atmosphere that could not be ignored. Yesterday it had snowed heavily, and the heat was now working on these great masses of snow which were on the point of sliding off. Nothing in Europe can give any idea of the force of these avalanches. They roll down over a distance of miles and are preceded by a blast that destroys everything in its path.

The glare was so terrific that without glasses it would have been impossible to keep one's eyes open. By good luck we were fairly well spaced out, so that the risk was diminished. The Sherpas no longer remembered the different pitches, and often with great difficulty, I had to take the lead and be let down on the end of the rope to find the right way. I had no crampons and I could not grasp an axe. We lost height far too slowly for my liking, and it worried me to see my Sherpas going so slowly and carefully and at the same time so insecurely. In actual fact they went very well, but I was so impatient I could no longer judge their performance fairly.

Lachenal was a long way behind us and every time I turned round he was sitting down in the track. He, too, was affected by snow-blindness, though not as badly as Terray and Rebuffat, and found difficulty in seeing his way. Rebuffat went ahead by guess-work, with agony in his face, but he kept on. We crossed the couloir without incident, and I congratulated myself that we had passed the danger zone.

The sun was at its height, the weather brilliant and the colours magnificent. Never had the mountains appeared to me so majestic as in this moment of extreme danger.

All at once a crack appeared in the snow under the feet of the Sherpas, and grew longer and wider. A mad notion flashed into my head – to climb up the slope at speed and reach solid ground. Then I was lifted up by a super-human force, and as the Sherpas disappeared before my eyes, I went head over heels. I could not see what was happening. My head hit the ice. In spite of my efforts I could no longer breathe, and a violent blow on my left thigh caused me acute pain. I turned round and round like a puppet. In a flash I saw the blinding light of the sun through the snow which was pouring past my eyes. The rope joining me to Sarki and Aila curled round my neck – the Sherpas shooting down the slope beneath would shortly strangle me, and the pain was unbearable. Again and again I crashed into solid ice as I went hurtling from one serac to another, and the snow crushed me down. The rope tightened round my neck and brought me to a stop. Before I had recovered my wits I began to pass water, violently and uncontrollably.

I opened my eyes, to find myself hanging head downwards, with the rope round my neck and my left leg, in a sort of hatchway of blue ice. I put out my elbows towards the walls in an attempt to stop the unbearable pendulum motion which sent me from one side to the other, and caught a glimpse of the final slopes of the couloir beneath me. My breathing steadied, and I blessed the rope which had stood the strain of the shock.

I simply *had* to try to get myself out. My feet and hands were numb, but I was able to make use of some little nicks in the wall. There was room for at least the edges of my boots. By frenzied, jerky movements I succeeded in freeing my left leg from the rope, and then managed to right myself and to climb up a yard or two. After every move I stopped, convinced that I had come to the end of my physical strength, and that in a second I should have to let go.

One more desperate effort, and I gained a few inches – I pulled on the rope and felt something give at the other end – no doubt the bodies of the Sherpas. I called, but hardly a whisper issued from my lips. There was a death-like silence. Where was Gaston?

Conscious of a shadow, as from a passing cloud, I looked up instinctively; and lo and behold! two scared black faces were framed against the circle of blue sky. Aila and Sarki! They were safe and sound, and at once set to work to rescue me. I was incapable of giving them the slightest advice. Aila disappeared, leaving Sarki alone at the edge of the hole; they began to pull on the rope, slowly, so as not to hurt me, and I was hauled up with a power and steadiness that gave me fresh courage. At last I was out. I collapsed on the snow.

The rope had caught over a ridge of ice and we had been suspended on either side; by good luck the weight of the two Sherpas and my own had balanced. If we had not been checked like this we should have hurtled down another 1,500 ft. There was chaos all around us. Where was Rebuffat? I was mortally anxious, for he was unroped. Looking up I caught sight of him less than a hundred yards away:

"Anything broken?" he called out to me.

I was greatly relieved, but I had no strength to reply. Lying flat, and semi-conscious, I gazed at the wreckage about me with unseeing eyes. We had been carried down for about 500 ft. It was not a healthy place to linger in – suppose another avalanche should fall! I instructed the Sherpas:

"Now – Doctor Sahib. Quick, very quick!"

By gestures I tried to make them understand that they must hold me very firmly. In doing this I found that my left arm was practically useless. I could not move it at all; the elbow had seized up – was it broken? We should see later. Now, we must push on to Oudot.

Rebuffat started down to join us, moving slowly; he had to place his feet by feel alone, and seeing him walk like this made my heart ache; he, too, had fallen, and he must have struck something with his jaw, for blood was oozing from the corners of his mouth. Like me, he had lost his glasses and we were forced to shut our eyes. Aila had an old spare pair which did very well for me, and without a second's hesitation Sarki gave his own to Rebuffat.

We had to get down at once. The Sherpas helped me up, and I advanced as best I could, reeling about in the most alarming fashion, but they realized now that they must hold me from behind. I skirted round the avalanche to our old track which started again a little further on.

We now came to the first wall. How on earth should we get down? Again, I asked the Sherpas to hold me firmly:

"*Hold me well because . . .*"

And I showed them my hands.

"Yes, sir," they replied together like good pupils. I came to the piton; the fixed rope attached to it hung down the wall and I had to hold on to it – there was no other way. It was terrible; my wooden feet kept slipping on the ice wall, and I could not grasp the thin line in my hands. Without letting go I endeavoured to wind it round them, but they were swollen and the skin broke in several places. Great strips of it came away and stuck to the rope and the flesh was laid bare. Yet I had to go on down; I could not give up half way.

"Aila! *Pay attention*! . . . *Pay attention*!"

To save my hands I now let the rope slide over my good

forearm and lowered myself like this in jerks. On reaching the bottom I fell about three feet, and the rope wrenched my forearm and wrists. The jolt was severe and affected my feet. I heard a queer crack and supposed I must have broken something – no doubt it was the frost-bite that prevented me from feeling any pain.

Rebuffat and the Sherpas came down and we went on, but it all seemed to take an unconscionably long time, and the plateau of Camp II seemed a long way off. I was just about at the limit of my strength. Every minute I felt like giving up; and why, anyway, should I go on when for me everything was over? My conscience was quite easy: everyone was safe, and the others would all get down. Far away below I could see the tents. Just one more hour – I gave myself one more hour and then, wherever I was, I would lie down in the snow. I would let myself go, peacefully. I would be through with it all, and could sleep content.

Setting this limit somehow cheered me on. I kept slipping, and on the steep slope the Sherpas could hardly hold me – it was miraculous that they did. The track stopped above a drop – the second and bigger of the walls we had equipped with a fixed rope. I tried to make up my mind, but I could not begin to see how I was going to get down. I pulled off the glove I had on one hand, and the red silk scarf that hid the other, which was covered in blood. This time everything was at stake – and my fingers could just look after themselves. I placed Sarki and Aila on the stance from which I had been accustomed to belay them, and where the two of them would be able to take the strain of my rope by standing firmly braced against each other. I tried to take hold of the fixed rope; both my hands were bleeding, but I had no pity to spare for myself and I took the rope between my thumb and forefinger, and started off. At the first move I was faced at once with a painful decision: if I let go, we should all fall to the bottom: if I held on, what would remain of my hands? I decided to hold on.

Every inch was a torture I was resolved to ignore. The sight of my hands made me feel sick; the flesh was laid bare and red, and the rope was covered with blood. I tried not to tear the strips right off: other accidents had taught me that one must preserve these bits to hasten the healing process later on. I tried to save my hands by braking with my stomach, my shoulders, and every other possible point of contact. When would this agony come to an end?

I came down to the nose of ice which I myself had cut away with my axe on the ascent. I felt about with my legs – it was all hard. There was no snow beneath. I was not yet down. In panic I called up to the Sherpas:

"Quick . . . Aila . . . Sarki . . .!"

They let my rope out more quickly and the friction on the fixed rope increased.

My hands were in a ghastly state. It felt as though all the flesh was being torn off. At last I was aware of something beneath my feet – the ledge. I had made it! I had to go along it now, always held by the rope; only three yards, but they were the trickiest of all. It was over. I collapsed, up to the waist in snow, and no longer conscious of time.

When I half-opened my eyes Rebuffat and the Sherpas were beside me, and I could distinctly see black dots moving about near the tents of Camp II. Sarki spoke to me, and pointed out two Sherpas coming up to meet us. They were still a long way off, but all the same it cheered me up.

I had to rouse myself; things were getting worse and worse. The frost-bite seemed to be gaining ground – up to my calves and my elbows. Sarki put my glasses on for me again, although the weather had turned grey. He put one glove on as best he could; but my left hand was in such a frightful state that it made him sick to look at it, and he tried to hide it in my red scarf.

The fantastic descent continued and I was sure that every step would be my last. Through the swirling mist I sometimes caught glimpses of the two Sherpas coming up. They had already reached the base of the avalanche cone, and when, from the little platform I had just reached, I saw them stop there, it sapped all my courage.

Snow began to fall, and we now had to make a long traverse over very unsafe ground where it was difficult to safeguard anyone: then, fifty yards further, we came to the avalanche cone. I recognized Phutharkay and Angdawa mounting rapidly towards us. Evidently they expected bad news, and Angdawa

must have been thinking of his two brothers, Aila and Pansy.
The former was with us all right – he could see him in the flesh –
but what about Pansy? Even at this distance they started up a
conversation, and by the time we reached them they knew
everything. I heaved a deep sigh of relief. I felt now as if I
had laid down a burden so heavy that I had nearly given way
beneath it. Phutharkay was beside me, smiling affectionately.
How can anyone call such people "primitive", or say that the
rigours of their existence take away all sense of pity? The
Sherpas rushed towards me, put down their sacks, uncorked
their flasks. Ah, just to drink a few mouthfuls! Nothing more. It
had all been such a long time . . .

Phutharkay lowered his eyes to my hands and lifted them
again, almost with embarrassment. With infinite sorrow, he
whispered: "Poor Bara Sahib   Ah . . ."

These reinforcements gave me a fresh access of courage, and
Camp II was near. Phutharkay supported me, and Angdawa
safeguarded us both. Phutharkay was smaller than I, and I hung
on round his neck and leant on his shoulders, gripping him
close. This contact comforted me and his warmth gave me
strength. I staggered down with little jerky steps, leaning more
and more on Phutharkay. Would I ever have the strength to
make it even with his help? Summoning what seemed my very
last ounce of energy, I begged Phutharkay to give me yet more
help. He took my glasses off and I could see better then. Just a
few more steps – the very last . . .

At Camp II Marcel Ichac had been following our movements
for the past two days, noting down the sequence of events,
minute by minute. Here are some extracts from his log:

Saturday June 3rd (I) – Camp II:
Oudot and Noyelle left at 9 o'clock; at 10.30 Noyelle arrived
back.
Something to do with the oxygen? Possibly the mask didn't
allow a sufficient flow? Oudot and the three Sherpas are going
very slowly up the funnel.
Meanwhile I am playing hide and seek with the clouds looking
through the telescope of the theodolite, and also watching the

parties above the seracs of the Sickle through field-glasses.
There are four of them; Lionel and Rebuffat, and behind them
Couzy and Schatz. No sign of Maurice. He must be on the final
slopes which are less steep, and so invisible from here. The
wind is blowing the powder snow violently. But he can't be far
from the summit now, perhaps even . . .

Sunday, June 4th
A dull day. Snow fell during the night – sleet, then fine snow
with a strong north wind. Annapurna is hidden in the mist.
Tired and anxious. What's happening to the others?
By midday eight inches of powder snow. Continual avalanches,
visibility nil.
Heard voices about 4 o'clock and in the mist, which continues
for about a hundred yards below the camp, four forms appeared
– Oudot and his three Sherpas. Obviously sinking in up to their
waists. Nothing to do but to get boiling water ready for them.
They arrived at 7 o'clock: that morning Oudot had remained in
his tent. Towards 1 o'clock the bad weather got worse and
Ajeeba had come to him and said: "It's the monsoon! If we stay
here we're done for."

Monday, June 5th
Will today end better than it has begun? What alarms there have
been – for us, anyway! At one time I thought Oudot and myself
were the sole survivors of the party of eight who left Le Bourget
on March 30th!
At 6 o'clock thought I heard someone calling and went outside:
the sun was rising through threatening clouds. Nothing to be
seen. Got back into my sleeping-bag; immediately heard two
distinct shouts and through the field-glasses saw two men on a
patch of ice at the height of Camp IV, but well over to the left.
They kept on shouting and signalling with their arms. Who
could they be – Oudot thought Schatz and Couzy. Their
immobility – particularly one of them – was most alarming.
Frost-bitten feet no doubt. What did they want? Normally it
takes six hours to get up so far in fine weather. But in powder
snow and with the monsoon striking repeatedly . . . They're
still shouting . . . things are getting urgent. Where are the other

eight? Higher up near the summit? Their position must be pretty precarious at Camp IV, but what can they be waiting for to descend to Camp III?

8 o'clock: Oudot is preparing a rescue party. He has no ice-pitons, etc. Noyelle is going down to Camp I with Ajeeba to bring up reinforcements (equipment and Dawathondup). Up here the Sherpas are uneasy. Three of them belong to the same family: Pansy, Aila and Angdawa.

8.30: Shouting continues. On the off-chance I'm tracing out the letters "VU" in the snow. A few minutes later a man moves quickly towards the seracs which must shelter Camp IV. He's stopped 300 yards away from it – on the same level – is making signs and has now gone back again. The others are getting up, apparently without difficulty, and are traversing across to Camp IV. Not two of them but four.
So there are four, plus the one who went to meet them, plus his companion or companions. The position of Camp IV near the funnel of the Sickle is more sheltered, and from there one can get down quickly to Camp III or Camp II. The avalanches have now stopped.

9.30: Saw Noyelle arrive at Camp I.

10 o'clock: At last – three men have appeared in the funnel of the Sickle coming down towards Camp III (one Sahib, two Sherpas?) Miraculously the weather is holding, with a west wind. Annapurna is completely clear – if only it lasts!
11 o'clock: Two men, unroped and therefore Sahibs, appear and come quickly down the former party's track. At the pace they're going, they should be here by evening. At last we'll know everything!

11.15: A man has appeared exactly at the spot where we saw one this morning, going *towards* Camp V. He has stopped and is evidently looking up. His appearance is comforting in one way, for he is certainly not alone at Camp IV. So that he and his probable companion make two, plus those coming down – three and two – seven in all. Seven out of ten. It looks, then, as if one party must still be somewhere higher up.

12.20: I'm watching the group of four crossing a very steep slope above Camp III. Behind them is one man alone, lagging a bit. Now, very high up, another man has just left Camp IV and is quickly descending: perhaps one of those I saw a short time ago? Suddenly a cloud of snow – like a volcano – appears to spurt out beneath the feet of the four near Camp III. They are knocked down and go rolling over and over. Then the avalanche passes on, leaving three figures stretched out on the snow; the lowest, who has been swept down 150 ft is now climbing up the slope again; now two more – ah, thank God! – they have separated and revealed a fourth. So they are all safe.
Our Sherpas have realized what's happened. Angdawa and Phutharkay have gone off to meet them with ice-axes and glasses which they have lost. The others are continuing to descend. At 3 o'clock they meet the two Sherpas at the top of the avalanche cone. At last we shall know everything . . .

We were now quite near the tents of Camp II and Ichac, Noyelle and Oudot rushed up to meet us. I was in a fever to tell them the good news.

"We're back from Annapurna," I shouted. "We got to the top yesterday, Lachenal and I." Then, after a pause: "My feet and hands are frost-bitten."

They all helped me; Ichac held something out to me, and Noyelle supported me, while Oudot was examining my injuries.

My responsibility was now at an end. We had succeeded, and I knew that the others would all be with us in a few minutes.

We were saved! We had conquered Annapurna, and we had retreated in order. It was now for the others to take the initiative, above all Oudot, in whom lay our only hope. I would put myself entirely in their hands; I would trust myself to their devotion. Henceforth only one thing would count – the victory that we had brought back, that would remain for ever with us as an ecstatic happiness and a miraculous consolation. The others must organize our retreat and bring us back as best they could to the soil of France.

My friends all rallied round – they took off my gloves and my cagoule and settled me into a tent already prepared to receive us. I found this simplification intensely comforting: I appreciated my new existence which, though it would be short-lived, was for the moment so easy and pleasant. In spite of the threatening weather the others were not long in arriving: Rebuffat was the first – his toes were frost-bitten, which made it difficult for him to walk and he looked ghastly, with a trickle of blood from his lips, and signs of suffering writ large on his face. They undressed him, and put him in a tent to await treatment.

Lachenal was still a long way off. Blind, exhausted, with his frost-bitten feet, how could he manage to follow such a rough and dangerous track? In fact, he got over the little crevasse by letting himself slide down on his bottom. Couzy caught up with him on his way down and, although desperately weary himself, gave him invaluable assistance.

Lionel Terray followed closely behind them, held on a rope by Schatz, who was still in fine fettle. The little group drew nearer to the camp. The first man to arrive was Terray, and Marcel Ichac went up towards the great cone to meet him. Terray's appearance was pitiful. He was blind, and clung to Angtharkay as he walked. He had a huge beard and his face was distorted by pain into a dreadful grin. This "strong man", this elemental force of nature who could barely drag himself along, cried out:

"But I'm still all right. If I could see properly, I'd come down by myself."

When he reached camp Oudot and Noyelle were aghast. Once so strong, he was now helpless and exhausted. His appearance moved them almost to tears.

Immediately after, Schatz and Couzy arrived, and then Lachenal, practically carried by two Sherpas. From a distance it looked as though he was pedalling along in the air, for he threw his legs out in front in a most disordered way. His head lolled backwards and was covered with a bandage. His features were lined with fatigue and spoke of suffering and sacrifice. He could not have gone on for another hour. Like myself, he had set a limit which had helped him to hold on until now. And yet Biscante, at such a moment, still had the spirit to say to Ichac:

"Want to see how a Chamonix guide comes down from the Himalaya?"

Ichac's only reply was to hold out to him a piece of sugar soaked in adrenalin.

It was painful to watch Terray groping for the tent six inches from his nose: he held both hands out in front of him feeling for obstacles. He was helped in, and he lay down; then Lachenal, too, was laid on an air mattress.

Everyone was now off the mountain and assembled at Camp II. But in what a state! It was Oudot's turn to take the initiative, and he made a rapid tour of inspection. Faced with the appalling sight that we presented, his countenance reflected, now the consternation of the friend, now the surgeon's impersonal severity.

He examined me first. My limbs were numb up to well beyond the ankles and wrists. My hands were in a frightful condition; there was practically no skin left, the little that remained was black, and long strips dangled down. My fingers were both swollen and distorted. My feet were scarcely any better: the entire soles were brown and violet, and completely without feeling. The arm which was hurting me, and which I was afraid might be broken, did not appear to be seriously injured, and my neck was all right.

I was anxious to have Oudot's first impression.

"What do you think of it all?" I asked him, ready to hear the worst.

"It's pretty serious. You'll probably lose part of your feet and hands. At present I can't say more than that."

"Do you think you'll be able to save something?"

"Yes, I'm sure of it. I'll do all I can."

This was not encouraging, and I was convinced that my feet and hands would have to be amputated.

Oudot took my blood pressure and seemed rather concerned. There was no pressure in the right arm, and the needle did not respond at all on my left arm. On my legs the needle oscillated slightly, indicating a restricted flow of blood. After putting a dressing over my eyes to prevent the onset of ophthalmia, he said:

"I'm going to see Lachenal. I'll come back in a moment and give you some injections. I used them during the war and it's the only treatment that's any use with frost-bite. See you presently."

Lachenal's condition was slightly less serious. His hands were not affected, and the black discoloration of his feet did not extend beyond the toes, but the sinister colour reappeared on his heels. He would very likely lose his toes, but that would probably not prevent him from climbing, and from continuing to practise his profession as a guide.

Rebuffat's condition was much less serious. His feet were pink except for two small grey patches on his toes. Ichac massaged him with Dolpyc for two hours and this appeared to relieve him; his eyes were still painful, but that was only a matter of two or three days. Terray was unscathed: like Rebuffat he was suffering from ophthalmia – most painful, but only a temporary affliction. Couzy was very weak, and would have to be considered out of action. That was the balance sheet.

Night fell gradually. Oudot made his preparations, requisitioned Ichac and Schatz as nurses, and Camp II was turned into a hospital. In cold and discomfort, and to the accompaniment of continual avalanches, these men fought, late into the night, to save their friends. Armed with torches, they passed from tent to tent, bending over the wounded and giving them emergency treatment, at this minute camp, perched 20,000 ft up on the flanks of one of the highest mountains in the world.

Oudot made ready to give me arterial injections. The lamp shone feebly and in the semi-darkness Ichac sterilized the syringes as best he could with ether. Before starting operations, Oudot explained:

"I am going to inject novocaine into your femoral and brachial arteries."

As I could not see a thing with the bandage over my eyes, he touched with his finger the places where he would insert the needle: both groins and in the bends of my elbows.

"It's going to hurt. Perhaps I shan't get the right place first shot. But in any case you mustn't move, particularly when I have got into the artery."

I was not at all reassured by these preparations; I had always had a horror of injections. But it would have to be done, it was the only thing possible.

"Go ahead," I said to Oudot, "but warn me when you are going to stab."

Anyhow, perhaps it would not hurt all that much in my present condition. I heard the murmur of voices – Oudot asking if something was ready, and Ichac answering: "Here you are. Got it?"

Oudot ran his fingers over my skin. I felt an acute pain in the groin and my legs began to tremble; I tried to control myself. He had to try again, for the artery rolled away from the needle. Another stab, and my whole body was seized with convulsions, I stiffened when I should have relaxed, and felt all my nerves in revolt.

"Gently!" I could not help myself.

Oudot began again: my blood was extremely thick and clotted in the needle.

"Your blood is black – it's like black pudding," he said in amazement.

"That's got it!" This time he had succeeded in spite of my howls which, I knew very well, made the operation all the more difficult to perform. The needle was now in position:

"Don't move!" Oudot shouted at me. Then to Ichac:

"Hand it over!"

Ichac passed him the syringe; I felt the needle moving in my flesh and the liquid began to flow into the artery. I should never, until then, have believed so much pain to be possible. I tried to brace myself to the utmost to keep myself from trembling: it simply had to be successful! The liquid went on flowing in.

"Can you feel any warmth?" asked Oudot, brusquely, while he was changing the syringe. Again the liquid went in; I gritted my teeth.

"Does it feel warm?"

Oudot was insistent – the point was evidently crucial; yet still I felt nothing. Several times the syringe was emptied, filled up, and emptied again:

"Now, do you feel anything?"

"I seem to feel a little warmth, but it's not very definite."

Was it auto-suggestion? The needle was withdrawn abruptly, and while Ichac sterilized the instruments, I had a few moments' respite.

"It's excruciating, the way it hurts," I said, just as if Oudot needed telling!

"Yes, I know, but we must go on."

The performance was repeated on the other leg. My nerves were all to pieces, and to brace myself like this took all my strength. In went the needle and I howled and sobbed miserably, but tried in vain to keep still. I could see nothing because of the bandage. If only I could have seen the faces of my friends it might perhaps have helped me. But I was in the dark – a terrible darkness – with nowhere to look for consolation but within myself. It was late and we had all had more than enough. Then for that day it was over and the first-aid party moved on to Lachenal's tent. Perhaps he would have more courage in face of physical pain.

It seemed to me, when I vaguely became aware of the end of the session, that things had gone more quickly for him. Terray slept in Lachenal's tent and Couzy and Ichac slept beside Rebuffat, who was delirious and moaned about his feet all night. Oudot came and lay down next to me. If anything were to happen, he would be there.

Next day plans were completed for the evacuation of the entire camp: the three injured men would be taken down on sledges, two would be able to walk, with assistance, and four were all right. There were miles of glacier to cover, rock barriers to get down, interminable moraines and screen slopes to skirt round or to traverse, a river to cross, and a pass of over 13,000 ft to negotiate – and all this in the monsoon!

It was now June 6th, and Ichac was worried; he remembered the Tilman expedition to Nanda Devi, which was held up for three weeks by rivers swollen by the torrential monsoon rains. Should we have time to reach the Gandaki Valley where the easier gradient would put fewer obstacles in our way? In a week's time we must be clear of the mountains. Soon Couzy would be fit again, Terray cured of his ophthalmia and Rebuffat able to walk. But there were two serious casualties who would have to be carried on the porters' backs under the most appalling conditions, as far as the main valley.

"I can't believe it," remarked Ichac, "it's actually fine today."

The medical supplies urgently demanded by Oudot had arrived from Camp I. He began his rounds with me, and was pleased because the injections had been effective and warmth had returned as far as my insteps. He put fresh dressings on my hands, and though I felt no real pain, there was, nevertheless, some sort of feeling in my fingers. Again I put my question:

"What shall I have left?"

"I can't exactly say. Things have not completely settled down yet and I hope to be able to gain an inch or so. I think you'll be able to use your hands. Of course," and he hesitated for a moment, "you'll lose one or two joints of each finger, but if there's enough of the thumbs left, you'll have a pinch hold, and that's of prime importance."

It was grim news, but still, only yesterday I had feared that the consequences would be far worse. For me this meant goodbye to a great many plans, and it also implied a new kind of life, perhaps even a new conception of existence. But I had neither the strength nor the wish to look into the future.

I appreciated Oudot's courage and was grateful to him for not being afraid to tell me the extent of the amputations which he foresaw would be necessary. He treated me as a man and as a friend, with courage and frankness which I shall never forget.

The injections, which had already done so much good, had to be repeated. This time the session would be even worse and I was terrified at the prospect. I am ashamed to say that the thought of this treatment daunted me – and yet so many people have had to endure it. This time it was to be an injection not of novocaine but acetyl-choline, of which a few ampoules had been brought up from Camp I. Terray joined me in the tent and stood close beside me. He, too, could see nothing under his bandage, and he had to be guided if he wanted to move about at all. I pictured his face, and touched his features with my forearms while Ichac and Oudot prepared the needles, ether and ampoules. I whispered to Lionel what a fearful ordeal I found it all, and begged him to stay close.

"Oudot will warn me before inserting the needle; I mustn't budge then, and you must hold me as tight as you can in your arms."

I hoped that Terray's presence would help me bear the agony. Oudot began with my legs; as on the day before, it was too awful for words. I howled and cried and sobbed in Terray's arms while he held me tight with all his strength. I felt as if my foot was burning – as if it had been suddenly plunged into boiling oil. Professionally, Oudot was in the seventh heaven and everybody shared his delight in my suffering, which was proof of the success of the treatment. This gave me courage and at last, after the fourth syringeful, the necessary 100 cc had been injected.

"Now for the arms," announced Oudot.

This session seemed to go on for ever and I was utterly worn out, but there was distinctly more feeling in my right arm. Oudot stormed away – the needles were either too thick or too small, too thin or too long: never just right, and each time it meant a fresh stab. I began to howl like a dog again.

"Hold me tighter," I gasped between sobs to Terray, who was already holding me as tightly as he could. I tried hard not to tremble, but Oudot was still not satisfied:

"Don't move, *nom d'une pipe!* We'll go on as long as we must. It's *got* to succeed."

"Sorry, I'm doing all I can; I'll bear it, never fear."

I held out my arm for a fresh attempt. When Oudot did find the artery, then it was the needle that got blocked – the too-thick blood clotted inside. From the bend of the elbow Oudot gradually tried higher and higher up towards the shoulder so as not always to stab in the same place. Twice he touched a nerve: I did not cry but sobbed spasmodically. What an eternity of suffering! I could do nothing. Oudot stopped for a moment. "We'll manage all right," Ichac assured me.

"Stick it, Maurice!" Terray whispered. "It'll soon be over; it's dreadful, I know, but I'm here beside you."

Yes, he was there. Without him I could never have borne it all. This man whom we thought hard because he was strong, who made himself out to be a tough peasant, showed a tenderness and affection towards me that I have never seen equalled. I hid my face against him and he put his arms round my neck.

"Come on! Get on with it!"

"Too small and too fine," shouted Oudot.

He began to lose patience. All this fuss with the instruments exasperated me, and I wondered if they would have succeeded "first go" in a nursing home.

After several hours, and goodness knows how many attempts, the injection was successfully made. In spite of frightful pain I remained still as the syringe was emptied. Deftly Oudot replaced it with another without removing the needle from the artery. With the second syringeful, I felt the warmth spreading, and Oudot was exultant. But this warmth became unbearable. I howled and clung to Terray in desperation, holding my arm out stiff, without, so I hoped, moving it a fraction of an inch. Then I felt the needle being withdrawn and cotton wool applied.

"Right arm finished! Now for the left!"

Oudot could not find the artery, and this puzzled him. I told him that when I was young I had seriously damaged this arm, and that explained everything: that was why there had been no blood pressure, and why he could feel no pulse. The position of the artery was not normal, and it was not possible to make an injection in the bend of the elbow; it would have to be done at the shoulder – much more difficult. I thought of what it had been like for the right arm! Suddenly, at the fifth or sixth attempt, Oudot shouted:

"I've got it!"

I kept absolutely still: syringeful after syringeful went in.

"I'll have to do a *stellaire*."

I had no idea what this was. Oudot explained that it meant injecting novocaine into the nerve ganglion to dilate the arteries and make them easier to find, and improve the blood supply. A long needle was necessary, to stick into the neck in the region of the pleura. I was in despair. It was just too much. For hours and hours I had endured this agony – I should never have the strength for more. But Oudot lost no time, the needle was ready, and he began to explore my neck:

"This is a tricky bit of work. You have to insert the needle in a certain direction, then, when you come up against an obstacle you have to push to the left, and you're bound to be in the right spot."

"Warn me before you stick it in."

In the silence that followed I heard things being moved around.

"I'm going to insert the needle," Oudot announced.

I braced myself immediately, and resolved to keep perfectly still. The needle went in – it must have been a tremendous length; it touched a very sensitive part and the pain made me cry out in Terray's arms. Oudot was now manoeuvring to get the needle into the ganglion, and I could feel it moving deep down. It was in! First shot! The liquid must have started flowing in, but I could not feel it.

"Will it take long?" I asked faintly.

"It's almost finished," he replied holding his breath. "Only another 20 cc to go in."

I felt the awful needle being pulled out: it was over, and now I could relax. Oudot was very pleased: it had been almost a whole day's work, but he had managed to do everything he wanted. Never had I suffered so much in my life; but if my feet and hands were saved it was thanks to Oudot and his perseverance. Ichac helped him collect the instruments to take along to Lachenal's tent. For the time being he was satisfied with my general condition, but what effect this generalized frost-bite would have on my body in the next few days remained to be seen. The camp was becoming more and more like a hospital: everybody's thoughts and actions were dictated by the condition of the casualties, and everybody hung on the surgeon's lips. From now on his word was law.

That same day began the incredible work of transporting the injured, which ended only after a long and painful retreat, lasting five weeks, beneath torrential rain and over dangerously steep ground. This retreat, during which all the injured slowly recovered, will for ever remain an achievement of the highest order, and it reflects great honour upon all the members of the Expedition.

The sledge we had at our disposal was an extra-lightweight

Dufour *luge* mounted on two skis for runners. Naturally, the Sherpas were not familiar with this contraption, so Oudot and Ichac decided to make the least injured of us, Rebuffat, the victim of the first try-out. Schatz took charge of operations, with four Sherpas whom he placed in V formation round the sledge, and the procession started off about 2.30. Rebuffat was well wrapped up and firmly tied to the sledge in case it should tip over. As night fell the four Sherpas arrived back in camp, bringing a note from Schatz advising the use of six men for subsequent descents.

Meanwhile Oudot had given all his patients injections and the evening was spent in changing the dressings. Soon after night-fall the weather worsened, and again it snowed heavily. The others were alarmed and decided to get the rest of the casualties down before it became too late. As luck would have it next morning, when we woke up, it was fine. I was to be taken down first, and before I left Oudot inspected my feet and hands and changed the dressings. He was very satisfied and described my progress as "spectacular"! I was dressed, put in a sleeping-bag and laid on the Dufour sledge, and Angtharkay directed the team of Sherpas. I could see nothing under my bandage, but I felt the air was warm and so knew it must be fine; I hated the thought of being transported without being able to see what was going on. I was very glad to hear that Ichac would accompany me down so that I should not be alone if I needed anything. In my heart I dreaded this descent, particularly the passage over the rock barriers. How would they manage? But the Sherpas were intelligent chaps and never had to be shown anything twice. Afterwards, when we were in camp, Ichac told me how much he had admired them: "It would have been difficult to find a team like this in France," he said; "every one of them did his utmost and every move was perfectly coordinated."

With a few jerks the sledge started off. I was weak and slightly deaf, but I recognized Oudot's voice in the climber's familiar *Bonne descente*! No doubt he was there behind us, waving a hand. Swaddled in all my clothes, I began to sweat; the sun must have been beating down. Sometimes my back skimmed the surface of the snow; now and again Ichac came close and said something, and it did me good to hear him and know he was there. Suddenly the slope steepened, and in spite of the straps holding me in position, I slipped forward. The Sherpas took up their positions in an inverted V in order to brake the sledge. We had reached the big rock band, and as far as I could remember the angle here was steep. I guessed that Ichac had driven his axe in to keep me in balance.

I heard a hollow echo – seracs – and the pace had to be forced now for there was danger of their collapsing. We came to the rocks – and how these Sherpas managed, I shall never know. The wall was very steep yet I was carried on the sledge itself; Ichac told me later that if my eyes had not been blindfolded I should never have been able to stand the sight of such acrobatics and of such impossible positions. I heard sighs of relief – we must have reached the glacier at last. The sledge reverted to a horizontal position, and I was on the snow. A few minutes rest, and on we went at what seemed to me a breakneck pace; I pictured the Sherpas pulling on the ropes all round me and running in the snow, though no doubt this was only imagination. Then we slowed up – we had reached the moraine of Camp I.

I was left alone for a moment while the Sherpas put up a big valley tent into which they carried me a few minutes later. Ichac settled himself beside me – from now on we always shared the same tent and he watched over me, day and night, like a brother. The descent had taken two hours and twenty minutes, and the Sherpas had been marvellous. What should we have done without them?

Ichac briefly explained what was going on. Being blind was most demoralizing; I felt I was nothing but a chattel to be carted about. I knew my ophthalmia was less serious than that of the others and I kept asking for the bandage to be taken off. But since I was nothing but a chattel I had no right to speak.

Although it had clouded over and had begun to sleet, the Sherpas went up again to Camp II with Schatz and Noyelle to fetch Lachenal. About 3 o'clock snow started to fall. Time dragged as I lay in my tent alone with my thoughts. The silence was broken only by the persistent sound of cracking ice, which rather alarmed me: where had they placed the tent? Suppose a crevasse suddenly opened? I was ashamed of these childish fears

– surely a mountaineer of many years' experience should know very well that a crevasse does not yawn open like that in a second!

Ichac, the only fit Sahib, supervised the organization of Camp I. Towards the end of the afternoon, at about 5 o'clock, he saw, to his great surprise, Noyelle and Lachenal's convoy emerge through the mist, covered in snow. This time the Sherpas had taken only an hour-and-three-quarters to come down – they had had a terrific day and were worn out. This resulted in some complaints: there was not enough food, and part of their equipment had remained up at Camp III and Camp IV! This last point especially bothered them, for on Himalayan expeditions the normal practice is for the Sherpas to keep their personal equipment as a perquisite. They bitterly regretted these clothes, which had to be considered as lost, and Angtharkay even declared his intention of going up to Camp III again.

I summoned Angtharkay and warned him that I expressly forbade anyone to return higher than Camp II to fetch anything whatsoever. But at the same time I told him of my very great satisfaction at the magnificent behaviour of the Sherpas under his orders, and assured him that they were not to worry about the clothes, for they would all receive generous compensation. Angtharkay went off to give the others the good news.

There was tremendous activity all over the camp, where Lachenal was being made as comfortable as possible. Tents seemed to have sprung up as if by magic, and what looked like a little village was formed at the foot of the great wall of ice.

The next day, after a fine start, the clouds collected again towards 11 o'clock, and it was not long before snow began to fall. Oudot had not yet come down from Camp II. I could hear the avalanches rumbling down in ever closer succession, making an appalling row which wore my nerves thin. Ichac tried to make a joke of it.

"Here we are – that's the 3.37 goods! Now for the 4 o'clock express!" He succeeded in making me smile.

Through the telescope he saw, towards the end of the morning, the last tents of Camp II being taken down, and in the afternoon our MO arrived with his Sherpas, laden like donkeys.

Before even putting down his sack he asked about the condition of his patients: any developments since yesterday?

There was marked improvement: Rebuffat could now walk and his ophthalmia was nearly cured. As for Lachenal, circulation had been restored to his feet, and warmth had returned, except to his toes, though the black patches on his heels would probably leave scars. Improvement was visible on my limbs, too, and Oudot was well pleased. He spoke with a frankness that touched me far more than he will ever know:

"I think that the fingers of your left hand will have to be amputated, but I hope to be able to save the end joints of your right hand fingers. If all goes well, you'll have passable hands. As for your feet, I'm afraid that all your toes will have to go, but that won't prevent you from walking. Of course to begin with it'll be difficult, but you'll adapt yourself all right, you'll see."

I was aghast at the thought of what would have happened if Oudot had not given me the injections so promptly and efficiently. Perhaps they had not yet produced all their effect. More sessions would be necessary and I wondered whether I should be able to overcome the immense lassitude that came over me after all these painful ordeals. In any case I wanted to take every advantage of the respite, and celebrate our success with due ceremony. For the first time since our victory the whole Expedition was assembled together and the condition of the casualties was now such as to warrant a little festivity. We gathered round the one and only tin of chicken in aspic and we uncorked the one bottle of champagne. There were already a lot of us who wanted a drink of it but I was determined that the Sherpas should, somehow or other, join in the general rejoicing. I invited Angtharkay and we drank with him to our victory. Ichac put our thoughts into words:

"You've taken a lot of punishment, but our victory will remain."

Aurora

Jonathan Waterman

An American climber and writer. In 1982 Waterman made a winter assault on Alaska's Mount McKinley, at 6,194 m (20,320 ft) the highest peak in North America. (The mountain is also well-known by its Indian name of Denali). A previous winter bid, in 1967, had left one team member dead and three frost-bitten.

On February 17, 1982, we flew onto the Kahiltna Glacier as Mike muttered about white beaches in the Caribbean. As we vaulted out of our ski-plane another team barrelled into a second plane, so grim-faced after their failed winter ascent that they stared straight ahead, refusing to acknowledge our ebullient waves.

The wind blew a thirty-below-zero chill through my zippers and into my crotch like liquid ice. Since Mike and Roger pretended not to notice my coughing, I pretended that the spasms were mere sneezes. True to form, Mike strutted around without a hat, remarking on how warm it was. And Roger discovered a *Penthouse* stashed in his haulbag by some joking torturer.

We set up a tent and promptly snapped a pole. The cold would continue to break stoves and lanterns and zippers and boots and cameras. Even removing a mitten to tie a knot could cost you your fingers. Because our cockiness was the only way to disguise the layers of terror in our hearts, we never openly discussed the cold, which shadowed us like an omniscient being.

Denali's winter mood was completely unlike the more benign and sun-kissed summer pastels. Even the sunset was violent: the orange light was plucked right off the mountain as it pulsed into abrupt nightfall. Unlike the perpetually lit summer climbing season, the sixteen-hour winter nights meant that camp chores began and ended in the dark. That night the Cassin Ridge stretched taut and arrow-straight beneath the rounded summit bow, tinted violet by stars.

In the morning we put our heads down and trudged into the relentless north wind, pulling loaded sleds ten miles toward the Cassin. We made pitiful progress. I coughed and limped behind Mike and Roger on the end of the rope, tilting back a bottle of cough syrup and chewing its frozen shards. Images of hot showers, warm beaches, and an ex-girlfriend plagued me like a toothache, while my ankle rode fat and unforgettable in its double-boot cast.

On the third morning our ten-foot-long snowcave tunnel filled in with wind-blown snow. Feeling a burgeoning morning urgency, I slipped out of my warm sleeping bag and struggled into my climbing suit, bracing myself for the inevitable hell outside. I wormed my way into the tunnel, shoveling and kicking back chunks of snow into our living quarters.

After twenty minutes of burrowing I poked my head up into a ground blizzard. When I stood up the wind blew me to my knees. Leaning into the gale, I staggered away from the cave and futilely searched for a windbreak. In this nether winter world where fantasy merges with reality. I imagined a toilet flushing; so I yanked off my mittens, unzipped my suit, and squatted until that loathsome wind blew me over and I was back in kindergarten, shame-faced, helpless, reduced to whimpering as I crawled back stinking into the cave. Unwilling to bear witness, Mike and Roger promptly exited and performed jumping jacks in the wind while I boiled my clothing.

Eventually, Mike tried to define the wind. As it whipped and whistled out in the tunnel, he waxed Shakespearean. With a sweeping gesture of his arms he announced that the wind was the breath of God. I never heard anything so untrue in my life.

On our fifth night we dug a palatial snowcave, with a customised "Quick Jonnie" chamber carved into the tunnel. Inside, Mike disgustedly swatted at Roger's clouds of burning dope – Roger assured us he would stop once we began climbing.

My bronchitis dried up and optimism warmed us as we approached the Cassin. Ten thousand feet above, the wind was like storm-driven surf. Its waves crashed and broke over the summit, swirling giant banners of foaming snow over the southwestern face. Our route, however, laid still and taunting.

Early on February 27 we emerged from a snowhole beneath the Japanese Couloir. Roger couldn't get over the bergschrund, so he stood on his pack, reached over the gap, and mantled up. We hoisted the packs up, chinned ourselves over, and pumped our legs, calf muscles screaming under huge packs, spurred on by the fear of changing weather.

It was impossible to avoid knocking plates of ice onto each other. When someone in the lead screamed "Ice!" the unhelmeted followers tried to duck beneath their packs. Four hundred feet up, Roger took a hit in the face and swore violently; his dark blood speckled the opaque ice like graffiti.

We swung our axes and kicked our feet repeatedly into the cold belly of the mountain. We were jumpy, nervous, yelling at each another to hurry. My left ankle felt good while frontpointing, but at each flatfooted twist electrical jolts shot up my leg.

We finished the 1,200-ft gully fumbling with our headlamps. The night hung above as if it were the mid-Atlantic becalmed: vast and black and mirror-still. We tied ourselves into pitons and made our beds on a narrow rock shelf, swinging and clomping our feet over the void with great delight. Getting off the avalanche-fired glacier and coming to grips with the climbing felt so nice that we temporarily forgot the business above.

The stove's flames licked at a pot full of ice. Two hours later we slurped down freeze-dried swill, and when Mike and Roger hurled my home-baked fruitcake into the void, I feigned indifference. We slept fitfully, wiggling toes and adjusting hoods, ogling the full moon as if it could offer the warmth of a lover.

Several hours before dawn we started melting ice for tea. Getting out of warm sleeping bags and pulling on frozen boots made us shut our eyes, clench our stomachs, and flutter our breath. Packing up was awkward with mittens, so we would take them off, make an adjustment, then rewarm our fingers in our armpits; our feet felt blocky and sore and distant.

Mike and Roger raced to the east, axes squeaking in the Styrofoam snow. As Roger led a hundred-foot cliffband with down-sloping 5.8, Mike and I looked away, cringing as we thought of Roger's 70 lb pack. His crampons raked the rock like fingernails screeching on a blackboard. Then, after a dutiful curse, he was up.

We followed him onto a long ridge that sliced the sky and, to my delight, made the wind hum in subjugation. *Au cheval* along this corniced arete, we kicked steps into the snow and ice for hours, weaving around cornices, oblivious to the space beneath. We laughed and taunted one another; I sang at belays. The mountain gave us what we had come for, and as we straddled it and held it and gently kicked it, I loved it more than I have ever loved a mountain before or since.

On such days you can see every snow crystal sparkle. You can even hear music, although the most elegant orchestra could play here and be horribly underdressed. Some might say that we had too many endorphins rushing around in our heads or that we were surfing a tsunami and staring down at our own reef of mortality, but those people will never hug sun-warmed granite in sub-zero cold, gnaw icicles from their moustaches, or hazard that a mountain and its wind have become a living, breathing entity.

We knew that we would suffer soon enough, but we did not know that the winter climb would prove to be a link to our later lives. Climbing the Cassin in winter put Mike's medical schooling in perspective, developed the pacing for Roger's march to the South Pole, and inspired my writing career. Even a decade later, I am still a captive of this climb.

Our competitiveness was one unfortunate by-product of both the climb and our personalities. The tension surged like a hot current along our climbing rope. If we didn't flash the Cassin, we would have to answer to weather conditions beyond any of our experiences. So, fervently kicking around a cornice, then running across a knife-edge, I pulled Roger off his feet behind me; snatches of blasphemy attached to my name blew past me in a fiery breeze.

That night's campsite was the only flatness of the route. Instead of pitching our tiny tent we jumped into a crevasse and chopped out a snowcave. Later, bathed in eerie ultraviolet glow, Mike and Roger gagged on freeze-dried chili and dumped it into the crevasse's bowels. I forced mine down, hoarding every calorie.

As we slept the wind gusted and swirled and shook at the cave entrance like a wolf worrying a caribou's flank. By morning our sleeping bags were frosted with snow.

There, at 13,500 ft, the climb became our only focus. We were married, chained, and bonded to Denali because a lesser dedication would have been dangerous luxury. Once we climbed higher, retreating during a winter storm, or even surviving a storm, seemed unthinkable. We had to get up.

That day the climbing was superb, albeit strenuous. After fun moves I'd shout, "Boy, that'd be great with light packs!" Roger and Mike replied with glowering anxiety on their faces. We clambered over tawny granite and gray ice, pinching rock with one hand, swinging an axe with the other. We rested on ledges, calves burning, chests heaving.

Because we couldn't afford to rest and acclimatise properly, we all had minor altitude illness. It was a question of getting pummelled by a storm, weakening to the cold, and being kited off by the wind versus dealing with headaches, weakness, and loss of appetite. We took the latter course, and if the cold had only tickled before, now we could feel its talons prickling our skin. Fear actually constipated me.

At the end of our third day of climbing we chopped a tent ledge into steep ice. Since it was too crowded for three, I built a separate platform with snow blocks and clipped into an ice screw. Then I lit the stove, put on a pot of ice, and hid inside my bag. Either gusts of wind blew out the stove, or the pot needed more ice, so I would emerge from my embryonic cocoon, shivering and hating the cold. My fingers turned wooden and the blood crept back all too slowly as I winced and thrust icy digits into my crotch.

When the northern lights first appeared, I dropped the

lighter in astonishment. A single ghostly strobe swept the horizon. Then the entire sky filled with tracers. I yelled, nearly knocking off the stove, while Roger opened the tent. Outer space was raining translucent bands of jade and saffron, stealing time and the cold away from us, reeling us beyond the bounds of our banal earthbound existence. Dinner somehow got cooked but had no taste; I no longer felt the cold.

Sleep was an elusive pursuit, so I gave a running commentary of the colors to Mike and Roger, burrowed inside their sleeping-bag wombs. I studied the heavens, raving like a lunatic.

I refuted Mike by saying that the wind is not God's breath, but Lucifer's; the northern lights are the aura of God. Every manmade monument – from Buddhist temples to cathedral frescoes to Louvre paintings – will remain forever artifices, forever cast into the shadow of this night and its aurora.

Although Roger and Mike kept rolling onto one another inside the tilted tent, their grumbling – like the neon glow of Anchorage – was eclipsed by the sublime spectre that blazed above and around us. I felt lifted and freed from earthly cares, while my anxiety about the next day was replaced by exhilaration and spiritual awe. Finally, the world was born anew as the northern lights dimmed into dawn.

The days blurred into one another. We grunted up rock pitches, leaning heads and knees wearily on the ice, always guessing how much further. I kept looking over my shoulder, wondering when the Great Fly Swatter in the sky would squash us like the insignificant insects that we were.

When Roger dislodged a boulder from a long chimney, he screamed "Rock!" and I shrunk under my pack. The 40-lb missile crashed a foot away and bounced fifty feet down, then crashed and gathered more rocks, pounding down until I could no longer see them. Ozone filled my nostrils. I imagined falling with the rocks as if I had become the clipped bird of my nightmares, down past the blinking blue eyes of tottering seracs, feeling the air burst from my lungs as I cartwheeled through wreaths of cloud and bounced off slabs of pebbled granite and slammed into the maws of the crevassed glacier below, finally free.

The falling rock had come and gone in a flash, but when fear is constantly thrown in your face and adrenalin surges through your vessels all day, you no longer recognize when you are supposed to be afraid. Roger shouted "Sorry!" and we blithely continued up the chimney together.

As the climbing became less difficult we grew weaker from the altitude. The thermometer read forty below at 16,500 ft, so Roger hid our "negativity indicator" in the bottom of his pack. Though we wore every piece of clothing we had, the wind came right through our customized suits. I didn't envy Roger, who was harassed by a headache and nausea that evening, taking his turn outside the tent like a Third World cur.

Morning fell loud and clear. We packed the rope away and I began stepkicking up a long couloir. Mike and Roger followed on my heels, grousing about the distance between my hard-won steps. So I cursed back at them – our tacit mode of climbing communication. Near the couloir's top, I felt dizzy and let them pass.

Stomach acid clung to the back of my throat. After a brief rest, panting over my ice-axe, I raced upward with a pulse drumming in my head. Lost in an other-worldly spell, I stepped on a patch of windslab snow, which broke away beneath my sore ankle and started me sliding. The world flashed around me: distant icefalls and endless peaks and cobalt sky whirled with flying saucer clouds. I jammed in my axe pick and clawed to a stop. Through the fog of my pom-pom head and my now-throbbing ankle, I forced myself to concentrate, then climb.

I caught up to them at 18,000 ft only because they had stopped. We chopped out a platform, then set up the tent, continually looking over our shoulders at the sky.

Inside my sleeping bag I assumed a praying position and whispered, "Please, please, please give us one more good day." In the grip of forces beyond your control, righteousness and prayer come to agnostic lips as if you had been born thumping the Bible. Such alchemy is frequently denied afterward, but during the heat of action it shrinks your skin with all the swiftness of a frigid baptism. No one could deny that Denali rose higher and whiter than any church on Earth.

We slept deeply and it dawned miraculously clear.

Up, up we went. The tempo of the drumbeat increased in my

head. My feet turned leaden. I could not find a rhythm, let alone go more than one step at a time. Mike and Roger yelled for me to hurry up but I could barely move, so after cursing like brigands they pulled gear out of my pack to lighten my load. Still, I stumbled back and forth, woozy with Denali's thin air, a derelict destined for the gutter.

Finally, after a paltry thousand feet, they stopped and chopped a platform. When I arrived, their anger hung indelibly, like the calm before a great storm. They could have gone on to the top. Bivouacs this high on the mountain were foolhardy, maybe even deadly. But short of being dragged I could not go on.

We piled into the tent. I was too weak to talk. My world spun and dipped and hovered as I held my head and tried to find my breath. Mike plied me with tea while Roger looked out the door and analyzed the sky; they took turns looking out the tent as if something were coming to get us. I'll never forget their wide eyes, the creases on their foreheads, the tension that shook the tent like the wind. Even sick, I knew how worried and scared and tiny we were.

I had destroyed our speedy climbing formula, so I closed my eyes and let sickness spin me away from the bitter realities into unconsciousness. That night the tent became a frozen coffin. We tossed and turned and rolled onto each other throughout the long, long night.

Just before the dawn I dreamed of drowning. I came alive thrashing and lunging for my sleeping-bag zipper, desperate for air. I sat up and realized that fluid had infiltrated my lungs; I could only steal panting breaths.

While the stove roared, Mike changed socks. His two big toes were black with frostbite, but when Roger peered closer, Mike yanked the socks back on. "Oh," he said, "it's nothing."

Stuffing my sleeping bag seemed to take hours. After breakfast, they left the tent, so I zipped the door shut, steepled my hands together, and begged for good weather and the strength to survive the coming ordeal.

Mike overheard me. He knew. "You say something, Jon?"

"No," I said, my breath bubbling. "Nothing."

I followed their steps, oblivious to the sea of clouds that had arrived, oblivious to the passage of time, and acutely aware of the terrible heaviness of the gravity that repeatedly sent me sprawling to the snow.

After several hours Mike and Roger topped out, dropped their packs, and walked the anticlimactic fifty yards to the summit. When they returned, they were not amused to see me crawling down below.

Mike jogged down and relieved me of my pack. Twenty minutes later, I finished my crawl to the summit ridge. I looked briefly upward, but on this day my success would be measured in survival, not a summit. I could manage only two steps before collapsing over my axe and fighting for the privilege of breathing. The wind was mild but the cold was vivid, and despite wearing three sets of layered mittens we couldn't touch our metal-topped axes. Somehow it registered that my toes had frozen.

We plungestepped down and after a dozen strides I was completely winded. Even the descent of Denali's standard route was going to be a battle. Roger and Mike were too cold to wait, so I urged them onward. After several minutes I caught my breath, although sitting down in the hundred-below temperature didn't seem to improve my mood. I shivered violently.

I had to pace myself. Breathe twice for each step, then rest for ten breaths. Again, again, and again. I forced myself into the rhythm, eyes locked on my feet. It became a game: how do you move forward when you can barely breathe?

Mike and Roger watched and waited as long as they could in the cold. They shouted at me in shrill voices, alternately mad and caring, then left me behind to keep me walking and ward off their own chill.

At Denali Pass I rested a long time, terrified I would fall asleep and never wake up. Just before dark, I caught up to them at 17,000 ft. Roger was curled outside the tent, so I crawled in with Mike. The tent shuddered with the cold, so I didn't bare my skin for more than a few seconds. Even while exhausted I could still enact my preprogrammed warming functions: brush off snow; remove Gore-Tex suit, mittens, boots; get in bag; dry feet; warm toes with hands. I turned on my headlamp. "Wait a minute," I thought. "White toes! Frostbite?" I massaged my swollen bluish ankle and toes until I fell into a sleep racked by coughing.

Strong winds blew in daylight and clouds as we fixed cocoa in the tent. Mike looked me in the eyes and told me I would die if I didn't get down. Then he dressed me like a child. I stumbled off into the wind as they pulled down the tent.

The sky darkened. Taking only three or four steps at a time was disheartening, but I thought I might get down. Mike caught up, then passed me, while Roger stayed with me, cajoling and coaxing me downward. At 16,200 ft I batmanned madly down the fixed ropes, stopping constantly to catch my breath, not sure how much longer I could continue. I tried to downclimb the bergschrund neatly, but in my sickened torpor I fell and landed next to Mike. He laughed – I'll never forget his laughter and the emptiness of our fallen friendship.

In the past, our partnership had rarely suffered because we had always been strong together. For seven years I had envisioned us laughing and hurting and starving and lusting after ice-blasted mountains that no one else gave a rat's ass for. Although we would later be hounded by the media and receive letters and phonecalls of congratulations, as I recoiled below the bergschrund I thought our expedition was a rout.

I lay gasping on my pack. In my delirium I suggested calling for a helicopter; Mike suggested leaving me. No sooner than the words left our mouths, the swirling clouds parted and we saw climbers below. The seriousness, the commitment, and the isolation all disappeared. We smiled for the first time in a week.

As we stumbled down, some Brits walked uphill with congratulations and hot tea. I stared at them, speechless, exhausted, elated. They pumped our hands. We looked up at the mountain wondering if we were dreaming. Someone helped me untie from the rope. "We're alive," I said to no one in particular. Later, in a snowcave, we warmed up and the mountain disappeared. While their nurse massaged my toes, the Brits confessed that when they had first seen us they thought we were crazed because our expressions had been those of asylum escapees.

In the morning Mike was angry, no longer willing to wait for me. His blackened toes mandated immediate descent. Fortunately, I had recovered in the thicker air, so we roped up and raced one another down the low-angled slopes.

We reached our 7,800-ft cache that afternoon and dug out some food. Mike apologized and said the frostbite was his own fault. But I wondered how we could ever set things straight. The words froze in my mouth and we both acknowledged without speaking that this climb had wrecked our friendship. Concealing our disappointment, we glutted ourselves with canned ham and pineapples. Then Mike reminded us of his toes, so with distended stomachs we packed up and trudged toward Base Camp in the gathering dusk.

Darkness hit quickly, and we became puppets jerking along to the pull of the rope. Unlike Mike, Roger and I had no snow-shoes and often broke through the crust, floundering in deep snow. Mincing strides seemed to give us a few more yards without smashing through the crust. Sometimes we crawled, which was slow, but this prevented us from wallowing. On the final Heartbreak Hill Mike snow-shoed ahead to dig out our landing-strip snowcave and fix hot drinks. Roger collapsed several times, and I went back to cajole and coax him onward. He murmured the name of Sir Robert Scott, who had died crawling back from the South Pole in 1912.

Recovering in the snowcave, I couldn't believe we had climbed the Cassin in winter. Roger came alive too, so we dug out a Walkman and listened to Judy Collins while sipping steaming cocoa. The music stirred me deeply. When I realized the extent of our sensory deprivation, how much we had suffered, how far the cold and the dark and the altitude had twisted us, I ducked into my sleeping bag and let the briny tears wash my face.

When I came out, Roger was grinning contagiously, holding his breath. Smoke filled the cave and Mike was coughing, trying to wave the cloud away. Mike said the climb hadn't really been difficult and he had never felt extended; I half-believed him. Roger's lungs were close to bursting and his eyes were narrow slits. He offered me the joint, but I waved it off, because I could scarcely control my emotions.

By our second day of waiting, our various irritations with one another and our tardy bush pilot would no longer permit normal conversation. The cave turned into a soot-blackened repository for all of our frostbitten misery. We ached to leave this frozen hell and endlessly fantasized of the pleasures we would own once we escaped.

Unbeknownst to us, our pilot flew in three Spanish climbers on our third afternoon of waiting. Although he saw our ice-axes and crampons lining the cave entrance, we could not hear his shouts, so he flew back out.

At dawn I hobbled out into the arctic gloom and discovered the Spanish tent. At this point I no longer knew what was real, so I shuffled over, yanked off my mittens, then rubbed the tent fabric between my fingers. The Spaniards woke up, unzipped their door, and jumped back when they saw my terrified face.

From then on the only subject Mike and Roger and I talked about with any mutual accord was our pilot's rationale in leaving us stranded in sub-zero anguish. Although Roger had been the only uninjured one among us, on the fifth day of waiting he fell into a crevasse and destroyed his knee cartilage so badly he could not stand. Thereafter, three derelicts grunted monosyllabically at one another, limping out of the cave only for matters of the toilet. Food rationing began.

Fortunately, the Spaniards swore they would not begin climbing Mount Hunter until we were successfully evacuated. On the eighth day, after our *compadres* dug the word *HELP* in forty-foot-high letters, a passing bush pilot came to our rescue.

The depressive ennui that followed our unsuccessful high adventure totalled me. Next to climbing Denali in winter, everything – relationships, work, exercise – seemed worthless. It took me months to readapt to normal living. While I recovered from my frost-bite (and inertia) in Colorado, a friend loaned me a room and a car, which I promptly crashed into the garage. Because I had squandered all on Denali, I had neither a cent nor a job.

Other climbers heard of our "success" and invited me on the big Himalayan trips I had always dreamed of. I told them that Denali had defeated me; I told them that I had quit climbing and I told them that summits had lost all meaning.

My inability to quit the climb, even with the red flags of injury and sickness waving in my face, can be written off as the

shining brashness of youth. But I am still haunted by a partnership that never happened, by a cold with claws, and by a wind so
corrupt I could smell its breath as it knocked me onto the
glacier, my pants fouled with shit. I did not lose my innocence
in 1964 when I saw my grandfather's corpse, nor with my first
lover in 1973. I lost my innocence on the Cassin Ridge in the
winter of 1982.

In the ensuing years my back stiffened as I heard about other
winter climbers on Denali. In February 1983, Charlie Sassara
was knocked off by his partner, Robert Frank. Sassara self-
arrested on the fifty-degree ice, then watched Frank plummet
thousands of feet, spraying flecks of bone and skin and blood on
the way down the west rib.

In January 1984, the Japanese soloist Naomi Uemura disappeared after trudging down alone from the storm-washed
summit on his birthday. That April I helped twenty Japanese
search for his body, but we never found it.

And in the winter of 1986, Vern Tejas soloed the west buttress.
Tejas, who had been inspired by Uemura, not only showed the
world that the mountain could be soloed in winter, but he
climbed it during a stormy February, sans frost-bite or epics.

The following winter, Dave Staeli walked in to solo the
Cassin. He took one look and wisely proceeded up the west rib.

Meanwhile, three Japanese alpinists, who had climbed several 8,000-metre peaks, were blown off the west buttress and
killed. Staeli abjectly snuck up to the summit a day later.
Although the Japanese autopsies read "hypothermia," anyone
who has withstood the breath of Denali in winter knows that the
wind murdered them.

During these climbs, I envied the climbers not a whit; I
worried about them a lot. Now I see Art and Dave and Charlie
and Vern and Dave infrequently. But when we greet one
another in Anchorage, we stop and look into each other's eyes
and beam at one another with little talk. We know full well what
we got away with.

Climbing changed for me because of the Cassin. Now I like to
revel in the mountain's virility rather than my own. I like to say
that in ten trips, I have gone to the summit only once, via the
west rib in 1981 – which is true and feels quite fair.

I like to say that we climb because mountains are sacred places and climbing is a form of worship. We climb because the mountains are our church. Indeed, *It* – the Creator, Allah, God, the Great Fly Swatter, or Buddha – can't be any greater than the sight of the aurora borealis at fifty below, where the wind hums over a fin of ice and the light cuts right through to your soul.

Roger wrote and expressed the "hollow feelings" the Cassin had left him with. After surgeons overhauled his knee, he returned to Alaska and limped up an unclimbed, sabre-edged ridge on coveted Mount Deborah. Afterward, he was nearly arrested in Cantwell for counting his own change out of the cash register, and when he got to Talkeetna his smile lit my afternoon.

Several years later, still gimpy, Roger pulled a sled to the South Pole, retracing the footsteps of Scott. He refused to carry a radio, his support ship sank with their plane, and he went into six-figure debt.

Meanwhile, Mike bagged a new route on Annapurna IV, got married, splintered his leg as a result of a long fall in the Alps, and fathered a daughter. In 1989, just before the sap ran in northern Vermont, we met again. He was 36, I was 32. Encountering Mike that day was extraordinary and unplanned. He lived in California and I lived in Colorado. Our spontaneous rendezvous at the house of some mutual friends could only be explained as one of the inescapable circles that connect climbers' lives. His arrival at the remote place I was staying was announced by four whitetail deer charging out of the clearing and into the forest. When he came through the doorway, surprise painted our faces because it had been a long time.

My skin prickled with terrible and textured remembrances: the acrid smell of falling rocks, Mike's anger when I dropped his water bottle into a crevasse, and the mountain trembling as an avalanche crashed down beside us.

The timbre of Mike's voice was as familiar as an old rock-and-roll tune from high school, and he telegraphed his thoughts before he spoke. Undoubtedly I did the same for him. I could scarcely imagine him playing the respectable faculty member at a Palo Alto hospital. His stately eyebrows jitterbugged above an unlined face, and he had the same untended chocolate mop of curls. I said that he looked no different than before.

"What did you expect," he asked, "an old man?"

Still, the climb would not go away, and we were held apart as if Denali sat between us on the table. We exchanged stilted formalities for a long hour. Finally I asked him if he wanted to go for a walk. He pulled on his boots.

We strolled side by side up the trail and sank into the snow rather than walk behind one another. Neither one of us knew exactly how or where to begin, although our intended destination was clear.

As a preamble, I called it providential that we had met again. Without knowing what my next words would bring, I told him I had been trying to forget what happened to us on Denali. I told him that nothing would make me happier than to go climbing or skiing together. In turn, Mike told me that he had recently climbed an ice gully on Mount Washington, our old stomping grounds. He had stopped midway and remembered our having climbed all of the gullies twice in five hours. Mike said that he treasured these memories, and I instantly recognized the kinder and higher-pitched burr to his voice. We both laughed. Too soon we were standing at the trailhead exchanging addresses.

A year and a half later, at the American Alpine Club meeting in San Diego, we met again. I was surprised to see him because he used to declare that formal climber gatherings – with all their attendant glad-handing and self-congratulation – were a waste of time. But he let it slip that he had come to be with friends. I knew that family dilemmas and city life offered him much more difficult mountains to climb, yet he never breathed a complaint.

Through all of the lectures about other climbers and different mountains, we hung close to one another and endured the weekend. It felt as if we were still relying upon one another, but uncomfortably so, as if still jailed in that putrid, soot-smeared cave during the winter of our discontent. Because of our competitiveness and our numbed toes and our mutual betrayals, we know one another better than I know any other climber, or any climber knows me. As those around us basked in their own deeds on warmer and higher peaks, Denali preyed on both of us. Finally, when no one could overhear, he said it: "You know, we really pulled off a coup up there, didn't we?"

The Climb

René Desmaison

Born in 1930, Desmaison was a French Alpinist and guide. He became a figure of controversy in 1966 when, aided by Mick Burke and Gary Hemming, he made an "unofficial" rescue of two German climbers from the West Face of the Dru – an "insuburdination" for which he was dismissed from the Guides Bureau. There was more controversy five years later when, accompanied by Serge Gousseault, he sought a new winter route on the left side of the Walker Spur of Grande Jorasses.

When daylight finally came, it was dull, sullen, overcast. A wan light filtered through the snow and the mist. When the clouds cleared momentarily, we could catch a glimpse of long trails of fresh snow across the face. And when the cloud closed in, all sound was muffled and deadened, and the snow fell softly, soundlessly, ominously. There would be a few moments' grace, then the wind would get up again and howl round the face, whirling, swirling, the snowflakes dancing round us in a mad dervish-dance. Then there would be another short lull, during which we could sense the storm gathering itself together, to hurl itself with demoniac energy against the immovable granite of the mountains, which had resisted storm and wind for aeon upon aeon of time.

Huddled in our sleeping bags, we watched the spindrift

swirling round and over us, at the whim of the winds. For a long moment we lay there silent, appalled, unable to bring ourselves to move.

Today, we must get off. At all costs, WE MUST GET OFF THE FACE. I could feel the phrase echoing round and round in my brain like a rat in a trap. But one step at a time – first, I had to get out of my sleeping bag.

"Serge, how do you feel? Did you get some sleep?"

"Yes, I slept for a bit. I'm not feeling too bad. How far do you think we are from the top?"

"No distance at all, really."

I struggled out of my sleeping bag and into the howl of the wind, then pushed what little gear we had left into my own rucksack. There was not very much: the stove, now on its last gas cylinder, three big channels, the sack-hauling rope, my crampons. All we had left to eat were four sachets of honey and six pieces of nougat. I divided them meticulously in half, gave half of them to Serge and thrust the other half into my anorak pocket. Then I threw the extra rucksack out into space – it was no longer serving any useful purpose. It whirled away into the air, swept along horizontally by the force of the wind.

Serge, too, was getting ready. I helped him to roll up his gear and pack it away, then to buckle his rucksack. I checked on our belay pegs and ropes.

"What did you do with the pegs from yesterday?"

"They're over there on that sling, clipped to the belay peg."

"What do you mean? Are you sure? There's only two of them!"

"That was all I managed to get out."

"How many have we got left, then?"

I did a very rapid count: there were the two we had used to belay for the night, then the two Serge had managed to bring up with him and five more clipped to my harness. That meant that we had just nine blade pitons and six big channels, counting the one I had left at the top of the flake before coming back down again the previous evening. But there were very few cracks on this face large enough to take a big channel. That meant that the channels were virtually useless, and what I needed, principally, were blades. What sort of problems was I likely to meet on the rest of the climb? How many pegs would I need to get up them?

"Serge, I know your hands are very painful, and believe me I do understand, but you must get the pitons out, you *must*, do you understand? All of them, every single one. I'll manage with as few as I possibly can, I'll hammer them in no farther than is absolutely necessary, but you must get them out, however much your hands hurt. If you don't, we've had it. Have you got that? – we've had it, we'll freeze to death on the face or else we'll fall. I know your hands arc in a bad way, but how do you feel in yourself? Not too bad?"

"Apart from my hands, I'm feeling all right. Do you think it's still far to the top?"

"No, we should make it by this evening. All right, bclay mc now. We'd better get started."

Snow was still driving out of the cloud, sweeping over the pall of ice on the diedre; when it met the overhanging wall it swirled upwards, caught in a violent updraught.

I used the yellow rope as a fixed rope, grasped the edge of the flake with both hands, set both feet on the rock, swung out and waybacked up the flake. I jammed my leg behind the flake, clipped into the peg and rubbed my hands together. They were already numb. The wind was whipping snow into my face, and I could feel my eyes watering and aching. I buried my face in my hands and rested for a moment, waiting for the burning sensation to go away. Would this wind never stop? I would have to get out my goggles.

Ten or twelve feet higher up was a little ledge. It looked as though it would make a good stance; if I could get a decent belay, I would be able to give Serge a tight rope. But there was one problem; how in heaven's name was I to stand up on the top of the flake?

The wind died away for a moment. It was now or never . . .

I grabbed the karabiner with my right hand, unjammed my left leg, twisted it out of the crack and got a foot up on top of the flake. My left hand groped frantically upwards and found a hold on a block a bit further up. I stood up . . .

"Watch out, Serge!! Below!!"

The block had come out. It shot over my shoulder,

rebounded once or twice from the slabs and flew out into the
storm. I was hanging from my right hand only, my fingers
hooked through the karabiner, both my feet dangling and
scrabbling at the face. With no time to spare, I clawed my left
hand over the top on the flake, pulled up with the strength of
desperation and jammed my leg back in the crack.

"Are you okay, Rene?"

"Yes thanks. Wait a minute, I need time to recover. What
about you, are you okay? The block didn't get you?"

"No, but I'm afraid it's cut right through the yellow rope.
You can see the cut end dangling behind you if you look down.
Watch it, you're not belayed any longer."

"Right, hang on a minute . . . All right, take in on red, I'm
coming down."

Once again I used the rope for an impromptu rappel and went
down to Serge's stance. The yellow rope was in an even worse
state than the red one had been: it was cut right through at about
one-third its length. We had just seventy-five feet of sound
climbing rope.

We untied from the shorter of the pieces of rope, coiled it and
put it away in my rucksack. I tied Serge by his harness to the
very end of the yellow rope.

"All right, Serge, I'll make a start. This time it should go.
After all, I've got rid of that loose block, so at least it shouldn't
happen again!"

Where the block had been was a little flat hold already
beginning to fill up with snow. I scrabbled under the snow,
found a little finger-hold, hooked my fingers round it. I pulled
up, mantelshelfed on to the little flat area on top of the flake and
stood up gingerly, with just enough space for the tips of my
boots.

I was now standing at the foot of a diedre, rigorously vertical
for the first few feet and sheathed with ice. There were a few
thin holds, the odd flake or spike sticking out of the ice. But
there was not a single peggable crack. It looked as if it might be
possible to get a peg into the back of the diedre fifteen or twenty
feet higher up, but first I would have to get that far. The diedre,
visibly, could not be taken direct. A little to the right was the
little ledge where I had intended to belay. And just above that

there was another little diedre, rather smaller than the first, separated from it by a rock corner and more or less parallel to it. Might that be the solution? Or could I start up the second diedre, and then traverse back left into the first a few feet higher up? I could only try . . .

"Serge, give me a bit of slack, I'm going to try moving up a bit right."

"All right, Rene, carry on."

Ten feet or so of relatively easy climbing, and I was on the ledge. I hammered in a piton and clipped in. I rubbed my hands together, slapped them against my body and put on my gloves. The movement brought some feeling back to my hands and took the stiffness out of the joints, so that I could use my hands. That was better: I could last out a bit longer yet. Provided that Serge remembered to get all the pitons out, we might yet make it. It was still snowing, true, but the wind was strong enough to blow the spindrift off the face and there was no drifting. On my right, a nose of rock prevented my seeing the rest of the face. I took off my belay, edged my way round the nose on small holds, leant out and peered round it. A violent gust of wind blew snow into my face and blinded me. No, it was a pointless exercise: what with the wind, the blizzard and the buffeting of the storm, it was impossible to make a leisurely study of the face. I retreated back to the peg.

And yet, back there, I thought I had glimpsed a giant groove slashing down the face, quite different from anything on our own route. If only I had been able to see more clearly! I was sure that the groove could only be part of the Cassin route on the Walker Spur. I tried to conjure up a mental re-run of the guidebook: the couloirs, the chimneys, the corners and diedres. Yes, surely the groove I had glimpsed must be the big gully between us and the summit ridge on the Cassin. It might well make a safer, easier route to the top. So why not traverse over to it? Perhaps I ought to try and abseil down and across into the groove? But suppose I was wrong? And besides it was all very well to talk of abseiling, but what were we to abseil on? A couple of ropes cut through and knotted halfway along? No, thank you very much. There was only one way out: up.

In the very back of the diedre was a thin, shallow crack, with a few little chockstones. We would have to use aid to climb it, but how much aid? How soon before a stance? Through the whirling snowflakes, the shreds and tatters of cloud, I could not even make a guess. It might be a very long pitch, and if so, Serge with his damaged, swollen hands would never be able to get the pegs out. We had so few, so desperately few of them left. I made the only possible decision: I would have to go back to the first of the diedres. And somehow or other claw my way up that. Surely there must be something, some little hairline crack for a peg or two?

To get back to the first diedre, I would have to go down a few feet. I took out the peg to which I had been belayed and yelled down to Serge to take in, very gently, very carefully, so as not to drag on me and pull me off.

Had he heard? More to the point; had he understood? Yes, I could feel very slight movements in the rope as he took in and it tightened a little.

My hopes were dashed: the first diedre would not go either. If I did try to fight my way up it, I would only, inevitably, come off, and Serge was no longer strong enough to arrest a fall. There was nothing for it: I would have to go back up right again. I was annoyed with myself for dithering and wasting so much time. You're losing your touch, I told myself, you're going bananas, and you couldn't have chosen a worse time.

There was only one thing for it: we would have to go up the second diedre so far, then traverse across back left to the first one. So be it: there was no point in hanging about any longer.

A gust of wind brought a gush of fresh snow down on my face, filling the diedre. I felt myself suffocating.

I went back to the foot of the second diedre and put the peg in again. "You can come up now, Serge!"

The wind carried my voice away; Serge had not heard.

"Serge, come on! Climb now! Can you hear me? Climb! Climb now!"

"Yes . . . coming . . ."

Thank God for that.

I clipped a jumar to the peg and put Serge's rope through it.

In lulls in the storm, I could hear occasional sounds of hammering. It sounded as though it was taking Serge a long time to get the belay piton out. I could tell that he was not managing very efficiently: the blows sounded feeble and inaccurate. Nevertheless, the pitons were indispensable.

Long minutes passed. The storm howled on.

Serge reached me. He was exhausted by the pull up over the overhang, although I had been able to hold him on a tight rope, had even pulled him up, inch by inch, hold by hold.

But at least there was now some legitimate grounds for a very faint hope. The overhang we had just surmounted was part of a rock band which marked the transition between two slab systems on the face, each more or less identical as to angle and seriousness. What was left should be no more difficult than the ramp we had earlier climbed. I turned to Serge and said: "Serge, I don't think there should be another overhang now. Once we're up this diedre, there'll just be the summit cornice. You've got to hold out, do you hear, got to!"

"Not to worry, Rene. I'll do it. I'll hold out."

That morning, Simone had not gone up to La Flegere. She had supposed, reasonably enough, that our radio set was broken, or even that we had dropped it.

Leo Filippo, a friend of ours who has a charming small hotel in Entreves just over the Italian border, had telephoned. "Serge and Rene should be down very soon. I should think they'll be there by tomorrow evening at the latest. Why don't you come and wait for them here?"

Simone, on whom by now the strain was beginning to tell, was only too ready to take his advice. All of a sudden, she was able to feel almost optimistic. Yes, of course, that was it, they would soon be back. In fact, they might be already on their way down.

She glanced at herself in the mirror. She looked like death warmed up. The result of so many sleepless nights, so many hours of worry. Rene certainly musn't see her like that! At three o'clock, she went to the hairdresser's. At five, along with Pierre and Marie-Claude, she took the Mont Blanc tunnel through to Entreves.

At Leo's, there was quite a crowd; journalists, television crews, a real circus. The hotel buzzed with an atmosphere of

almost feverish impatience. God, what awful weather conditions up on the face! They must be having one hell of a struggle!
By the following evening, they would be down.

"Where are your goggles, Serge?"

"In the front pocket of my rucksack."

I got out the goggles, brushed caked snow and ice off his
eyebrows and eyelashes, and put them on for him. Then I found
my own and put them on.

"Did you manage to get all the pegs out of the stance?"

"Yes, here they are, I even managed to get the big channel."

"Well done, that's great! How about your hands? All right?"

"Not so bad. But don't hammer the pegs in too hard, will
you?"

"I'll do my best, but there's not much point if they pop out as
soon as I put my weight on them!"

I untied Serge from the red rope and tied it firmly to the belay
piton.

"When I get up to a belay, I'll call you. Then I'll hold you on
the yellow rope, and you can jumar up the red one. But until
then, you can belay me on both."

I traversed diagonally upwards for about thirty feet, taking
out most of my own pegs as I went. But some I had to leave for
Serge, about four of them, so that as he prussicked, or if he came
off, he would not pendulum across left out of control. And now
there was a new problem: I had to make a tension traverse into
the first of the diedres, fifteen or twenty feet below me.

I explained to Serge what I intended to do. In short lulls in
the blizzard, through blinding swirls of snow, I cold see his face,
intent, looking up at me. Had he understood?

"When you get up to where I am now, you can let yourself
slide down the rope from the karabiner I'll leave in the peg here.
We'll have to leave the peg and the krab in place, but don't
bother about them. I'll hold you from below. Give me some
slack on yellow."

I gripped the red rope with both hands and let myself slide
slowly down into the back of the diedre. I felt both feet land on a
patch of sheer ice where they could get no purchase at all. For
several heart-stopping moments, my feet scrabbled and slid,

trying to find some pebble sticking out of the ice, some little rugosity in the ice, so that my feet would grip. Finally I managed it. There was a crack just to my right. I hammered in a piton and belayed myself securely.

"Taking in on yellow . . . I'm on belay."

The rope came inching in. I pulled it determinedly until it came taut. Now for my crampons; at all costs I must not drop them down the mountain. I entrusted all my weight to the peg and hung my rucksack on it while I got out my crampons. What a position to try to fasten crampons on to your boots! Finally I managed it, taking infinite precautions to avoid dropping them.

"Okay, Serge! Climb when you're ready."

"Yes."

"The pitons – for God's sake don't forget the pitons!"

Whatever time could it be now? Serge seemed to be crawling up the face like a snail on a leaf. We were in an insane world, a world in which every minute seemed an hour, but where the hours were hurrying past at terrifying speed. Suddenly I heard a shout:

"I can't get the pegs out. I can't . . ."

Just those few terrible words, floating up out of nothingness, blown by the wind.

"Serge, you *must* get the pegs out! Do you hear me? You *must*!"

Finally he reached the last peg.

"Just let yourself go. I'll lower you on the rope."

Serge let himself hang on the rope. Very slowly, using the friction of the rope over my shoulder to provide a brake, I let him down to the stance beside me. I tied his ropes to the peg and took in both ropes.

"I've left two of the pegs behind. I just couldn't get them out."

Serge was exhausted, at the end of his tether. There was no point in blaming him. And anyway, it was probably quite true – his hands must have been virtually useless.

"Look, Serge, if you look up it seems a bit less steep. It'll be easier from now on, you'll see. I'll help you get your crampons on."

I got his crampons out of his rucksack and strapped them

securely to his boots. Out of my anorak pocket I took three pieces of nougat and unwrapped them.

"Here, open your mouth. And here's another one. And here's a sachet of honey."

I took one piece of nougat and one sachet of honey myself. We would have to conserve the rest; they would be needed that night and the next day.

"Right, I'm carrying on."

I passed the rope round Serge's shoulder and under one arm, then turned to continue my struggle upwards, in quest of the summit which seemed to be becoming more elusive, less attainable with every foot we climbed.

The storm had eased momentarily, but now it came on again worse than ever. Would this face ever have an end? Were we condemned to a hell in which we would go on climbing endlessly, laboriously, upward?

The worn front points of my crampons bit less and less into the ice. To my right was rock; I had hoped to find it climbable, but it was disappointingly compact and smooth. No escape that way. I could only kick my front points into the ice as securely as possible, and use each piton as I placed it as a foot-hold on which I could stand to place the next.

By the time I had done forty feet or so, I had just one peg left, one blade: the channels were useless here in any case. There was a crack just in front of me. I hammered the blade in securely. A crack like that was a real piece of good luck. Real good luck – for once fate was on our side. A decent crack! Suddenly I saw the irony of what I was thinking. Luck, indeed! If we had had any luck, we would have been off the face and down in the valley hours ago. Hours ago . . .

I cut a step in the ice to use as a stance.

"Come on, Serge! And don't forget the pegs! Hey, Serge, Can you hear me? Serge! Come on! Come on, come up now!"

No reply from Serge. Perhaps he had not heard me.

"Hey, Serge! Serge, you can climb! Come on!"

What in God's name was he up to? Why wasn't he replying?

"Can . . . you . . . hear . . . me? Come on!!"

Serge did not seem to be moving; he was standing there

motionless, his arms by his sides, staring into the void. Through the howling of the wind I could not hear him.

"What's going on, Serge? What's the matter?"

And then, finally, I caught a few words as his voice floated up to me.

"Not coming . . . can't make it . . . hands . . . completely dead."

An icy hand clutched my heart; my blood drummed in my ears. A feeling of intense grief, nameless horror swept over me, and left me momentarily helpless. Serge had given up. I could see him not far away below me, a remote and motionless figure silhouetted against the whirling snow, resigned and apathetic before the assaults of the storm. I found it difficult to believe that this was really happening. It must be a nightmare! And yet could any nightmare be as detailed, as complete, as this? Never, never as long as I live will I forget that second, that instant of searing, appalling realization.

Serge had given up. He had no more fight left in him, and he could no longer climb.

Despair and fear swept over me. I felt helpless, broken. It was too much. I stood there motionless too, as if turned to stone, my forehead pressed to the ice. We were finished. The ship was foundering in the still, dark, sinister waters of death. For the first time I felt truly afraid.

But no! I had to go on. I had to. I could not give in, not when I at least still had some fight left in me. My hands after all were undamaged. If necessary, I could let myself down on the rope as far as the stance where Serge was standing, climb up again de-pegging as I went, and then haul Serge up bodily foot by foot, inch by inch, to the stance. Every little inch we made would be one inch nearer to the cornice, which so short a time before – could it really be only twenty-four hours? – we had seen shining like a friendly beacon in the sun.

We had to get off. Somehow or other, by hook or by crook, we had to get off.

I untied both ropes from my harness, threaded them through the belay peg and abseiled down to Serge.

"Come on, mate, this is no time to be giving up. We're very nearly at the top."

"I can't go on. My hands are finished. If you want to go on, you'll have to pull me up. Don't be angry. I've done my best."

"Don't worry, Serge, I'm not angry. I'll pull you up, and you'll see, it'll all be quite easy and comfortable. All you have to do is walk up the ice on your front points, and I'll do the rest. Come on, cheer up. We'll be out of here before very long."

My heart ached as I spoke. I could feel weak tears gathering in my eyes. But this of all times was no time to start weeping; now, if ever, was the time to be strong, stronger than ever before. Death in circumstances like these is merciless, pitiless. You must gird yourself up and fight back with everything you've got – fight it every inch of the way, until it draws back, defeated.

I unclipped Serge's rope from the peg. He was held firmly now on the yellow rope tied off to the peg at the stance fifty feet or so higher up. I tied on to the red rope, and started to prussick up it, step by step, de-pegging as I went.

"All right, Serge, come on, I'm taking in. I've got you, all you have to do is walk up on your front points."

I took in the rope, heaving on it with all my strength, in a back-breaking, muscle-tearing, last effort.

"Come on, Serge, just one more step . . . and another . . . and another."

All fear had left me. No longer was I mesmerized by the tragedy that menaced us, the probable uselessness of these last efforts. I was fighting back – no, *we* were fighting back. And if we were to succeed, I must generate hope. Nobody can fight properly on a diet of despair.

The following pitch was even more harrowing than the previous one, even more desperately dangerous. My second was no longer in any fit state to give me a belay. The ropes hung loose behind me. This time, I simply de-pegged as I went. I held on to the latest piton with one hand, leant out and down and removed the previous one. It only needed one peg to give way, just one, and that would be the end: a last, fearful fall into nothingness and oblivion.

The ice as it formed had glued my eyelashes and my eyelids to my goggles. I tore them off and threw them out into the void.

Almost immediately I regretted my action and realized it had been one of those meaningless gestures of defiance in the face of fate.

And then another realization swept over me. Night would fall before too long, and I could see no sign of a ledge, no sign even of a marginally flatter spot.

Despairing of finding a ready-made bivouac, I set to and cut a little scoop where the ice was thickest, a small refuge where we could wait for the next day.

"Go on, sit down – there, in the little scoop. I'll tie you on. There, that's it, you can relax, you're belayed."

I organized the bivouac tent round us. Snow fell, softly, with deadly persistence. I took off Serge's crampons and fastened them to the belay peg, along with our rucksacks. We must not lose those, above all we could not afford to lose our crampons. I got out Serge's sleeping bag.

"Put your feet in the sleeping bag, I'm holding it. Sit up a bit so that I can get it under you. What? You can't quite manage it? All right then, put your arms round my neck . . . yes, that's right, now hold on tight and I'll raise you up a bit. There you are, the sleeping bag's on, you can sit down again now. Put your arms in the bag. All right? You're comfortable? Is the rope okay? Sure? All right, then, just hang on a minute while I get comfortable."

I wriggled into my sleeping bag and curled up on the little scoop in the side. Then I jammed the stove between my knees and the ice and got it alight.

"I've got a few mints left in my anorak pocket," said Serge, "you could put them in the hot water, it would make it taste better . . ."

Only later, a long time later, was I to understand what was the matter. Months later, some friends of Serge told me: "But Serge wasn't at all well, you know. He'd been suffering all winter from a calcium deficiency, he'd been having medical treatment."

Everyone knew about it; everyone but me.

"But why on earth didn't he say anything?"

"Because you wouldn't have taken him with you, of course!"

Yes, it was only months later that they were to tell me the

truth, the incredible, the unbelievable truth. Oh yes, yes indeed, certainly I would never have taken him with me.

"All right, Serge, you can have a drink now, here's the pan, I'm holding it. The water's really quite hot. That'll feel better. And with the mints in it, you're right, it does taste better. Wait a moment, here's a piece of nougat, and a sachet of honey. We'll have to keep a few for tomorrow. You're not feeling too cold? We'll be at the top tomorrow. If you're not too cold, you'd better try to get a bit of sleep. Don't worry, you'll feel much better tomorrow. We'll be all right. Yes, of course we'll get off the face. And then we'll be able to eat as much as we want. And we'll be able to sleep. You'll see – for days on end we'll just eat and sleep, eat and sleep."

They'll be up at the top by tomorrow night. Down in the valley, in the little hotel, there were comings and goings, cigarette smoke, reassuring words, the beginnings of a crowd. Yes, of course, no question, they'll be at the top. After all, yesterday, they were only 600 ft from the summit.

"Look, Simone," said Leo, "there's no point in worrying, they can't possibly come down this evening, it's too late and too dark. If they're somewhere on the way down, they'll be bivouacking. You might as well go and get some sleep, there's a bedroom ready."

But . . . the night was a succession of buts. But what about the weather? Anything can happen, up there.

It was to be a long, a weary night.

Would daylight never come? My legs were cramped and painful, curled up under me. I could no longer stand the foetal position I had had to adopt. Only one thing would bring some relief; I stood up, carefully, gingerly, hunching over almost double to avoid dislodging the bivouac tent. The scoop I had hollowed out in the ice was not big enough for both of us to be able to sit down at once.

When, *when* would it be daylight? An act of faith told me it would come – difficult, impossible to believe, but it would come.

Friday, 19 February

Daylight came. Creeping, pale, and sullen, but it came, through the driving snow, the mist and cloud. The wind had dropped a little during the night, but now it rose again, blinding, tearing, exhausting.

We shared about a pint of tepid water, no more. We had very little fuel left, and that evening we would need enough to heat a little more water.

Serge, superficially, seemed no worse. But I was aware, terrifyingly aware, of how every hour, every minute that passed must be sapping the little strength he had left, wearing away his resistance, weakening his muscles.

Suddenly, my own courage drained away. I sat there, motionless, beaten, defeated, overcome by a wave of panic fear at the realization of all the difficulties that I would have to overcome single-handed, with no physical or moral support. I had no hope left; there could be no way out, no ground for optimism. But even in that blackest of moments I was conscious, deep inside me, of a will to live. And if I wanted to live, I must climb on. I must not give in – I must carry on the fight, even if it seemed hopeless, crazy. I must carry on, over the ice and the rock, up to the summit whose whereabouts above me was by now only an article of faith. I could scarcely remember what we were doing here, scarcely even remember the name of the face. Life was reduced to the elemental, to the endless, hopeless battle for survival. How long had we been here? A week? A month? An eternity? How much longer would we have to spend in this hell?

And then, by a supreme effort, I turned my thoughts elsewhere. I looked back into my past and tried to remember other occasions. Just as hopeless, just as desperate, from which I had emerged alive and which might provide some ground for hope. If I had done it once, I could do it again . . . But there was nothing; never had I been in a situation so terrible, so desperate. In twenty years of climbing at the highest standard of difficulty, never had the prospect of survival seemed so black. Nothing; never; never, except yesterday. What I had done yesterday, I would have to do today. The waves of fear had to be overcome . . . I would have to get my head up, conquer gloom and despair. Bloody hell, Rene, you're not finished yet. If the only way out is to climb, climb! And the only way I could do that was to take it one step at a time, forget the future, forget the past, simply climb.

The face here was a jumble of boulders, rounded, ice-covered. You wondered why they didn't simply cataract down the mountain, away from this featureless, murderously steep face.

That was another three feet gained, anyway, and even three feet was something. But there were so many feet to the summit cornice high above us. And even if we got there, what would the summit mean for us? Life? Death? Or just nothingness?

"Simone Desmaison, how do you rate your husband's chances of survival now?"

"How long do you think they can last out without food or drink?"

"Are you worried?"

"They'll come back," said Simone, "of course they will, they'll come back."

It is hard to believe the sort of questions that get asked at times like these. But we musn't grumble: the journalists are only doing their job. Their role is to be there so that the overfed "general public", smugly asleep in its warm, cosy bed, does not miss out on anything: happiness and suffering, peace and war, poverty and riches, starvation and glut, the gallows and the firing squad, death and despair.

During the course of the morning, Nanouk, Serge's fiancee, came over to be with Simone. She was alarmed, of course, but still confident. Patiently, gently, Pierre with his instinctive kindness did his best to reassure.

"Look, Serge, there's the cornice, not so far above us. It's only about 300 feet away. All right, we won't make it this evening, but we'll be there by tomorrow. Just one more night, and that'll be it."

Serge looked up, but made no reply.

"Can you see it all right, the cornice?"

"Yes, I can see it. Do you really think we'll be there tomorrow?"

"Yes, of course we shall. Look, we're not going to spend the rest of the winter perched on this bloody face!"

Seventy feet above us I could see a bulge of granite, and a few feet further on there was a big block. At last we would be able to sit down, sheltered from the wind by the big block. There was an overhanging wall just above, and once we won over that, two pitches should take us to the top.

There was a very steep, difficult pitch between ourselves and the top of the bulge. I struggled up it. My arm was painful. There was a recurrent stabbing pain up my spine. And when I got there, there was no terrace; the top of the rock bulge was downward sloping. Not even a ledge big enough to sit down. Just as disappointing, the big block which had looked so promising from below was actually almost ridiculously small. Everything on this face was deceptive, nothing was what it seemed; no hope was ever fulfilled. And yet we had no choice: we had to bivouac as best we could, get through the night somehow. Life seemed to be turning into one long waiting game . . .

"Come on, Serge, you can take off your belay now."

Serge could no longer take his belay off; his fingers were not strong enough to open the gate of the karabiner. I had to go down, unclip him, then climb up again. That night I was exhausted but at least, thanks to that last effort, Serge was beside me.

Each of us hung from his separate piton, slung from a series of nylon webbing slings under his thighs and round his waist. Each of us had a precarious foot-hold on the edge of the rock bulge. So suspended, we embarked on the night, the night I could only pray would be our last on the face.

I had used my peg-hammer to break off some little slivers of ice from the rock around us. We would be able to melt them, and that night, at least, we would each have an inch or two of water to drink.

There was no point in even thinking of sleep. The webbing slings would eventually cut off the circulation and, where they went under our thighs, we would begin to feel first an uncomfortable throbbing, then real pain. We would have to keep moving, shifting the slings, relieving the aches in our muscles.

It was agonizing, even more trying and more exhausting in fact than the febrile activity of the day.

Saturday, 20 February
A pale daylight filtered through the cloth of the bivouac tent. Pale, but clear and bright with no haze.

"Serge, it's a fine day. The good weather's back. We'll make it, do you hear? We're going to make it, we'll be at the top today."

Serge groaned, rolled his head from side to side, made no answer. I turned to him, took him by the shoulders, shook him slightly.

"Serge, wake up!"

"No, I don't want to. I've had enough, I can't go any further!" his voice finally came, slow, dragging.

"Oh, come on, Serge! It can't be more than a couple of pitches, it may even be less. We've got to get out of here!"

"No, I've had enough, I'm not moving."

"Don't worry, I'll pull you up as I did yesterday. You won't have to make the slightest effort, just hang on the rope and walk up on your crampons. Look, we're not just going to give up here, a couple of pitches from the top!"

"Had enough . . . Don't want to . . ."

That did it. "Serge, you chose to come here – I didn't make you. So you can damn well climb, you can put one bloody foot in front of another until we get off this mountain, do you hear? Once we're up, we're all right, friends will come and get us off, but until then, until we get to the top, you'll climb, and no bloody arguing!"

It was no use. Serge was no longer open to curses or pleas. He had sunk into a silent, deadly lethargy from which nothing could rouse him, and which simply became deeper and deeper. And so that was it. We could go no further. There was nothing more I could do. We had simply to give up and wait. Wait for the inevitable helicopter. Today was fine, clear, almost windless. Almost certainly a helicopter would come. They would see us and guess that we were stuck just below the summit. They would realize from our immobility that something was wrong; you don't sit around resting just a short distance from the top, not if the weather is good and after ten days on the climb. Never in my climbing career had I sat around, even in the worst conditions. That had always been my rule: never wait, go either up or down.

The sky was clear at last. At last, those in the valley could make out what was going on on the face. At Entreves, everyone was up at dawn. Binoculars and telescopes were focused on the South Face of the Jorasses. Watchful, experienced eyes raked up and down the descent. Nothing. Not the slightest trace, no small black dots between the summit and the Boccalatte Hut 5,000 ft below. They must still be on the North Face.

At eleven o'clock, Simone telephoned the Chamonix police force in charge of mountain rescue and made a formal request for a helicopter reconnaissance flight. She was told: "We'll try to land somewhere near them and speak to them by loud-hailer."

"Serge, listen! Can you hear that? It's a helicopter and it's coming nearer."

Louder and louder came the characteristic noises of the helicopter: the turbo-prop engine, the clatter of the rotor, almost deafening after the long silence of the face. The machine came nearer, and hovered level with our belay, very close, certainly no more than 150 ft away and maybe even less. It hung there motionless for a few seconds. I could see the passengers looking at us. One of them waved an arm at us, first with his thumb up, then with it turned down.

I was more accustomed to the signals used in underwater diving than to those used by pilots. I took them to mean: up or down, or more precisely, are you going up or going down? I flapped my arms horizontally across my chest then outwards, in a wide extravagant gesture intended to convey that we were stuck, that in fact we could go neither up nor down. Then, again making an exaggerated gesture, I pointed several times to my companion, immobile, slumped beside me.

It seemed to me perfectly obvious, inevitable, that the passengers in the helicopter would see what was wrong. They were quite close enough to see that we were not comfortably and securely installed in our bivouac tent on a good ledge, but perched precariously on a spider's web of slings and pegs, and wrapped only approximately in the tent – so approximately that it could give us scarcely any protection from the wind and the cold. And surely they would be aware that after ten days on the face, two of them in the most appalling weather conditions, it would be absurd of us to sit around inactive only a short distance below the summit, on the very day when the weather had finally improved.

Later they were to claim that I had made a thumbs-up sign, which in the gesture language of aeroplane pilots would have implied that everything was all right. I don't remember having done so, but if I did, I certainly did not mean to imply that everything was all right, but rather that I thought our only hope of escape was upwards.

It is true enough that on that occasion I did not make the recognized mountain distress signal: moving my arm slowly and regularly up and down six times in a minute. As I have already said, the helicopter was so close that I was absolutely sure that the passengers would see for themselves what was the trouble.

Every year, dozens, hundreds maybe, of rescue operations in the Alps are performed by helicopter. I took part in a number myself when I was a guide-instructor at the Ecole Nationale in Chamonix, and I can state categorically that never, in all my experience, had it been necessary for climbers in difficulty to use the recognized distress signal. Anybody of any experience realizes very quickly and easily, from their position on the face and their lack of movement, that the climbers need help. And it is worth adding that up to that time the recognized distress signal had never been taught at the Ecole Nationale on the guides' course.

The helicopter veered away. Of course it would come back – we never doubted it for a second. The wind was not particularly strong, and any pilot used to flying in these mountains would be quite undeterred by it. It should be perfectly possible to land in the breche between the Pointe Walker and the Pointe Whymper.

An hour later, the mountain-rescue service telephoned Simone at Filippo's hotel: "We weren't able to land, but we saw them all right. They're about 300 feet below the summit. We waved to them and then communicated with gestures. They waved back very enthusiastically. They looked quite well and happy. There's a fair amount of wind up there."

As a result, Simone and our friends could only suppose that we were waiting for the wind to drop before making a final push for the summit.

And yet, in spite of herself, Simone was not quite convinced. She was restless, uneasy, tense. She tried to hang on to one certainty: at least we were alive: alive, and the weather was good, and we were not far from the summit. We would make it, we would soon be off the face, it could only be a matter of a few hours.

She decided to go back to Chamonix. She would come back when Leo telephoned to say that she should.

Why, *why* had the helicopter not come back?

Vainly, hopelessly, I peered into the empty sky; vainly, I strained my ears for any murmur of sounds other than the usual ones of wind and flapping canvas.

Night fell. Nobody would come now. The helicopter would not return. I told myself that of course it takes time to get together a rescue team, get it equipped and organized, get it up to the top of the Jorasses: more time than I had allowed.

The next morning they would be there. For us it was a simple matter of surviving the night. We would make it. Serge would make it. We had no choice.

The slings and rope-loops in which we sat became more and more agonizing. All restraint lost, we moaned aloud, groaned, muttered. Every minute, every second, dragged past, and every hour seemed endless, an eternity. That night was the torture of the damned.

Sunday, 21 February

Cold, bleak, grey, daylight filtered back on our eleventh day on the face. Gusts of wind blew sudden flurries of snow from the ridge. It was over; the long night was over. Serge's condition was worsening. His lips and nose were swollen with the cold. He could no longer feel anything, and I could only be grateful that he could no longer suffer. He was hungry and thirsty. All our food had gone. We had nothing whatsoever left. There was just a little gas in the bottom of one cylinder. I managed to melt just one more cupful of water before the stove finally gave out. Very gently, I poured a little of the warm water between my companion's lips. I was no longer thirsty or hungry. My stomach felt knotted, hard, completely insensible. Physically, I could feel nothing but a dull, continuous ache. Much more insistent was my gnawing sense of urgency. If no one came today, Serge would be finished. I could not imagine he would survive another night.

What *could* they be doing down there in the valley? Yesterday the weather had been good. They must surely have guessed something was wrong, otherwise we would hardly be sitting motionless like that, cramped and contorted on our little cornice.

What time could it be? Was it morning, or was it already afternoon?

Serge could not survive long like this. I would have to go and get help. Perhaps I could go and meet the mountain-rescue caravan which must already be winding up the South Face. Perhaps I could get down to the valley and get together a team of friends. Come and give me a hand – Serge is dying.

Even alone I could do something. I could take the last few pitons, five or six of them, scramble down to get the ones ten feet below, get up to the summit – I might even make it before nightfall – and then at least start down. By evening on the following day. I should be down in the valley. And then I could hurry up again with a rescue-team!

But they might already be on their way. And how long would it take me, all this? Serge would not last out. So what was I to do? Save my own skin, get out while there was still time? Get off the face, get down to the valley, and safety, and Simone? No; there is a law of the mountains, just as there is a law of the jungle: until death us do part. You don't leave your companion to die alone. And this was no longer some boy-scout code: it was a question of simple humanity. Serge needed me: he had no defence, now, against the cold and the wind. I had no choice: I must stay, look after him, protect him, help him to hold out.

And yet – for how long *could* be hold out? How long could I survive myself?

That morning, at nine o'clock, Edouard arrived. Edouard Martin, a friend, a pillar of strength – a sort of elder brother whose sympathy and affection gave Simone a much-needed feeling of confidence. Together they went to see Charly Dessertenne. He runs a cafe in Chamonix which we usually use for telephone calls, and where messages are left for us. They decided that in the next clear spell they would ask for another helicopter reconnaissance flight. They were all quite clear in their minds: something was wrong, and our immobility just a few feet below the summit was alarming. At eleven o'clock, Simone rang the mountain-rescue service.

"They're coming back, Serge, I can hear them! Didn't I tell you? They're coming back!"

I pushed back the bivouac tent which I had pulled over our heads. I could see the machine edging closer to the face, athough it could not come as close as yesterday's. There was more turbulence today, and I could see that the pilot was having trouble. I pulled a red anorak out of my rucksack and held it up at arm's length over my head. It flapped in the wind, then streamed out horizontally. Had they seen it? Had they been able to distinguish it from the red of the bivouac tent? The helicopter veered away, circled once and came back. I put my anorak back in the rucksack, waited until the machine came back close enough, then stuck out my arm and waved it slowly up and down six times. The helicopter seemed to come a little closer, then went away. Even now, Serge's voice comes back to me as he registered what was happening: clear, composed, calm: "Rene, the helicopter's gone away. It's gone again . . ."

"No, Serge, don't worry, it'll come back. I swear it'll come back."

Of course it would come back; I had no doubt of that. But if the weather got any worse, the helicopter would not be able to come back. That knowledge, that painful truth, I kept to myself.

*   *   *

At midday, Simone telephoned the police mountain-rescue service.

"They're still in the same place, but you can see that everything's fine. They were waving at us quite happily, and you could see they were quite all right. There's nothing wrong with Rene, don't you worry."

"But look here," replied Simone, "that can't be right, there *must* be something wrong. Rene isn't the sort of man to just sit there waiting a few feet below the summit. There *must* be something wrong."

And it was then that they asked the unbelievable, the unforgivable question: "Your husband couldn't just be putting it on, could he?"

Simone was so flabbergasted, so horrified, that she thought she must be hearing things.

"*What* did you say?"

"I said, your husband couldn't just be putting it on, could he?"

"What do you mean? You surely can't imagine that Rene is 'putting it on' after eleven days on that face, and when they can't have any food or water left?"

Shocked and shaken by such hostility, Simone hung up. She was distraught, unable to decide what was going on and what she ought to do. The day before they had told her that everything was fine. Today, apparently, everything was still all right. So what ought she to do? Should she call out the rescue service immediately? But nothing could be done that night: the weather was getting worse. She made up her mind: she would wait until the following morning, and then, come what might, she would call out a rescue team. If Rene was really refusing to be rescued, as the police rescue service seemed to be claiming, then he must have gone quite mad. It would not be the first time that a climber had gone mad in the mountains. The next morning, a rescue team would be sent up to get him off the face, to drag him off bodily, if necessary.

"Will it soon be dark, Rene?"

"Yes, quite soon, Serge."

"Why hasn't the helicopter come back?"

"The cloud is right down. But don't worry, there'll be a team coming up the South Face. They know we're stuck."

"Do you really think they'll be here tomorrow?"

"Oh, come on, Serge, of course they will! What would you do if you were in their place?"

"Yes, of course, you're right."

"The rope isn't hurting you too much?"

"Actually, it feels more comfortable than it did yesterday."

"Your sleeping bag is slipping off. Try to raise yourself a bit, I'll tuck it round you again."

I tucked the bivouac tent around us again like a sort of blanket, hoping that the wind would not tear it off us.

Yet another long night began, cramped and painful, during which I hovered in and out of nightmare. From time to time, Serge dozed off, then jerked awake again, moaning softly. I wriggled and shifted constantly, trying to find a less painful position, and every few minutes tucking in the bivouac tent that the wind threatened to tear away.

Monday, 22 February

My eyes strained towards the horizon where I knew that, eventually, day must come. And than at last, at long last, I could see, dimly, a line of contrast between earth and sky, then a faint, a very faint band of grey; finally, a pale blurred light spread from the east.

As we hung there suspended between earth and sky, my mind wandered off. Our planet was hurtling through space at some 1,250 mph. And life went on. Just as the earth would turn and turn eternally, so life would come and go, bringing deaths and endings, new beginnings and new life. At this very moment thousands of workers all over France would be setting off to earn their daily bread. They would be condemning themselves to a long eight hours shut up in gloomy workshops, deafened by noise, suffocated by fumes and dust. Did I, in the last analysis, envy them?

And nearer at hand, down in the valley, workmen would be setting cable-cars and ski-tows in motion; the sno-cats would be lurching out to prepare the pistes. Life would be going on, peacefully, heedlessly, to a prearranged and regular pattern.

But up there, on the Jorasses, time had come to a halt. There was no longer any such thing as time – only an eternity of waiting . . .

The faint, grey, diffused light turned to a golden, rosy glow. The sun, the life-giving sun was not yet in sight. We could only guess at its presence behind the Hirondelles Ridge, but we could see evidence of it on the gilded sky, the far bright peaks of the Matterhorn and Monte Rosa. On the South Face of the Jorasses, there must now be dazzling sunshine. But for us, on the North Face, there was no light, no warmth, only the harsh, freezing, deadly shadows. We could only wait, patiently, nursing the small remaining spark of life, putting our trust in the self-sacrifice and goodwill of our fellows.

We might be content to wait, but the time had come when Simone could no longer bear to do so. The reassuring words, the placating phrases were no longer enough. She had made up her mind. At eleven o'clock, she made an official request for a rescue.

Serge's parents had arrived the previous day. They were out of their element, uncomfortable in the mountains, in this bleak landscape and cruel climate which they could only admire without affection, and which they found profoundly disquieting. Gentle and a little lost, they felt isolated in the atmosphere of unease and alarm of which they soon became conscious.

How had it come about that Serge, a product of the quiet, tranquil countryside of the Touraine, with its sleepy rivers and lush orchards, had fallen in love with mountains?

Mme Gousseault talked freely about her son. That winter, she told Simone, Serge had not been well – had not been himself at all . . .

Once again a sound of turbo-prop engines, once again the clatter of the screws, echoed in the cold clear air of the face. I felt a surge of renewed hope. The helicopter soared up to us, disappeared, came in again. A gust of wind brought the smell of kerosene wafting over to our bivouac. The machine seemed so close I almost felt I could put out a hand and touch it. And with a sudden pang I realized that there, a few yards away, was life itself, sealed and apart in that bubble of perspex and metal.

Endlessly, unstoppably, the bivouac tent flapped noisily in the wind. It was the wind that was our enemy, sapping what little strength we had. We must not give in, we must hold out.

Serge was in a worse state than ever. He had sunk into a torpor, his head bent forward and resting on his folded arms which in turn rested on his bent knees. When I spoke to him, he no longer heard, no longer answered. All I could do for him now was to tuck the bivouac tent round him over and over again, and retrieve his sleeping-bag every time it threatened to slip off and disappear into space. He moaned gently, fell silent, moaned, fell silent, moaned . . .

We seemed to have travelled out of normality altogether, to be living in a timeless, featureless hell which could offer no hope to man. We had dared too much, gone too far, broken the barriers decreed by fate. And inexorably the barriers had closed behind us: we could not go back.

Serge suddenly raised his head and looked at me. I shall never forget his face as it looked at that moment; as long as I live, his expression will be engraved on my heart. "Rene, we'd better get on. If we don't get up to the meadows soon, we'll not have time to go to the cafe for lunch. We can always come back later."

My heart turned over. Serge had lost his reason. In spirit he was no longer with me, but somewhere off in the Calanques on the Mediterrean coast, in one of his favourite climbing grounds. Somewhere there, there must be a climb with meadows at the top and a cafe not too far away where after a climb in the blazing southern sun you could go and get a long cool drink.

"Yes, Serge, of course, we'll take the easy route up to the meadow, and then we'll come back later."

In 1961, on the Freney Pillar, I had heard that Pierrot Kohlmann and Antoine Vieille, too, had lost their reason just before they died.

Serge had fallen silent again. He lowered his head back on to his folded arms.

I have never known how many more minutes or hours went past before Serge raised his head again. He looked up and gestured wildly. "My helicopter! Look, Rene, it's coming back for me, my helicopter is!"

This with a joy and enthusiasm that was even harder to take than his torpor of earlier on.

"Yes, Serge, of course it's coming. It's almost here! I can see it. It's here, waiting for you! It's like a great dome of glass, with golden blades!"

Serge straightened. His back arched, then he fell back, slowly, and sat unmoving, his eyes wide open, staring into space and into worlds beyond my seeing.

My heart ached. My head felt empty. I felt nothing. I sat there unmoving, unable to think, my head on my knees.

Serge had gone. Serge had gone. I was alone, quite alone. And all of a sudden a wave of despair and rage swept over me, and something like madness took me. I screamed into the wind, at the top of my lungs: "You bastard! You hear me? You bastard! I stayed with you, didn't I? I didn't leave you, and now you've left me. You bastard, you've left me all alone."

And then suddenly I came back to myself. I too was losing my reason. I chided myself: "Come on, Rene, pull yourself together. You'd better tuck in the bivouac tent, it's come untucked and the wind will blow it away." I pulled it down, tucked it round the pair of us and jammed it in behind my back. Now I could only wait for the night.

Serge is dead. Serge is dead. The words echoed and re-echoed round my head. Except for that one terrible thought, my head was an empty drum.

The wind had dropped. To the east, the darkness rose and spread. A great calm grew in me. I felt completely indifferent, unconcerned about myself. Yet every so often I would become aware again of the agony of the slings and the rope-loops round my thighs. Physical suffering was the only thing of which I was now conscious, the only thing that had any reality for me. Before you die, you must suffer. Such is the law of life . . .

Why, at that moment, did I not think of escaping from the face? Why, the next day, did I not make a last, hopeless, desperate dash for the summit? I had at least a little physical strength left – after all, I had enough strength to be aware of my suffering. So why?

It would be difficult to give any coherent answer.

It was not, as people might imagine, some sort of expiatory

self-sacrifice, a penance paid to God or to man because I had been unable to save Serge. It was not some sort of death-wish, inspired by a tragic sense of personal failure. No, it was that some spring had broken in me.

By dying, Serge had given me back my freedom of action, and yet I could not leave him. Alive or dead, he was there, beside me. We were still, in some mysterious way, one flesh.

At six o'clock that evening, down in a little room in the Chamonix town hall, a meeting was held. At one end of the room was a platform, and there a few public figures from the valley, among them Gerard Devouassoux, held a press conference. They described the events of the day. A helicopter pilot called Nogues had tried to land on the summit of the Grandes Jorasses, but there had been serious air-pockets and turbulence, and the helicopter had had considerable trouble. The pilot and his passengers had not surprisingly had a fright. There would be further attempts the following day.

Simone had been present at the conference, one of quite a crowd. That night she went back to our chalet and wrote me a letter begging me to accept any offers of rescue made; like everyone else she believed that I was refusing help. "Please come back, we need you." Simone was convinced of one thing at least: if either of us was still alive to make signals, it must be me. She handed the letter over, the next day, to the rescue-team on the helicopter which was to try to land on the Jorasses, but she made one mistake, as it later turned out: she sealed the letter. That she should not have done: she should have left it open so that it could be generally read. In any case, the letter was never given to me; it was never necessary. It was given back later to Simone, who threw it in the wastepaper basket. Later, during the police inquiry, they asked me what had been in the letter, and I repeated exactly what is written here.

"Well, of course, you would say that, but what guarantee have we that that is really what was in the letter?"

What else in Heaven's name would poor Simone have written? Did they imagine she'd written me a little note suggesting I make myself comfortable and stay up there a few days longer? Incredible as it seems, that may have been the thought in their

minds: they were saying in the valley that every day I stayed up
there on the face meant another thousand pounds or so in my
pocket. And it was for that, apparently, they thought I had
played fast and loose with Serge's life, and risked my own neck –
a few miserable extra noughts on the francs in my bank balance.

Robert Flematti came to see Simone. Along with Lieutenant
Marmier and Sergeant Georges Nomine, both of them from the
crack Alpine troops of the Chasseurs Alpins, they wanted to go
up the Italian side of the Jorasses, that is the *voie normale* on the
South Face. All three were Alpine guides attached as instructors
to the Ecole Militaire de Haute Montagne, the premier training
school in France for Alpine troops. Nomine and Marmier, in
fact, had just come off the winter ascent of the North Face of the
Grandes Jorasses by the Croz Spur. Of all those at that time in
the valley, they were undoubtedly the most experienced, the
best-qualified and the fittest, as well as the most accustomed to
winter ascents. Moreover, because of their work at the Ecole
Militaire, they were particularly well qualified in all the techniques of mountain rescue. But in order to absent themselves
from the Ecole Militaire and take part in a rescue, they needed
permission from their commanding officers.

It was night. The sky was a profound black pricked with stars,
like diamonds on a black velvet dress. High up, way above the
Jorasses and directly above the Hirondelles Ridge, I watched an
aeroplane wing across the sky from south to north. I could just
catch the sound of its engines – I listened hungrily, avidly. It
seemed in a hurry – to escape from the dark, perhaps. I could
visualize the warm, well-lit cocoon of the cabin, the passengers
leaning back at their ease. In just a few minutes, the air-hostess
would be saying: "Fasten your seat-belts, please, we are beginning our descent to Paris Orly." Unimaginable world. Could it
be real? For several evenings now I had heard the plane go over,
and I knew it would be the last before morning. The morning
plane usually went over at dawn. I could always distinguish it
from the night plane – its engines sounded more muffled and its
drone more leisurely. Maybe it was simply at a higher altitude.

The friendly little winking light of the plane had gone,
disappearing at last into the far, far distance. Now there would

be only a long, dark tunnel until morning. A long silent tunnel, its silence broken only by the whine of the wind and the incessant, irritating flap of the bivouac tent.

I was neither hungry nor thirsty. Simply, I knew that my throat was very sore. It felt as though it was being slowly squeezed in a red-hot, relentless iron neck-ring.

I was not even conscious of the cold. It was just that my body, every so often, was racked by fits of convulsive shivering.

"Poor old lump of flesh! We've been through a lot together, you and I. You've not done too badly – you deserved better than this. Now look what I've got you into!"

I became aware that I was talking aloud. Now come on, mate, watch it; just pull up your sleeping-bag, otherwise the wind will have it off you. I realized dimly that I was now slipping from delirium to consciousness and back again almost without noticing the transition. I dragged up my sleeping bag and tried to relax on the rope loops, my head leaning on Serge's shoulder. Was it day? Or night? I could no longer be sure . . .

Ah, there it was, the dawn plane going over. I recognized the distinctive sound of the engines, but I could no longer tell if it was coming from the north or from the south.

Oh God, now I'd lost the bivouac tent! This time the wind must have got it. No, there it was, on the other side of Serge. Luckily it was securely guyed to Serge's belay peg. When it was light I'd bring it over and tuck it round me. It would be a good idea to tie it to my belay peg so that it wouldn't fly away again – but that would be no good; if I did that I wouldn't be able to shift around any more, and the slings were an agony. I must just sit there, staring into space, patiently waiting for the first sign of dawn: a faint ribbon of grey light over beyond the Matterhorn and Monte Rosa.

Patiently, vacantly I stared at the horizon, hoping for that first sign. The wind had dropped long before. There were tears trickling from my eyes. It must be the cold – after all, it must be very cold . . . Agonizing, endless wait for the dawn. And suppose dawn never came? No, that was impossible. In any imaginable world, dawn must come. Nothing, no human agency, no natural disaster, could prevent the dawn. The cosmic clock works perfectly, always. Man may come and man may go, but dawn goes on for ever . . .

At last! There it was. Suddenly the peaks in the distance looked blacker, silhouetted against the paler sky. I remembered a legend from my childhood – somewhere out there, over the great oceans, a little black boy was sitting on a hill playing a pipe, and as he played the sun rose, rose, rose . . .

Tuesday, 23 February

At 6.30 in the morning, Simone, clutching her letter, was waiting patiently in front of the police mountain-rescue head-quarters. Finally, at 7.30, a man appeared. He was to be one of the team in the helicopter on the first overflight on the Jorasses that morning. Simone gave him the letter and explained what it was for.

"Okay, then, we'll give it to him – if he's not already dead, that is."

Simone burst into tears. With Edouard Martin, who was looking after her, she went into the helicopter landing pad. They waited – there was nothing else to do . . .

Daylight. The mountains emerging from the blue haze. A magnificent sight, a fairyland. They are the mountains I have loved for years, my own playground: the Argentieres, the Chardonnet, the Weisshorn, Monte Rosa. They look on impassive, stare uncaring at the last act of our tragedy. I look up – and there above me is the cornice, the promised land, dark still but soon to be touched by the golden fingers of the sun. To my left is Serge, stiff and still in his blue down jacket. He used to smile and call it his sunsuit. I'll wake up in a moment – in my own bed, in my own chalet, with my friends, with Simone. It's just a nightmare – if I rub my eyes, pinch myself, I'll wake up. But no. However hard I pinch, I'll never wake up. It's no nightmare – or rather it's a sort of living nightmare. Horror of horrors, life itself has become a living nightmare.

How long has it been daylight? Now the wind's getting up. Wait a minute – there's a noise. Yes, it's the helicopter all right – it's coming closer – it's only a few feet away. If I don't watch out they'll think I'm dead. I'd better get up, get on my feet – that'll show them!

Why haven't they come back? It's odd – after all, there wasn't that much wind. If only the helicopter had got here a bit earlier this morning!

But I expect they were just flying over to check up on the latest situation. Because of course, by this time, there must be rescue teams coming up the South Face.

Chamonix, nine o'clock
"There was too much wind, we couldn't land."

Simone realized that they should never have placed all their reliance on the helicopters. They should have sent off a team on foot, as Robert Flematti had wanted. And now it was too late.

In the course of the morning, Simone telephoned the French War Office. Very soon afterwards Flematti, Nomine (who was to be killed soon afterwards on the Aiguille du Midi) and Lieutenant Marmier were given leave to take part in a rescue attempt. The three of them were among the best guides of their generation, trained to the highest standard and very experienced in mountain rescue. But there was a problem: they were soldiers, not Chamonix guides. Maurice Herzog, conqueror of Annapurna, president of the mountain-rescue services in the Chamonix valley and Mayor of Chamonix said: "We've already got a full team. And I know all about you, of course, but you must remember that a good climber doesn't necessarily make a good mountain-rescue man."

But when exceptional measures are called for, good climbers are precisely what are needed. Herzog should have remembered Annapurna, and recalled just what sort of men saved him then, rescuing him from certain death.

It might have been possible, and it certainly would have been worth trying, to land three men not on the summit of the Jorasses where the wind made it impossible, but 600 ft lower down on the South Face on the glacier. The helicopter would surely have been able to hover for a few seconds above the snow, long enough for the men to jump out safely into the snow, and then once they were down they could have scrambled fairly easily up to the summit. That part of the South Face is nearly always sheltered, and in any case it's easier for the helicopters to land there than on the narrow summit.

In February 1963, when I had done the Walker Spur by the Cassin route with Jacques Batkin, we had gone down that way to the valley. On the summit there had been a howling gale, but 600 ft further down it had been almost still.

In January 1973 Giorgio Bertone, Michel Claret and I were to be caught in bad weather and bivouac on the South Face of the Jorasses. As before, there was to be a hundred-mile-an-hour gale on the summit; and as before, 600 ft down, we were quite comfortable.

In my opinion they should have brought in the most experienced helicopter pilots. They had only to call on Jean-Louis Lumper, for instance, from the Protection Civile, who had spent the previous seven years piloting helicopters around the Mont Blanc range. Not only would he not have refused but I know for a fact that he volunteered. Or they could have tried Georges Rigaud, a pilot of quite exceptional skill who used a helicopter more powerful than those on normal service in Chamonix. In the event Rigaud was forbidden to try, on the pretext that he was under contract to the French television service and that meant he must take a photographer with him on any flight he might make. "No free publicity from mountain rescue", the authorities stated – this despite the fact that the television photographers swarmed quite unchecked around the Chamonix helicopter pad.

Towards the end of that morning, another machine arrived in Chamonix: the SA 330 known as the Puma. It was piloted by a remarkable man: Jean Boulet, chief engineer and chief pilot for Sud-Aviation who had for some years held the helicopter altitude record.

Simone dared to feel a little whisper of hope.

At the helicopter pad, they had set up barriers and brought in police to control the crowds. No one was allowed through – except of course the camera crews. Simone was kept outside, as if she had been one of the sensation seekers or souvenir hunters who surged round the barriers. For hour upon hour, she stood waiting in the cold, trying to find out what she could from gossip, rumour, second-hand sources . . .

*   *   *

I can't see it but this time I know it's not an Alouette III. The beat of the engine seems slower, more powerful. Ah, there it is! I can just see it, at the extreme range of my field of vision, just above the summit ridge of the Walker Spur. It's a fair size – much bigger than the Alouette III. It's camouflage-coloured – an army helicopter, perhaps? But that's odd – it's got wheels, not skis. You can't land a helicopter on a glacier on wheels! Through the cabin windows, I can see faces peering out at me. The machine hangs motionless for a moment or two, soars upwards again, then disappears. It must have come up to do an equipment drop for the rescue teams on the South Face.

Simone had been too long without any real news. She decided to go down to the police mountain-rescue headquarters. Surely there they'd be able to give her some definite news. She hovered patiently for a while in a corridor. Nobody. She opened a door at random and peered in.

"Excuse me, do you think perhaps today . . .?"

No reaction. They simply shut the door in her face. There are some things it is very difficult to forgive.

Meanwhile, at last, something was being done. A team composed of French and Italian guides had been dropped by helicopter at the Boccalatte Hut, which is at about 9,000 ft on the South Face of the Jorasses; that meant about 5,000 ft of vertical height below the summit, but about two miles in distance to cover.

The Boccalatte Hut, after all that time! You'd have thought they could do better than that, better than wasting precious time trudging up a track, when the helicopter could have dropped them a good 4,000 ft higher up. Was it just a gesture? Did they want to give the impression that at least *something* was being done?

A pink glow steals over the mountains. A last golden ray of sunlight lingers on the snow-capped summit of Monte Rosa, then, abruptly, is gone. Day is coming to an end. Great violet shadows come creeping stealthily over the glaciers, crawling up the couloirs. Upwards and upwards, engulfing each summit in turn. Already the valleys are invisible, swamped in a tide of darkness. Like sandcastles that children build in the path of the incoming tide, one after another the mountain-tops sank into the ocean of the dark.

What am I doing, still up here on the face? I ought to have gone on this morning. Serge doesn't need me any longer. What has come over me? I can't understand why I'm feeling so lethargic, so unwilling to move . . . I should have gone on, should have put everything into a last dash for the summit. This is not how I want to die, sitting hunched up on a lump of rock. If I must die, I want to die on my feet, on the move – a fall perhaps, a last flashing fall, not a long, slow lingering death from cold and starvation. I ought to have tried to get out, so that I could explain what had gone wrong . . . And yet – it was not a question of failure. We had fought to the very end. To lose a fight is not dishonour. The mountain had won, that was all. And sometimes, after all, the mountain must win, or where's the point of it all?

Ah, there you are – there's the aeroplane back again with its little winking light. You might wait for me . . .

Let's have a look at my right hand – it's feeling worse. Yes, very swollen, and there's a sort of big spot just on top of the swelling. Must be an abscess. God – you wouldn't think you could get an abscess when it's as cold as this. Tomorrow, as soon as it's light, I'd better do something about it. And tomorrow I'd better get out of here. Oh, hell, the wind's got under the bivouac tent again – it's blown off me and over beyond Serge. Don't worry, Serge, I'll soon have us both comfortable and warm again, we can't sit here all night without the bivouac tent, can we? There we are, Serge, that's nice and comfy, isn't it? Yes, I know, I know, you can't hear me – but I've got to talk to someone, haven't I? Haven't I, Serge? Now let's both have a nice little sleep. Down there in the valley, they must all be fast asleep. Except Simone, of course – Simone won't be asleep – how could she be? But I don't feel she's real any more . . . So I'll just put my head on your shoulder, shall I? You don't mind do you? That's better!

A long column of men, like black ants, trudge on and on along a dusty road. A grey sky. Endless grey, endless despair. Hundreds of us – thousands of us. When did we start? Where are we going? Why are we here? I no longer know. All I know is that we must keep walking, walking. We can sleep sometimes, for a moment or two, only chained together, chained to stakes on the long road – to a piton on the vertical rock-face . . . Yes, you can see that's how it's done – you have to hang in a sort or rope hammock. If you let yourself hang flat, it's a lot more comfortable. The really important thing is to have a good long anorak, that'll keep your back warm . . .

I shiver uncontrollably and wake up. Out of the nightmare. I have fallen off the scoop in the ice and I'm hanging from the peg. My sleeping bag is round my knees. I come back to myself and realize where I am. The bivouac tent is still not tucked in – good job it's tied on. And now I've only the one sleeping-bag left – the other has disappeared, finally and completely, down the face. Whatever happens, I must not lose the other one. How can I prevent it from slipping off? Sitting in a spider's web of slings like this, I can't pull it up properly and zip it. I tug it back over my shoulders. I mustn't go to sleep again. I mustn't go to sleep, otherwise I'll probably never wake up.

Wednesday, 24 February
That's odd. It's daylight and I haven't heard the morning plane going over. Surely I can't have been asleep?

There's the big helicopter back again. What can have happened to the others? My hand is agonizing. Let's have a look at it. Yes, very swollen. I'd better do something about that big white spot. Fingers pretty sore too. Frostbite, perhaps? Silk gloves aren't really enough protection. So what's happened to my woollen mittens? They must have got lost. When? I don't know.

And what's that yellow slimy stuff running out of my nose? It's all clogged up round my mouth. I don't know. Well, I suppose it must mean it'll soon all be over. Can't be long, now . . . I'll have to remember to keep on wiping my mouth on my sleeve. I don't want them to find me up here dead with my face all covered with yellow slime. I must make sure I stay conscious as long as possible . . . What shall I do about my hand? If I rub the big white spot on the back of my hand on the rough granite – rub it hard – really hard, just once, like that – God that hurt! –

but that's done it, it's broken. That's odd, nothing's coming out, no pus, just a bit of blood. Strange, that, after all the hand's really swollen. What's that helicopter up to? I can just see its tail over the edge of the cornice. I suppose it's too much to hope it's landed? No, there it goes, disappeared again over the other side, can't see it any longer. Considering how long it's been, there ought to be an army of them up there. Still, mate, you're on your own now. Better make a little collection of bits of ice to suck, soon you won't be able to move. Can't? Hands hurt? Too bad, mate: just get on with it, break off bits of ice with your peg-hammer, and put them in the rucksack ready. Too bad if they're cold, too bad if they hurt your throat, you've got to suck them. Your body needs moisture, and the wind and the cold are drying you up.

Back at our chalet it was bedlam. All our friends were gathering to support Simone. My little sister Marie-Lou had travelled up from Perigueux. She didn't understand the mountains and had very little idea of what it was all about. She was frightened by all the tension, all the comings and goings. What could she do to help? Nothing. Why wasn't anything being done? Nanouk, Serge's fiancee, was staying at the chalet, too, but that night nobody slept much.

Down in the village, the helicopter circus went on. Behind the police barriers, our friends waited, in growing anguish and despair. It was now our fourteenth day on the face. Could we still, possibly, be alive?

My mouth is now so dehydrated that the bits of ice stick to my lips, then to the roof of my mouth, and only then begin to melt. The moisture trickles down into my burning throat. I am no longer really conscious of the agony of thirst; the larger agony, the agony of cold, is more immediate.

Each little morsel of ice melting in my mouth will prolong my life at least for a minute or two and, God knows why, I cling to those few minutes. Death's icy fingers are crawling over my face, and death is too close now for me to have any real hope left. Just a few hours more, and it could all be over. If I just sat here quietly and shut my eyes, I could slip down into a long peaceful sleep, full of dreams, full of illusions, a long sleep which would lead unnoticed into the sleep of death, into the light or into the dark, whichever would be waiting for me. But it's not that simple; in my heart, death is now a fact, but my head is still clinging on to a spark of life, still refusing to give up and lie down and sleep. I must not give up, I must not go to sleep, I must meet death still awake and in my right mind.

And I am still conscious enough to be capable of self-analysis, to notice what is happening to me, to be aware when I have slipped over into delirium and hallucination. I'm too well-acquainted with the symptoms, too experienced not to realize what is going on: the toxins are gradually poisoning my body. The nightmare I have just had is, as I know only too well, a foretaste of the crisis which will finish me off.

As madness had threatened, as I had seemed to be slipping quietly over the edge of reason, I had felt a sudden overwhelming sense of serenity. Now that I am myself again, aware once again of the horrors of my situation, I am still calm, still oddly relaxed, in spite of the physical agonies. And my hallucinations are now more like mirages in the desert; in my mind's eye I can see that enormous Tokyo skyscraper, with its neon sign advertising beer: beer in gigantic glasses, capped with monstrous foaming heads.

As that hallucination fades, I can see another: a deep gorge and on its floor a crystal, cool mountain stream – the stream where we used to swim after a long hot day's climbing.

Way up above me, a jet leaves a white vapour-trail across the sky. I am back in a plane . . . flying and swooping far above the earth . . . I'm on my way to India . . . Nepal . . . I can smell the acrid, overpowering smell of the East. I can hear the mountain rivers soaring in my ears . . . I can see Jannu soaring, perfect and white, into the sky. "Whisky and soda, please . . ." I'd like to die up there, up in the sunshine. If only I could get away, cast off my body. Then I'd go off down to Simone and tell her: "Here I am, don't worry, it's all over now. Up there it's all over, but here I am."

Watch it, mate, you're going mad. Look, you're standing up, leaning out. If you carry on like that, you'll have the peg out –

you know the peg's none too sound. And your sleeping-bag's round your ankles. If you don't do something, you'll lose it.

In the valley nerves were beginning to crack under the strain. A friend took Simone back home: she had fainted and was in a state of collapse. At the end of the afternoon she insisted on going back to the helicopter launch pad. As often happens morning and evening, the wind had almost completely dropped. It was about 5.30. As Simone sat there in the car, Maurice Herzog passed by. Simone said: "But why have you stopped the helicopter flights? The wind's almost dropped and it's still light enough."

"I'm sorry, madame," he replied, "but those are my orders. No risks are to be taken."

I know, of course, that according to the rulebook helicopter take-offs and landings must take place at sun-up, not at first light. But in a place like Chamonix, in the bottom of a valley, the sun sinks below the horizon much earlier than it would on the plain. And so I have often seen the helicopters taking off at the first glimmer of light and coming in to land in the dark.

Simone was thinking: "Rene is going to die up there on a clear day, in bright sunlight, with no wind to speak of. An absurd, an unnecessary death."

The blue haze on the North Face darkens, the grey of the rock goes black. For a few hours there has been no wind. The bivouac tent dangles limply from its peg. There is a stony, terrible silence, a biting cold.

All of a sudden I am afraid. Afraid of the silence, of the cold. Afraid of the agony I have already undergone, the agony ahead. I can no longer face the nightmare night again, no longer risk slipping into hallucinations from which I may never awake. How long will I be able to resist this intolerable urge to sleep? I must keep my brain working . . . I must not stop thinking . . . And indeed perhaps I should think – after all there may still be time, still time before I cross over to the other side – think about God. And why not? You were born a Christian, so why not . . .? Too easy? Too obvious? Belief, faith, coming a bit too pat . . .? And yet there have been times, out on the seared yellow plains of India, in the lush and secret valleys of the Himalayas, when you thought you caught a glimpse of a sort of truth, when you wondered if the peasants might not have something you had not. They *could* just have been poor fools, of course, convincing themselves of the existence of unreal gods. And you're not really very convinced, are you? But it's difficult to resign yourself to the thought of nothing, of a great non-being . . . It would be nice to *know*. Perhaps it's all a great big cosmic joke – not with a bang but with a whimper. But what's the point of the joke? It would take a supernatural, a "divine" sense of humour to enjoy a joke for aeons of time and not get bored with it.

Look up at the stars – their beauty, their everlasting dance. Each could be a new, a fantastic world. And even the mountains which will kill you are a part of a vast, an awesome creation. Is that *it*? Is that what it all means?

Little light up there, aeroplane light twinkling up there like one of the stars, don't go away! Please, please, wait for me, come and get me. Don't leave me alone. I can't stand any more.

Odd, I've forgotten what I'm doing here. Why am I hanging here on the face with my arms jammed behind me through the bars of the gate? The gate over the mouth of the tunnel; if I could just get into the tunnel it would bring me out on the South Face. My legs are dangling, my arms are aching, my hand is agonizing. I don't think I'll be able to hang on much longer, I'll have to leave go. That's what I'm trying to tell all those people milling about in the tunnel-mouth, behind the gate. But they won't even listen.

"Nothing we can do – you'll just have to stay there."

I can hear them muttering, whispering, behind their hands, and I can't hear what they're saying, and I can't even turn round to get a good look at them.

"Get me out of here – save me – I'm cold – oh God, I'm cold!"

I'm flailing around, struggling. I'm shivering with cold. The peg! If I don't keep still, the peg will come out of the crack. Too bad if the peg does come out, I don't want to stay here like a coat on a hook any longer. My God! The sleeping-bag! Where in God's name is it? Gone! The last disaster. And the bivouac tent? That at least is still there, on Serge's other side. I must wrap it round me, it's all I've got left.

Uneasily wandering between dream and reality, I search, despairingly, for the gate into the tunnel, unable to kill the faint hope that that at least is real, not part of the nightmare.

Thursday, 25 February
Through the bivouac tent tucked round me and over my face, I can see the first faint glimmers of daylight. I put my head on Serge's shoulder and feel almost comfortable. I am almost oblivious to the pain from the cat's cradle of slings and ropes. My flesh must have become hardened, and perhaps the cold has made me less sensitive. I am shivering, but I can no longer really feel the cold biting into my hands, my feet. The only thing that worries me is the horrible yellow slime oozing out of my nose so that I can't breathe properly. I wipe if off, slowly with my sleeve. My throat is dry, burning, painful. I put a hand in my rucksack to get a bit of ice. Nothing – empty. Sometime in the night, as I tossed and turned, I must have tipped the rucksack up. To get some more bits of ice would mean getting up and edging over several feet to my left. I don't feel strong enough – and anyway, what's the point? I know by now that no one is going to come up the South Face to get me down. Gary Hemming is dead, he won't come. It's a very long time since that rescue operation on the Drus, and perhaps, now, I'm having to pay the price for that long-past epic. It seems a bit hard to have a price to pay for rescuing two other men, two total strangers. But it had been worth it – yes, it had been worth it.

Over on the horizon, the outline of the mountains blurred and cleared, blurred and cleared. My eyesight was failing. I realized with perfect clarity, almost dispassionately, that it could not be very long now . . .

It was nothing short of a miracle that the weather was still good, thought Simone. She telephoned to the weather bureau. At 13,000 ft the wind speed was about 20 mph. At seven o'clock prompt she was at the helicopter landing pad.

"The wind has dropped a lot," she said to Gerard Devouassoux.

"You're quite right," he replied, "we ought to be able to land."

At 7.25, the SA 330 took off from Chamonix. Four guides were on board.

There they are – two of them. God, they're mad, if they fly that close together they'll collide. No, there's only one. No, there's the other one after all. No, I've lost him again where's he got to? Ah yes, I understand now, there *is* only one helicopter. It's me who's seeing double.

8.15
Total failure. The SA 330 arrived back at the landing pad. "Too much wind. We couldn't land."

The wind again – always the wind. And yet that morning it had felt as if there was scarcely a breath. Simone collapsed, exhausted and hopeless. They took her to a doctor, and then back home. They tried injections, sedatives, sleeping-tablets, but to no avail.

Back at our chalet, no one dared speak above a whisper. Simone was in a bad enough state already – how were they to give her the news that would so inevitably come, if not that day then the next, or the one after? How would they be able to tell her, when the two bodies were carried back to the valley: "Here they are." Of course they would make all the right comforting noises: "Would he have wanted to live, with no feet and no hands? Would life have meant anything to him?"

But for Simone, rather a Rene without hands and without feet than no Rene at all. Days ago in fact, she had faced up to that possibility. After fifteen days on the face, six of them totally immobile in sub-zero temperatures, she could not expect hands and feet to survive. But she would be able to help him adjust, she would make life happy and fulfilling even if he was crippled.

Poor Serge, now you've lost your sleeping-bag, too. Is it still morning? If I could be sure of the light over on the mountains, if I could see the sunlight, I'd be able to guess what sort of time it is. Everything is blurred. I can't remember Simone or the children. What do they look like? They seem to have receded into a dream. But I must try to remember . . . Their faces . . . No, it takes too much effort . . . No, it's coming back to me . . . I must hold on to the image, not let it slip away . . . I must work on it – what shape? what colour hair? I must remember – concentrate. There's nothing else to do now, anyway. I'll wrap the bivouac tent round me. I'll give up. I'll just think of Simone and the children – I'll never leave them again . . .

Grenoble, 9.10
On the helicopter pad at Versoud, an Alouette III is starting up. A long strident roar from its engine: 20,000 revs – 25,000 – 30,000. The automatic torque switches in, the long flexible blades turn, slowly at first and then quicker and quicker: 100,000–150,000. The machine vibrates and trembles on its skis. The rotor is now turning so fast it's invisible: 350,000 revs. The rev counters both reach maximum take-off revs. The helicopter, freed, soars up into the blue sky of the Isere. On board is the pilot Alain Frebault from the CRS and his technician Roland Pin, both of them accredited to the mountain-rescue service in Grenoble. Unlikely as it may seem, this was a miracle; there is no other word.

Alain Frebault had taken part in a number of rescues in the Dauphine Alps as part of the CRS, sometimes in extreme conditions. He knew nothing whatsoever about the Grandes Jorasses. He had never even set eyes on them. At about 9.50 he flew directly over the summit of Mont Blanc, then over the Col du Geant where the CRS post gave him the wind speed (which incidentally had not changed since earlier that morning), and the bearings for the Grandes Jorasses. He could scarcely miss them. There in front of him was the great face. He saw the summit ridge and realized it was too narrow for him to land in those wind conditions. But just a little further on, between the two summits, was a breche. He did not hesitate – calling on all his experience, all the skill of the great pilot which he was, he slipped quietly into the breche and touched down lightly on the snow. It was exactly 10.15. At that precise second Alain Frebault saved my life. He stayed there for a few moments, then took off again and flew calmly down to Chamonix.

Alain Frebault landed, got out of his machine and announced calmly that he had just landed on the Grandes Jorasses. Consternation! Reactions varying from incredulous delight to sheer pique.

Alain Freret, an old climbing partner of mine, exploded: "What the hell's going on around here? Wind conditions terrible, none of the helicopters can land, and this bloke comes straight up from Grenoble, doesn't even need to ask the way, just goes up there and lands."

At 10.45 Alain Frebault set off again with his technician and the guide Claude Ancey. A few minutes later he clattered composedly into the breche, touched down, stayed down for about a minute, then took off again with his passenger still aboard to prove he could repeat the manoeuvre even if conditions became worse. Then he did it again. Another helicopter, this time piloted by a Chamonix pilot called Violeau, put down and left another guide on the breche. Frebault circled, came in again touched down and dropped Claude Ancey.

By eleven o'clock there were five guides up at the breche. At 11.30 they started up the Pointe Walker. It was only about 350 ft above the breche. The ridge was windswept, bare ice. They had steps to cut, rescue gear to carry up to the summit. "Hello! Hello!"

From far away the call floated down to me. Dimly I thought I could hear it, but it didn't seem real.

"Hello! Hello!"

A call? Surely it couldn't be? No, just another hallucination. But what if it was real? And suddenly a feeling of wild hope swept over me. They were calling. They had come for me. Somewhere up there, someone was calling me. I got to my feet and looked up. There, above the overhang, was a man. A man, coming down on a cable.

"Hello! I'm here!"

He came down. He was beside me. I recognized him: Gerard Devouassoux.

"You're a hard man, Rene! God, but you're a hard man!"

"Yes, I'm still alive. Gerard, I'm glad it was you who got to me first."

I was remembering that epic rescue on the Drus, all those years ago, when Gerard and I had quarrelled after Gary Hemming and I insisted on bringing down the Germans from the West Face. Surely that old quarrel could be healed now? Nothing unforgivable, surely, had been said or done? Here I had been, lost and near death, and Gerard Devouassoux had come and got me; that made everything all right. In my naivety, in my state of physical weakness and heartfelt relief and gratitude, I was sure that it would all be as simple as that.

They clipped me on to the cable with Gerard Devouassoux. They pulled me up slowly, foot by foot; I had nothing to do but steady myself with my feet. The thin steel cable drew me up and up, out of the dark well into which I had fallen and back into the sunlight. I got my first proper look at those last 300 ft of face, and realized to my consternation that only the first 150 ft or so presented any difficulties at all. However had it happened that so small a distance had been fatal? It seemed a particular cruelty of fate; it made Serge's death seem more absurd than ever.

We stopped for a time while the guides made some adjustment to the steel cable. Then we went on. There were just a few more feet to the cornice, the almost transparent ice-barrier marking the frontier between light and shadow, life and death. I hungered for it, thirsted for it as if it had been a draught of pure, clear water from a crystal stream. Only six feet more – only three – and then suddenly I was over the edge, and a shaft of brilliant sunlight struck my face, and I fell to my knees on the ice, I was on my knees on the summit cornice. I wanted to look up, to raise my eyes to heaven, but I was twisted and wracked by emotion. Joseph Cornier put his strong arm round me and drew my head down to his shoulder. I felt sobs rising in my throat.

"Don't give way now, Rene, don't give way. You must hold out for a little longer. You remember me, don't you? We were in the same year on the guides' course."

"Yes, of course I remember. I'll hold out."

His mouth was working at the emotion of the moment. His eyes filled with tears. But don't worry, Joseph, I'll hold out, I'm not giving up now.

Olier and Zapelli from Courmayeur were there at the top, with Claude Ancey in charge of the stretcher.

Everything now took place in a dream. The breche where I sat, the helicopter that lifted me off the mountain and took me down to the valley, the door opening, the friendly hands supporting me, helping me to walk across to the waiting ambulance. I could still stand, I wanted to walk under my own steam . . . friends supported me, Jean Franco gave me a shoulder to lean on. I looked everywhere for Simone, but she was not there. They had not yet dared to give her the news, because they did not yet know which of us it was who was still alive – were not yet sure, even, that one of us was still alive.

I lay down on a stretcher in the ambulance. The doors were slammed shut, the ambulance set off.

At the hospital they took me straight to intensive care. Seconds later, it seemed, I was undressed, laying down, with tubes up my nostrils and tubes into my bladder. They hung bottles of yellow and colourless liquids above me, pushed needles into my veins, stuck electrodes into my chest. Nothing had yet been said, no promises had been made. Rene Christen the surgeon was quite aware of the problems. Terminal renal failure could have been only an inch away; I ought to have been dead. The mere fact that I was still alive was miracle enough. I could only have lived for a few more hours, he told me later.

I could feel oxygen flooding into my lungs. My blood was pumping itself back to normal. A delicious warmth stole over me. In the shaded room I felt good. I need no longer think of anything at all.

Simone came. Rene Christen had warned her.

"I'll do all I can, but I can't promise anything. The next forty-eight hours will be critical. He's in a state of extreme physical exhaustion."

I felt her presence before I actually saw her. She had not dared come too near. I turned my head slowly towards her and saw her drawn, weary face. How she too had suffered! And the fears were not over: I could read all her apprehension in her eyes.

"Don't worry, I'm back now, and I don't intend to die yet."

Through the window of my hospital room, warm and golden in the sunlight, I could see the Aiguilles dusted with frost and new snow. The temperature had fallen yet further.

The Loneliest Place on Earth

Hermann Buhl

Buhl was an Austrian mountaineer who, in 1953, made the first ascent of Nanga Parbat, 8,125 m (26,666 ft). This solo climb involved a tent-less, emergency bivouac at around 8,000 metres (26,000 ft), something previously considered impossible to survive.

"As I had been quite unable to sleep I was glad when it was 1 o'clock and time to get up. The storm had abated somewhat but it was still pitch-dark. Otto was well tucked into his sleeping bag and seemed oblivious to everything. He did not stir although I made a terrific clatter as I rooted around in the tent, brewed tea, dressed and packed my rucksack. Several times I urged him to get up, but he kept saying that it was too early and that yesterday I had said we would rise at 3 o'clock. I reminded him that we must make the fullest possible use of the day ahead of us and that we should be glad later on of every minute we gained now. I added that in any case I should be setting off at two and that if he were not ready I should have to go on alone. For the time being I packed everything necessary into my own rucksack, which made it quite a weight.

"Eventually Otto emerged from his chrysalis. I now thought that if I went on ahead and made the trail Otto would easily overtake me, and so that I should not have to carry everything myself I left some of the stuff behind for him, among other things Kuno's bacon, which was to be the summit ration. I was later to regret this bitterly. At 2.30 a.m. I crawled out of the tent and started on my way.

"The night was star-lit and the crescent moon threw her silvery light along the ridge which stretched away ahead of me. It was calm and cold. I put on everything I could. Across a hard, steep spur of compressed snow I regained the top of the ridge. Here on the spine the going was treacherous. I buckled on my crampons and felt able to move with greater freedom. In thrilling soaring leaps the ridge rose steeply before me. To the right giant snow slopes, broken by icy barriers, plunged to the plateau above Camp II; to the left my way was skirted by dark rock formations, while beyond the eye was lost in unimaginable depths. A biting wind came up from the south and forced me on to the Rakhiot side. At the start of the traverse to the Silver Saddle I paused for a rest. It was 5 a.m. and behind the Karakoram the sun was rising in golden splendour. Caught in the brilliance of the first rays an undulating sea of summits greeted me: beautiful Chogori, trapezoidal Masherbrum, the bishop's mitre of Rakaposhi, the black granite of the Mustag Tower. In the valleys a fine mist hovered, the best of weather portents. Blissfully I basked in the early sunshine as I took my morning refreshment. Otto was still a good way behind me – I estimated it at an hour's climb – but I never doubted for a moment that he would eventually catch up with me.

"The *Firn* was hard and in places patches of bare, bluish irridescent ice came to the surface. Distances were most deceptive. The rocks of Silver Crag stubbornly refused to come any nearer and another two hours had passed before I was standing on the Silver Saddle, at the edge of the great *Firn* plateau. How often had I dreamed of this moment!

"My altimeter registered 24,275 ft. So far I had made pretty good time. I was not terribly affected by the height. I was having to take two breaths for each step. After another short rest I continued on my way. The *Firn* plateau went on for about two miles, at first rising gently but later inclining steeply up to the Fore-Summit; the difference in height amounted to about 1,500 ft.

"The *Firn* had been ploughed by the high winds into undulations three feet high. This meant a perpetual clambering up and down which greatly slowed down progress. At 25,000 ft I seemed to reach the limit of my capacity. Suddenly my body felt paralyzed, my lungs could not expand, and every step demanded tremendous effort. My pauses for rest became more and more frequent, and I was acutely conscious of the thinness of the air.

"Otto did not seem to be faring any better. It was quite some time before I caught sight of his figure on the Silver Saddle advancing slowly, silhouetted against the skyline. I saw him stop and then sink down. Otto had given up. This in itself was more or less immaterial to me but with my tongue parched and my stomach rumbling I could not but think of the bacon in Otto's rucksack which was now lost to me.

"On the Silver Plateau the sun was scorching, the air was terribly dry and not a breath of wind was stirring. After each rest I had to force myself to get up and carry on, so great was the temptation to go on lying where I was. The steep rise to the Fore-Summit seemed to get not one whit nearer although I had now been pegging away for hours. My idea that I should reach the summit by midday was completely set at naught. I now directed my steps over to the extreme edge of the plateau where it dropped away into the southern face. I hoped that a cool breeze might be coming up from the south. But here too the air was perfectly still.

"The weight of my rucksack became intolerable and when at length I reached the foot of the rise to the Fore-Summit I took it off and left it behind. I reckoned on being back there before nightfall. I tied my anorak round my waist by the sleeves, having first stuffed the summit flag, my camera, spare gloves and drinking flask in the pockets. I also stowed away some Pervitin, and also Padutin in case of frost-bite, picked up my ice-axe and continued on my way.

"The going was now decidedly easier; the pauses became less frequent and, summoning all my will-power, I tracked along below the Fore-Summit to the right in the direction of a declivity between the Fore-Summit and the Diamir depression. Once more the distance proved to be greater than it had appeared. I began to have doubts whether I should be able

to keep going long enough, but in any case the Fore-Summit
was within my grasp. It just missed being in the 26,000 ft class,
but anyhow mine would be the first ascent. The Pervitin I was
carrying gave me confidence; I felt I could rely on it in case of
emergency. Just 300 ft below the Fore-Summit I set foot on the
above-mentioned declivity."

Buhl had now reached the highest point hitherto attained.
This was just about where Aschenbrenner and Schneider had
stood when in 1934 they had climbed to within 150 ft of the
Fore-Summit. It was also roughly the point where all possible
ascent routes converged. Mummery in 1895 had aimed at the
Bazhin Gap, and the route over the North Summit reconnoi-
tered by Harrer, Aufschnaiter and Lobenhoffer in 1939 would
also run into the Rakhiot route at approximately this point.
From this juncture Schneider had conjectured that the route to
the summit continued by a descent to the snowfield below the
Bazhin Gap and then up the summit shoulder either by a central
rib on its north-eastern flank or by a traverse of the main east
ridge from the Bazhin Gap. Buhl decided to traverse direct from
the declivity towards the Bazhin Gap and the main east ridge,
without descending to the snowfield below. His narrative continues:

"My traverse across the rocks to the Bazhin Gap took me over
snow and ice, deeply terraced and strewn with boulders. It was
already 2 p.m. A steep rocky ridge crowded with snow towers,
vertical pitches of sharp-edged granite, badly exposed cornices
and steep flanks of compressed snow, now lay between me and
the shoulder. Assessing all these difficulties I remembered the
Pervitin and took two tablets. I should need every ounce of
energy and will-power I could muster. I knew that the drug
would remain effective for only six to seven hours and that I
must reach some resting place by that time.

"A steep ridge of compressed snow led to the foot of the
rocks. At this point the mountain-face plunged in a vertical
drop of several miles direct from the ridge. Once or twice I
looked through crevices which had formed between the rock
and the ice into the gaping void below. Never had I seen such an
abyss.

"I laboured doggedly on from one rise to the next, treating

every single pitch as an objective in itself. When once more the summit revealed itself far above me I simply could not realize that that was my ultimate objective. Finally I had to scale a thirty-foot overhang which obstructed the access to a *couloir* which in turn led farther up. At the end of the ridge, which was in parts very severe, a massive and upright gendarme still barred the way. It was impossible to climb over it so I had somehow to circumvent it. The rock was very brittle and called for extreme care. The last rise before the shoulder consisted of a very steep and long slope of hard compressed snow. This presented no special problem but it demanded great exertion. With my last reserves of energy I managed to work myself up the few feet which still separated me from the ridge. At 6 p.m. I stood at last on the shoulder at an altitude of about 26,250 ft.

"I felt that I had reached the limit of my endurance.

"Naturally, as a climber, I realized that I was now on the last lap to the summit. But it might just as well have been any other summit in my native Tyrol. This may seem incredible but that was how I felt. I was simply not conscious of the fact that I was at that moment at grips with our own Nanga Parbat, an untrodden peak of over 26,000 feet, the summit to which no less than seven expeditions had gone forth, the mountain which had claimed so many lives . . .

"I took a last gulp of coca-tea, which offered some fleeting refreshment. Then I traversed into the northern face. Steep and rough, a tumbled mass of boulders now led up to the summit, still about 300 ft above me. I now left the ski-sticks behind and – I could do it in no other way – scrambled up on all fours. Suddenly I realized that I could go no higher . . . I was on the summit.

"I was not, I must confess, at the time fully conscious of the significance of that moment, nor did I have any feeling of elation at my victory. I simply felt relieved to be on top and to know that all the sweat and toil of the ascent were behind me.

"It was about 7 p.m. I at once took the small Tyrolese pennant from the pocket of my anorak, tied it to my ice-axe, took a photograph and tucked the pennant away again to take back to my club. Then I got out the flag of the country whose guests we were, Pakistan, fastened it to my ice-axe, changed films and took some more photographs – down towards Rakhiot Peak, towards the Fore-Summit, the Plateau and the Silver Saddle. My eye scanned the three mile drop into the Rupal valley where the setting sun was throwing the mighty shadow of the mountain on which I stood far out into the land. I looked all round me, eastward into the Himalaya, northward to the Karakoram with the Pamirs and the Hindukush adjoining farther west. To the south I could see over and beyond many 16,000 ft peaks.

"It was 7.10 p.m. when I left the summit pyramid. The sun was just disappearing on the horizon, and although the rocks still held some of the heat of the day, it immediately became very cold. The ridge seemed to me to be too difficult and dangerous for the purposes of descent, so I thought of trying to get down across the *Firn* flank facing the Diamir side. Unaccountably I had left my ice-axe on the summit so I had only the two ski-sticks with which to keep my balance. This carelessness might well have proved to be my undoing, for I was standing right in the middle of the traverse when suddenly my right crampon slipped off my boot. I just managed to grab it in time but the strap went overboard.

"I was left like a stork standing on the smooth, hard surface on one crampon, supporting myself on the two ski-sticks and without an idea as to how I should extricate myself. With extreme caution I finally succeeded in reaching some rocky ground.

"When I had dropped about 450 ft from the summit, night suddenly closed in on me. Some distance away I could just see the outline of a large rock and I now groped my way towards it. Supporting my body against the mountainside which inclined at an angle of about 50 degrees, I spent the night standing on this rock.

"I thought longingly of my bivouac equipment which was waiting for me in my rucksack at the foot of the Fore-Summit. I only had my thin pullover on; my heavy one, the tent-sack and my other spare clothing were all in the rucksack.

"Finally, as Karl had been at great pains to impress on me that I should do in case of an emergency bivouac, I took a few pills of Padutin.

"It was 9 p.m. when the darkness forced me to bivouac against the mountain, standing on that unsteady chunk of rock. To the west the last light of day was gradually being extinguished. My rest did me good, even if I was standing all the time. The hours passed surprisingly quickly. I dozed, nodding a little now and again, then jerking myself upright once more. Then a cold shiver would run through me. But it was all quite bearable. The only trouble was that my feet gradually lost all feeling, for I could not keep them moving sufficiently. It was not until nearly 2 a.m. that the moon appeared. Its silvery crescent hung just above the summit, lighting up miraculously the slopes of the North and Fore-Summits below me and casting its light right over to the Bazhin Gap. But I was not in its floodlit path; the flank remained in shadow. So I had to go on waiting until dawn should break.

"As the morning of 4th July approached it became increasingly cold. On the eastern horizon a pale streak showed in the sky. But it was still too dark for climbing and it was not until 4 a.m. that I was able to continue my descent. I had no feeling whatsoever in my feet, my boots were frozen stiff and the rubber soles were glazed with ice. All this called for extreme care. Every step had to be well considered even where the gradient was not particularly steep; the smallest error of judgment could have been fatal.

"If I did only one slight slip in the snow this took so much out of me that I needed minutes to collect myself again. After overcoming a difficult pitch which once again left me completely out of breath I stood at last on the steep iron-hard snowfield which led up to the Bazhin Gap. At around midday I eventually reached the rocks at the Diamir depression. As these offered but very slight hand-holds I took off both pairs of gloves and stuffed them in my pockets. When later I went to put them on again I found that one pair was missing. I have no idea what could have happened to them.

"Throughout this day I had the feeling that I was not alone, that someone was accompanying me. Many times I found myself in the act of turning round to address my companion, and when I was looking for my gloves he told me that I had lost them. It was only when I looked round that I realized that I was alone.

"The sun beat down without mercy. I took a rest and fell asleep for a short time. I awoke feeling ravenously hungry and with a raging thirst. I was so absolutely parched that I was obsessed with the thought of drinking. Now and again I heard voices above me and hoped it might be Hans or Walter coming to meet me with a flask of tea. But no one came. I continued to drag myself on with what help I could get from the ski-sticks, to the Diamir depression which lay about 100 ft up. It seemed quite incredible now, that only the day before I had been able to climb to the summit.

"At last I reached the Diamir depression. Before me lay once more the vast sweep of the Silver Plateau. I could no longer swallow nor speak. Bloodstained slaver oozed from my mouth. I longed to get at my rucksack, for hunger was torturing me no less than thirst. I stumbled about among the hard furrows. It was some time before I could locate the rucksack, then finally I fell down beside it. I could not swallow dry food, but I made myself a wonderfully refreshing concoction of Dextro-energen and snow and after a prolonged rest began to feel better again. Far away on the Silver Saddle I saw two specks. Oh, the joy of it! Someone was coming! I heard voices too, calling my name.

"But what was wrong? The two specks remained static. There was no movement in them. Then I realized that they were rocks. How bitter, how painful was this disillusion! My rests became more and more frequent, the pauses ever longer. I would struggle along for twenty or thirty yards then once more would I be fettered and held in total collapse. Two to three steps demanded ten rapid gasps for breath, then twenty, then still more, until eventually I could go on no longer. Then would follow another long rest, and then the agony would start all over again.

"In this fashion I reached the lowest point of the plateau. I was on the very brink of despair as I floundered among the petrified waves of this vast expanse of fluted *Firn*.

"The counter-gradient to the Silver Saddle seemed endless. I now resorted once more to Pervitin. Whatever reserves of energy were left must now be mobilized, otherwise I should be finished.

"At 5.30 p.m. I stood at last on the Silver Saddle and, looking down, saw two men standing near the Moor's Head. The sight of them gave me fresh impetus and as though buoyed up anew by some secret force I went ahead with greater ease."

The Gods Giveth, the Gods Taketh Away

Kurt Diemberger

In 1957, Diemberger, an Austrian alpinist, accompanied the legendary Hermann Buhl – the conqueror of Nanga Parbat – on an expedition to the Himalayas where, after climbing Broad Peak, they turned to the ascent of Chogolisa.

June 27th dawned clear, fine and calm, a veritable gift of the Gods. We were happy beyond words. Our rest-day had done us good, and we felt brimming over with fitness, and a burning zeal to bag the summit.

We were off at about a quarter to five. It was still very cold, but we knew it couldn't be for very long. The sky grew lighter and lighter above Baltoro Kangri. To the south lay a sea of summits, peaks about 20,000 to 23,000 ft high, and hardly even explored. To the north the sun was already touching K2. Between us and it, Broad Peak displayed only its main summit, masking the other two.

Almost as soon as we had got our legs moving, the warmth of the sun reached us. We tramped happily up over the glittering snow. Free of our loads, we made unbelievably easy progress. The going was excellent on the very crest of the ridge, but the snow was deep and trying on either side; besides which, the wind had formed dangerous wind-slabs on the slope. One of them broke away quite close to us and went thundering down in a fair-sized avalanche to the level plateau of the Kaberi Saddle

below. It made quite an impression on us and we stuck carefully
to the crest of the ridge, which was so far uncorniced. But how
would things go up there on Ridge Peak, where we could see
cornices several yards wide projecting unpleasantly in a continuous hem? No doubt the storm of the previous day had
notably increased their size.

At 23,000 ft we left the ridge, by now corniced, and traversed
a little way across a smooth ice-slope to reach a projection
farther up. There were actually a few rocks here, quite a
curiosity on this mountain. And what about the route above?
Ye Gods! There was the summit, just over there! It couldn't be
any great distance and it certainly didn't look difficult. We
ought to be up on it by midday, we thought.

Indeed, the next bit was easy; the slope flattened out appre-
ciably and all we had to do was to keep along it to the deep notch
beyond Ridge Peak. We made light of turning the huge cornices
which towered over us to the right. Chogolisa's immense roof
drew rapidly nearer, but after a quarter of an hour we had to
admit it wasn't going to be easy. The slope grew steeper and the
sector of ridge rising behind it had a distinctly airy look. Then
suddenly we could see the whole route, and there was nothing
about it to be lightly dismissed. The ridge down to the notch
was as sharp as a knife-blade, its left-hand side a giddily steep
precipice of rock and ice, to its right great cornices hanging far
out over the North Face. We should have to be very careful
there. The rock precipices below us kept on forcing us farther
up towards the jagged white crest. We belayed carefully with
the rope, watching for avalanches. A small wind-slab did in fact
break away and went sliding away into the abyss. The snow
conditions were really a curse. Just as we got to the rocks,
Hermann went through to his waist, and hardly had he
scrambled out when he was sitting in another hole. Damn it,
the slope was a positive honeycomb! Hermann balanced his way
forward as if walking on eggshells – lucky man, he didn't weigh
much. He reached ice-plastered rocks and moved from foothold to foot-hold with incredible delicacy of balance, hardly
touching the holds as he moved. A moment later he disappeared
over a rib. "Up you come!" I could hear him calling.

Rope's length by rope's length, we worked our way along the

ridge, sometimes on the slope, sometimes right up at the edge of the cornices. Steadily, the wind passed over the crest; glittering snow rose towards the deep blue dome of the sky. Down in the south there were huge clouds now. But they did not move.

We had made good time in spite of the unexpected difficulties. It was only 9 o'clock when we reached the saddle at 23,000 ft. And there, only 2,000 ft above us, was the sharp tip of the turret on the long crest of the summit-ridge. A steep, but for the most part broad, ridge of snow led up to it.

We sat down in a sheltered hollow, in glorious warm sunshine, and took off the rope. We were ravenous; what about a drop of tea and those delicacies we had saved up for our trip to the top? "This is the best day for me since I came out with the expedition," mused Hermann. How well I understood him. Climbing a seven-thousander in three days . . . not in three weeks! This was just his pigeon – very different from what he went through on Broad Peak. I shared his obvious delight.

We didn't move on for a whole long hour. When we did, we took alternate leads in deep snow. We were unroped now. It was enough to carry the rope with us in the rucksack, Hermann said, so I did not think much about it. A steep pitch with a short ice-cliff called for work with the axe; after that it was easy again. Occasional cracks in the slope spelled avalanche-danger. They pushed us out farther on to the brink of the precipice than we had intended.

Ridge Peak was gradually sinking below and behind us. To the south, the great mountainous banks of cloud were moving very slowly nearer. The sky was calm and of a deep, deep blue. The banner of snow blowing from Ridge Peak seemed to have grown a little. To the north lay a tremendous prospect: all the giants of the Baltoro lined up in a row, a whole chain of peaks 26,000 ft high or only just less. We let our gaze range in wonderment from K2 to Hidden Peak. We took photographs and then moved on again.

How quickly the clouds were coming towards us now! We hoped they wouldn't interfere with our view from the top. We quickened our pace. The last steep pitch began a little way up there, and close above it we could see the tower that was the summit – 1,500 feet at the most – *that* couldn't take so very long.

Presently a little cloud came climbing up the slope below us. It grew larger, enveloping us, enveloping the peak. Without any warning, all hell broke loose. Grey veils of mist scurried across the ridge. Unnatural darkness swamped us. We fought our way forward through clouds of blown snow, bending double to meet the fury of the gale. On the crest of the ridge it flung itself upon us in full blast, snatching at our clothes, trying to claw us from our footing. It was terribly cold and the needles of ice blowing down into our faces hurt savagely. We could only see the next yard or two ahead. We kept on changing the lead, struggling grimly upwards.

It didn't seem possible. I thought of the blue sky such a short time back. It had all been so quick. I had an uncanny feeling – hadn't exactly the same thing happened to the Duke of the Abruzzi, quite close to the summit? Were we going to be robbed, too? Away with such stupid thoughts; it was only a few hundred feet, and we had *got* to do it.

It grew lighter for a moment, as the wind parted the driving clouds. We stood rooted, looking up to where the summit must be. There it was, near enough to touch, looming darkly above us. An instant later the wrack had swallowed it up again.

The storm continued its horrific din. Laboriously we moved up, with a steep, bottomless precipice below us, keeping close to the ridge crest. Everything was white now and we could hardly see.

We were at about 24,000 ft. Only another thousand to the summit-tower. Suddenly Hermann spoke: "We've got to turn back at once, or the wind will cover our tracks up, and then we shall stray out on to the cornices!" He was quite right. We hadn't given a thought to it; and now visibility was almost nil.

We should have to hurry. We turned then and there. Hermann had been leading, so I was in front now. He followed at a safe distance of ten to fifteen yards, which was all that visibility would permit.

Bent double, I felt my way downwards. It was incredible – only 150 ft down, there was no trace to be seen of our upward trail, except the deep holes made by our axes. Very soon there wouldn't be very many of *them*. And still the tempest kept up its infernal din.

I reckoned we must be at about 23,600 ft, and that we must be near the steep avalanche slope which had pushed us so close to the cornices. If only one could see a bit more! I turned and saw Hermann coming after me, keeping the distance unaltered, following in my actual steps. As I moved down, I kept on looking across to the left, trying to see through the mist. All I could see was that it was getting a bit darker overhead and a bit lighter below. That must be the edge of the cornices. It seemed a safe distance away, but in mist distances can be deceptive. Perhaps it would be better to keep a bit to the right, but then I should have to look out for the precipice. It ought to be here by now. Ah, there's another axe-hole . . .

I looked anxiously to the left and then down to the surface at my feet. I was at a loss; it was almost impossible to see anything at all. *Crack!* Something shot through me like a shock. Everything shook, and for a second the surface of the snow seemed to shrink. Blindly, I jumped sideways to the right – an instantaneous reflex action – two, three great strides, and followed the steep slope downwards a little way, shattered by what I had seen at my feet – the rim of the cornice, with little jagged bits breaking away from it. My luck had been in, all right! I had been clean out on the cornice. What would Hermann have to say about that, I wondered? I stopped and turned, but the curve of the slope prevented my seeing over the crest as I looked up. The light was improving a little. Hermann must bob up any moment up there. I still couldn't fathom that extraordinary shaking sensation; had the snow really settled under my weight?

Still no Hermann. "Hermann!" I shouted. "For God's sake, what's up? Hermann!" I rushed, gasping up the slope. There it was, the crest . . . and beyond it, smooth snow . . . and it was empty . . . Hermann . . . You! . . .

Done for . . .

I dragged myself up a little farther. I could see his last footmarks in the snow, then the jagged edge of the broken cornice, yawning. Then the black depths.

The broken cornice – that had been the quaking beneath my feet, then.

I couldn't get a sight of the North Face from anywhere near. I should have to get down to Ridge Peak for that. As I went down, the storm gradually abated, and the mists lifted from time to time. I was utterly stunned. How could that have happened just behind me? I had the greatest difficulty in getting up the short rise to Ridge Peak, but even before I got there it had cleared up. I hurried out to the farthest edge of the cliffs.

The storm was hunting the clouds high into the heavens. Above the veils of mist and through them a ridge loomed up – a tower – a great roof with tremendous banners of blown snow streaming from it. Chogolisa, the horrible. I could see the spot where we had turned at about 24,000 ft. Our trail down the broad snow-field below was crystal clear. Then that fearsome drop to the north – into the clouds. And there, even closer to our tracks as they ran straight downwards, the encroaching precipice. And then I could see it all with stark and terrible clarity. Just at that point, Hermann had left my tracks at a slight bend, where I was hugging the rim of the precipice, and gone straight on ahead, only three or four yards – straight out on to the tottering rim of the cornice – straight out into nothingness. Of the foot of the wall I could see nothing. Stupidly, I stared upwards again.

If we had been roped . . .

I looked down along the face, shuddering . . .

No, I should never have been able to hold him there; at the moment of his fall I myself was too far out on the overhanging snow.

At last I could see clearly down below, where the broad snow-masses of an avalanche fanned out. The crashing cornice had set it off and it had swept the face clean. Hermann was nowhere to be seen. He must have fallen at least 1,000, maybe 2,000 ft and was lying there buried under the piled-up snow. Could he have survived that? There was no answer to my shouts and I had no way of getting down there. I should have to fetch the others and we should have to come from below. That was the only faint possibility. I strained my eyes, searching every cranny, searching for a rucksack, a ski-stick, a dark blob. But there was nothing to be seen – absolutely nothing. Only our tracks – up there . . .

Clouds blotted the mountain out again. I was alone.

★   ★   ★

Mists and a high wind were sweeping the corniced ridge as I tried to find the way down. At times I could see nothing at all and could only tell from rifts in the snow that I had strayed too far down the slope. After what seemed an age, I found our tent. It was a horror of emptiness. I took the absolute essentials for the descent and went on down. At the Kaberi Saddle there was knee-deep fresh snow, through which only a tiny corner of the marker-pennants showed. I probed with my feet under that smooth expanse of white to find out from which side our ascent-route had come, then went straight on into the whiteness . . . to the next pennant. I wandered vaguely down endless hollows, over crevasses, through fog, then into the darkness of night. For long, indescribable hours of horror – during which I at times had a feeling that Hermann was still with me – I managed, by some miracle, to find my way, onwards, downwards. Then, just before the great ice-falls, my pocket-lamp failed; so I had to bivouac at 18,000 ft. In the first pale light of dawn I made my way down the ice-falls. On and on . . . endlessly on . . . till, 27 hours after Hermann's fall, I tottered into Base Camp.

The search which followed found absolutely nothing.

Once again, the monstrous rubble-covered river of ice lay freed of all human presence. The sun burned down on it with scorching intensity. The snow was rapidly vanishing, melting into the waters of gurgling glacier-streams. Chogolisa's white roof-tree seemed to lift into the very sky itself. The great peaks stood silently all around. Were they, too, mourning? Or was this only the great healing silence which eternally enfolds all living and dying?

The Hard Way

Doug Scott and Dougal Haston

The British climbers Doug Scott (1941–) and Dougal Haston (1940–77) made the first ascent of Everest's difficult South-West face. The expedition, which took place in 1975, was led by Chris Bonington.

Dougal Haston

I hauled onto the proposed site of Camp VI. Straight away my energy and upward urges came rushing back – there ahead in reality was the way we'd been hypothetically tracing for so long with fingers on photographs and making us forget everything else was the fact it looked feasible. There was a steepish-looking rock pitch just ahead, but after it seemed like unbroken snow slopes to the couloir. It looked as if progress was inevitable as long as the others were successful in their carry. Ang Phurba kept muttering about a campsite further up under some rocks, but this looked like wasted effort to us, as the traverse line started logically from where we were at the moment. Diplomatically we told him that we were staying there, it being mainly Doug's and my concern, as we were going to have to occupy the camp, and he started off down, leaving his valuable load. We began digging in spells, without oxygen, but using some to regain strength during the rests.

Mike Thompson, Chris Bonington and Mick Burke arrived one after the other, looking tired, as well they should be. Carrying heavy loads at over 27,000 ft is no easy occupation.

Doug Scott

Theirs had been a magnificent carry, especially Chris, who had now been at Camp V and above for eight days, and also Mick, who was carrying a dead weight of cine equipment. He had been at Camp V for five days, and Pertemba had worked hard practically every day of the expedition carrying heavy loads and encouraging his Sherpas, while Mike Thompson, who had never been above 23,000 ft before, had arrived carrying a heavy sack with apparent ease at 27,300 ft. We sat there talking confidently in the late afternoon. There was a strong bond of companionship as there had been all the way up the Face. One by one they departed for Camp V and they left us with the bare essentials to make this last step to the top of our route and perhaps the summit itself. I yelled our thanks down to Mike as they were sliding back down the rope. He must have known his chances of making a summit bid were slim, yet he replied, "Just you get up, that's all the reward I need." And that's how it had been from start to finish with all members of the team. It had taken the combined effort of forty Sherpas, and sixteen climbers, together with Chris's planning, to get the two of us into this position. We knew how lucky we were being the representatives of such a team and to be given the chance to put the finishing touches to all our efforts. Finally Mick left, having run all the film he had through the cameras. Dougal and I were left alone to dig out a more substantial platform and to erect the two-man summit tent. We were working without oxygen and took frequent rests to recover, but also to look across the Upper Snow Field leading up to the South Summit couloir. After the tent was up, Dougal got inside to prepare the evening meal, whilst I pottered about outside stowing away equipment in a little ice cave and tying empty oxygen bottles around the tent to weight it down. They hung in festoons on either side of the snow arete. Finally I bundled rope and oxygen bottles into our sacks for the following morning and dived into the tent to join Dougal.

Dougal Haston

Inside, we worked on plans for the next day. We had 500 metres of rope for fixing along the traverse and hoped to do that, then come back to [Camp] VI and make our big push the day after.

I was higher on Everest than I'd ever been before, yet

thoughts of the summit were still far away in the thinking and
hoping process. It had all seemed so near before in 1971 and
1972: euphoric nights at Camps V and VI when progress had
seemed good and one tended to skip the difficult parts with
visions of oneself standing at the top of the South West Face,
then reality shattering the dreams in progressive phases as
realization of certain failure burst the bubble. There had been
an inevitability about both previous failures, but still carrying a
lot of disappointment. Failure you must accept, but that does
not make it any easier, especially on a project like the South
West Face, where so much thinking, willpower and straight
physical effort are necessary to get to the higher points. This
time it seemed better. We were above the Rock Band and the
ground ahead looked climbable, but I kept a rigid limit on my
thoughts, contemplating possible progress along the traverse to
the exit couloir, nothing more. If that proved possible then I
would allow for further up-type thinking.

Our physical situation felt comfortable. Maybe that is a
reflection of the degree of progress that we have made in our
adaptation to altitude. Many the story we had read or been told
about assault camps on the world's highest peak. No one ever
seemed to spend a comfortable night at Camp VI on the South
Col route. Their nights seemed to be compounded of sleeplessness, discomfort and thirst. Here there was none of that.
The situation was very bearable. We weren't stretched personally, didn't even feel tired or uncomfortable, despite a long day.
The stove brewed the hours away – tea, lemon drinks and even a
full-scale meal with meat and mashed potatoes. Each was deep
into his own thoughts with only one slightly urgent communal
reaction as a change of oxygen cylinder went wrong and the gas
stove roared into white heat. Order was restored before an
explosion, with Doug fixing the leak at the same time as I
turned off the stove. Emergency over, we laughed, conjuring
visions of the reaction at Camp II as Camp VI exploded like a
successfully attacked missile target. It would have been a new
reason for failure!

Thereafter sleep claimed its way, and I moved gently into
another world of tangled dreams, eased by a gentle flow of
oxygen. The night was only disturbed by a light wind rocking

our box and a changing of sleeping cylinders. One would need to be a good or very exhausted sleeper to sleep through a cylinder running out. From a gentle warm comfort one suddenly feels cold, uneasy and very awake. Just after midnight and the changeover, we gave up sleeping and started the long task of preparing for the morning's work.

Shortly after first light I moved out into blue and white dawn to continue the upward way, leaving Doug wrapped in all the down in the tent mouth, cameras and belays set up for action. There was a rock step lurking ahead that had seemed reasonably close in the setting afternoon sun of the previous day. Now in the clear first light, a truer perspective was established as I kept on thrusting into the deep-powdered fifty-degree slope, sliding sideways like a crab out of its element reaching for an object that didn't seem to come any closer. One hundred metres of this progress it was, before I could finally fix a piton and eye the rock step. It wasn't long, seven or eight metres, but looked difficult enough. Downward-sloping, steep slabs with a layer of powder. Interesting work. Grade 5 at this height. Much concentration and three more pitons saw a delicate rightwards exit and back, temporarily thankful, into deep snow to finish the rope length and finally give Doug the signal to move.

Doug Scott
I traversed across on his rope and up the difficult rocks to his stance. I led out another 400 ft over much easier ground, parallel with the top of the Rock Band. We gradually armed to the task and began to enjoy our position. After all the months of dreaming, here we were cutting across that Upper Snow Field. Dougal led out the next reel of rope.

Dougal Haston
The conditions and climbing difficulty began to change again. Kicking through with crampons I found there was no ice beneath. Rock slabs only, which have never been renowned for their adherence to front points. A few tentative movements up, down, sideways proved it existed all around. It seemed the time for a tension traverse. But on what? The rock was shattered loose and worse – no cracks. After I had scraped away a large

area a small moveable flake appeared. It would have to do. Tapping in the beginnings of an angle, which seemed to be okay to pull on but not for a fall, I started tensioning across to an inviting-looking snow lump. Thoughts flashed through my mind of a similar traverse nine years before, near the top of the Eiger Direct. There it would have been all over with a slip, and suddenly, as I worked it out, things didn't look too good here, if you cared to think in those directions. Not only didn't I care to, I also didn't dare to think of full consequences, and chasing the dangerous thoughts away, I concentrated on tiptoeing progress. Slowly the limit of tension was reached and my feet were on some vaguely adhering snow. This will have to do for the present, were my thoughts as I let go the rope and looked around. A couple of probes with the axe brought nothing but a sense of commitment.

"No man is an island," it is said. I felt very close to a realization of the contrary of this, standing on that semi-secure snow step in the midst of a sea of insecurity. But there was no racing adrenalin, only the cold clinical thought of years of experience. About five metres away the snow appeared to deepen. It would have to be another tension traverse. Long periods of excavation found no cracks. Tugs on the rope and impatient shouting from Doug. Communication at altitude is bad in awkward situations. One has to take off the oxygen mask to shout. Then when one tries to do this, one's throat is so dry and painful that nothing comes out. Hoping that Doug would keep his cool, I carried on, looking for a piton placement. A reasonable-looking crack came to light and two pitons linked up meant the game could go on. This time I felt I could put more bearing weight on the anchor. Just as well. Twice the tension limit failed, and there was the skidding movement backwards on the scraping slabs. But a third try and a long reach saw me in deep good snow, sucking oxygen violently. The way ahead relented, looking reasonable. My voice gained enough momentum to shout to Doug, and soon he was on his way. Following is usually monotone – sliding along on jumars. This one was not so. I could almost see the gleam in Doug's eyes shining through his layers of glasses as he pulled out the first tension piton with his fingers.

"Nasty stuff, youth."

I had to agree as he passed on through.

Doug Scott

I continued across further, using up one of our two climbing ropes, before dropping down slightly to belay. We had probably come too high, for there was easier snow below the rocks that led right up towards the South Summit couloir. However, avalanches were still cascading down the mountain, so we climbed up to the rocks in an effort to find good peg anchors for the fixed ropes. We didn't want to return the next day to find them hanging over the Rock Band. Dougal led a short section on easy snow, then all the rope was run out and we turned back for camp.

I sat in the snow to take photographs and watched the sun go down over Gaurishankar. What a place to be! I could look straight down and see Camp II 6,000 ft down. There were people moving about between tents, obviously preparing to camp for the night. Mounds of equipment were being covered with tarpaulins, one or two wandered out to the crevasse toilet, others stood about in small groups before diving into their tents for the night. A line of shadow crept up the face to Camp IV by the time I was back to our tent. I again sorted out loads and pushed in oxygen bottles for the night, whilst Dougal melted down snow for the evening meal.

We discovered over the radio that only Lhakpa Dorje had made the carry to Camp VI that day. He had managed to bring up vital supplies of oxygen, but unfortunately the food, cine camera and still film we needed had not arrived. Anyway they were not essential, so we could still make our bid for the summit next day. There was also no more rope in camp, but I think we were both secretly relieved about this. Chris had always insisted that whoever made the first summit bid should lay down as much fixed rope as possible so that if that first attempt failed the effort would not be wasted. This made good sense, but it did take a lot of effort up there and we all longed for the time when we could cut loose from the fixed ropes. It was a perfect evening with no wind at all as we sat looking out of the tent doorway sipping mugs of tea. Finally the sun was gone from our tent and lit up only the upper snows, golden turning red, before all the mountain was in shadow. We zipped up the tent door and built up quite a fug of warm air heating up water for corned beef hash.

Dougal Haston

Five hundred metres of committing ground was a good day's work on any point of the mountain. The fact that it was all above 27,000 ft made our performance level high and, more to the point, we hadn't exhausted ourselves in doing it. This was crucial because deterioration is rapid at such altitudes. Over tea we discussed what to take next day. I still reckoned deep down on the possibility of a bivouac. Doug seemed reluctant to admit to the straight fact, but didn't disagree when I mentioned packing a tent sac and stove. The packs weren't going to be light. Two oxygen cylinders each would be needed for the undoubtedly long day, plus three fifty-metre ropes, also various pitons and karabiners. Even if a bivouac was contemplated we couldn't pack a sleeping bag. This would have been pushing weight too much. The bivouac idea was only for an emergency and we would have hastened that emergency by slowing ourselves down through too much weight – so we tried to avoid the possibility by going as lightly as possible. The only extra I allowed myself was a pair of down socks, reckoning they could be invaluable for warming very cold or even frostbitten feet and hands. There was no sense of drama that evening. Not even any unusual conversation. We radioed down and told those at Camp II what we were doing, ate the rest of our food and fell asleep.

Doug Scott

About one in the morning we awoke to a rising wind. It was buffeting the tent, shaking it about and pelting it with spindrift, snow and ice chips. I lay there wondering what the morning would bring, for if the wind increased in violence we should surely not be able to move. At about 2:30 we began slowly to wind ourselves up for the climb. We put a brew on and heated up the remains of the corned beef hash for breakfast. The wind speed was decreasing slightly as we put on our frozen boots and zipped up our suits. Dougal chose his down-filled suit, whilst I took only my windproofs, hoping to move faster and easier without the restriction of tightly packed feathers around my legs. I had never got round to sorting out a down-filled suit that fitted me properly.

Because of the intense cold it was essential to put on crampons, harnesses, even the rucksack and oxygen system in the warmth of the tent. Just after 3:30 we emerged to get straight on to the ropes and away to the end. It was a blustery morning, difficult in the dark and miserable in the cold. It was one of those mornings when you keep going because he does and he, no doubt, because you do. By the time we had passed the end of the fixed ropes the sun popped up from behind the South Summit and we awoke to the new day. It was exhilarating to part company with our safety line, for that is after all what fixed ropes are. They facilitate troop movements, but at the same time they do detract from the adventure of the climb. Now at last we were committed and it felt good to be out on our own.

Dougal Haston
There's something surrealistic about being alone high on Everest at this hour. No end to the strange beauty of the experience. Alone, enclosed in a mask with the harsh rattle of your breathing echoing in your ears. Already far in the west behind Cho Oyu a few pale strands of the day and ahead and all around a deep midnight blue with the South Summit sharply, whitely, defined in my line of vision and the always predawn wind picking up stray runners of spindrift and swirling them gently, but not malignantly, around me. Movement was relaxed and easy. As I passed by yesterday's tension points only a brief flash of them came into memory. They were stored for future remembrances, but the today mind was geared for more to come. Not geared with any sense of nervousness or foreboding, just happily relaxed, waiting – anticipating. Signs of life on the rope behind indicated that Doug was following apace and I waited at yesterday's abandoned oxygen cylinders as he came up with the sun, almost haloed in silhouette, uncountable peaks as his background. But no saint this.

"All right, youth?" in a flat Nottingham accent.

"Yeah, yourself?"

A nod and the appearance of a camera for sunrise pictures answered this question, so I tied on the rope and started breaking new ground. The entrance to the couloir wasn't particularly good, but there again it was not outstandingly bad by Himalayan standards, merely knee-deep powder snow with the occasional make-you-think hard patch where there was no snow base on the rock. On the last part before entering the couloir proper there was a longish section of this where we just climbed together relying on each other's ability, rope trailing in between, there being no belays to speak of.

The rope length before the rock step changed into beautiful, hard front-pointing snow ice but the pleasure suddenly seemed to diminish. Leading, my progress started to get slower. By now the signs were well known. I knew it wasn't me. One just doesn't degenerate so quickly. Oxygen again. It seemed early for a cylinder to run out. Forcing it, I reached a stance beneath the rock step. Rucksack off. Check cylinder gauge first. Still plenty left. That's got to be bad. It must be the system. Doug comes up. We both start investigating. Over an hour we played with it. No avail. Strangely enough I felt quite calm and resigned about everything. I say strangely because if the system had proved irreparable then our summit chance would have been ruined. There was only a quiet cloud of disappointment creeping over our heads. Doug decided to try extreme unction. "Let's take it apart piece by piece, kid. There's nothing to lose." I merely nodded as he started prising apart the jubilee clip which held the tube onto the mouthpiece. At last something positive – a lump of ice was securely blocked in the junction. Carving it out with a knife, we tentatively stuck the two points together again, then shut off the flow so we could register oxygen being used. A couple of hard sucks on the mask – that was it. I could breathe freely again.

Doug started out on the rock step, leaving me contemplating the escape we'd just had. I was still thinking very calmly about it, but could just about start to imagine what my feelings of disgust would have been like down below if we'd been turned back by mechanical failure. Self-failure you have to accept, bitter though it can be. Defeat by bad weather also, but to be turned back by failure of a humanly constructed system would have left a mental scar. But now it was upward thinking again. Idly, but carefully, I watched Doug. He was climbing well. Slowly, relaxed, putting in the odd piton for protection. Only his strange masked and hump-backed appearance gave any indication that he was climbing hard rock at 28,000 ft.

Doug Scott

At first I worked my way across from Dougal's stance easily in deep soft snow, but then it steepened and thinned out until it was all a veneer covering the yellow amorphous rock underneath. I went up quite steeply for thirty feet, hoping the front points of my crampons were dug well into the sandy rock underneath the snow. I managed to get in three pegs in a cluster, hoping that one of them might hold, should I fall off. However, the next thirty feet were less steep and the snow lay thicker, which was fortunate seeing as I had run out of oxygen. I reached a stance about a hundred feet above Dougal, and with heaving lungs, I started to anchor off the rope. I pounded in the last of our rock pegs and yelled down to Dougal to come up. Whilst he was jumaring up the rope I took photographs and changed over to my remaining full bottle of oxygen. I left the empty bottle tied on the pegs.

We were now into the South Summit couloir and a way seemed clear to the top of the South West Face. We led another rope length each and stopped for a chat about the route. Dougal's sporting instincts came to the fore – he fancied a direct gully straight up to the Hillary Step. I wasn't keen on account of the soft snow, so he shrugged his shoulders and continued off towards the South Summit. I don't know whether the direct way would have been any less strenuous, but from now on the route to the South Summit became increasingly difficult.

Dougal Haston

The South West Face wasn't going to relax its opposition one little bit. That became very evident as I ploughed into the first rope length above the rock step. I had met many bad types of snow conditions in eighteen years of climbing. Chris and I had once been shoulder-deep retreating from a winter attempt on a new line on the North Face of the Grandes Jorasses. The snow in the couloir wasn't that deep, but it seemed much worse to handle. In the Alps we had been retreating, but now we were trying to make progress. Progress? The word seemed almost laughable as I moved more and more slowly. A first step and in up to the waist. Attempts to move upward only resulted in a deeper sinking motion. Time for new techniques: steps up, sink in, then start clearing away the slope in front like some breast-stroking snow plough and eventually you pack enough together to be able to move a little further and sink in only to your knees. Two work-loaded rope lengths like this brought us to the choice of going leftwards on the more direct line I had suggested to Doug in an earlier moment of somewhat undisciplined thinking. By now my head was in control again and I scarcely gave it a glance, thinking that at the current rate of progress we'd be lucky to make even the South Summit.

It seemed that conditions would have to improve but they didn't. The slope steepened to sixty degrees and I swung rightwards, heading for a rock step in an attempt to get out of this treadmill of nature. No relief for us. The snow stayed the same, but not only was it steeper, we were now on open wind-blown slopes and there was a hard breakable crust. Classic wind slab avalanche conditions. In some kind of maniacal cold anger I ploughed on. There was no point in stopping for belays. There weren't any possibilities. I had a rhythm, so kept the evil stroking upwards with Doug tight on my heels. Two feet in a hole, I'd bang the slope to shatter the crust, push away the debris, move up, sink in. Thigh. Sweep away. Knees. Gain a metre. Then repeat the process. It was useful having Doug right behind, as sometimes, when it was particularly difficult to make progress, he was able to stick two hands in my back to stop me sliding backwards. Hours were flashing like minutes, but it was still upward gain.

Doug Scott

I took over the awful work just as it was beginning to ease off. I clambered over some rocks poking out of the snow and noticed that there was a cave between the rocks and the neve ice – a good bivvy for later perhaps. Just before the South Summit I rested whilst Dougal came up. I continued round the South Summit rock whilst Dougal got his breath. I was crawling on all fours with the wind blowing up spindrift snow all around. I collapsed into a belay position just below the frontier ridge and took in the rope as Dougal came up my tracks. After a few minutes' rest we both stood up and climbed onto the ridge, and there before us was Tibet.

After all those months spent in the Western Cwm over this and two other expeditions now at last we could look out of the Cwm to the world beyond – the rolling brown lands of Tibet in the north and north east, to Kangchenjunga and just below us Makalu and Chomo Lonzo. Neither of us said much, we just stood there absorbed in the scene.

Dougal Haston

The wind was going round the South Summit like a mad maypole. The Face was finished, successfully climbed but there was no calm to give much thought to rejoicing. It should have been a moment for elation but wasn't. Certainly we'd climbed the Face but neither of us wanted to stop there. The summit was beckoning.

Often in the Alps it seems fine to complete one's route and not go to the summit, but in the Himalayas it's somewhat different. An expedition is not regarded as being totally successful unless the top is reached. Everything was known to us about the way ahead. This was the South East ridge, the original Hillary/Tenzing route of 1953. It was reckoned to be mainly snow, without too much technical difficulty. But snow on the ridge similar to the snow in the couloir would provide a greater obstacle to progress than any technical difficulties. There were dilemmas hanging around and question marks on all plans.

My head was considering sitting in the tent sac until sunset or later, then climbing the ridge when it would be, theoretically, frozen hard. Doug saw the logic of this thinking but obviously wasn't too happy about it. No other suggestions were forthcoming from his direction, however, so I got into the tent sac, got the stove going to give our thinking power a boost with some hot water. Doug began scooping a shallow snow cave in the side of the cornice, showing that he hadn't totally rejected the idea.

The hot water passing over our raw, damaged throat linings brought our slide into lethargic pessimism to a sharp halt.

Swinging his pack onto his back Doug croaked, "Look after the rope. I'm going to at least try a rope length to sample conditions. If it's too bad we'll bivouac. If not we carry on as far as possible."

I couldn't find any fault with this reasoning, so grabbed the rope as he disappeared back into Nepal. The way it was going quickly through my hands augured well. Reaching the end Doug gave a "come on" signal. Following quickly, I realized that there were now summit possibilities in the wind. Conditions were by no means excellent, but relative to those in the couloir they merited the title reasonable. There was no need to say anything as I reached Doug. He just stepped aside, changed the rope around and I continued. Savage, wonderful country. On the left the South-West Face dropped away steeply, to the right wild curving cornices pointed the way to Tibet. Much care was needed, but there was a certain elation in our movements. The Hillary Step appeared, unlike any photograph we had seen. No rock step this year, just a break in the continuity of the snow ridge. Seventy degrees of steepness and eighty feet of length. It was my turn to explore again. Conditions reverted to bad, but by now I'd become so inured to the technique that even the extra ten degrees didn't present too much problem.

Doug Scott
As I belayed Dougal up the Hillary Step it gradually dawned upon me that we were going to reach the summit of Big E. I took another photograph of Dougal and wound on the film to find that it was finished. I didn't think I had any more film in my rucksack, for I had left film and spare gloves with the bivvy sheet and stove at the South Summit. I took off my oxygen mask and rucksack and put them on the ridge in front of me. I was seated astride it, one leg in Nepal, the other in Tibet. I hoped Dougal's steps would hold, for I could think of no other place to put his rope than between my teeth as I rummaged around in my sack. I found a cassette of colour film, that had somehow got left behind several days before. The cold was intense and the brittle film kept breaking off. The wind was strong and blew the

snow Dougal was sending down the Nepalese side right back into the air and over into Tibet. I fitted the film into the camera and followed him up. This was the place where Ed Hillary had chimneyed his way up the crevasse between the rock and the ice. Now with all the monsoon snow on the mountain it was well banked up, but with snow the consistency of sugar it looked decidedly difficult.

A wide whaleback ridge ran up the last 300 yards. It was just a matter of trial-breaking. Sometimes the crust would hold for a few steps and then suddenly we would be stumbling around as it broke through to our knees. All the way along we were fully aware of the enormous monsoon cornices, overhanging the 10,000 ft East Face of Everest. We therefore kept well to the left.

It was whilst trail-breaking on this last section that I noticed my mind seemed to be operating in two parts, one external to my head. It warned me somewhere over my left shoulder about not going too far right in the area of the cornice, and it would urge me to keep well to the left. Whenever I stumbled through the crust it suggested that I slow down and pick my way through more carefully. In general it seemed to give me confidence and seemed such a natural phenomenon that I hardly gave it a second thought at the time. Dougal took over the trail-breaking and headed up the final slope to the top – and a red flag flying there. The snow improved and he slackened his pace to let me come alongside. We then walked up side by side the last few paces to the top, arriving there together.

All the world lay before us. That summit was everything and more that a summit should be. My usually reticent partner became expansive, his face broke out into a broad happy smile and we stood there hugging each other and thumping each other's backs. The implications of reaching the top of the highest mountain in the world surely had some bearings on our feelings, I'm sure they did on mine, but I can't say that it was that strong. I can't say either that I felt any relief that the struggle was over. In fact, in some ways it seemed a shame that it was, for we had been fully programmed and now we had to switch off and go back into reverse. But not yet, for the view was so staggering, the disappearing sun so full of colour that the

setting held us in awe. I was absorbed by the brown hills of
Tibet. They only looked like hills from our lofty summit. They
were really high mountains, some of them 24,000 ft high, but
with hardly any snow to indicate their importance. I could see
silver threads of rivers meandering down between them, flowing north and west to bigger rivers which might have included
the Tsangpo. Towards the east, Kangchenjunga caught the
setting sun, although around to the south clouds boiled down
in the Nepalese valleys and far down behind a vast front of black
cloud was advancing towards us from the plains of India. It
flickered lightning ominously. There was no rush, though, for it
would be a long time coming over Everest – time to pick out the
north side route – the Rongphu Glacier, the East Rongphu
Glacier and Changtse in between. There was the North Col,
and the place where, in 1924, Odell, who had climbed to 28,000
feet on the North Face, was standing when he last saw Mallory
and Irvine climbing up toward the summit of Everest. Wonder
if they made it? Their route was hidden by the convex slope – no
sign of them, edge out a bit further – no nothing. Not with all
the monsoon snow, my external mind pointed out.

 The only sign of anyone was the flag; it was some time before
I got round to looking at it. It was an unwelcome intrusion and
there had been more to do than look at manmade objects. Still,
you couldn't help but look at it, seeing as how it was a tripod and
pole nearly five feet high with a rosary of red ribbons attached to
the top. Take a photograph. Ah, yes! Dougal ought to get some
of me. He hadn't taken a single photograph on the whole trip.
"Here you are, youth. Take a snap for my mother." I passed
him my camera. "Better take another one, your glove's in front
of the lens. Now a black and white one." He's never been keen
on photography, but he obliged.

Dougal Haston
We were sampling a unique moment in our lives. Down and
over into the brown plains of Tibet a purple shadow of Everest
was projected for what must have been something like 200
miles. On these north and east sides there was a sense of
wildness and remoteness, almost untouchability. Miraculous
events seemed to be taking place in the region of the sun. One

moment it seemed to dip behind a cloud layer lying a little above the horizon. End Game – thought we. But then the cloud dropped faster than the sun and out it came again. Three times in all. I began to feel like Saul on the road to Tarsus. More materially, right in front of me was an aluminum survey pole with a strip of red canvas attached. The Japanese ladies in the spring hadn't mentioned leaving or seeing anything. Puzzlement for a moment. Then the only answer. There had been a Chinese ascent of the North East Ridge claimed, just after the Japanese ascent. Some doubt, however, had been cast on the validity of this, due to the summit pictures lacking the detail associated with previous summit shots. It was good to have the ultimate proof in front of us. Having to play the doubt game in climbing is never a pleasant experience.

Slowly creeping into the euphoria came one very insistent thought as the sun finally won its race with the clouds and slid over the edge. The thought? Well, we were after all on the top of the world, but it was still a long way back to Camp VI and it was going to be dark very soon and then what would we do? We knew we could get back to the South Summit in the half light. On the previous nights there had been a very bright moon, and it seemed reasonable to assume we could retrace our steps down the Face if this came out. If it didn't, as a last resort we could bivouac. That, after all, was the reason for bringing the tent sac. I'd always reckoned a bivouac possible at such altitude, but that doesn't mean to say I looked upon the project with a great degree of enthusiasm. We finally turned our backs to the summit and set off down.

Our tracks were already freezing up, making the going reasonable. An abseil got rid of the Hillary Step with the rope left in place. Moving together we were soon back at our little cave. Much cloud activity didn't bode well for the appearance of a moon. The oxygen cylinders dribbled out their last drops of usefulness and became mere burdens. Standing vaguely waiting for some light to happen it was good to take off the tanks and mask. Lighter feeling but not lighter-headed. Slowly, as it clouded over, the choices were gradually cut down. We decided to have a look at the possibility of a descent in the dark, knowing the up-trail to be deep and maybe now frozen, but a tentative fifty-foot grope on the South-West Face side of the ridge into the strong night wind with finger and toes going solid finally slammed all the alternative choices to a bivouac out of mind. Dropping back to the sheltered side I told Doug the news. There was nothing really to say. He started enlarging the hole.

Doug Scott

Dougal melted snow on the stove once again whilst I continued digging into the hillside. After we had had a few sips of warm water, Dougal joined me and we quickly enlarged the snow cave, digging away with our ice-axes, pushing the loose snow out through the entrance. By nine o'clock it was big enough to lie down in; we pushed out more snow against the entrance and reduced it to a narrow slit. We were now out of the wind, which was fortunate, as already our oxygen bottles were empty, or our sets had refused to function. The little stove, too, was soon used up. So there we lay on top of our rucksacks and the bivvy sheet, wishing perhaps we had given more thought to the possibility of bivouacking, for we had no food and no sleeping bags. I was wearing only the clothes that I had climbed up in, a silk vest, a wool jumper, a nylon pile suit and my wind suit. I don't think we were ever worried about surviving, for we had read of other climbers who had spent the night out on Everest without much gear, although lower down. However, they had all subsequently had some fingers and toes cut off. What worried us was the quality of survival, and we brought all the strength of our dulled listless minds to bear upon that. I shivered uncontrollably and took off my gloves, boots and socks to rub life back into my extremities for hours at a time. We were so wrapped up in our own personal miseries that we hardly noticed each other, though at one point Dougal unzipped the front of his duvet suit and kindly allowed me to put my bare left foot under his right armpit and my other at his crotch, which seemed to help. Without oxygen there didn't seem to be any internal heat being created, so I mostly sat and rubbed and rubbed my fingers and toes. This was no time for sleep. It needed the utmost vigilance to concentrate on survival, keeping my boots upright out of the snow, keeping the snow off my bare hands and feet, warming my socks against my stomach, keeping my head from brushing snow off the roof of the cave. The temperature was probably – thirty degrees Centigrade. It was so cold that at first when I left a sock on my rucksack the foot of the sock went as stiff as a board. Most of the night I dug away at the cave just to keep warm, hacking away at the back with the ice-axe into the hard snow and pushing it out through the doorway. By the dawn it was to be big enough to sleep five people lying down!

Our minds started to wander with the stress and the lack of sleep and oxygen. Dougal quite clearly spoke out to Dave Clarke. He had quite a long and involved conversation with him. I found myself talking to my feet. I personalized them to such an extent that they were two separate beings needing help. The left one was very slow to warm up, and after conversations with the right one, we decided I had better concentrate on rubbing it hard. And all the time my external mind was putting its spoke in as well.

Dougal Haston
I was locked in suffering silence except for the occasional quiet conversation with Dave Clarke. Hallucination or dream? It seemed comforting and occasionally directed my mind away from the cold. That stopped, and then it was a retreat so far into silence that I seemed to be going to sleep. Shaking awake, I decided to stay this way. We'd heard too many tales of people in survival situations falling asleep and not waking up. It seemed as if we'd both come to this conclusion and Doug's incoherent speech served to keep both awake. There was no escaping the cold. Every position was tried. Holding together, feet in each other's armpits, rubbing, moving around the hole constantly, exercising arms. Just no way to catch a vestige of warmth. But during all this the hours were passing. I don't think anything we did or said that night was very rational or planned. We were suffering from lack of oxygen, cold, and tiredness but we had a terrible will to get through the night; all our survival instincts came right up front. These and our wills saw the night to a successful end.

First light came, and we were able to start the process of preparing for downward movement. Checks showed an ability to stand up and move. Extremities had slight numbness, but no frostbite. Kidney pains were locking us in an almost bent-in-two position. Boots were difficult to get on. I gave up my frozen inner boots and used downfilled boots as a replacement. The sun came up, but with no hope of getting any warmth to our bodies. Movement was the only way, and soon we were across the cornice, saying adieu to Tibet and starting off back down the Face. The warmth of movement was almost orgasmic in its intensity as the blood started recirculating. Aware of the possibilities of lack-of-oxygen hallucinations and their potentially dire effects, we kept a wary eye on each other as we belayed down the first few pitches.

Doug Scott
We had not slept or eaten for nearly thirty hours, we had actually spent the night out in China, and we had done it at 28,700 ft without oxygen. Eventually we made the fixed rope and at 9 a.m. fell into our sleeping bags at Camp VI. I put the stove on and looked around for something to eat and came across the radio. We had been so absorbed in surviving the night and the descent that at times it had all seemed so much like a dream, just the two of us and no one else in the world to share the cold swirling snow. The radio brought us back to reality; it crackled into life. Answering voices – Chris concerned, relieved – happy with the success. Put on a good voice, I thought, don't want to sound slurred, although I felt it. "No, I don't think we are frostbitten," I said, for by then our fingers and toes were tingling.

The quality of survival had been good.

Attack on Kangchenjunga

F. S. Smythe

Frank Smythe was a British mountaineer and the first to climb the Himalayan peak of Kalmet. He was a member of three Everest expeditions (1933, 1936 and 1938) and during the Second World War led the Commando Mountain Warfare School. Here Smythe (1900–49) recalls his part in the dogged German ascent of the avalanche-stricken Kangchenjunga peak of the Sikkim Himalaya in 1930.

On May 10, the day after the accident, Professor Dyhrenfurth, Kurz and Dr Richter arrived from Base Camp, and a conference was held on the situation. "Conference" is perhaps a little misleading. It is a word conjuring up a picture of frock-coated gentlemen seated round a long mahogany table, the highly polished surface of which reflects waistcoats ornamented with gold watch-chains, and earnest countenances on which responsibility and a heavy lunch sit heavily. In the present instance I must ask the reader to imagine the sombre interior of the large porters' tent, the thick canvas of which reduces the light within to a faint depressing green, whilst a pungent reek of smoke struggles with a faint, yet perceptible odour of unwashed bodies that have lain there during the previous night. In the middle a heterogeneous collection of packing cases do duty as a table. Seated on other packing cases are a number of unsavoury looking ragamuffins with unkempt hair, frowsy beards, cracked sun-scorched countenances, and eyes bleared by the snow glare.

The first suggestion made by those who had remained at the Base Camp was that the attack on the ice wall should be renewed, but this was very properly rejected by all those who had shared in the attack. The sole remaining alternative was to attempt the North-West Ridge which rises from the western tributary of the Kangchenjunga Glacier. This ridge ends in a snow and ice terrace beneath the Kangbachen summit, 25,782 ft, of Kangchenjunga. Even supposing the terrace to be reached, however, the most we could hope for was to ascend the Kangbachen summit, as there was no possibility of traversing to the highest summit, as both distance and difficulty were too great. Personally, I must confess to a longing to flee from the mountain altogether, and be able to lie in a sleeping bag at nights and sleep undisturbed by the fear of annihilation from ice avalanches. I suggested, therefore, that we should retire, cross the Jonsong La, and attempt the Jonsong Peak, 24,344 ft high. This idea met with no support, and it was decided to attempt the North-West Ridge. Should we fail, as it seemed certain we must do, judging from appearance, at all events we could ascend the Western Tributary Glacier, explore its head, and possibly climb the Ramthang Peak.

In order to do this, it was decided to move Camp I across the glacier to the foot of the rocky spur separating the Western Tributary Glacier from the glacier falling between the Wedge Peak and the Ramthang Peak. This new site would have the advantage of being considerably safer than the present one, for it was by no means certain that we were safe in the event of an exceptionally large ice avalanche falling from Kangchenjunga or the Twins. This uncertainty was emphasized the same after-noon in a startling fashion.

We were aroused from an after-lunch siesta by the thunder-clap of a great avalanche. We issued from our tents in alarm. Thousands of feet above us on the face of Kangchenjunga masses of hanging glacier were collapsing. Sweeping the pre-cipices with appalling violence, the avalanche crashed down to the glacier, and roared straight across at us.

Huge clouds of snow were raised by the wind blast from the surface of the glacier, and came rushing down upon the camp. They concealed the falling ice, and it was hard to tell whether the camp was safe or not. My own inclination was to run for it, and I was about to bolt precipitately when I saw Duval calmly turning the handle of his cine camera with that sang-froid peculiar to his calling, the tradition of which demands that the handle of a cine camera shall be turned in the face of charging elephants, and at shipwrecks, fires, explosions, earthquakes and other catastrophies. Fired by his example, I pulled out my own folding camera and took a hurried snap. The avalanche resembled the white clouds of some new and deadly form of gas attack. The God of Kangchenjunga is evidently well up in the technique of modern warfare. The roar of the avalanche subsided. We knew that we were safe from ice debris, but the clouds of snow continued to pour down the glacier towards the camp with extraordinary velocity. The next moment a wind blast struck the camp, and a blizzard of snow sent us scuttling into shelter.

The blizzard lasted some minutes, and when it had cleared the upper part of the glacier was seen to be covered in nearly an inch of wind-blown snow. The actual ice debris of the avalanche had stopped well short of the camp, but it had swept quite half a mile down the glacier. This was not the only avalanche; other lesser ones fell, but none of such terrifying dimensions. It was obvious, however, that it was a mere question of volume and momentum whether or not the camp was to be swept away by a future avalanche. If it was a rest day for tired bodies, it was scarcely so for nerve-racked minds.

It was a simple matter moving camp the next day, and the new site on the other side of the glacier was safer than any we had yet discovered. We had not been able to bring down all our equipment from Camp II, so some porters under the charge of Kurz went up to fetch it. Schneider and Duvanel, meanwhile, descended to the Base Camp, the former in order to make a new track up the glacier to our new camp, the latter to develop some cine film. I was left in charge of the evacuation of the old camp, and took the opportunity of donning a pair of skis, and making short runs on the glacier. The snow was excellent and similar to late spring Alpine snow.

The new Camp I was pitched in a fine situation. There was a delightful view northwards up the moraine-stacked Jonsong Glacier winding sinuously up towards the little notch of the Jonsong La. The background was dominated by the rocky mass of the Jonsong Peak. Farther to the east, rose a ridge of icy peaks running northwards from Kangchenjunga and the Twins, from which the Tent Peak, 24,089 ft, rose head and shoulders above everything else. It is as aptly named as the Wedge Peak, for its horizontal summit ridge with its small points at either end resembles a tent, the ridge of which sags between its supporting poles.

Some useful stores arrived from the Base Camp that day, among them being synthetic rubber ground-sheets for the tents. Though light and spongy, and weighing but a pound or so each, the difference they made to our comfort was amazing, and we were able to sleep then and afterwards far more warmly and comfortably than we would have done otherwise, insulated as we were from the snow. There is no question that they are far superior to any ground-sheet, and form an item of equipment that no future Himalayan expedition can afford to leave out, for they induce the sleep which is so essential if climbers are to keep fit.

Relieved by the thought that we were tolerably safe from avalanches, we slept well that night. It would have been wise to have started early the next morning while the snow was still hard from the overnight frost, but we did not get away until the sun had thawed its crust sufficiently to let it break beneath our weight. The obvious route up the Western Tributary Glacier was a trough between the glacier and the rock ridge forming its northern containing wall. The trough was snow-filled for most of its distance, except for one section where a scree slope interposed. These troughs, which form such a convenient line of least resistance up the glaciers of this district are perhaps the only thing vouchsafed by Kangchenjunga which seems to have been intended for the benefit of the long-suffering mountaineer.

Wieland and I, with some porters, were the first to set off. Hoerlin, Kurz, and some more porters were to follow, but at the last moment Kurz, who was again not feeling well, decided to return to the Base Camp.

The snow in the trough was in the worst possible condition. We floundered waist-deep into holes between concealed snow-covered boulders, and wallowed in hollows where the snow was soft and watery. An hour passed; we had made but little progress. I suggested to Wieland that we should leave the trough in favour of the ice-fall of the glacier. In making this suggestion I was actuated by the fact that at one place the trough seemed likely to be swept by falling stones from the cliffs above. Hoerlin, was of a different mind; he would stick to the trough. As things transpired, he was right; the danger was more apparent than real.

Ascending the ice-fall was fatiguing work on account of the soft snow. Snow-shoes eased the porters' labours to some extent, but there were not enough pairs to go round. Considering how broken was the ice, it was remarkable how few crevasses there were, but these few were dangerous ones, subtly concealed. We toiled up and down over hummocks, or threaded our way between pinnacles. The devil of doubt began to gnaw at our hearts; would we be able to get through the ice-fall? The sun beat down upon us mercilessly, and glacier lassitude sapped the strength of sahib and porter alike. At last we saw a sort of corridor leading from the ice-fall into the upper part of the trough. We could see that the trough was perfectly safe, but had it been dangerous, we should still have preferred it to the sweltering gullies and hollows of the ice-fall, for glacier lassitude tends to undermine the judgment and warp the conscience of the mountaineer.

A crevasse barred the way. We stepped gingerly on to a fragile snow bridge. Icicles were dislodged and went tinkling down into the green depths with a noise like the banging together of small chandeliers. The corridor stretched ahead; its smooth, snow floor looked innocuous, but Wieland suddenly disappeared up to his waist in a concealed crevasse: it was merely one of Kangchenjunga's little jokes.

At the top of the trough, where it debouches on to the glacier, above the worst of the ice-fall, there is a short section liable to be swept by ice avalanches from a hanging glacier forming the edge of a snow plateau on the Ramthang Peak. While still within the danger area we were startled by a sudden crash, but all that came down were a few boulders and blocks of ice.

The porters were by now very tired, and they begged us to camp as soon as possible. We promised to do so as soon as we were out of range of ice avalanches. The sun was declining, and evening mists gathering around us as we reached the smooth slopes above the ice-fall, where stretched Hoerlin's straggling track, man's first score on these snow-fields. Here we decided to camp, while Wieland went on with ski to bring down Hoerlin, who had camped some distance farther up the glacier.

The evening was strangely still save for an undercurrent of sound, as though the goblins and witches who haunt the cliffs of Kangchenjunga above were murmuring at our coming. As usual, it was the wind. An upward glance disclosed the snow eddying and swirling from the polished ice cliffs defending the snowy terraces. The sun set calmly. Barely had its last rays faded when they were replaced by silver moon sheen behind the North Ridge of Kangchenjunga. The snow blown off the ridge by the wind was illumined from behind, and Kangchenjunga took to itself a glowing aureole of light. Imperceptibly the upper snow-slopes were resolved from the darkness; ghostlike, unreal, they shimmered far above the world. Mindless of the cold, we stood outside our tents entranced by the glorious spectacle. At long last the laggardly moon peered over the ridge in a shy, self-deprecating sort of way. It seemed to wither and shrivel as it mounted into the frosty sky and its radiance, at first soft and wan, became a hard, cold electric blue. Details stood forth as clearly as in daylight. Only the shadows were black, and in these lurked the darkness of a pit.

The cold gripped us. We crawled into our tents, and with numbed fingers laced-to the flaps. As Sir Leslie Stephen wrote: "Bodily fatigue and an appreciation of natural scenery are simply incompatible." He might have added cold and discomfort.

The sun reached us early the next morning, and we were off betimes. Our first business was to move camp farther up the glacier to a site that would form a convenient upper base for operations against the North-West Ridge. As we marched up the glacier we were able to examine the latter. First impressions are not always accurate and it is never easy to assess the difficulties of a mountainside or ridge at their true worth. As that great mountaineer, Captain J. P. Farrar used to remark:

"You can never tell what rocks are like until you have rubbed your nose against them." Yet, even bearing these things in mind, no ridge I have examined affected me with the same feeling of utter and complete hopelessness as that of the North-West Ridge of Kangchenjunga. Picture a ridge rising 4,000 ft. Thin, trim and whittle down its edges until they are as keen as a Gurkha's *kukri*; then hack deep gaps into these edges and perch rocky towers hundreds of feet high on them. Armour every smooth bit with ice, and mask every ledge with snow, and you will perhaps obtain a faint glimmering of an idea of the North-West Ridge of Kangchenjunga. The ridge attempted by the Munich party is formidable, but it cannot compare to the North-West Ridge. Ice pinnacles alone had to be surmounted on the former; spiky rock pinnacles bar the way on the latter, and between these are some of those extraordinary ice ridges peculiar to the Himalayas. In appearance and sensationalism they are comparable to those on the Wedge Peak. There are the same tottering masses, the same biscuit-like flakes through which the sun gleams, the same extravagant forms, hacked and torn by the wind, lurching and tottering at the behest of gravity, and the same ice flutings to emphasize by their graceful lines the appalling steepness of the slopes they decorate. If we had been forced to attack the ridge from its base, I think we would have relinquished any idea of attempting it at the outset, for the lowest rock towers are hopeless from a climbing point of view. It looked possible, however, to gain the crest of the ridge above these initial pinnacles, by a steep snow-filled couloir about 600 ft high, leading upwards from the glacier to one of the gaps in the crest of the ridge.

Camp was pitched on the glacier, and leaving the porters to make it comfortable we set off to climb the couloir. The lower half was simple; then the angle steepened. It was not difficult, but care had to be taken that the footsteps kicked in the floury snow that masked rock slabs and ice did not collapse. The last hundred feet was very steep. The angle must have exceeded sixty degrees, but we were comforted by the thought that we could fix a rope to facilitate the descent. A small cornice leaned over the summit. The leader, Hoerlin, hacked and flogged it down, and squirmed through and over to the gap, Wieland and

I following one by one. The ascent had taken only forty-five minutes, indicating that we had become well acclimatized to altitude.

My first impression was probably somewhat similar to that experienced by a house-breaker, not a burglar, but one of those phlegmatic gentlemen who stands on the dizzy edges of aged and tottering walls knocking bricks off into space with a pick-axe. But surely no house-breaker has ever stood on top of such an unstable wall as we found ourselves on. A modern £25 down and balance in rent villa could scarcely be more "jerrybuilt" than the place on which we stood. On either side of us the rocks were piled in loose masses needing but a touch to send them crashing down on either side of the ridge below us. On the opposite side of the ridge to that which we had ascended loose yellowish precipices dropped to the head of the Ramthang Glacier. From our gap it appeared possible to descend to the glacier down another steep gully, scarred with falling debris. Such a descent would, however, involve unavoidable dangers. And far above this scene of perpetual decay rose the great ice slopes and ice walls of Kangchenjunga.

Is there any hope of ascending Kangchenjunga from the Ramthang Glacier? The answer must be, no, unless the climber is prepared to take his life, *and* the lives of his porters in his hand. Like the face above the Kangchenjunga Glacier, that above the Ramthang Glacier is defended by enormous walls of ice running across the mountainside. At one point only is there any hope of climbing the *lowest* of these ice walls, and this point is also liable to be swept at any moment by ice avalanches from another and tottering ice wall above. Kangchenjunga was not built for the mountaineer.

Leaving rucksacks and spare rope, we commenced to climb along the unstable ridge. Almost immediately, we were forced off the crest to avoid a decrepit rocky tower. A traverse had to be made on the southern side of the ridge over steep, loose rocks, here and there treacherously covered in snow. It was a place not so much difficult as dangerous. There was not a reliable rock round which a rope could be placed to secure the party, and had a slip occurred, it would in all probability have been attended by the worst results.

From the traverse, an upward ascent brought us into the mouth of a loose gully, the head of which consisted of slippery slabs disagreeably covered by a few inches of unstable scree.

It is curious how on any climb the mental equilibrium of the mountaineer is liable to be upset by bad rock. Difficulty is one thing, danger another. The nerve-stressed mountaineer needing a safety valve for his feelings frequently finds an outlet for them in forceful language. I make no excuses, therefore, for certain improper remarks when clambering up these rocks. I cannot remember what Hoerlin and Wieland said, I had not yet learned the English translation of the German epithets that they held in reserve for such occasions, but once, Hoerlin turned and remarked to me in perfect English, "These rocks are ——!" sentiments which, happily, I was able to return with interest.

The principal advantage of taking photographs on a mountain is that the mountaineer is thus enabled to stop at frequent intervals and recover his breath. That is why most elderly mountaineers carry cameras. Taking a photograph is a much more convincing excuse for a halt than a boot-lace or braces that need adjusting. All those liable to be touched in the wind should take a camera. With what the reader will no doubt consider admirable foresight, I had brought up my camera with me, and not left it at the gap. I was not blown, but the ridge beyond the top of the little gully appeared so uninviting that I decided to stop there and photograph Hoerlin and Wieland doing it.

Seated in a sheltered place, with the sun glancing warmly down upon me, I was able to appreciate the situation to the full. For a short distance the ridge appeared possible, and although extremely loose, not excessively difficult. But beyond the next tower it was very different. It rose abruptly in a huge pinnacle, quite 300 ft high, and above this pinnacle, connecting it to the next pinnacle, was the first of those appalling ice ridges. As I sat there I tried to think of an Alpine ridge comparable to it, but I could think of none. The Peteret, the Brenva, the East Ridge of the Jungfrau, none would fit.

How were porters to be got up? Even supposing ropes were to be fixed the whole way up the smooth slabs of the first great pinnacle, they would not be able to climb with anything but a light load; also we had lost so much rope in the avalanche that we certainly had not enough to spare for even this first pinnacle. There was, however, no necessity for experiencing renewed pessimism. What we were now seeing simply confirmed the opinion that some of us had formed when gazing from the glacier below.

Hoerlin and Wieland were moving slowly and carefully, but even so they could not avoid dislodging many rocks which thundered down the precipices of the Ramthang Glacier. They turned a corner, and disappeared from view, but presently I saw them on the top of another minor pinnacle. There they remained, and I formed the conclusion that they could not advance farther.

The usual mists gathered, but without threatening anything beyond desultory snow flurries. Occasionally, they rolled aside to disclose a beautiful snow mountain, unknown and unnamed in a south-westerly direction, apparently on the ridge separating the Yalung and Ramthang Glaciers. This peak was in shape something like the Ober Gabelhorn, and possessed the same sweeping lines as the graceful Zermatt peak. Jannu should have been visible beyond, but mists obscured it. Almost immediately beneath us was the camp we had just established. We seemed to be looking almost vertically down upon it so steep were the precipices below. It seemed that a jump would have landed us on our tents. Above the camp, the Western Tributary Glacier swept up serenely to the col separating the Ramthang Peak from the first rock towers of the ridge we were on. The Ramthang Peak itself was playing hide-and-seek in a fitful mist but what was visible of it reminded me forcibly of the Monch seen from the Jungfrau Glacier. There were the same graceful lines, the same flowing yet defiant massiveness.

It was late when we returned to camp, where we found Professor Dyhrenfurth, Schneider and Duvanel, who had come up that day from Camp I. I fear none of us was particularly optimistic over the day's work, and it was refreshing to find that Professor Dyhrenfurth did not agree with an opinion that the ridge was hopelessly inaccessible and considered that we should continue with the attack towards the terrace above.

For once, the afternoon clouds, instead of thickening for a snowstorm, dissolved. The evening was a calm and beautiful one, sky and world were unsullied by a single speck of cloud, a profound silence brooded over the sanctuaries of the snows, and only an occasional streamer of wind-blown snow sallied into space from the upper reaches of Kangchenjunga. Slowly night's floods filled the valleys, and the peaks became steeped in gaudy hues, like waxen deities covering their countenances with rouge and lipstick. Imperceptibly, the aerial pageantry died, but its riot of colourings was superseded by an afterglow which released the peaks from night's bonds for a few instants revealing them as cold statues of purest alabaster against a sky of deepest indigo. It was of such a day's end that Mr G. Winthrop Young once wrote:

> When in the hour of mountain peace
> The tumult and the passion cease,
> As the red sunfloods sink,
> And the pale lords of sovereign height,
> Watch the cold armies of the night
> Mustering their first assault.

Who would suspect evil to lurk in such a sunset? Yet, somehow, its superlative colourings put me in mind of a sunset I had once watched from a tiny ledge 12,000 ft up on the south face of Mont Maudit. *That* had been a sunset preceding a heavy snowstorm in which retreat had been no easy matter.

I awoke some hours later to hear the pattering of snow on my tent. In the quietude it sounded like the light tread of fairy feet. Presently I became aware of a faint under-current of sound like the far-off throb of a train down some pastoral valley. The train approached, its distant murmurings rising gradually to a booming crescendo of sound. A gust of wind struck the tent, hurling the snowflakes against it with rude fierce spatterings. The gust passed, but soon came another and stronger gust. In a few minutes the blizzard burst, furiously sweeping upon our encampment. I snuggled more closely into my sleeping bag, for strong though the tent fabric was, it was not entirely proof against this bitter onslaught at a height of 20,000 ft. We had thought to be sheltered by the North-West Ridge, but it afforded no protection, for the wind seemed to pour over it like a cataract, and descend almost vertically upon the camp.

The gusts grew stronger, they wailed and shrilled, rising to a roaring sort of boom like an express train racing through a tunnel. I could feel the tent floor rise as though malicious wind devils were undermining it with the object of my abode flying upwards into space. The wind dug viciously at the sides, or strove with strong fingers to tear apart the flaps, and burst the tent asunder. I prayed that Nemu had driven the pegs firmly and deeply into the snow, and then I recollected that the guy ropes were pitifully thin, no thicker than a sashline. There seemed every possibility of the tent carrying away; if it did, there would be little fun in being overtaken by such a disaster clad only in underclothes, so I struggled out of my sleeping bag, pulled on my climbing clothes, and packed my rucksack with some necessaries.

The storm had now reached a pitch of intensity I had never before experienced when camping, and the night was filled with thunderous volleyings. Sometimes the wind would sink to a mysterious calm, during which it was possible to hear the storm snarling and worrying on the North-West Ridge as a preliminary before gathering its forces for a fresh charge on the camp. It was during one of these temporary lulls that I heard a sort of wailing outside, a wailing more human than storm-like. Peering through the flaps, I could just perceive a figure crawling through the snow. It approached my tent. In the light of my electric torch I saw the white, frightened face of Nagpa, the cook. "Sahib! Sahib!" he cried, "Tent go! Tent go!" Opening the flaps wider, I glanced out, the porters' tent was intact; the cook had merely lost his head. I was unwilling to have him for a bedfellow, and told him to go back. The cook, however, was completely demoralized, and shielding his face from the blast, he crawled down the line of tents with his constant wailing of "Sahib! Sahib! Tent go! Tent go!" Eventually, he found sanctuary with Wieland and Schneider, but as they explained later, they took him in not for love or charity, but simply as additional ballast for their own tent! It was the solitary untoward incident of the storm. Well and truly had our tents been pitched.

An hour or two later the wind began to subside, and ere dawn it withdrew with some last mutters and snarls, leaving a clean sky picked out with stars against which the windy banners of Kangchenjunga softly lit by moonlight streamed in ghostly rivalry to the starry constellations.

We awoke to a warm sun glancing benevolently over the Twins. The North-West Ridge was plastered with new snow, and our steps in the couloir had been obliterated. As there was a possibility of avalanches occurring, we decided not to renew the attempt that day, and devoted the morning to building a wall of snow blocks on the windward side of the camp. Hoerlin was not feeling well; somehow he had contracted a severe chill. Duvanel was also by no means fit, and only his devotion to his cinematographic duties had torn him away from the Base Camp.

At the head of the glacier on the ridge separating the Ramthang Peak from the North-West Ridge of Kangchenjunga is a small point about 20,800 ft high. This Wieland climbed by himself, using ski most of the way, and returned reporting that he had had a splendid view of the Ramthang Glacier and the North-West Ridge. It was decided, therefore, that the whole party should ascend to this point the following day, and carefully examine the latter to see whether it was worth while persisting in the attempt to climb it.

The following morning, May 15, dawned fine. Unfortunately, Hoerlin was so ill that there was no option but for him to return to the Base Camp. This was a serious loss to the climbing party; at the same time, the prospect of getting any distance up the North-West Ridge was so utterly hopeless that it did not really matter.

After the experiences of the past fortnight, it was with something more than relief that we set out to climb something that could be climbed. It has been said that on Everest the climbing party were so heartily "fed up" with the mountain, its weather, and the effects of altitude that their sole wish was to get the job over and done with, no matter who did it. Our attitude towards Kangchenjunga was the same. I do not think there was one of us who was not sick to death of work on the mountain. At exactly what height mountaineering ceases to be pleasurable is not easily defined, the matter is rather one of individual temperament, but I do not think there is one mountaineer who has

climbed on Everest or Kangchenjunga who can honestly say
that he enjoyed the work. Achievement may be good for the
soul, but it is not necessarily enjoyable. It was a relief to turn
away from our exacting opponent for a day and *enjoy* ourselves.

The 20,800 ft point is easily reached along the ridge connecting it to the Ramthang Peak, but from sheer exuberance we
chose to ascend by a little rock face rising from the glacier. We
raced each other up by various routes, and subsided puffing and
blowing on the summit. What a summit it is – one of the most
extraordinary that I have ever stood upon. From the Western
Tributary Glacier it appears a mere knob, an insignificant
excrescence, but had we stood on the Ramthang Glacier we
should have seen an "impossible" peak. Seldom have I gazed
down such abysmal precipices as those falling to the Ramthang
Glacier. They were as long as the south-eastern face of the
Finsteraahorn, and as steep as the Dolomite wall of the Wink-
lerthurm. The seamed and wrinkled surface of the Ramthang
Glacier was spread out beneath us like a relief map, and we
gazed down upon it like pilots from the nose of a bombing
aeroplane. The upper portion of the Ramthang Glacier rises
very steeply in an almost continuous ice-fall. From the col we
had reached in the North-West Ridge we had been separated by
but a few hundred feet from it, but the drop from Point 20,800
must be at least 4,000 ft and as this point is separated from the
col by only about a mile, the inclination of the glacier is a steep
one.

At its extreme head the Ramthang Glacier forms a snowy
plain beneath the west face of the Kangbachen summit of
Kangchenjunga Glacier. This face resembles closely the north
face above the Kangchenjunga Glacier. There are the same
impregnable ice walls stretching across it from which ice avalanches fall at least as big as those that fall from the north face.
At the southern end of the face where it abuts against the main
West Ridge of Kangchenjunga, which separates the head of the
Ramthang Glacier from the Yalung Glacier, there appeared to
be a remote possibility of ascending between the ice walls and
gaining the West Ridge. But, like the route we had already tried
to the North Ridge, the possibility of success was more than
counterbalanced by the possibility of annihilation, for the whole

of the route was liable to be swept at any moment by ice avalanches. Even if the West Ridge was gained, what then? At the best it could only lead to the Kangbachen summit. To traverse the ridge between the Kangbachen summit and the highest summit, over the third highest summit, would be beyond the powers of any party. Therefore, it can be said without hesitation that Kangchenjunga is definitely unassailable from the Ramthang Glacier.

But if this side of Kangchenjunga is disappointing as regards its climbing potentialities it is hardly so otherwise. Great tiers of ice, gleaming steeps, and terrific red granite precipices combine to form a mountain face of a magnificence and grandeur worthy of the high summits it defends.

We had looked upon the last portion of Kangchenjunga to be properly seen by man, and what we had seen but confirmed our opinion that there are no groups of mountain tops defended so impregnably as the "Five Treasures of the Snows". We tore our eyes away from those terrible ice walls and glanced for relief along the winding trench down which flows the Ramthang Glacier, and up over the sea of peaks to the west. Woolly clouds were rising from the valleys and draping themselves about the shoulders of the peaks. Once the cloudy waves rolled back; in a distant trough a great peak rose in noble solitude above the world. Someone said, "Everest". Then the mists closed in, and we saw it no more.

We turned to the North-West Ridge. Our view of it was an end-on one, but if it was impossible to gauge its length, its height and difficulty were apparent. Below us on the glacier was the camp, a mere smudge on the immaculate expanse of snow. The terrace we must gain was 4,000 ft higher. The North-West Ridge was the connecting link. I have already described its knife-like edges of ice and its rocky towers. Seen thus, end on, they were jumbled one against the other, and one gained but little idea of the real length of the ridge. Perhaps it was this that deceived Professor Dyhrenfurth into deciding to continue with the attack. To those used only to Alpine scale, it is easy to be misled by the length of these Himalayan ridges. But if the length was not apparent, the difficulties were, and one could not but wonder how porters were to be got up, and camps established along that tremendous crest. There was no answer to this question. Even supposing the upper ice wall, against which the ridge abutted, to be climbed, and the terrace gained, what next? There was no possibility whatever of reaching any of Kangchenjunga's summits. The terrace did not extend right across the mountain to the North Ridge, there was a cut-off of impassable precipices. At the best, we could only hope to reach the Kangbachen summit, and that was separated from the terrace by 1,500 ft at least of formidable granite precipices. The most we could do was to climb as high as possible, perhaps even as high as the Bavarians, but what was the practical use of that? I fear my companions thought me a pessimist, but what else could one be taking everything into consideration? Anyway, the decision was made. We were to go on. This settled, we sat and lazed two or three hours away in the warm sun, happy hours, but trammelled by the thought of the morrow. The evening mists saw us jogging down the glacier to the camp.

The party that left the next morning consisted of Professor Dyhrenfurth, Schneider, Wieland and myself, with two porters, Lewa and Nima, the last named not to be confused with Nemu, my servant, both experienced Everest men. The couloir was in bad condition, and steps had to be kicked or cut through an upper layer of powdery snow a foot deep. The porters were not happy; neither of them had experienced similar climbing before. Lewa stuck gamely to the task, but Nima was constantly slipping from his steps. I was next to him on the rope, and had several times to hold him. The ridge itself was also in a worse condition than it was during our reconnaissance.

We climbed on two ropes, Schneider, Wieland, and Lewa on the first, and Professor Dyhrenfurth, Nima, and myself on the second. The duty of the second party was to drive in pitons and fix ropes to the rocks. Nima caused us some anxious moments. It made one shudder to see the way he climbed on the loose rocks, hauling himself up on his hands without testing loose holds. So poor a show did he put up that we decided to leave him on a broad and safe part of the ridge, a decision that relieved him as much as it did us. Lewa was, however, an excellent rock climber, and followed Schneider and Wieland without difficulty to the top of the pinnacle, which had been the farthest point reached during the reconnaissance.

From the top of the pinnacle a vertical and holdless slice of granite drops to a gap. The climber must descend the granite slice on the rope, and alight on a sharp edge of snow. A piton was driven into a crack on the pinnacle, and a double rope fixed to it. Schneider and Wieland then descended hand over hand down the fixed rope, while being held at the same time from above on another rope by the remainder of the party. It was the sort of place fiction writers would make much of. Their descriptions would bristle with "unfathomable abysses", "like a fly on a wall", "beetling precipices", and so forth. The mountaineering guide-book writer would, however, describe it simply as "a twenty feet abseil," and as a grudging compliment to the place add "sensational". In this case, however, the fiction writer would convey a better picture to the mind of even the most sophisticated reader than the guide-book writer. To add to the sensationalism might be added the fact that the cracked and disintegrating pinnacle on which we stood exhibited a distinct tremor if rudely handled. I distinctly remember thinking, a trifle morosely, what a grand finale it would make to the expedition if the thing collapsed, and toppled into the "unfathomable abyss" with its human load.

As Wieland swung over the edge, the dirty and battered topi he was accustomed to affect looked strangely incongruous in these surroundings of rock, snow and ice, and, as he bumped and rasped down the rough granite, I half hoped that it would be knocked from his head and go spinning down the precipices, arriving at the camp below a pulped and shapeless mass. No such diversion occurred, and soon he had joined Schneider in the gap on the snow ridge.

Professor Dyhrenfurth and I remained on the pinnacle for an hour or two. We were privileged in witnessing one of the finest feats of climbing we had ever seen. Immediately above the gap rose a semi-detached mass of rock; beyond was another small gap, above which rose the great pinnacle in 300 ft of slabs set at an angle not far removed from the vertical. Ice in the interstices of these slabs had forced them apart in many places and dangerously unstable flakes rested against the face. Every ledge was loaded with snow or ice. On an Alpine climb of exceptional severity the ascent of this pinnacle would be a formidable task; at 20,000 ft it seemed impossible.

Wieland ensconced himself on top of the semi-detached mass, and Schneider descended, without much difficulty, into the secondary gap, and began the ascent of the slabs. Methodically he worked his way upwards. The exertion of hard rock climbing at such an altitude was obviously severe, and after each upward heave he was forced to halt and rest. At length he reached a small stance, a tiny triangular recess, where Wieland joined him. Above this rose a slanting crack formed by the edge of a projecting flake the upper part of which bulged out unpleasantly. It was not a place to linger over, and Schneider did not linger. A foot scrape on the wall, a hand wedged in the crack, a quick upward caterpillar-like movement with naught but tiny hand-holds to prevent a backward topple, and the hardest part had been accomplished. In the silence, unbroken save by an occasional whisper of wind, I could hear the sibilant sucking in of breath by sorely stressed lungs. A few feet more of difficult, but not such exacting climbing brought him to a sloping shelf. Wieland followed, and although burdened by both ice-axes and a rucksack, he came up without relying on the rope.

So far, so good. For a few feet the work was easier; then the slopes steepened once more. In places they were dangerously ice glazed, and their sloping icy shelves were masked by snow. Ice-axes were called into play to clear holds. Now and again loose flakes of rock were dislodged. Hurtling madly down the cliffs they loosed other rocks and sent the echoes thundering.

Two hours' work, 200 ft of ascent, such was the climbing on the great pinnacle. Professor Dyhrenfurth and I watched the struggle with intense interest. It was, probably, the finest piece of rock climbing ever done at such an altitude. We forgot for the moment that the real problem was not the ascent of the ridge by the Europeans but the establishing of camps and the getting up of porters over this gaunt backbone of rock and ice.

The weather restored pessimism, grey mists came flying up from the west, a chill wind sobbed over the ridge, driving before it small moths of snow. Schneider and Wieland were out of sight now. Occasionally we could hear their voices, whilst an occasional stone crashed out news of their advance. We rose, stretched our cramped limbs, tied on Lewa, and started to descend.

We had collected Nima but were still above the col when we were startled by an enormous roar. Millions of tons of ice had broken away from the ice wall and were thundering down to the Ramthang Glacier. Instantly, the whole upper basin of the glacier was filled with a writhing hurricane of snow. Whirling up at us, it enveloped us in a blizzard, that whitened and sheeted our clothes in snow. The sky was darkened; the whole district seemed filled with wind-blown snow dislodged by this monstrous avalanche.

Such an avalanche, had it occurred in the Alps would command widespread attention, newspapers would refer to it as a "Cataclysm of Nature", and questions would be asked in the Swiss Parliament about it. But on Kangchenjunga, such avalanches are not the exception, but the rule – almost an everyday occurrence.

Kangchenjunga is by no means the only Himalayan peak to discharge avalanches of such magnitude, but it is probably safe to say that there is no other Himalayan peak that discharges them with such frequency. This is due, of course, to its great snowfall, the quick downward movement of its glaciers. A good instance of the size of a Himalayan avalanche is that which occurred during the late A. F. Mummery's attempt on Nanga Parbat. The party had bivouacked on a rock rib which projected some 500 ft from the mountainside, but when they returned to their bivouac site after an unsuccessful attempt on the mountain, they found that their gear had been swept away by an ice avalanche. The avalanche had fallen diagonally and taken the 500 ft rib in its stride! The size and destructive power of Himalayan avalanches is the first thing that should be studied when climbing in the Himalayas. A purely Alpine-trained mountaineer finds it difficult to appreciate the scale on which such avalanches occur. Mummery paid the penalty of not realizing this when he made his final and disastrous attempt on Nanga Parbat. No trace of him and his two Gurkha followers was ever discovered. We narrowly missed paying the same penalty too, and had we been wiped out during our attempt to reach the North Ridge of Kangchenjunga, we should have received our just deserts.

It must be remembered that Himalayan ice avalanches *habitually* sweep the whole breadth of glaciers. To illustrate this I can but add that were the peaks in the vicinity of the well-known Concordia Hut in the Bernese Oberland enlarged to Himalayan scale, the mountaineer staying at the hut would not be safe from ice avalanches falling from the peaks on the opposite side of the Aletsch Glacier.

It was a relief to leave the rotten rocks, and to stand once more in the col; and it was pleasant to escape from the cutting wind, and seizing the fixed rope that hung down the steep upper part of the couloir step blithely down the ladder of holds to the camp.

We glissaded down the lower part of the couloir, and for the first time that day Nima's worried expression gave place to a broad grin of delight. The porters are children at heart, and they have all the enthusiasm for a glissade down snow that a child has for a toboggan. For the benefit of the uninitiated I should explain that there are two methods of glissading. One is to stand upright, and the other is to sit down. The former is best employed on hard snow, the latter on soft snow. A certain degree of expertness is necessary for the stand-up glissade. Many commence in elegant style. With ever increasing speed, they slide down the slope. Presently, as the speed becomes faster and faster, they become flustered. From stability, they are reduced to instability; their elegance, their dignified deportment is lost, their balance is upset, they struggle wildly to regain it, then the snow comes up and hits them on the nose. They go head over heels, their ice-axes are snatched from their hands, their hats torn from their heads, their rucksacks wind themselves round their necks, endeavouring to strangle them, snow is forced down their collars, up their sleeves, and into their pockets and trousers. Over and over they go in a series of somersaults, to subside finally at the bottom where they rise to their feet vowing it was good fun.

There is one other variety of glissade worthy of mention, and that is glissading on a rope. This is one degree worse than skiing on a rope. What usually happens is this: the leader, without troubling to enquire whether the second man is ready, shoots off with great velocity, despite the agonized cries of the latter. In a moment or two, the rope tightens on the second man who has barely had time to start, snatching him forward on to his head, and squeezing the breath out of him. The jerk arrests the leader, who hurls an uncomplimentary remark over his shoulder at the unfortunate second man, who meanwhile slides, or somersaults pell-mell past the leader. Then, before the leader has time to continue, he is in his turn dragged in the wake of the second man. And so it goes on, a vicious cycle, until they have reached the bottom, where they sit in the snow roundly abusing one another.

We reached camp in desultory snow squalls. Mists concealed the North-West Ridge, but now and again they blew aside and we scanned the rocks a little anxiously for signs of Schneider and Wieland. It was not until evening that we saw them descending, mere dots silhouetted against the jagged skyline. Dusk was falling when they returned. They reported immense difficulties, difficulties both of rocks and ice. Short of roping the great tower up from top to bottom, there was no possibility of getting the porters up it, and even with ropes, it would most likely prove impossible for laden men. The prospect of farther advance beyond the tower was doubtful in the extreme. The whole crest of the first knife-like ice ridge would have to be hacked away before a passage could be won. At the end of this ridge, there was another tower, not so high as the first, but more difficult, in fact, probably impassable. Its summit was capped by a boss of ice which flowed down its sides like icing on a cake. There was no avoiding this tower, for the precipices on either side were sheer and offered no hope of a traverse. Above this tower, other ice ridges rose, a whole series of them, up to the terrace. Nowhere, said Schneider, was there a place on which a camp might be pitched. There were not even any ice pinnacles of a type suitable for bivouac caves. And the weather? What would be the position of a party caught high up on this great ridge in bad weather or high winds? The storm on the glacier three nights previously had been bad enough, but what would it have been like on the ridge? Retreat would be impossible. It would probably mean two weeks hard work to reach the terrace, even supposing camps could be established, and porters brought up, and by then the monsoon would most likely have broken. Each of these facts taken separately was sufficiently weighty to militate against any attempt.

There was no alternative but to abandon the project, and the following day Wieland and I accomplished the dreary task of collecting and bringing down the fixed ropes. Kangchenjunga had beaten us, beaten us not by bad weather, so much as by sheer difficulty. We had examined every portion of the faces above the Kangchenjunga and Ramthang Glaciers. Nowhere was there a chink in the armour of the giant; nowhere was there a route at which the mountaineer might look and say, "Well, it *might* go." Others sceptical as to the truth of these assertions may follow in our footsteps, but they too will return disappointed, and tremble, even as the ground trembles, at the roar of the great ice avalanches that seek their destruction, and like us, their hope and optimism will be ruthlessly crushed beneath the icy heel of Kangchenjunga.

The Ridge

Tom Hornbein

An American physician and mountaineer, Hornbein was born in 1930. Together with Willi Unsoeld he summitted Everest via the unclimbed West Ridge. They then traversed Everest (another first), to descend the South Ridge. To cap one of mountaineering's greatest exploits, they also survived – like Herman Buhl before them (see pp 218–226) – an emergency bivouac at 8,000 m (26,000 ft). The year was 1963.

A t four the oxygen ran out, a most effective alarm clock. Two well-incubated butane stoves were fished from inside our sleeping bags and soon bouillon was brewing in the kitchen. Climbing into boots was a breathless challenge to balance in our close quarters. Then overboots, and crampons.

"Crampons, in the tent?"

"Sure," I replied, "It's a hell of a lot colder out there."

"But our air mattresses!"

"Just be careful. We may not be back here again, anyway. I hope."

We were clothed in multilayer warmth. The fishnet underwear next to our skin provided tiny air pockets to hold our body heat. It also kept the outer layers at a distance which, considering our weeks without a bath, was respectful. Next came Duofold underwear, a wool shirt, down underwear tops and bottoms, wool climbing pants, and a lightweight wind parka. In spite of the cold our down parkas would be too bulky for difficult climbing, so we used them to insulate two quarts of hot lemonade, hoping they might remain unfrozen long enough to drink during the climb. Inside the felt inner liners of our reindeer-hair boots were innersoles and two pairs of heavy wool socks. Down shells covered a pair of wool mittens. Over our oxygen helmets we wore wool balaclavas and our parka hoods. The down parka-lemonade muff was stuffed into our packs as padding between the two oxygen bottles. With camera, radio, flashlight, and sundry mementos (including the pages from Emerson's diary), our loads came close to 40 lb. For all the prior evening's planning it was more than two hours before we emerged.

I snugged a bowline about my waist, feeling satisfaction at the ease with which the knot fell together beneath heavily mittened hands. This was part of the ritual, experienced innumerable times before. With it came a feeling of security, not from the protection provided by the rope joining Willi and me, but from my being able to relegate those grey brooding forbidding walls, so high in such an unknown world, to common reality – to all those times I had ever tied into a rope before: with warm hands while I stood at the base of sun-baked granite walls in the Tetons, with cold hands on a winter night while I prepared to tackle my first steep ice on Longs Peak. This knot tied me to the past, to experience known, with that which man might do. To weave the knot so smoothly with clumsily mittened hands was to assert my confidence, to assert some competence in the face of the waiting rock, to accept the challenge.

Hooking our masks in place we bade a slightly regretful goodbye to our tent, sleeping bags, and the extra supply of food we hadn't been able to eat. Willi was at the edge of the ledge looking up the narrow gully when I joined him.

"My oxygen's hissing, Tom, even with the regulator turned off."

For the next twenty minutes we screwed and unscrewed regulators, checked valves for ice, to no avail. The hiss continued. We guessed it must be in the valve, and thought of going back to the tent for the spare bottle, but the impatient feeling that time was more important kept us from retracing those forty feet.

"It doesn't sound too bad," I said. "Let's just keep an eye on the pressure. Besides if you run out we can hook up the sleeping T and extra tubing and both climb on one bottle." Willi envisioned the two of us climbing Everest in lockstep, wed by six feet of rubber hose.

We turned to the climb. It was ten minutes to seven. Willi led off. Three years before in a tent high on Masherbrum he had expounded on the importance of knee-to-toe distance for step-kicking up steep snow. Now his anatomical advantage determined the order of things as he put his theory to the test. Right away we found it was going to be difficult. The Couloir, as it cut through the Yellow Band, narrowed to ten or fifteen feet and steepened to fifty degrees. The snow was hard, too hard to kick steps in, but not hard enough to hold crampons; they slid disconcertingly down through this wind-sheltered, granular stuff. There was nothing for it but to cut steps, zigzagging back and forth across the gully, occasionally finding a bit of rock along the side up which we could scramble. We were forced to climb one at a time with psychological belays from axes thrust a few inches into the snow. Our regulators were set to deliver two litres of oxygen per minute, half the optimal flow for this altitude. We turned them off when we were belaying to conserve the precious gas, though we knew that the belayer should always be kept at peak alertness in case of a fall.

We crept along. My God, I thought, we'll never get there at this rate. But that's as far as the thought ever got. Willi's leads were meticulous, painstakingly slow and steady. He plugged tirelessly on, deluging me with showers of ice as his axe carved each step. When he ran out the hundred feet of rope he jammed his axe into the snow to belay me. I turned my oxygen on to "2" and moved up as far as I could, hoping to save a few moments of critical time. By the time I joined him I was completely winded, gasping for air, and sorely puzzled about why. Only late in the afternoon, when my first oxygen bottle was still going strong, did I realize what a low flow of gas my regulator was actually delivering.

Up the tongue of snow we climbed, squeezing through a passage where the walls of the Yellow Band closed in, narrowing the Couloir to shoulder width.

In four hours we had climbed only 400 ft. It was 11 a.m. A rotten bit of vertical wall forced us to the right onto the open face. To regain the Couloir it would be necessary to climb this sixty-foot cliff, composed of two pitches split by a broken snow-covered step.

"You like to lead this one?" Willi asked.

With my oxygen off I failed to think before I replied, "Sure, I'll try it."

The rock sloped malevolently outward like shingles on a roof – rotten shingles. The covering of snow was no better than the rock. It would pretend to hold for a moment, then suddenly shatter and peel, cascading down on Willi. He sank a piton into the base of the step to anchor his belay.

I started up around the corner to the left, crampon points grating on rusty limestone. Then it became a snowplowing procedure as I searched for some sort of purchase beneath. The pick of my axe found a crack. Using the shaft for gentle leverage, I moved carefully onto the broken strata of the step. I went left again, loose debris rolling under my crampons, to the base of the final vertical rise, about eight feet high. For all its steepness, this was a singularly poor plastering job, nothing but wobbly rubble. I searched about for a crack, unclipped a big angle piton from my sling, and whomped it in with the hammer. It sank smoothly, as if penetrating soft butter. A gentle lift easily extracted it.

"Hmmm. Not so good," I mumbled through my mask. On the fourth try the piton gripped a bit more solidly. Deciding not to loosen it by testing, I turned to the final wall. Its steepness threw my weight out from the rock, and my pack became a downright hindrance. There was an unlimited selection of handholds, mostly portable. I shed my mittens. For a few seconds the rock felt comfortably reassuring, but cold. Then not cold anymore. My eyes tried to direct sensationless fingers. Flakes peeled out beneath my crampons. I leaned out from the rock to move upward, panting like a steam engine. Damn it, it'll go; I know it will, T, I thought. My grip was gone. I hadn't thought to turn my oxygen up.

"No soap," I called down. "Can't make it now. Too pooped."

"Come on down. There may be a way to the right."

I descended, half rappeling from the piton, which held. I had spent the better part of an hour up there. A hundred feet out we looked back. Clearly we had been on the right route, for above the last little step the gully opened out. A hundred feet higher the Yellow Band met the grey of the summit limestone. It had to get easier.

"You'd better take it, Willi. I've wasted enough time already."

"Hell, if you couldn't make it, I'm not going to be able to do it any better."

"Yes you will. It's really not that hard. I was just worn out from putting that piton in. Turn your regulator clear open, though."

Willi headed up around the corner, moving well. In ten minutes his rope was snapped through the high piton. Discarding a few unsavoury holds, he gripped the rotten edge with his unmittened hands. He leaned out for the final move. His pack pulled. Crampons scraped, loosing a shower of rock from beneath his feet. He was over. He leaned against the rock, fighting for his breath.

"Man, that's work. But it looks better above."

Belayed, I followed, retrieved the first piton, moved up, and went to work on the second. It wouldn't come. "Guess it's better than I thought," I shouted. "I'm going to leave it." I turned my oxygen to four litres, leaned out from the wall, and scrambled up. The extra oxygen helped, but it was surprising how breathless such a brief effort left me.

"Good lead," I panted. "That wasn't easy."

"Thanks. Let's roll."

Another rope length and we stopped. After six hours of hiss Willi's first bottle was empty. There was still a long way to go, but at least he could travel ten pounds lighter without the extra cylinder. Our altimeter read 27,900. We called Base on the walkie-talkie.

Willi: West Ridge to Base. West Ridge to Base. Over.

Base (Jim Whittaker, excitedly): This is Base here, Willi. How are you? How are things going? What's the word up there? Over.

Willi: Man, this is a real bearcat! We are nearing the top of the Yellow Band and it's mighty tough. It's too damned tough to try to go back. It would be too dangerous.

Base (Jim): I'm sure you're considering all about your exits. Why don't you leave yourself an opening? If it's not going to pan out, you can always start your way down. I think there is always a way to come back.

Willi: Roger, Jim. We're counting on a further consultation in about two or three hundred feet. It should ease up by then! Goddammit, if we can't start moving together, we'll have to move back down. But it should be easier once the Yellow Band is passed. Over.

Base (Jim): Don't work yourself up into a bottleneck, Willi. How about rappeling? Is that possible, or don't you have any *reepschnur* or anything? Over.

Willi: There are no rappel points, Jim, absolutely no rappel points. There's nothing to secure a rope to. So it's up and over for us today . . .

While the import of his words settled upon those listening 10,000 ft below, Willi went right on:

Willi (continuing): . . . and we'll probably be getting in pretty late, maybe as late as seven or eight o'clock tonight.

As Willi talked, I looked at the mountain above. The slopes looked reasonable, as far as I could see, which wasn't very far. We sat at the base of a big, wide-open amphitheatre. It looked like summits all over the place. I looked down. Descent was totally unappetizing. The rotten rock, the softening snow, the absence of even tolerable piton cracks only added to our desire to go on. Too much labour, too many sleepless nights, and too many dreams had been invested to bring us this far. We couldn't come back for another try next weekend. To go down now, even if we could have, would be descending to a future marked by one huge question: what might have been? It would not be a matter of living with our fellow man, but simply living with ourselves, with the knowledge that we had had more to give.

I listened, only mildly absorbed in Willi's conversation with Base, and looked past him at the convexity of rock cutting off our view of the gully we had ascended. Above – a snowfield, grey walls, then blue-black sky. We were committed. An invisible barrier sliced through the mountain beneath our feet, cutting us from the world below. Though we could see through, all we saw was infinitely remote. The ethereal link provided by our radio only intensified our separation. My wife and children seemed suddenly close. Yet home, life itself, lay only over the top of Everest and down the other side. Suppose we fail? The thought brought no remorse, no fear. Once entertained, it hardly seemed even interesting. What now mattered most was right here: Willi and I, tied together on a rope, and the mountain, its summit not inaccessibly far above. The reason we had come was within our grasp. We belonged to the mountain and it to us. There was anxiety, to be sure, but it was all but lost in a feeling of calm, of pleasure at the joy of climbing. That we couldn't go down only made easier that which we really wanted to do. That we might not get there was scarcely conceivable.

Willi was still talking.

Willi: Any news of Barrel and Lute? Over.

Jim: I haven't heard a word from them. Over.

Willi: How about Dingman?

Jim: No word from Dingman. We've heard nothing at all.

Willi: Well listen, if you do get hold of Dingman, tell him to put a light in the window because we're headed for the summit, Jim. We can't possibly get back to our camp now. Over.

I stuffed the radio back in Willi's pack. It was 1 p.m. From here we could both climb at the same time, moving across the last of the yellow slabs. Another 100 ft and the Yellow Band was below us. A steep tongue of snow flared wide, penetrating the grey strata that capped the mountain. The snow was hard, almost ice-hard in places. We had only to bend our ankles, firmly plant all twelve crampon points, and walk uphill. At last, we were moving, though it would have appeared painfully slow to a distant bystander.

As we climbed out of the Couloir the pieces of the puzzle fell into place. That snow rib ahead on the left skyline should lead us to the Summit Snowfield, a patch of perpetual white clinging to the North Face at the base of Everest's final pyramid. By three we were on the Snowfield. We had been climbing for eight hours and knew we needed to take time to refuel. At a shaly outcrop of rock we stopped for lunch. There was a decision to be made. We could either cut straight up the north-east ridge and follow it west to the summit, or we could traverse the face and regain the West Ridge. From where we sat, the Ridge looked easier. Besides, it was the route we'd intended in the first place.

We split a quart of lemonade that was slushy with ice. In spite of its down parka wrapping, the other bottle was already frozen solid, as were the kippered snacks. They were almost tasteless but we downed them more with dutiful thoughts of calories than with pleasure.

To save time we moved together, diagonalling upward across downsloping slabs of rotten shale. There were no possible stances from which to belay each other. Then snow again, and Willi kicked steps, fastidiously picking a route between the outcropping of rocks. Though still carting my full load of oxygen bottles, I was beginning to feel quite strong. With this excess energy came impatience, and an unconscious anxiety over the high stakes for which we were playing and the lateness of the day. Why the hell is Willi going so damned slow? I thought. And a little later: He should cut over to the Ridge now; it'll be a lot easier.

I shouted into the wind, "Hold up, Willi!" He pretended not to hear me as he started up the rock. It seemed terribly important to tell him to go to the right. I tugged on the rope. "Damn it, wait up, Willi!" Stopped by a taut rope and an unyielding Hornbein, he turned, and with some irritation anchored his axe while I hastened to join him. He was perched, through no choice of his own, in rather cramped, precarious quarters. I sheepishly apologized.

We were on rock now. One rope length, crampons scraping, brought us to the crest of the West Ridge for the first time since we'd left Camp 4W yesterday morning. The South Face fell 8,000 ft to the tiny tents of Advanced Base. Lhotse, straight across the face, was below us now. And near at hand 150 feet higher, the South Summit of Everest shone in the afternoon sun. We were within 400 ft of the top! The wind whipped across the ridge from the north at nearly sixty miles an hour. Far below, peak shadows reached long across the cloud-filled valleys. Above, the Ridge rose, a twisting, rocky spine.

We shed crampons and overboots to tackle this next rocky bit with the comforting grip of cleated rubber soles. Here I unloaded my first oxygen bottle though it was not quite empty. It had lasted ten hours, which obviously meant I'd be getting a lower flow than indicated by the regulator. Resisting Willi's suggestion to drop the cylinder off the South Face, I left it for some unknown posterity. When I resaddled 10 lb lighter, I felt I could float to the top.

The rock was firm, at least in comparison with our fare thus far. Climbing one at a time, we experienced the joy of delicate moves on tiny holds. The going was a wonderful pleasure, almost like a day in the Rockies. With the sheer drop to the Cwm beneath us, we measured off another four rope lengths. Solid rock gave way to crud, then snow. A thin, firm, knife-edge of white pointed gently toward the sky. Buffeted by the wind, we laced our crampons on, racing each other with rapidly numbing fingers. It took nearly twenty minutes. Then we were off again, squandering oxygen at three litres per minute since time seemed the shorter commodity at the moment. We moved together, Willi in front. It seemed almost as if we were cheating, using oxygen; we could nearly run this final bit.

Ahead the North and South ridges converged to a point. Surely the summit wasn't that near? It must be off behind. Willi stopped. What's he waiting for, I wondered as I moved to join him. With a feeling of disbelief I looked up. Forty feet ahead tattered and whipped by the wind was the flag Jim had left three weeks before. It was 6.15. The sun's rays sheered horizontally across the summit. We hugged each other as tears welled up, ran down across our oxygen masks, and turned to ice.

Just rock, a dome of snow, the deep blue sky, and a hunk of orange-painted metal from which a shredded American flag cracked in the wind. Nothing more. Except two tiny figures walking together those last few feet to the top of the earth.

For twenty minutes we stayed there. The last brilliance of the day cast the shadow of our summit on the cloud . . . plain a hundred miles . . . to the east. Valleys were filled with the indistinct purple haze of evening, concealing the dwellings of man we knew were there. The chill roar of wind made speaking difficult, heightened our feeling of remoteness. The flag left there seemed a feeble gesture of man that had no purpose but to accentuate the isolation. The two of us who had dreamed months before of sharing this moment were linked by a thin line of rope, joined in the intensity of companionship to those inaccessibly far below, Al and Barry and Dick – and Jake.

From a pitch of intense emotional and physical drive it was only partly possible to become suddenly, completely the philosopher of a balmy afternoon. The head of steam was too great, and the demands on it still remained. We have a long way to go to get down, I thought. But the prospect of descent of an unknown side of the mountain in the dark caused me less anxiety than many other occasions had. I had a blind, fatalistic faith that, having succeeded in coming this far, we could not fail to get down. The moment became an end in itself.

There were many things savoured in this brief time. Even with our oxygen turned off we had no problem performing those summit obeisances, photographing the fading day (it's a wonderful place to be for sunset photographs), smiling behind our masks for the inevitable "I was there" picture. Willi wrapped the kata given him by Ang Dorje about the flag pole and planted Andy Bakewell's crucifix alongside it in the snow; Lhotse and Makalu, below us, were a contrast of sun-blazed snow etched against the darkness of evening shadow. We felt the lonely beauty of the evening, the immense roaring silence of the wind, the tenuousness of our tie to all below. There was a hint of fear, not for our lives, but of a vast unknown which pressed upon us. A fleeting disappointment – that after all those dreams and questions this was only a mountaintop – gave way to the suspicion that maybe there was something more, something beyond the three-dimensional form of the moment. If only it could be perceived.

But it was late. The memories had to be stored, the meaning taken down. The question of why we had come was not now to be answered, yet something up here must yield an answer, something only dimly felt, comprehended by senses reaching farther yet than the point on which we stood; reaching for understanding, which hovered but a few steps higher. The answers lay not on the summit of Everest, nor in the sky above it, but in the world to which we belonged and must now return.

Footprints in the snow told that Lute and Barrel had been here. We'd have a path to follow as long as light remained.

"Want to go first?" Willi asked. He began to coil the rope.

Looking down the corniced edge, I thought of the added protection of a rope from above. "Doesn't matter, Willi. Either way."

"OK. Why don't I go first then?" he said, handing me the coil. Paying out the rope as he disappeared below me I wondered, Is Unsoeld tired? It was hard to believe. Still he'd worked hard; he had a right to be weary. Starting sluggishly, I'd felt stronger as we climbed. So now we would reverse roles. Going up had been pretty much Willi's show; going down would be mine. I dropped the last coil and started after him.

Fifty feet from the top we stopped at a patch of exposed rock. Only the summit of Everest, shining pink, remained above the shadow sea. Willi radioed to Maynard Miller at Advance Base that we were headed for the South Col. It was 6.35 p.m.

We almost ran along the crest, trusting Lute and Barrel's track to keep us a safe distance from the cornice edge. Have to reach the South Summit before dark, I thought, or we'll never find our way. The sun dropped below the jagged horizon. We didn't need goggles any more. There was a loud hiss as I banged against the ice wall. Damn! Something's broken. I reached back and turned off the valve. Without oxygen, I tried to keep pace with the rope disappearing over the edge ahead. Vision dimmed, the ground began to move. I stopped till things cleared, waved my arms and shouted into the wind for Willi to hold up. The taut rope finally stopped him. I tightened the regulator, then turned the oxygen on. No hiss! To my relief it had only been jarred loose. On oxygen again, I could move rapidly. Up twenty feet, and we were on the South Summit. It was 7.15.

Thank God for the footprints. Without them, we'd have had a tough time deciding which way to go. We hurried on, facing outward, driving our heels into the steep snow. By 7.30 it was dark. We took out the flash-light and resumed the descent. The batteries, dregs of the Expedition, had not been helped by our

session with Emerson's diary the night before; they quickly
faded. There was pitiful humour as Willi probed, holding the
light a few inches off the snow to catch some sign of tracks. You
could order your eyes to see, but nothing in the blackness
complied.

We moved slowly now. Willi was only a voice and an occasional faint flicker of light to point the way. No fear, no worry,
no strangeness, just complete absorption. The drive which had
carried us to a nebulous goal was replaced by simple desire for
survival. There was no time to dwell on the uniqueness of our
situation. We climbed carefully, from years of habit. At a rock
outcrop we paused. Which way? Willi groped to the right along
a corniced edge. In my imagination, I filled in the void.

"No tracks over here." Willi called

"Maybe we should dig in for the night."

"I don't know. Dave and Girmi should be at six."

We shouted into the night, and the wind engulfed our call. A
lull. Again we shouted. "Helloooo," the wind answered. Or was
it the wind?

"Hellooo," we called once more.

"Hellooo," came back faintly. That wasn't the wind!

"To the left, Willi."

"OK, go ahead."

In the blackness I couldn't see my feet. Each foot groped
cautiously, feeling its way down, trusting to the pattern set by
its predecessor. Slowly left, right, left, crampons biting into the
snow, right, left . . .

"*Willeeee!*" I yelled as I somersaulted into space. The rope
came taut, and with a soft thud I landed.

"Seems to be a cornice there," I called from beneath the wall.
"I'll belay you from here."

Willi sleepwalked down the edge. The dim outline of his foot
wavered until it met my guiding hand. His arrival lacked the
flair of my descent. It was well that the one of lighter weight had
gone first.

Gusts buffeted from all directions, threatening to dislodge us
from the slope. Above a cliff we paused, untied, cut the rope in
half, and tied in again. It didn't help; even five feet behind I
couldn't see Willi. Sometimes the snow was good, sometimes it

was soft, sometimes it lay shallow over rocks so we could only drive our axes in an inch or two. With these psychological belays, we wandered slowly down, closer to the answering shouts. The wind was dying, and so was the flashlight, now no more than an orange glow illuminating nothing. The stars, brilliant above, cast no light on the snow. Willi's oxygen ran out. He slowed, suddenly feeling much wearier.

The voices were close now. Were they coming from those two black shapes in the snow? Or were those rocks?

"Shine your lights down here," a voice called.

"Where? Shine yours up here," I answered.

"Don't have one," came the reply.

Then we were with them – not Dave and Girmi, but Lute and Barrel. They were near exhaustion, shivering lumps curled on the snow. Barrel in particular was far gone. Anxious hungering for air through the previous night, and the near catastrophe when their tent caught fire in the morning, had left him tired before they even started. Determination got him to the top, but now he no longer cared. He only wanted to be left alone. Lute was also tired. Because of Barrel's condition he'd had to bear the brunt of the climbing labour. His eyes were painfully burned, perhaps by the fire, perhaps by the sun and wind. From sheer fatigue they had stopped thinking. Their oxygen was gone, except for a bit Lute had saved for Barrel; but they were too weak to make the change.

At 9.30 we were still 1,000 ft above Camp VI. Willi sat down in the snow, and I walked over to get Lute's oxygen for Barrel. As I unscrewed Lute's regulator from the bottle, he explained why they were still there. Because of the stove fire that had sent them diving from the tent, they were an hour late in starting. It was 3.30 p.m. when they reached the summit. Seeing no sign of movement down the west side, they figured no one would be any later than they were. At 4.15 they started down. Fatigue slowed their descent. Just after dark they stopped to rest and were preparing to move when they heard shouts. Dave and Girmi, they thought. No – the sounds seemed to be coming from above. Willi and Tom! So they waited, shivering.

I removed Barrel's regulator from his empty bottle and screwed it into Lute's. We were together now, sharing the support so vigorously debated a week before. Lute would know the way back to their camp, even in the dark. All we had to do was help them down. Fumbling with unfeeling fingers, I tried to attach Barrel's oxygen hose to the regulator. Damn! Can't make the connection. My fingers scraped uncoordinatedly against the cold metal. Try again. There it goes. Then, quickly, numb fingers clumsy, back into mittens. Feeling slowly returned, and pain. Then, the pain went and the fingers were warm again.

Willi remembered the Dexedrine I had dropped into my shirt pocket the evening before. I fished out two pills – one for Barrel and one for Lute. Barrel was better with oxygen, but why I had balked at his communal use of Lute's regulator, I cannot say. Lack of oxygen? Fatigue? it was fifteen hours since we'd started the climb. Or was it that my thoughts were too busy with another problem? We had to keep moving or freeze.

I led off. Lute followed in my footsteps to point out the route. Lost in the darkness sixty feet back on our ropes, Willi and Barrel followed. The track was more sensed than seen, but it was easier now, not so steep. My eyes watered from searching for the black holes punched in the snow by Lute's and Barrel's axes during their ascent. We walked to the left of the crest, three feet down, ramming our axes into the narrow edge. Thirty feet, and the rope came taut as Barrel collapsed in the snow, bringing the entire caravan to a halt. Lute sat down behind me. Got to keep moving. We'll never get there.

We had almost no contact with the back of the line. When the rope came taut, we stopped, when it loosened we moved on. Somewhere my oxygen ran out, but we were going too slow for me to notice the difference. Ought to dump the empty bottle, I thought, but it was too much trouble to take off my pack.

Heat lightning flashed along the plains to the east, too distant to light our way. Rocks that showed in the snow below seemed to get no closer as the hours passed. Follow the axe holes. Where'd they go? Not sure. There's another.

"Now where, Lute?"

"Can't see, Tom," Lute said. "Can't see a damn thing. We've got to turn down a gully between some rocks."

"Which gully. There's two or three."

"Don't know, Tom."

"Think, Lute. Try to remember. We've got to get to six."

"I don't know. I just can't see."

Again and again I questioned, badgering, trying to extract some hint. But half blind and weary, Lute had no answer. We plodded on. The rocks came closer.

Once the rope jerked tight, nearly pulling me off balance. Damn! What's going on? I turned and looked at Lute's dim form lying on the snow a few feet further down the Kangshung Face. His fall had been effectively if uncomfortably arrested when his neck snagged the rope between Willi and me.

We turned off the crest, toward the rocks. Tongues of snow pierced the cliffs below. But which one? It was too dangerous to plunge on. After midnight we reached the rocks. It had taken nearly three hours to descend 400 ft, maybe fifteen minutes' worth by daylight.

Tired. No hope of finding camp in the darkness. No choice but to wait for day. Packs off. Willi and I slipped into our down parkas. In the dark, numb fingers couldn't start the zippers. We settled to the ground, curled as small as possible atop our pack frames. Lute and Barrel were somewhere behind, apart, each alone. Willi and I tried hugging each other to salvage warmth, but my uncontrollable shivering made it impossible.

The oxygen was gone, but the mask helped a little for warmth. Feet, cooling, began to hurt. I withdrew my hands from the warmth of my crotch and loosened crampon binding and boot laces, but my feet stayed cold. Willi offered to rub them. We removed boots and socks and planted both my feet against his stomach. No sensation returned.

Tired by the awkward position, and frustrated by the result, we gave up. I slid my feet back into socks and boots, but couldn't tie them. I offered to warm Willi's feet. Thinking that his freedom from pain was due to high tolerance of cold, he declined. We were too weary to realize the reason for his comfort.

The night was overpoweringly empty. Stars shed cold un-shimmering light. The heat lightning dancing along the plains spoke of a world of warmth and flatness. The black silhouette of Lhotse lurked half sensed, half seen, still below. Only the ridge on which we were rose higher, disappearing into the night, a last lonely outpost of the world.

Mostly there was nothing. We hung suspended in a timeless void. The wind died, and there was silence. Even without wind it was cold. I could reach back and touch Lute or Barrel lying head to toe above me. They seemed miles away.

Unsignalled, unembellished, the hours passed. Intense cold penetrated, carrying with it the realization that each of us was completely alone. Nothing Willi could do for me or I for him. No team now, just each of us, imprisoned with his own discomfort, his own thoughts, his own will to survive.

Yet for me, survival was hardly a conscious thought. Nothing to plan, nothing to push for, nothing to do but shiver and wait for the sun to rise. I floated in a dreamlike eternity, devoid of plans, fears, regrets. The heat lightning, Lhotse, my companions, discomfort, all were there – yet not there. Death had no meaning, nor, for that matter, did life. Survival was no concern, no issue. Only a dulled impatience for the sun to rise tied my formless thoughts to the future.

About 4.00 the sky began to lighten along the eastern rim, baring the bulk of Kangchenjunga. The sun was slow in following, interminably slow. Not till after 5.00 did it finally come, its light streaming through the South Col, blazing yellow across the Nuptse Wall, then onto the white wave crest of peaks far below. We watched as if our own life was being born again. Then as the cold yellow light touched us, we rose. There were still miles to go.

The rest is like a photograph with little depth of field, the focused moments crystal sharp against a blurred background of fatigue. We descended the gully I had been unable to find in the dark. Round the corner, Dave and Girmi were coming toward us. They thought they heard shouts in the night and had started up, but their own calls were followed only by silence. Now as they came in search of the bodies of Lute and Barry they saw people coming down – not just two, but four. Dave puzzled a moment before he understood.

The tents at Camp VI – and we were home from the mountain. Nima Dorje brought tea. We shed boots. I started blankly at the marble-white soles of Willi's feet. They were cold and hard as ice. We filled in Emerson's diary for the last time, then started down.

With wind tearing snow from its rocky plain, the South Col was as desolate and uninviting as it had always been described. We sought shelter in the tents at Camp V for lunch, then emerged into the gale. Across the Geneva Spur, out of the wind, onto the open sweep of the Lhotse Face we plodded in sombre procession. Dave led gently, patiently; the four behind rocked along, feet apart to keep from falling. Only for Willi and me was this side of the mountain new. Like tourists we looked around, forgetting fatigue for a moment.

At Camp IV we stopped to melt water, then continued with the setting sun, walking through dusk into darkness as Dave guided us among crevasses, down the Cwm. It was a mystery to me how he found the way. I walked along at the back, following the flashlight. Sometimes Willi stopped and I would nearly bump into him. We waited while Dave searched, then moved on. No one complained.

At 10.30 p.m. we arrived at Advance Base. Dick, Barry, and Al were down from the Ridge, waiting. Frozen feet and Barrel's hands were thawed in warm water. Finally to bed, after almost two days. Short a sleeping bag, Willi and I shared one as best we could.

May 24 we were late starting, tired. Lute, Willi, and Barrel walked on thawed feet. It was too dangerous to carry them down through the Icefall. Willi, ahead of me on the rope, heeled down like an awkward clown. The codeine wasn't enough to prevent cries of pain when he stubbed his toes against the snow. I cried as I walked behind, unharmed.

At Camp I Maynard nursed us like a mother hen, serving us water laboriously melted from ice samples drilled from the glacier for analysis. Then down through the Icefall, past Jake's grave – and a feeling of finality. It's all done. The dream's finished.

No rest. The next day, a grim grey one, we departed Base. From low-hanging clouds wet snow fell. Willi, Barrel, and Lute were loaded aboard porters to be carried down over the rocky moraine. It was easier walking.

At Gorak Shep we paused. On a huge boulder a Sherpa craftsman had patiently carved:

IN MEMORY OF JOHN E. BREITENBACH,
AMERICAN MOUNT EVEREST EXPEDITION, 1963.

Clouds concealed the mountain that was Jake's grave.

As we descended, the falling snow gave way to a fine drizzle. There was nothing to see; just one foot, then another. But slowly a change came, something that no matter how many times experienced, is always new, like life. It was life. From ice and snow and rock, we descended to a world of living things, of green – grass and trees and bushes. There was no taking it for granted. Spring had come, and even the grey drizzle imparted a wet sheen to all that grew. At Pheriche flowers bloomed in the meadows.

Lying in bed, Willi and I listened to a sound that wasn't identifiable, so foreign was it to the place – the chopping whir as a helicopter circled, searching for a place to light. In a flurry of activity Willi and Barrel were loaded aboard. The helicopter rose from the hilltop above the village and dipped into the distance. The chop-chop-chop of the blades faded, until finally the craft itself was lost in the massive backdrop. The departure was too unreal, too much a part of another world, to be really comprehended. Less than five days after they had stood on the summit of Everest, Barrel and Willi were back in Kathmandu. For them the Expedition was ended. Now all that remained was weeks in bed, sitting, rocking in pain, waiting for toes to mummify to the time for amputation.

Up over barren passes made forbidding by mist and a chill wind, we travelled. Hard work. Then down through forests of rain-drenched rhododendrons, blossoming pastels of pink and lavender. Toes hurt. Two weeks to Kathmandu. Feet slipped on the muddy path. Everything was wet.

We were finished. Everest was climbed; nothing to push for now. Existence knew only the instant, counting steps, falling asleep each time we stopped to rest beside the trail. Lester, Emerson, and I talked about motivation; for me it was all gone. It was a time of relaxation, a time when senses were turned to perceive, but nothing was left to give.

Pleasure lay half-hidden beneath discomfort, fatigue, loneliness. Willi was gone. The gap where he had been was filled with question: Why hadn't I known that his feet were numb? Surely I could have done something, if only . . . I was too weary to know the question couldn't be resolved. Half of me seemed to have gone with him; the other half was isolated from my companion by an experience I couldn't share and by the feeling that something was ending that had come to mean too much. Talk of home, of the first evening in the Yak and Yeti Bar, of the reception that waited, was it really so important? Did it warrant the rush?

We'd climbed Everest. What good was it to Jake? To Willi, to Barrel? To Norman, with Everest all done now? And to the rest of us? What waits? What price less tangible than toes? There must be something more to it than toiling over the top of another, albeit expensive, mountain. Perhaps there was something of the nobility-that-is-man in it somewhere, but it was hard to be sure.

Yes, it satisfied in a way. Not just climbing the mountain, but the entire effort – the creating something, the few of us moulding it from the beginning. With a lot of luck we'd succeeded. But what had we proved?

Existence on a mountain is simple. Seldom in life does it come any simpler: survival, plus the striving toward the summit. The goal is solidly, three-dimensionally there – you can see it, touch it, stand upon it – the way to reach it well defined, the energy of all directed toward its achievement. It is this simplicity that strips the veneer off civilization and makes that which is meaningful easier to come by – the pleasure of deep companionship, moments of uninhibited humour, the tasting of hardship, sorrow, beauty, joy. But it is this very simplicity that may prevent finding answers to the questions I had asked as we approached the mountain.

Then I had been unsure that I could survive and function in a world so foreign to my normal existence. Now I felt at home here, no longer overly afraid. Each step toward Kathmandu carried me back toward the known, yet toward many things terribly unknown, toward goals unclear, to be reached by paths undefined.

Beneath fatigue lurked the suspicion that the answers I sought were not to be found on a mountain. What possible difference could climbing Everest make? Certainly the mountain hadn't been changed. Even now wind and falling snow would have obliterated most signs of our having been there. Was I any greater for having stood on the highest place on earth? Within the wasted figure that stumbled weary and fearful back toward home there was no question about the answer to that one.

It had been a wonderful dream, but now all that lingered was the memory. The dream was ended.

The Upper Tower

Peter Boardman

The British climbers Peter Boardman and Joe Tasker formed one of the most dynamic climbing partnerships of the late 1970s. Below Boardman recounts their negotiation of the Upper Tower during their ascent (the first) of the awesome 6,844 m (22,462 ft) Changabang West Wall of Kumaon Himalaya in 1976. Six years later Boardman and Tasker disappeared whilst attempting the unclimbed North-East Ridge of Everest.

9th–13th October
Camp I shrank below me, a blue dot on the curve of the ridge that swept from far beneath my feet towards Bagini Peak and Dunagiri. The only sounds were the wind whipping the corners of my down hood, and my own heavy panting as I pushed and pulled myself up the rope with the jumars. I was returning to the problem, feeling strong. Everything around me was pure in the light of receding dawn. The fresh powder snow, the harsh crystalline granite, the air itself, seemed newly created. There was even a terrible cleanliness about the danger to which I was exposed.

Two hundred feet below me, Joe was fixing a few short lengths of the rope from Shipton's Col, over the rock steps above Camp I. He had agreed to continue up behind and do the finger work of dismantling the fixed ropes beneath the Balcony and bringing them up with him. To compensate his extra burden, I was carrying all the down equipment.

It had been the earliest start we had ever made on the mountain. I had not slept well. I had kept on waking up and thinking about the route. At three in the morning I had decided I was certainly not going to get any more sleep. Silently resenting Joe's peaceful doze, I had leant out of the door in the darkness and smashed some snow off the ever-retreating section of the cornice outside the tent and put the brew on. "Typical!" I had thought. "I bet he hardly stirs for another three hours." And he did not. Nevertheless, we had moved off by half past six, at first light.

The plan was to pull up all the six terylene ropes hanging below the spike beneath the Balcony, where we had spent our first hammock bivouac. These, combined with the ropes on the icefield, ought to be enough to fix the Upper Tower. In this way we could still leave two ropes tied through the overhangs. We knew that if we retrieved these, we could never get back again. We had mused morbidly that it was retrieving the rope after the first crossing of the Hinterstoisser traverse on the Eiger that had cut off the retreat and precipitated the tragic deaths of the four climbers in 1936, including Toni Kurz. Joe and I were not prepared to cut off our retreat completely. If the hammock plan had worked, then we would have moved slowly up the mountain, stopping whenever we finished the day's climbing. But now, if we could establish the tent on the icefield, we would have to work every day from there, and take all the risks of jumaring and prusiking that it entailed.

I was astonished how smoothly the jumaring went. I was carrying two long sticks of bamboo that we had rescued from one of the Japanese expedition camps. I had pushed them as far as possible to the bottom of my sack. Now their ends wavered in the air above my head like bizarre antennae, as if they were rendering mysterious aid to my progress. I was wearing my one-piece down suit, yet even when the sun came out I was not too hot. The weather was steadily becoming colder. As I negotiated the vertical jumaring onto the foot of the icefield above the Toni Kurz pitch, I was bouncing about as usual when I ripped a large tear in the suit. For the rest of the journey up the ropes, I was accompanied by a trail of down, which rose, hovered and plummeted on the up-and-down draughts of air that sailed around the West Wall. Now, instead of staring glumly at the ice as I recovered between bursts of effort, I watched feathers soar hundreds of feet, with the intensity of a child at a balloon competition at a fair. Yet this was a more expensive game, I decided, and determined to wear my oversuit on top of my down suit in the future.

I reached the high point at half past two in the afternoon, thankfully to find that all the equipment, food and fuel we had left there was still intact. Combined with the food and fuel we were bringing up with us, we had a week's provisions – or ten days in an uncomfortable emergency. We were still feeling fit and fresh. I knew that I had lost a lot of weight, and that my body had become hardened and sinews become wiry with the effort of the previous few weeks. And I knew, also, that this feeling might not last for long. However, for the moment my mind and body felt in perfect accord, as if my will could force my limbs into any situation, as long as it entailed reaching the summit of the mountain.

The critical problem then was to find a site for us to pitch Camp II. I unclipped from the rope and started soloing around the mixed ground above the fixed rope. After climbing about fifteen feet, I came to my senses and decided to clip back on. It was stupidity to deny myself some sort of chance if I were to slip. Joe was still a long way behind me on the icefield, so I pulled through fifty feet of the spare rope we had left up there and tied on to it. Then, with more confidence, I started climbing. I ran half the rope out, by which time Joe had arrived. Joe belayed me and I looked at all the area within seventy feet above our high point. Every time a line of rock promised a ledge, on inspection I always found its top stacked steeply with hard water ice. I crept back to Joe. I could not talk to him because of the wind, until I had reached him.

"Well, there aren't any good ledges. We might as well try and hack a platform out of this bit of ice as any other."

We tied off to fifteen-foot lengths of rope and started slicing into the ice with our axes.

We set about the work with enthusiasm. This was mountaineering at its most basic; serious play. As a child I had loved building tree-top dens and digging dug-outs. This was similar elemental home building, except the difference was the situation and the materials. Now we had the threat of bad weather and avalanche hanging over our heads if we did not do a good job. Secure shelter would make the difference between success and failure.

The ice-cutting was exhausting work. We hacked furiously until stopped by shortness of breath or cramp in the forearms. We soon hit the rock of the slab under the ice, and this forced the limit on the width of the ledge. By the time the sun was sinking into the cloud beyond Dunagiri, we had enlarged a ledge six feet long, two feet six inches wide at one end and tapering to two feet at the other. Whilst I tensioned the tent off from a system of nuts, spikes and rock and ice pegs I had fixed above, Joe lashed two sticks of the Japanese bamboo together and bent them across the entrance like a hoop. He improvised guylines from little stones knotted into the walls of the tent and hammered our hammock spacer bars into the ice for tent pegs.

Before the afternoon sun disappeared, I finished off the pitch I had started leading earlier. The climbing was quite awkward, but it was mere scrambling compared to that beneath the icefield. My thoughts raced ahead with the hope that the Upper Tower would be quickly climbed if it were all like that.

The last rays of the sun had moved off the Wall high above us and "home" was ready.

"There doesn't seem to be much room in there," I commented.

"We'll have to tie on well," said Joe.

"Yeah, that's a drag, we'll have to leave part of the tent open to let the line through. And we'll have to keep our harnesses on inside our sleeping bags."

We had left our full body harnesses at Camp I, and put on our sit harnesses, hoping to save weight and also because the full body harnesses got in the way of the pockets of our oversuits. Now we regretted having made this decision, for the point of attachment of the sit harnesses was so low down. Outside the tent there was a chaos of equipment, slings and ropes, and after we had sorted them out the question that had been in the backs of our minds came out into the open. "Who's going to sleep on the outside then?" If Joe was still insisting that I cooked breakfast, then I was not going to give in on this question. To my surprise, he agreed to sleep on the side of the tent overhanging the edge.

"Only for a couple of nights, mind you," he said.

The tent was so cramped there was only room for one of us to sort himself out at a time. I went in and laid the insulating mats and the hammocks down, took off my boots and got into my sleeping bags. Joe squeezed in and did the same.

"Christ, my knees protrude over the edge," he said.

"Isn't it cosy?" I said.

"Good job we've got our pee bottles with us," said Joe. "I wouldn't fancy getting up in the middle of the night for a piss!"

"Make sure you pour it out on the left-hand side, we don't want our cooking ice polluted," I said.

We wedged the stove in between the soles of my boots in the tent entrance and put a brew on. The wind did not seem to be penetrating the thin fabric.

"You taking Dalmane or Valium tonight?" asked Joe.

"Dalmane, Dalmane, all around my brain, please."

Saturday, October 9th. I had missed the BMC Peak Area Meeting!

The improvised tent was protecting us – the problem of shelter had been solved, and my heart warmed to the action to come.

We had decided that on the Upper Tower we would do two leads each in succession. We expected to go just as slowly on the Upper Tower as we had done below and had found that leading four rope lengths each was too much – two days' consecutive leading had been exhausting, and if you were seconding, you lost a feel for the action. The next day I was intending to run out another rope length before Joe took over.

It was an exciting change to start climbing in the cold of the morning, straight from the camp and without any jumaring. But the optimism of the previous afternoon was short lived.

The only line that offered any feasibility of progress was a bottomless groove that was guarded from me by a bulge of ice. As I moved up to the bulge I started feeling tired. The climbing became hard and the wind and cold were sapping my strength. I was now wearing both down and nylon Ventile oversuits – far more than I had ever found it necessary to wear on Everest the year before. With my overmitts off and dangling from my wrists, and wearing only the pairs of gloves underneath, my fingers quickly became cold. I wanted to avoid making them colder by trying to put my crampons on. I traversed left on the rock to below where a bulge turned into a rock overhang. This was slit by a ramp, which I managed to step onto, and I traversed across to the side of the ice that filled the back of a hanging groove. Rather than put crampons on, I tapped a drive-in ice peg into the ice. It went in a couple of inches before stopping against the rock underneath. I tied a nylon rope sling around it where it came out of the ice, and stepped into it. Then I repeated the same movement further up the groove twice, before I could bridge out with my feet on either side on to rock. A few feet of climbing and I had reached the top of the groove.

The groove was capped by a six-foot overhang. I saw one ledge eighteen inches wide over on the left that ran around the corner onto the North Face and, after shouting a few warning words to Joe, I crawled along it. The wall above me bulged out and I was virtually on all fours. The ledge was in a horrifying position, without the icefield to soften the view downwards. Below me was a sheer drop of 4,000 ft onto the Bagini Glacier. By curling my fingers around narrow sideholds, I braced myself sideways and peered round the corner. We had seen, through our binoculars from the glacier, a long slanting groove line high on the edge of the Upper Tower between the West and North Walls. It had been the only obvious feature on the Upper Tower and we had hoped it would offer some straightforward crack climbing. We had called it "the Niche". Looking upwards now I could see it, and it scared me even to look at it! The corner was vertical, ice-smeared and 200 ft high. I shouted down to Joe.

"I've seen the Niche. It's around the corner. It overhangs the North Face and looks bloody impossible – to reach it, climb it, or get upwards from the top of it. We'll only get up if we climb the right side of the Upper Tower for the next few pitches!"

It was a measure of our trust in each other's climbing judgment that Joe accepted all this immediately, without demanding a look of his own.

The right-handed exit offered the only option – a fifteen-foot leaning crack. I tried to climb it by artificial aid, but none of the pegs or nuts I had with me would fit the crack. "Don't be such a chicken," I told myself inside. "If this was on gritstone you'd bomb up it. It's obviously a lay back crack and doesn't look as if it'll play any tricks. Just take a few deep breaths and fight up it."

I felt as if I had lead in my boots and my weight had doubled as soon as I swung my weight onto my arms. Half-way up the lay back, my fingers started to unfold from the edge of the crack so I rammed my fist round and into the back of the crack and squeezed it in a hand jam. I locked my arm straight from the jam and hung there until my breathing returned to normal. Then I returned to the lay back position and fought, with continually draining strength, upwards. My fingers curled over the edge of the arete that bounded the top of the crack. The arete rocked a little – it was a granite block of dubious quality. But I was past caring about that. One last heave and I swung up onto some footholds and gasped for air. A momentary feeling of nausea welled up from my stomach; I thought I was going to vomit. I managed to bang a peg in, tied the rope off and shouted down into the wind to Joe that he could start jumaring.

"That would have been quite a respectable grade on gritstone," I thought, and resolved to avoid such strenuous climbing in the future. I looked down past Joe at the buff-coloured tent of Camp II, now two hundred steep feet below. Beyond that was the sweep of the icefield and then nothing. The Wall seemed to breathe in under that. There was only the Rhamani Glacier, and the tiny dot of the Ridge Camp I was just visible. Joe was dangling beneath me, all arms and legs, braced across the groove, hanging from a thread. He was unscrewing the ice pegs.

"A pity you'll miss the lay back," I said.

It was an uncharitable sentiment which back home on rock I used to relish when I watched seconds struggling up something difficult that I had led. Joe heard me from beneath his layers of balaclava, helmet and hood.

"It looked quite hard," he muttered. With a few upward strokes of his jumars, he had joined me. Now it was his turn.

With confident balance, Joe moved up a few feet above my head and then traversed diagonally rightwards under a line of overhangs, placing his feet carefully on a narrow sloping granite shelf. He placed a runner around a spike and looked around, obviously enjoying himself:

> The climbing was delicate and thrilling, tip-toeing up the edge with stupendous exposure below. At the end of the shelf was a magnificent groove, steep and reminiscent of a Scottish climb. I put on my crampons. I found it hard, but on the right side of the borderline. Rocks frozen in place provided welcome holds and, when loose, added an extra thrill to the climbing. I was bridged across the icy runnel for most of the way. It was just the kind of pitch I enjoyed most, varied, intricate, uncertain.

I was watching the progress of the sun. The shadow crept back towards me imperceptibly, but inexorably. It had long since moved down the Bagini Peak and past Camp I. As the Wall steepened, so its speed increased. For a few moments I could see the icefield crystals shimmering in the sun's halo above the windswept South-West Ridge. Then the sun came out and the shadow ran away up the Wall. But the wind and the altitude were fighting away the warmth that should have come with the light.

The rope stopped moving, and there was not much of it left. The restless wind swept our shouts aside and threw them around the mountain. I decided that Joe must have tied on. I pulled on the terylene rope. Yes, it seemed secured. I shouldered the sack and moved off.

I was tense with concentration as I crossed the shelf that Joe had appeared to stroll across with such ease. "Perhaps my boots are too big. Perhaps it's the weight of the sack. Perhaps I'm having an off day. I wish he'd put more runners in, I might swing off," I thought. The thought that Joe was climbing well, was not allowed. I swallowed my moans.

The groove up which he had disappeared looked as if it had been fun to climb, with a succession of spikes to haul up on – held on to the mountain by hard water ice. But now I had swung into the line of the rope and was jumaring past them. Above the groove there was some easier angled rock and the rope whipped back left around the edge of the Upper Tower. I followed it and found Joe standing at the bottom of an over-hanging groove that split the edge of the mountain for about 300 ft. We both hoped it would not be necessary to climb that, and called it the "Big Groove". However, the alternative over on the right did not look much more attractive – massive blank walls stepped by overhangs looming upwards for over 500 ft confronted us.

"There might be some easier angled ground on the left between us and the top of the Niche," said Joe. And he disappeared round the corner, leaving me standing at the foot of the Big Groove.

For two hours, Joe fought a hard and cunning battle with the rock and ice of the North Face on the left of the Big Groove:

I came to a long, slightly overhanging crack. I chose to look further left. The crack was feasible but would have been very strenuous. Another corner had a tongue of ice running up into it – this seemed a better proposition. The ice was steep, a lot steeper than it had looked from below and, as I gained height, the tongue of ice became narrower and thinner. I had difficulty in maintaining my balance. I hammered a thin blade piton into a crack above. It only went in an inch, but gave me a little more support. I wondered whether to come down and try the other corner. It would be time-wasting to start again; I could see nothing of Pete. He would be wondering at the slow movement of the rope. I hoped he had secure hold of it. The next few moves would depend on everything working together just right.

I hammered the pick of an axe into the ice; carefully, I balanced up and stood on the head of the axe protruding from the ice. Gently I reached down and undid my crampons. With my boots free of the crampons I stepped up onto small footholds on the rock, feeling strangely naked. I bent down and yanked out the axe.

There were some delicate moves to make on the rock, but the friction of the rope pulled me back. I had to strain furiously to pull sufficient rope through to allow me to move up a few feet.

Above was another ice slope. It seemed like a haven of security. On the rock I had been exposed and vulnerable. I drove the pick of my axe into the ice and went through the procedure of refixing my crampons.

With my crampons on, I climbed up the ice to a grotto where I could see some boulders to which I attached the rope, and relaxed.

It was obvious that this lead had been desperately hard and, for Joe, the most demanding of the climb so far. I found it very difficult leaving Joe's last runner without swinging off further over the North Face like a pendulum – a sixty-foot swing could do a lot of damage and I would have difficulty getting back. I felt mentally and physically tired when I reached Joe. "It's getting late," I said.

Joe, full of accounts of sliding feet and frightening hops with ice hammers, was obviously thirsting for more action. It was 4.30. We had not far to descend back to the tent, but we knew it would start getting dark at five. There were seventy feet of steep ice above us on the North Face. It was my turn to lead but Joe was obviously more in tune than I. He set off up it, after agreeing to stop at five. He climbed it carefully but quickly and hammered in two pegs. The shadow that had climbed upwards six hours before was now returning. It was good to have snatched those extra feet at the end of the day. We swung quickly down the ropes to Camp II, feeling happy. Things were going well.

Back in the tent, we peered at our photographs of the Face, trying to calculate our latest high point. We knew that we could not continue up the North Face any further, for we wanted to reach a feature which we had named "the Ramp" – a thin line of snow that appeared from our photographs to stretch down from the summit snowfield, through an area of steep rock to the top of the Upper Tower. If we became committed to the upper section of the North Face, we would inevitably miss that exit. We only had five lengths of rope left which we could fix in place. After that we would have to climb away from our lifeline, and the Ramp seemed to be the only feature that would not trap us on the Wall or dangerously slow us down, but would offer us a slim chance of success. So the next day we would have to try and regain the crest of the Upper Tower above the Big Groove. And that would be my task.

It was morning.

"Bloody hell, no lumps of ice left." I swore violently.

Joe's eyes shuttered open briefly. "What's up, hasn't it been delivered?"

All my pent-up fears and frustrations were being released in curses into the morning wind. I had forgotten to break any ice the night before for the breakfast cooking and, in the darkness, was having to stretch out and claw at the ice hanging above the tent. Slowly, I accumulated a pile of ice chips on the side of the level patch outside, shouting loudly and angrily at the fragments that splintered off into the air and bounced down the mountain-side. Back inside the tent, I tried to warm myself up again and started melting the ice, chip by chip. "I'll be glad when we've got up this mountain!" I mumbled, as it started becoming lighter. "I'm fed up with this view, I hope we can see Nanda Devi from the top."

The reality that soon I was going to have to do two hours of frightening jumaring was gnawing at me and I was irritable. I crushed thoughts that Joe, lying snoozing peacefully, was deliberately obstructing my cooking, and felt embarrassed about my morning moaning. I had not been shouting at him; I wanted to say I wasn't blaming him for suggesting this climb, for not cooking breakfasts. I was just exploding with the tension and shouting at everything – it did not mean anything and I was all right now. But our conversation had died to a basic mini-mum. I tried to rouse him with some talk about how settled the weather was. I felt that we ought to talk about something. But Joe hated small talk and platitudes, and felt as if I were treating

him as if he were on one of the BMC Committees. He preferred
to keep his brain ticking over in neutral.

It was the lonely hour of dawn. Joe went down to the icefield
to pick up three ropes which we would need for climbing on and
fixing on the Upper Tower. We had done a lot of diagonal
climbing backwards and forwards the previous day, and I went
up to straighten out the first three rope lengths. By removing
the first two anchors, I hoped to be able to save a hundred and
fifty feet of rope for higher up. It all seemed feasible in theory.
On reaching the second anchor, I wanted to swing the rope into
line below Joe's shelf pitch. I took the peg out and leaned
sideways on the rope. But I had miscalculated the distance I was
going to swing. Time closed up before me, like the progression
of incidents in a split-second dream. I was soon hurtling
through the air with a momentum that would not have been
out of place on an Outward Bound ropes course. Too late I tried
to spin my legs round to take the impact, but was not fast
enough and I crashed into a wall, vertically below the next
anchor, with a sickening thud that squeezed all the wind out of
me. I had swung forty feet – half a pendulum, stopped abruptly
by a rock wall.

I wriggled as much as I was able, whilst suspended from my
jumars. No, nothing seemed to be broken. My mind shrugged
grimly, "Well, I'm still here." I looked down at Joe, a tiny dot
on the icefield. He probably had not seen my mishap, and why
should he bother about it anyway? There was nothing he
could do. We were further apart than we had been for a long
time.

It was strange deciding the line of the ropes, by myself, after
days of deciding all tactics by consultation. I laughed at how
dependent I was becoming, and moved on. I chose to keep the
line of the rope going through Joe's groove in the overhangs, so
as to avoid any overhanging jumaring. Soon after eleven, I was
established at the previous day's highpoint and waiting for Joe,
feeling determined to maintain the momentum he had set in his
lead the previous day.

The problem was to try and move back right to the edge of the
Upper Tower. There was a line of cracks stretching across a
steep wall in between us and the sky line. Guarding any

entrance to them was an enormous flake. It was angular and about ten feet across, and it was possible to see light behind it in places. It seemed to be glued to the side of the mountain by a few patches of ice. Wearing my crampons, I front-pointed up to it and thumped it hard with my hammer. "BOOMM!" it replied threateningly.

"What do you think to this, Joe, do you think it'll be safe? It might skate off with me riding it."

"Oh, it'll be all right," he replied. "It must have been there long enough. Anyway," he added reassuringly, "it's not my lead, is it?"

Nervously, I draped a sling over the top of the spike, as if I were conferring a holy order. I curled my fingers around the edge of this spike and swung my weight onto it. Nothing moved, except my mind, which was whirring with thoughts of the sweeping action this great tonnage of rock would have on us if it decided to detach itself. What would Joe do with me if I broke my back up here?

I slotted the front points of my crampons into a tiny lip of granite on the block and edged across. Leaning across the wall I could just reach a crack about two inches wide. At full stretch, I managed to prod a large bong peg into it, and this I patted in until it seemed to stay there by itself. Using this as a hand hold, I traversed out a little further. I reached high above my head with my hammer pick and hooked it into a little niche in the rock, then, pulling myself up onto this, made a lunge with my feet for a foothold on the edge of the buttress. Gently, I eased my weight over my feet until I was in balance. The foothold was a good one and I relaxed, detachedly amused at myself for reaching such an extraordinary position.

The sun had moved onto us whilst I had been climbing and I could see my shadow silhouetted on the rock above Joe. Beyond his self-absorbed form hanging in slings, I could see the for-bidding sweep of the North Face and the brown lines of moraine on the Bagini Glacier, far below. I was directly above the Big Groove, and could now see parts of the West Wall again. I leant across and screwed a good hand jam into the top of the crack at the back of the Big Groove, and bridged across. A few feet above, the Big Groove reached an apex, like a pea pod, and I swarmed up to it. Above this, there was a ten-foot-high iceslope and I planted my ice-axe and hammer into this and pulled up until I was teetering on the ice with my front points. My calves were quivering with the strain and I battered the ice with my axe until a foothold splintered into existence and I could rest my foot sideways. Above me, the Wall reared up again, split by a thin crack. Longing for security, I pounded three pegs into it, a blade, a soft steel blade and a leeper. These three pegs provided a welcome refuge after the sixty feet of instability beneath me.

Joe jumared up to me and we quickly discussed the situation. We had generated such unified intensity of purpose that whatever Joe said I had been thinking at the same time. Yes, we would straighten the fixed ropes the next morning. Yes, the next pitch should bring the Ramp into view. Yes, the crack looks the best line to follow until I can tension around the corner. The wind and the sunshine were forgotten.

The crack line became continually thinner, but there were no other features to use to climb this blank wall. After twenty feet, it faded out among the granite crystals. I leant down and sideways until it seemed every muscle in my body was taut. My balance was wobbling on the point of swinging me round and off the rock like an unfastened barn door in a draught. I was able to place a one-inch long knife blade peg in upside down, and this enabled me to reach another crack line which took me around an arete into a groove. For twenty feet I was able to establish a pattern of movement as the pegging became straightforward, and there was no hope of free climbing, since the rock was either vertical or overhanging. However, soon I was running out of equipment and above a short overhang I could see the back of the upper part of the groove gleaming with bulging ice. "Nothing's ever simple," I thought. I took out two pegs I had used below me and placed them, and then knocked two ice pegs into the ice-filled crack. As I moved my weight onto them, I was not quite sure if it was the rock, ice or just a lot of luck that held them there. Now I only had small angle pegs left, and there were no ledges in sight.

Our route seemed to be forcing us up into ever more bleakly exposed fly-on-the-wall situations. However careful we always were at retrieving pegs, there were always some that were dropped or were left behind, and now we were running short of many sizes. The three angles that I had hammered in did not inspire my confidence, but I convinced myself that, on the law of averages, one of them would stay in, and I tied the rope off. "Joe can sort it out from here in the morning," I decided.

"Can you see the start of the Ramp?" shouted Joe.

"Yes, I think so." I returned to him, de-pegging as I descended and it was nearly dark when I reached him. We were late and, for the first time, I realized the full consequences of the loss of my descendeur as I struggled down with my complicated karabiner brake, past pegs and knots. The difficulty of this descent was a harbinger of the nightmare descents to come.

Dawn, the following morning, was the time of reckoning. I was going to have to go to the loo. I had been fighting this moment off all the previous day. Crawling out of the tent was a problem in itself, there were so many things I could knock over, including Joe and the tent. Only one person could move at a time and it was my turn. I imagined that I was at the fairground, trying one of those games where you have a circle of wire in your hand which you have to thread along another meandering piece of thicker wire without touching it. If you do touch it, a buzzer rings and you lose your money. Joe, the tent door, the pan on the stove, I thought, would all buzz loudly if I touched them as I threaded myself past them. Once outside the tent the game was just as delicate. On the third night, in Camp, II, we had not bothered to tie ourselves on whilst we slept, because the crisscrossed ropes inside the tent made the simplest movement too complicated. Once outside, however, to move anywhere you had to climb, and it was important to tie on. We had cut a line of steps underneath the tent and these I followed until I reached the back of the ledge. There, leaning out on the rope, I wrestled with the specially-designed zips of the oversuit, down suit and polar fibre undersuit. As soon as they were undone, my trousers started flapping agitatedly upwards, like medieval streamers in the bitter wind that was rolling up the Wall. Occasionally, my face or backside was lashed by a volley of spindrift or a flailing zip. The whole bizarre procedure took half an hour and, at the end of it, the word "masochism" had taken on a new meaning.

We had decided it was Joe's turn to go up the fixed ropes first that morning, and this gave me a feeling of relief – we were sharing the risk. Joe was to go up and straighten the fixed rope and sort himself out at the high point of the previous day. The first one up always took the risk that the wind might have frayed the rope against a sharp edge of rock somewhere. Nevertheless, following him I was still apprehensive, even though he had tested the rope and anchors like the jester sampling the king's food for poison. When we had climbed the rock below the icefield we had thought it steep, but it seemed that now the Wall was rearing even steeper. The jumaring was correspondingly more exhausting. My thoughts, refreshed by the night's sleep, were alert to all the dangers. I was delayed by still having some rearranging of the anchors to do on the ropes above Camp II, and when I arrived at the foot of the Big Groove a shock was awaiting me. Joe had de-pegged the anchors from the three rope lengths above me and, on reaching the three peg crack, he had swung all the rope round in a great loop like a 400-ft skipping rope until he had lodged them in the Big Groove. Then he pulled them up tight. As a result I was confronted by nearly 200 ft of eight-millimetre terylene rope hanging out from the rock down towards me.

"Joe's put it there, so he must be prepared to jumar it," I thought as I started up, the competitive urge the only motivation. All the instances I had ever known of ropes snapping flashed through my mind like slides on a projector on auto-change, interspersed with pictures of me spread out in the air in the apparent standstill of a free fall. "Still, at least terylene doesn't saw up and down," I thought. But as I got higher, this rope started to shudder sideways on an edge of rock at the top of the Big Groove. The apex was far away. I moved very stealthily, trying not to jerk the rope, looking at my jumars, eyes focused only on the umbilical cord that held me. The uncanny double-take, a constant companion at altitude, moved in. Was my mind here? My body seemed to be, but my mind felt free and uninvolved. Suddenly it was the top of the apex – there was the short ice slope, Joe, and the three peg crack. Joe was preparing to jumar up the last pitch to our high point.

"That last bit was exciting – it's in a good position," I said.

"It's saved a lot of rope," said Joe.

I knew that we could not afford to go up and down that length of rope many times without it wearing through, but did not mention it. Joe could see it as well as I, and he would find out all about what it was like to jumar the Big Groove when we next came back up! But did he worry as much as I did? I was filled with envy – I was seeing his existence from my separateness, and it seemed to possess a coherence and unity that mine did not.

I followed Joe up to the high point I had reached the previous day. It was a tangled procedure, interlocking me onto the hanging belay. I noticed he had only clipped into two of the three angle pegs I had placed so apprehensively before.

"Why have you only clipped onto two, Joe?"

"They look all right. Two should be enough," he said.

I hastily clipped into the third one. Pegs always give an illusion of safety if you have not put them in yourself.

The sun was filtering around on to us, as Joe set off in the lead. At first the climbing was almost identical to that of the pitch before. Joe did a few feet of pegging until the crack disappeared. He drove a blade peg until it stopped half way, and then passed the climbing rope through a karabiner on the peg. As I held the rope taut he leaned across rightwards, his weight supported by the tension in the rope. Using tiny flakes on the slab, he pulled himself across to the arete. Soon all that I could see were his left hand and foot, scything the arete. It was a fascinating puppet show. The hand and the foot jerked up and then scuttled down. Up, and then down. Up, and then down. Then suddenly they disappeared.

Around the corner, Joe was having a grim struggle:

From the arete I could see a groove with a crack in the back about six feet away. The groove continued upwards towards the corners above.

I pulled myself round the arete. The rope was horizontal between my waist and the peg; it was still holding my weight. I tried to reach the groove but as I stretched further right I tended to swing away from the rock. There were no holds big enough to hang onto; I relied on friction to keep me in place. Moving further rightwards round the arete was to move beyond the balance of friction maintained by the rope taking much of my weight and the rugosities of granite beneath my boots and hands. If I parted company, I would swing back twenty feet and the peg would probably come out.

I juggled with the precarious balance for a while, stretching slightly further each time by clinging to tiny flakes discovered by my groping fingers. My body was almost horizontal and still I could not reach the groove. I glanced at the rope – it was rubbing, every time I moved, up and down the sharp edge of the arete. There was a sense of detachment about this observation; I wondered if I would reach the safety of the groove before the rope was cut through.

I was quite exhausted by now and as a final resort took a nylon sling from around my neck. It had an aluminium chockstone on it, which I threw towards the crack. It lodged there first time, and I pulled myself to the crack on the nylon tape. The groove was overhanging; I didn't look down to soak in the atmosphere, but hammered in a peg immediately, fastened myself to it and rested.

A few feet of free climbing took him to a large granite block, which he flopped his arm around and rested again.

From the block Joe could see on his right an enormous hanging corner, 200 ft high. Above that hung tendrils of ice, signifying the start of the Ramp. Towards the middle of this corner, across an overhanging wall, ran a two-foot wide sloping ledge, thirty feet long and banked high with ice. Joe gingerly put his crampons on and kicked his way across it until he was barred by an overhang. This he pegged over. Then he hammered two pegs in to hang from, and waited:

I shouted for Pete to follow. When I remembered to examine the rope which had been wearing away on the arete I saw that it had been half cut through. I felt a lot more frightened now that I was safe and just thinking about what could have happened, than what I had actually been when involved with the situation. I cut away the frayed part and re-fastened the good rope to my waist.

Joe's tension traverse was difficult to follow, and I moved the diagonal line of his ropes by a series of swings as I knocked pegs out. It was acrobatic, and I felt like Tarzan swinging on a long vine that kept on snagging amongst twigs and branches. When I reached the big block, I peered around the corner and could see Joe, roosting forlornly above the overhang, like a big black hooded bird.

"Where are you going from there?" I shouted.

It looked like a dead end to me. The corner above him that stretched up to the Ramp would take a whole day to climb, if it was possible at all.

"Don't worry," came the habitual reassurance, with its over-emphasized, patronising tone. "I can see a way."

Feeling thankful that he did not sound frightened, I tightened up the rope along the ledge like a handrail on a catwalk, and set off along it. I had decided not to waste time putting my crampons on and my feet felt very insecure in the footholds Joe had hacked in the ice. Most of my weight was on the rope, which felt even thinner than normal, since it was stretched sideways. I remembered that the breaking strain of the rope was even lower when it was stretched horizontally. It had started to snow, and Joe was busily recording the dramatic situation and the snow and cloud effects with his camera.

Joe was right, there was a way out. Between the overhangs, and out of sight from below, a stepped corner reached up leftwards for sixty feet back to the crest of the Upper Tower. "Good route-finding," I complimented him, wondering if he had been led there by his sixth sense, blind luck or just because he could not climb up anywhere else. At first the crack in the corner was blind and he reached another crack on the left wall by a tension traverse. This crack he followed into the corner, and proceeded to climb it by a series of delicate free moves. After an hour he reached the crest. "Can you see the Ramp? Will it go?"

"Yes, it only looks one rope length away. Hurry up, it's a hell of a way down and it will be dark in a minute."

The snow shower had passed and rock was turning red around us. But I felt relaxed. I took some pictures of Joe, varying the exposures so as to catch the lighting.

"Hurry up, there's no time for taking photographs." It was the first time Joe had sounded angrily impatient.

"Don't worry," I shouted back. "You'll be glad of them when you are an old man!"

It was another diagonal swinging pitch to follow. I retrieved all the pegs and nuts so that we could fix the edge out straight down the over-hanging wall to the big block. Joe was perched on one foothold and I hung off the slings of his spike belay whilst he sorted the equipment out for his descent. I had taken half an hour longer than he did the day before to descend back to Camp II, because I had to use a karabiner brake.

"Don't forget to put the brew on," I reminded him.

"See you soon," he said as he reeled off down the rope and out of sight.

Irrationally, I did not share Joe's sense of urgency. I looked up and saw an overhanging groove reaching up to the Ramp. For me it was a golden line of promise through an area of turmoil, as if parted by the rod of Moses. At the top it was crowned by an enormous block of granite bridging across the walls of the groove like a beam across the corner of a roofless house. Perhaps we could peep beneath the crown? Nothing could stop us now.

The rope that had been my tormentor in the harsh light of early morning awareness, had now become a friend. I was descending in a trance. The swooping slides, the dancing traverses and swings, were part of the pattern deeply hidden within the game of the descent. The complicated procedures for passing knots and pitons were factual procedures to be mastered as part of the choreography. The consequences of a mistake were forgotten. The emphasis of progress and the numbness induced by the cold, altitude and fatigue had put me in a state of reverie. A fantasy world had grown around me assuming nonsensical names and nationalities. The knots in the rope I called "cows", the pegs became "Americans", the karabiners at my waist all took the names of different girls. I was a big spider scuttling down.

There was a blue light inside the tent, telling me that the stove was purring. The brew was on. I crouched in the darkness, sorting and clipping my equipment to the slings outside, ready to crawl in for shelter.

"I nearly left you to finish the climb on your own, whilst I was up there," said Joe. He was shaken and unnerved.

At the point where there were three pegs together, the rope was criss-crossed between them. Whilst Joe had been passing this section, he had realized something was amiss, and had noticed that his jumar had become unclipped from his waist, his descendeur was in his right hand and all his weight was hanging from his left hand on the jumar.

It was really weird, odd thoughts kept on spinning round like "Is this it?" and "Is Pete going to have to finish the climb on his own?" and "I don't want to drop my descendeur." Eventually I fumbled a nylon sling from my neck, wrapped that round the rope and put my arm through it, so that I could get myself clipped in.

Joe said little as we ate our evening meal. It was the usual Oxo with freeze-dried meat and mashed potato and a cup of tea, followed by a nibble of chocolate. I dozed out of his way, as he cooked. What a day it had been – from doubt and fear to resolution. Then from intense effort to joy – all the emotions of a lifetime had been carried to my heart with extraordinary power. Yet our conversation reflected no more than a quiet, calculated hopefulness. In the morning we would move away as early as possible, pack food for two days, and push, alpine style, for the summit.

It was as if our subconscious was plugged into the same internal clock. We both woke late, having already made the decision whilst we were asleep to have a rest day. Now we were waiting for the other one to suggest it. Eventually I asked Joe what he thought about the idea since I had to decide whether to start cooking or not.

"I'm glad you suggested that," he said. And we laughed and slid back onto our imaginations, comforted by the thought that we could wait for the sunshine before starting the cooking or venturing outside into the wind to go to the toilet. That morning at least our internal clock could rest unwound.

During the afternoon, I started to feel claustrophobic inside the tent. When crawling out I accidentally knelt on some of Joe's camera equipment. He snapped at my clumsiness. I had not understood until that point his enthusiasm as a photographer. He had brought his lens tissues and brush up with him and was fastidiously cleaning his equipment.

"I had to buy my cameras," he said. "They weren't given to me, you know."

I had been given an Olympus OMi camera for the Everest climb, which I had brought up with me, fitted with a wide-angle lens. But I wasn't lavishing it with the attention that Joe thought it deserved. As usual, Joe's precise, orderly approach to bivouacking and equipment made me feel muddled and clumsy, like a small boy told off for touching in a china shop. Some people judge mountaineers by their speed, and by the difficulty of the rock they can climb. But on Changabang the real test was more how efficiently you could put a brew on, warm your fingers or take your boots off.

Outside I drank in the view in the afternoon sunshine. All the mountain shapes nearby were so familiar. Was that the Holy Kailas I could see, I wondered, looking at a solitary white-topped mountain above the distant brown plains of Tibet? Kailas – the throne of Shiva, the precious ice mountain, the crystal one, the centre of the universe. The waters of Kailas fed some of the greatest rivers of Asia and before politics and a war changed borders and religions, thousands of pilgrims travelled to walk or crawl around it. To me it was a white signpost to a forbidden land. Soon, I thought, I would see Nanda Devi from the Summit Ridge, and we would have worked hard for that view. It was now the 13th October, and soon the winter would come. We had not much time.

As I began to squirm back inside the tent I noticed some dark stains on the snow just outside the door, where Joe had been coughing. He had been spitting blood. Since he had not talked about it to me, I decided not to mention it. Inside the tent he was lying in his sleeping bag with an ecstatic look on his face.

"What's making you look so pleased with yourself?" I asked.

"Ooh," he said, "have you felt the tent fabric? It's sort of billowing down over my face, and when you touch it it sort of bulges in soft round yielding curves. Ultimate Bill says that it's the same material used for making women's underwear."

The rest of the day floated past in idle banter. Changabang did not worry us any more.

White Spider

Heinrich Harrer

Harrer was an Austrian climber, born in 1912, who was a member of the team which made the first ascent of the notorious Eigerwand. This 1938 epic is described below. During the Second World War Harrer was detained by the British in India, from whence he escaped to Tibet, where he became a friend of the Dalai Lama. His internationally famous memoir Seven Years in Tibet *(1953) details this time.*

The summer of 1938 began sadly enough, with the death of two young Italian climbers. Bartolo Sandri and Mario Menti, employees in a wool factory at Valdagno in the Province of Vicenza, were both respected members of the Italian Alpine Club though only 23 years old. Sandri, especially, was known to be an unusually fine rock-climber, who had done a number of super-severe climbs ranking as "Grade VI", among them some first ascents. True they had hardly any experience of ice-climbing in the Western Alps. Like all true mountaineers, they came to Alpiglen and the Scheidegg quietly, without any fuss, indeed almost secretly. They studied the Face, tried themselves out by a reconnaissance of its lower structure and came down again. They decided that the direct route, followed three years before by Sedlmayer and Mehringer, was easier than that discovered by Hinterstoisser. But it wasn't any easier. The fact is that the Face was not yet fit for climbing at all.

None the less Bartolo and Mario started up it early on June 21st. They reached a greater height than Sedlmayer and Mehringer had on their first day. Their courage and enthusiasm ran high, and they were driven on by a burning urge to succeed. They just couldn't wait. Nature, however, followed her own laws, heedless of courage, enthusiasm or ambition. Late in the evening one of the Eiger's notorious thunderstorms set in . . .

The very next day a search-party of Grindelwald guides, led by Fritz Steuri Senior, found Sandri lying dead on a patch of snow at the foot of the Face. Menti's body was only recovered with some difficulty a few days later from a deep crevasse.

That was a bad enough start to operations on the Eiger in the summer of 1938, but it could not hold up the developments which were due. The memory of the successful retreat of Rebitsch and Vorg, which had been the turning point in men's minds, was still vivid. So was the lesson that it was impossible to capture the Face by surprise. *Veni, vidi, vici* wouldn't work on the Eiger. Endless patience was required and long waiting . . . for days, even weeks.

Meanwhile, Fritz Kasparek was waiting impatiently for my arrival. That tremendous climber from Vienna, bursting with life, blessed with an optimism nothing could destroy, had already been in Grindelwald for some time, skiing around the Bernese Oberland, keeping a constant watch on the Eiger's mighty Face. Though, so far, there hadn't been much to watch except continual avalanches, sufficient in themselves to nip in the bud even the thought of an attempt. All the same, Fritz would have liked by now to have had with him his partner on the big climb they had planned to do together; for one never knows what may happen to interrupt one's plans. Sepp Brunnhuber, too, with whom Fritz had done the first winter ascent of the North Face of the Grosse Zinne as long ago as February – to some extent as a training climb for the Eiger project – could still not get away. I had promised Fritz to arrive at Grindelwald by July 10; but at the bottom of his heart he had good grounds for mistrusting students' promises.

Actually I was no longer a student by the time I got to Grindelwald. My tutors at the University of Graz were greatly astonished at the speed with which I suddenly attacked my

Finals. I could hardly explain to them that I wanted my studies out of the way before I climbed the North Face of the Eiger. They would certainly have shaken their heads and – not without some justification – reminded me that it was quite in order to "come off" that climb without having graduated first. I told nobody of our plan, not a fellow-student, not a mountaineering or sporting acquaintance. The only person I let into the secret was that wise, practical and plucky woman, my future mother-in-law, Frau Else Wegener. In 1930 her husband Professor Alfred Wegener had given his life for his companions on Greenland's inscrutable inland ice, when he perished in a blizzard; so she might well have had strong grounds for being fiercely opposed to ventures involving a risk to life. She, however, uttered no warning word; on the contrary, she encouraged me, though well acquainted with the reputation of the Eiger's North Face.

My last paper was on the morning of July 9th. At lunch-time I mounted my heavily laden motor-bicycle; and I arrived at Grindelwald punctually on July 10th, as promised. Fritz Kasparek, burnt brown by the glacier sun, his fair mop almost bleached white, greeted me in unmistakable Viennese.

He was blessed with the gift of the gab. His was a positively original gift for inventing expletives when faced with apparently insurmountable difficulties of the kind he was never in the habit of giving in to – both in the mountains and in ordinary life. However, he never used to parade his feelings; nor did he waffle about companionship and friendship. But his nature was such that, at times of crisis, he would not only share his last crust of bread or crumb of chocolate with his companions, but would give the whole of it away to them. And then not as a pathetic gesture, but to the accompaniment of some good nervous Viennese expression or other.

With friends of that kind one could go horse-rustling, invite the Devil to a picnic or – attempt the North Face of the Eiger.

Fraissl and Brankowski, those two old Eiger-hands, were also in Grindelwald. We strolled up to a pasture above Alpiglen together and there set up house. It was our firm intention to avoid the errors which had proved fatal to previous parties. The most important thing was to get to know our mountain as a whole, before attempting its most interesting and difficult face. So we first of all climbed from the "Hoheneis" diagonally across the (north-east) flank to the Mittellegi Ridge, then up it to the summit and down again by the normal route. In addition we climbed the Monch by the "Nollen".

Meanwhile cows had been driven up on to our idyllic pasture. Fritz and I decided to move our abode, and pitched our little tent in a small meadow close under the Face. Fraissl and Brankowsky stayed on the pasture. It was a fine day when Fritz and I started up the lower part of the Face and after climbing about 2,300 ft, to the so-called "Bivouac Cave" above the "Shattered Pillar", parked a rucksack full of provisions and equipment there. We attached a label to it, which read: "The property of Kasparek and Harrer. Don't move."

This notice did not indicate any particular mistrust of other North Face climbers. It was simply that, thanks to the many attempts and frequent rescuc- and recovery-operations, the Face was littered with pieces of equipment, ropes and pitons, which served as very welcome aids and additions to the equipment of subsequent parties. This made it absolutely necessary to mark clearly any rucksack intentionally parked on the Face like this one of ours.

We climbed down again to our tent. Conditions would not yet allow of an attempt with the slightest prospect of success. We had taken a firm stand not to let ourselves be pushed, driven or goaded. Past tragedies and particularly the deaths of the two Italians earlier in the summer had taught us that unseemly haste can ruin every sober consideration and lead to the direst results. We could wait and we meant to wait.

Days of fine weather set in; and still we waited, watching how the snow which had fallen during storms and been whipped against the rocks altered in consistency, melted away, settled and bound firmly with the old underlying layer. It now seemed reasonable to hope that conditions up on the higher, unknown sector of the Face too would be bearable.

By July 21st we decided that everything was in order. At about 2 a.m. on that day we started up the Face, crossing the edge-crevasse in the dark, climbing independently, unroped, up towards the "Shattered Pillar". We moved in silence, each of us picking his own line, each of us thinking his own thoughts.

Those hours between night and day are always a keen challenge to one's courage. One's body goes mechanically through the correct movements essential to gaining height; but the spirit is not yet awake nor full of the joy of climbing, the heart is shrouded in a cloak of doubt and diffidence. My friend Kurt Maix once described this diffidence as Fear's friendly sister, the right and necessary counterweight to that courage which urges men skywards, and protects them from self-destruction. It is certainly not fear which besets the climber; but doubts and questionings and "butterflies" are human failings. And climbers are after all only human beings.

They have to reconcile themselves with their own shortcomings and with constraining feelings; they have to subject themselves to the will-power already geared to the enterprise in hand. And so the first hour, the hour of the grey, shapeless, colourless dusk before dawn, is an hour of silence.

Sheer thrustfulness is false, indeed fallacious, at times when a man is struggling to achieve a balance and is busy trying to reconcile subtle *nuances* of feeling with his will-power. And the glorious thing about mountains is that they will endure no lies. Among them, we must be true to ourselves, too.

Fritz and I climbed on up, in the darkness before dawn, to the right of the "Shattered Pillar". From time to time we heard voices behind us, could distinguish individual words. It was Fraissl and Brankowsky, who like ourselves had waited for the fine weather, and had started up the Face behind us. We would get on well enough with them. Two parties on that great precipice are no hindrance to one another; indeed, they can help each other in a variety of ways.

The rocks looked grey, even the snow looked grey in the first livid light of dawn. And there was something else grey moving in front of us. Not rocks this time, but people, peeling out of their tent-sacks in front of the bivouac-cave.

In an instant all thought, doubts and self-questionings which had risen up out of the secret depths of our *ego* had sunk back again. We did not talk about them, least of all in front of strange fellow-climbers who were at one and the same time comrades and competitors.

Strangers? Climbers are never really strangers, least of all on this Face. We introduced ourselves to these two who had only just woken up from their night's sleep. Then they told us who they were: Andreas Heckmair and Ludwig Vorg. It was a unique place for such an introduction. The light of an unborn day was strong enough for each of us to be able to see the faces of our opposite numbers clearly, to sample their features, to assess their characteristics.

So this was the famous Andreas Heckmair. At 32 he was the oldest of us four. His face was limned by the hills themselves, spare, deeply lined, with a sharp, jutting nose. It was a stern, bold face, the face of a fighter, of a man who would demand much of his companions and the last ounce of himself.

The other man, Ludwig Vorg, seemed to be exactly the opposite type; a well-rounded, athletic type, not in the least sinewy or spare, nor were his features as prominent as Heckmair's. They radiated amiable relaxation; his whole being personified latent strength and an inner peace. His friends with whom he had been to the Caucasus two years before had nicknamed him the "Bivouac King". Even those nights in the open on the 7,000 ft ice-face of Ushba, the "Terrible Mountain", had failed to rob him of his sleep. On a snap judgment one would attribute the dynamic force to Heckmair, the stamina to Vorg. In any case two such diverse and complementary characters couldn't help making up a rope of quite extraordinary climbing ability and strength.

We couldn't tell if the two men were disappointed at our all being on the Face at the same time. If they were, they certainly didn't show it. Heckmair said: "We knew you were trying the Face too. We saw your rucksack and read the label." We couldn't quite grasp why we had been in the dark about the presence of these two men, who hadn't been living in a tent either at Alpiglen or Kleine Scheidegg, nor in the hay on any of the pastures. We only found out later that this time they had completely covered their traces. They had come to Grindelwald with luggage and taken a room in one of the hotels at Kleine Scheidegg. Who ever heard of a candidate for the North Face of the Eiger sleeping in a hotel bedroom? The ruse had worked perfectly.

Heckmair and Vorg had with them the best, most up-to-date equipment. They were in fact just as poor as we were, but had raised a sponsor for their climb in advance and had therefore found themselves for the first time in their lives in a position to buy to their hearts' desire at Munich's best sports shop, and even to order gear which had to be specially manufactured. Of course they both had the twelve-pointer crampons which had just become fashionable. Fritz had ten-pointers, but I hadn't any at all. Admittedly this was a mistake, but it wasn't the result of carelessness, but rather of over-careful consideration. We had taken the view that the North Face was a rock-wall with aprons of snow and ice embedded in it. A pair of crampons weighs a good deal, and we felt that if we did without it, we could take more equipment or provisions along. My boots were nailed with the well-known claw system popular in Graz, a lay-out providing an equally good grip on rock and ice. Our plan was for Fritz to lead on the ice pitches and me to take over on the rocks. We also hoped to avoid the irksome and time-wasting necessity of strapping crampons on and taking them off again all the time. We were quite wrong, and it was a mistake; but it did not prove disastrous, for all it did was to lose us time and provide me with extra exertion. But we hadn't yet discovered that as we stood talking to Heckmair and Vorg outside the bivouac-cave.

Vorg, used to bivouacking in all sorts of conditions and places, was grousing about the night they had just spent. "It was cold and uncomfortable," he complained. "Falling stones wouldn't allow us to stay outside the cave, and the cave itself was narrow and wet. It dripped steadily on our tent-sack all night long."

Heckmair studied his altimeter and shook his head dubiously. "It has risen about sixty metres." he announced, "which means the barometer has fallen about three points. I don't like the look of the weather."

Just at that moment Fraissl and Brankowsky came up with us. Introductions and friendly greetings followed, but by now there was a note of real concern detectable in Heckmair's voice. Like a

good trouper he concealed his disappointment. He just pointed
to a fish-shaped cloud on the horizon and said: "I'm sure the
weather's breaking. We're not climbing any further."

We ourselves felt certain that the weather would hold, and
Fritz put forward that viewpoint in his optimistic way: "Oh,
sure, the weather'll hold all right. And someone's got to climb
the Face sometime, after all!"

Heckmair and Vorg were getting ready to go down, as we
moved on up. I kept on thinking about the retreat of those two
superb climbers and remembering the look of utter disappointment on Vorg's face. And what about Heckmair? I soon realized
that his fishy cloud and the "rise in the altimeter" were only
excuses. He knew that the presence of three ropes on the Face
could mean serious delays, but he was too good a sport to stand
on his rights of "first come, first served" and ask one of our
parties to turn back. So he turned back himself: instead of
saying "you're in the wrong", he remarked that he didn't like
the look of the weather. It was a decision dictated by a true sense
of mountaineering responsibility.

Time and again climbers on the North Face had got into
difficulties, through allowing themselves to be hurried not only
by the state of the Face or by weather conditions, but by the
competition of others. Vorg, one of the finest climbers ever to
attempt the climb, was not going to let himself be hurried.

At the moment there was little time for psychological studies
or similar problems. The Face itself was providing our immediate problems, as we reached the "Difficult Crack". Twilight had at last been forced to yield to the first full light of
morning. We roped up, and Fritz tackled the first severe pitch
with his own personal craftsmanship. The heavy Eiger-pack on
his shoulders brought his first swift upward drive to a halt.
Down he had to come and leave his rucksack at my feet. Then he
began his second assault. It was a pleasure to watch him. Higher
and higher he went, stylishly, using every projecting wrinkle,
never breaking his rhythm, never struggling. And in a stagger-
ingly short time he had mastered this first great defence-work
on the Face.

The job of roping Fritz's rucksack up after him was difficult
and time-wasting; it kept on jamming under overhangs. How-

ever, the first one got up there in the end; the second, weighing
55 lb, followed, but on my shoulders. We just hadn't time to
indulge in another bout of roping-up. Fritz hauled on my rope;
his assistance at least offset the weight of my pack, and I too was
soon at the top of the crack. The pitch gave me a gentle foretaste
of what the Face had in store; but the fact that I hadn't lost my
breath coming up the crack strengthened my confidence that I
was up to the work in hand. There is, of course, a huge
difference between balancing upwards like a gymnast totally
unencumbered on even the hardest Dolomite wall and climbing
heavily-laden up the Face of the Eiger. But then isn't the ability
to hump heavy loads a requisite for every successful major
climb?

Many climbers still to come will use rope slings on the
"Difficult Crack". We preferred to climb it free. A rock-
climber of Kasparek's supreme skill only resorts to slings where
they are absolutely unavoidable.

By now we were just below the Rote Fluh, that sheer wall,
hundreds of feet high, which goes winging up to the sky in a
sweep of incomparable smoothness. According to the book of
the rules, based on man's experience, the mountain walls sleep
quietly in the early morning, blanketed by the night frost. Even
the stones are supposed to be frozen into inactivity. But the
Eiger's Face doesn't go by any Queensberry rules; this was just
another instance of the way it tips human experience overboard.
Down came the stones. We could see them taking off over the
top edge of the Rote Fluh and whizzing out through empty
space in a wide arc. The Face was raking us with defensive fire.
We hurried on upwards, for the nearer we got to the foot of the
Rote Fluh, the safer we should be.

We could hear another heavy block coming. It landed below
us, splintering into a thousand pieces.

Then we heard Fraissl's voice, Not a call for help or an SOS,
just a communication; one of them had been hit on the head and
hurt.

"How bad is it? Do you need help?" we asked.

"No, but I'm pretty giddy. I think we've had it. We'll have to
turn back."

"Can you manage it alone?"

"Yes, we can."

We were sorry that our two Viennese friends couldn't keep us company, but we didn't try to dissuade them. So Fraissl and Brankowski started to climb down again.

Now, before sunrise, we two were alone on the Face again. Only a little while ago there had been six of us; now Fritz and I had only each other to rely on. We didn't discuss it, but subconsciously it strengthened our feeling of mutual dependence and comradeship. We made rapid progress over easier ground; and then, suddenly, we were at the passage which Rebitsch and Vorg had christened the "Hinterstoisser Traverse" the year before.

The rocks across which we now had to traverse to the left were almost vertical, plunging away beneath into thin air. We were full of admiration for Hinterstoisser's brave achievement when he opened up this rope-assisted traverse across to the First Ice-field for the first time, feeling his perilous way from hold to hold. We were full of gratitude too to Vorg and Rebitsch for having left a traversing-rope – shouting a welcome to us, it seemed – in place here. We tested it and found it firmly anchored and secure against any strain, although it had been exposed for twelve months to storms and showers, to the wet and the cold.

We knew from reports, descriptions and photographs how to effect the traverse. Nobody, however, had described the pitch when heavily iced over. The rock was absolutely glazed, offering no hold whatever to a frictioning foot. None the less, Fritz led off into the traverse with that tremendous skill of his, fighting for his balance on smooth holdless film, winning his way, inch by inch, yard by yard, across that difficult and treacherous cliff. In places he had to knock away snow or a crust of ice from the rock with his ice-hammer; the ice-splinters swept down the slabs with a high whirring sound, to disappear into the abyss. But Fritz held on, pushing, feeling his way over to the left, climbing, hanging right away from the rock on the rope, from hold to hold, till he reached the far end of the traverse. Then I followed, shoving Fritz's rucksack along ahead of me on a snap-link in the traversing-rope, and soon joined him at the other end.

Soon after the traverse we came to the "Swallow's Nest", the bivouac place already made famous by Rebitsch and Vorg, and there we halted for a rest and some breakfast. The weather was holding, and a fine dawn had turned into a lovely day. The light was so good that it had already been possible to take pictures down on the traverse, a traverse which is certainly one of the most photogenic pitches in all the Alps. That one prosaic epithet tells the whole story – the extreme difficulty, the exposure, the daring of the traverse. And I should at once like to take the opportunity of correcting a misapprehension: the Hinterstoisser Traverse is one of the key pitches to the climb, not the only one. There are numerous critical places on this incredibly huge Face, which – thanks to the safe return of Rebitsch and Vorg – had by now been reconnoitred as far as Sedlmayer and Mehringer's "Death Bivouac". As yet we didn't know what key-pitches lurked up there on the final precipice. All we knew was that, wherever it might rise in the Alps, it would by itself have been an object of wonder to the beholder and a highly-prized objective for the best rock-climbers alive.

We were going splendidly, the weather was fine, and we had no doubt that we stood a good chance of success; but we also knew that the very best of climbers had had to beat a retreat. So we equipped the "Swallow's Nest" as a strong point in case of a withdrawal. The old rope left by the 1937 party on the traverse was not enough. We proposed to assure the direct line of descent, which in 1936 had proved fatal to the party of four, a tragedy which only reached its appalling end with the ghastly death of Toni Kurz. At the "Swallow's Nest" we left behind us 330 ft of rope, pitons, snap-links, rope-slings and provisions.

It was July 21st 1938. Exactly two years ago to a day Hinterstoisser had spent hour upon hour in desperate attempts to climb back along the traverse he himself had been the first to discover. All in vain. He, and with him Angerer and Rainer, died on that same day. We were tremendously impressed by that memory. If those four men had only left their traversing-rope in place at the Traverse, if they had only had a long enough rope at the "Swallow's Nest", if only . . . We had to thank the dead for our knowledge. The memory made us both proud and said, but it did not scare us. Life has its laws, which we unconsciously obey. They pointed to the way up.

Fritz had strapped on his crampons; soon he was on his way up the First Ice-field. Here was no neve, but hard, brittle somewhat watery ice. I assessed the angle at from fifty to fifty-five degrees, that is, somewhat steeper than the average slope of the Grossglockner's Pallavicini Couloir. After the first rope's-length, Fritz cut a big stance and drove in an ice-piton, to protect me on my ascent. We were already beginning to realize that our calculations had gone astray when we decided to leave my crampons behind. I now had to make up for lack of equipment by a considerable increase in muscular energy. Never mind, my training in several forms of sport would be a great asset . . .

We were aiming for a vertical cliff, which leads from the First to the Second Ice-field. The only possible way seemed to be through an icy groove, later to be known as the "Ice-Hose". This barrier between the two shields of ice is one of the many snares and delusions on this Face. Optically, a wall in the Dolomites is far more impressive than any single pitch on the Eiger's Face. When I recall the great Dolomite faces, there is much which seems more difficult, steeper, more inaccessible than it really is. But when you lay your hand on the Dolomite rock, you immediately delight in the rough surface, the horizontal stratification, the resulting proliferation of holds and of the never-failing crannies and cracks into which pitons may safely be driven.

But here? The first illusion — the ice-covered rock-barrier doesn't look particularly difficult. All you have to do is to hammer in a belaying-piton below it . . . but it doesn't offer a belay. In fact there isn't a cranny anywhere for a reliable piton, and there aren't any natural holds. Moreover, the rock is scoured smooth by falling stones, bread-crumbled with snow, ice and rubble. It isn't an invitation to cheerful climbing, it offers no spur to one's courage; it simply threatens hard work and danger. All the same, it is a part of the Eiger's North Face, which we are trying to climb . . .

The "Ice-Hose" does justice to its name. The rock was thickly plastered with the stuff; but even the hose part couldn't

have been more accurate. Water was pouring down under the
frozen layer, between the ice and the rock. The only way was up
through it. The water poured into our sleeves, flowing right
down our bodies, building up for a short time above the gaiters,
which were supposed to separate our trousers from our boots,
before finding its way out. There were practically no holds in
this crack consisting of ice, rock and water. It is severe, calls for
the best climbing technique and demands the most ingenious
balancing manoeuvres. Here too Fritz showed his supreme skill;
but it took hours to reach the Second Ice-field. We were wet to
the skin when we got there.

It was still early in the afternoon. High and wide above us
loomed the Second Ice-field. Our way led diagonally up to the
left towards the arete of the "Flatiron", in the direction of the
last bivouac of Sedlmayer and Mehringer. The huge ice-apron
was greatly foreshortened from where we stood; but even
allowing for the optical illusion and remembering that it had
taken first-class ice-exponents like Rebitsch and Vorg five
hours – twenty rope's-lengths – to reach its upper rim, we still
had plenty of time to do it and probably even to reach the
"Death Bivouac". For there would still be at least six hours of
daylight.

In spite of all that, we decided to climb not to the left but to
the right, to a little knob of rock sticking out of the snow above
the upper edge of the Rote Fluh. The fine afternoon was letting
the sun beat diagonally down on the upper part of the Face – up
there where the "little icicles blow their noses". That was what
started the avalanches; and stones, once released from the
imprisoning ice up there, were in the habit of following the
laws of gravity.

And further over to the west – for one has to traverse
diagonally across the Face for hundreds of feet on those ice-
shields – snow-slides, stone-falls and cascades of water were
coming down in their vertical, unhampered course from the
"Spider".

Admittedly, every stone doesn't find a target. But we hadn't
carefully built a strong-point for a retreat down at the "Swallow's Nest" in order to be knocked out by stones or wiped off
the Face by avalanches up here. Falling stones are numbered

among the "objective" dangers of climbing or in other words as circumstances over which man has no control; but to venture with one's eyes open into the line of fire of falling stones is no longer an objective but a subjective exposure to danger, the outcome of sheer carelessness or stupidity. This huge ice-apron was a place to be climbed during the morning. Even then the danger from stones wouldn't be entirely eliminated, but it would be considerably less.

We reached our knob and were able to fix two belaying-pitons; then we spent hours in digging a small seat out of the ice below it. It was still daylight when we began to make the final preparations for our bivouac. We tied ourselves and our belongings to the pitons for security's sake, furnished our seat with coils of rope, and started to cook our meal. The knob of rock afforded us complete protection from stones; the view from our perch was magnificent. All the conditions for a happy bivouac were present; but we hadn't a dry stitch on us. Yet, although we had warm clothing and a change of underwear in our rucksacks, we dared not risk getting it, too, damp by putting it on under soaking clothes. We didn't know what the weather might do, or how often, where and under what conditions we should have to bivouac. So we would have to keep our spares dry against nights yet to come; but it needed some strength of mind not to fetch them out of the packs and put them on, even though we knew better.

The night was long, cold and uncomfortable. The bivouac was not a good one. We were only to know later on that it was the worst on the whole Face, in spite of its comparatively good sitting-space. Our wet clothes made us doubly susceptible to the cold; our minds and spirits were as busy as our bodies trying to cope with the discomfort. No training in the world is proof against that.

Every night has to come to an end sometime. In the grey light of dawn we got up with chattering teeth and prepared the ropes for the day's climbing. The weather was still good and the frost had anchored all the stones, as we started on the diagonal climb across the Second Ice-field. It was only now that we realized to the full what a mistake we had made in leaving my crampons behind. Fritz counteracted the error by a tremendous output of

energy, as he built a positive ladder of steps. It was amazing to
see how expert with his ice-axe was this best of all Vienna's
rock-climbers. For hours on end he swung it rhythmically to cut
step upon step, resting only when he stopped to safeguard me
up them. And the steps were so good that my claw-nails gave me
excellent holds in them.

From down below, the Ice-field looks like a smooth surface;
but that is pure illusion. Huge waves in the ice constantly gave
the impression that we were quite close to the safety of the rocks
above; but we soon realized that we had only reached another
bulge in the ice and that there was yet another ice-valley to be
crossed. It was the phenomenon the climber so often experiences in the Western Alps, when he mistakes one of many
subsidiary excrescences for the main summit.

The fully-equipped modern mountaineer handles his ice-axe
like a guide of the classical Alpine era. Speed is the essence of
modern climbing; steady, slow progress that of the classic past.
We were naturally taking longer because we were using the
technique of the past. Even Rebitsch and Vorg had taken five
hours the year before to cross this huge patch of ice. We took
exactly the same time.

Just before the rocks separating the Second from the Third
Ice-field, I looked back, down our endless ladder of steps. Up it
I saw the New Era coming at express speed; there were two men
running – and I mean running, not climbing – up it. Admittedly, practised climbers can move quickly in good steps; but
for these two to have reached this point quite early in the
morning was positively amazing. They must have bivouacked
last night on the lower part of the wall; it hardly seemed possible
that they had only started up it today. But it was, in fact, the
case.

These two were the best of all the "Eiger Candidates" –
Heckman and Vorg – wearing their twelve-pointer crampons. I
felt quite outmoded in my old claws. We exchanged a brief
greeting; then they went on up to Fritz. I knew my friend and
his highly developed set of alpine etiquette pretty well; I knew
he preferred to find his own way, and that, though he wore the
honourable badge of the Mountain Rescue Service, he himself
didn't like assistance. Even Heckmair's obviously joking en-

quiry whether he wouldn't prefer to turn back only brought a good strong Viennese reply from Fritz.

But Anderl didn't mean to start a squabble. His is a character with no touch of malice in it; moreover, Kasparek and Heckmair had far too great a respect for one another, and so the result of the encounter was neither discord nor rivalry, but a teaming-up such as has rarely been seen on this mighty Face. We naturally continued to climb as two separate ropes, with Heckmair and Vorg now taking over the lead. They told us later how they had seen Fraissl and Brankowsky turn back; after that there had been no holding them. They had started up the Face early in the morning and now they had already caught us up. And now, too, we would be staying together . . .

We moved on up the steep ridge towards the "Death Bivouac" at a uniform pace. During our extended midday rest at that point we felt completely united. Not a word was spoken indicative of any sense of disappointment. It was just as if we had always intended to climb together and now we were glad to have joined up at long last.

There could be no difference of opinion as to the continuation of the route. It led from our resting place diagonally downwards across the Third Ice-field towards the foot of the "Ramp", the rock-feature rising steeply towards the ridge up which lies the Lauper Route; then from the "Ramp" a right-hand traverse to the "Spider"; across the "Spider" and then up the adjacent exit-cracks to the summit-neve, crowning the final wall. It all sounds so easy. Yet each of the pitches named has its own big question-mark. But when I looked at my companions, Fritz, Anderl and Wiggerl, I felt quite certain that any pitch which offered the faintest possibility of a route up it would be climbed by our party of four.

It might perhaps have been possible to climb straight up the cliff from the "Death Bivouac" to the "Spider", but we could not see very far as we looked up the precipice. Mists were closing in on the mountain, and beginning to drift gently down to us. These were the mists which are known "out there" as the Eiger's "Wad of cotton-wool" and hug every contour of its ice and rock. That didn't upset us very much. It is one of the Eiger's regular features to put on a skull-cap for its after-lunch nap, much to the fury of the inquisitive people milling round the telescopes. We, of course, couldn't know the intensity of that fury, stemming from the fact that queue-tickets were being issued and that their purchasers had to pay for three minutes' viewing, whether they saw anything or not. Meanwhile, unobserved by the great world outside, we were traversing across an ice-slope, whose inclination exceeds sixty degrees, to the start of the "Ramp".

The "Ramp" – well, it fits that Face, on which everything is more difficult than it looks. You cannot run up it, for there are no rough slabs, no good foot- or hand-holds. Here too the rock-strata slope outwards and downwards, and the crannies into which a piton can be driven can be counted on one hand. At all events, I had a good belaying-piton at the foot of the "Ramp". I stood watching Fritz as he moved upwards with even, rhythmic movements, to a point some eighty feet above me.

Suddenly he slipped. I couldn't tell whether a hold had come away in his hand or whether he had failed to find a foot-hold. Everything went so quickly – he was already out of sight. I took in as much slack as I could and stood there waiting for the shock. I knew the piton was firmly in and would hold. And the rope, cushioned by the belay round my shoulders, ought with any luck to take the strain. Anybody coming off unbelayed at this point would go winging straight down to the outcrops at the bottom of the Face . . .

Luck was with us. The rope ran out over a little ridge of snow, cutting into the surface neve. This checked the velocity of Fritz's fall to such an extent that the shock I had to withstand was perfectly bearable. But was Fritz hurt?

My mind was soon at rest. Up from below came a couple of words only intelligible to one who knows Viennese slang inside out – a good aggressive oath. Then Fritz was climbing again. Soon he was at the top of the "Ramp", moving on above it, just as if nothing had happened, till presently I shouted up to him that there was no more rope. On my way up, I took a look at the place where he had come off. Fritz had fallen sixty feet through thin air straight down from the diagonal "Ramp" and had then calmly climbed back again by a difficult crack. We didn't mention the mishap again. Fritz carried it off as quietly as a player whom the dice condemn to go back to the start at "Snakes and Ladders". We weren't in the least upset: we just laughed because we were enjoying life. No sentimental hand-shakes either. Back to the start – and then six forward up the next waterfall – that was the way we looked at it. It was quite natural for Fritz to have climbed straight up again after his fall, for he hadn't hurt himself. And it was quite natural for me to have held the rope because that was what I was there for. Fritz was just the right companion for this great Face. He treated irrelevancies as such, never burdening his friends with "if" and "suppose", nor with the thought "what might have happened", or the question "why did it happen?" What really mattered was that nothing *had* happened.

Late in the afternoon the four of us were all together again. Above us the "Ramp" had contracted to a narrow gulley with a crack blasted out of it. Water was running down the crack. None of us wanted to bivouac in wet clothes – our own had dried out during the morning, while we were traversing the Second Ice-field; moreover, we were beginning to find the day's labours sufficient. The crack would be a good prelude to the next day's work; so we prepared to bivouac.

That sounds easy enough. And we had thought it would be easy enough when we were looking at the "Ramp" in photo-graphs or through a telescope. We even thought we could pick our seats. Actually there were no seats, in fact not a single seat. Indeed, good stances were a rarity.

We arranged our bivouac about 8 feet below that of Heckmair and Vorg. We managed to drive a single piton into a tiny crevice in the rock. It was a thin square-shafted piton. It held after only a centimetre, but it was just jammed. Obviously, once we hung our whole weight on it, it would very likely work loose with the leverage. So we bent it downwards in a hoop, till the ring was touching the rock. In this way we did away with any question of leverage and knew we could rely on our little grey steely friend. First we hung all our belongings on to it and, after that, ourselves.

There was no room to sit down. The "Ramp" was very narrow and very steep at this point; but we managed to man-ufacture a sort of seat with the aid of rope-slings, and hung out some more to prevent our legs dangling over the gulf. Next to me there was a tiny level spot, just big enough for our cooker, so we were able to brew tea, coffee and cocoa. We were all very much in need of liquids.

Heckmair and Vorg were no more comfortably lodged. The relaxed attitude of Vorg, the "Bivouac King" was quite remarkable; even in a place like this he had no intention of doing without every possible comfort. He even put on his soft fleece-lined bivouac-slippers, and the expression on his face was that of a genuine connoisseur of such mattters. It is absolutely no exaggeration to say that we all felt quite well and indeed comfortable. Experienced climbers will understand that statement, and laymen must simply believe it. A famous philosopher, when asked what true happiness was, replied; "If you have some broth, a place to sleep in and no bodily pains, you are well on the way." We can improve on that definition. "Dry clothes, a reliable piton and precious revivifying drinks – that is true happiness where the North Face of the Eiger is concerned."

Yes, we were quite happy. This huge mountain-face had brought our lives down to the lowest common denominator. After cooking for hours we pulled the Zdarsky-sack over us and tried to find as comfortable a position as possible, so that we could at least doze off occasinally. It was great to be able to look forward to a night in dry clothes. Our perch was about 4,000 feet above the snow-fields at the base of the precipice; if one of us fell off now, that was where he would certainly finish up. But who was thinking about falling off?

It was a good bivouac. Bodily aches and discomfort made no disturbing intrusion on the train of our thoughts. As I fell asleep, I saw a picture, a happy, sunny picture of something that happened when I was very young; no mirage of a sheltering roof over my head or a warm bed, but a memory of one of my first experiences in the mountains.

It happened when I was only 15. I had climbed all alone to the top of the Mangart, that proud summit in the Julian Alps, and was coming down, very impressed by my great experience. I reached a huge scree-slope, of the kind one so often finds in the Julians, miles long. Down it I went, through the bleak hanging-valley, taking long bounding strides. The sun was scorching and my tongue was sticking to my gums. There in the middle of the rubble, I saw two eagles tearing huge lumps of flesh from the carcass of a chamois. The birds of prey only flew away reluctantly as I came by. I was so fascinated by the sight that I momentarily forgot my thirst. Young as I was, the knowledge that the death of one thing can mean the life of another was borne in on me ineradicably. Was that an immutable law of Nature, I wondered? Was it true for people as well as for animals? Every fibre of my being protested against the notion.

I came down to the shore of the Weissenfelser See. There, by the lake, stood a shepherd's hut, next to a spring, from which fell a glittering column of water. I bent down and let the water run down over my wrists. Then I drank and drank and drank. . . .

Suddenly I felt a sharp box on my ears. The tall, white-haired herdsman was standing there, his sharp-etched face burnt mahogany by the sun.

"Boy, why are you drinking water?" he asked. "There in my hut I have cool milk and sour cream. You can quench your thirst and drink your fill indoors."

I shall never forget that old man, who allowed his tongue to grow sharp in order to do me a good turn. I remained for days as his guest, eating and drinking everything the little farm produced, milk and cream and cream-cheese. He was a proud, hospitable man and, what is more, educated and much-travelled, who could speak eight languages fluently. For many years he had been a ship's cook over the face of the seven seas; and all his life's experiences added up to kindness towards his fellow men. I remembered the horrible picture of the eagles and the dead chamois. And instantly I realized, with the receptive idealism of early youth, that Nature's cruelty didn't hold among men. Men must be kindly . . .

With that memory of the old man by the Weissenfelser See I nodded off, into a deep and dreamless sleep. I don't know how long I slept like that. Suddenly, dreaming now, I saw the old man there again in front of me. His face was no longer kind; he was angry as he tugged at my breast. I tried to shake him off, wanting to go on sleeping, but I could not, he was so strong. He tugged at me and shook me harder still.

I only half woke up, but could still feel the fierce pressure on my chest. It was the rope. I had slid off my perch as I slept, and was hanging on it with my full weight. I knew then that I was on the "Ramp", on the Eiger's North Face, and that I really ought to straighten myself out, raise myself and resume a proper sitting posture; but I was too lethargic and only wanted to go on sleeping. Vaguely I recognized that one shouldn't for a moment longer than necessary weigh down a piton which is only a centimetre deep into the rock; but it was so pleasant to snatch just a few more minutes before straightening everything out. So I fell asleep again.

The moment I nodded off, there was the dream, back again. This time the old man shook me properly awake. I stood up in the slings, resumed my sedentary posture on that vertiginous little stance. Fritz mumbled something in his sleep.

Then I heard Andreas and Ludwig talking overhead. Vorg's voice sounded worried, so I asked what was the matter.

"Anderl feels sick," came the answer. "The sardines he ate last night have upset his tummy."

I was wide awake by now and fully restored. I could hardly feel the cold any more. There, close by me, on its little level spot, stood the cooker.

"I'll brew you some tea, Anderl," I said. "It always helps."

Tea is surely the king of all drinks. It helps against cold, it helps against the heat, against discomfort and sickness, against weariness and weakness. And it helped on this occasion too. The sardines quietened down in Anderl's tummy. We dozed and slept till the stars began to pale and the light of a new day crept through the twilight before dawn. Night was over; it had not been a bad one.

Vorg began cooking at about four o'clock. Like everything else, he did it thoughtfully, unhurriedly and thoroughly. He cooked porridge and coffee in large quantities. That cheered us up and drove away the cold. It was seven o'clock before we finally started to climb again. To have to cope with the crack in the gully as early morning physical training was quite a big demand on bodies still stiff from a bivouac. It didn't look any easier this morning than it had yesterday evening, except that the waterfall had stopped. In its place there was a thin armouring of ice on the rocks. Even Anderl, leading up it, looked a little doubtful.

He seemed to think straight on up was the best way and took the gully direct, knocking in a piton wherever he could. One of them actually held safe. He worked his way higher and higher with supreme technical skill, trying to get off the ice by climbing into the overhanging cliffs on the Face. He was nearly up the overhang, trying out a hold from which to get a final pull-up; but it wasn't a hold, it was a loose block, and it broke away bringing him down with it. A second or two later our friend was hanging safely from the good piton below the overhang. That wouldn't do at all for Andreas Heckmair: overhangs can't behave like that. He was very cross indeed. If it wouldn't go on the ice-free stuff, then it had better go right up the middle of the ice itself. So he put on his famous twelve-pointer crampons.

Then he treated us to an acrobatic *tour de force*, an exhibition exercise, such as we had rarely witnessed before. It was half superb rock-technique, half a toe-dance on the ice – a toe-dance above a perpendicular drop. He got a hold on the rock, a hold on the ice, bent himself double, uncoiled himself, the front points of his crampons moving ever upwards, boring into the ice. They only got a few millimetres' purchase, but that was enough. Heckmair defeated that difficult pitch, cut foot-holds and banged pitons into the ice slope which began above it, then safeguarded Vorg up it after him.

We were still climbing as two separate ropes. It was now Kasparek's turn to tackle the crack in the gully. Not only had he no twelve-pointer crampons, he had a completely different conception of the pitch. He took it direct, avoiding entanglements with the icy and the ice-free containing walls alike. By a masterly piece of climbing he got up the crack as if climbing in the Gesause at home rather than on the great Face of the Eiger.

I came up last. Then we were all four together again on the ice, looking up in incredulous astonishment at the menacing bulge of ice which here threatens finally to bar all progress up the "Ramp". Could anybody climb that?

The cliff was more than thirty feet high. I had never seen anything to match it; even the others at first seemed flabbergasted. Would it go on the left? No. On the right? No. Straight up seemed to be the best bet: but was this "best" a possible one? Heckmair had a go. He began by banging pitons into the ice below the bulge. One of them went in and held like a vice. Then he balanced his way delicately upwards. There were icicles hanging from the bulge; to one of these he fastened a sling and pushed himself up a bit in it. It looked terrifying, but he didn't seem in the least impressed by the danger; inch by inch he moved upwards, but as soon as he trusted his weight to the icicle, the pretty glittering thing broke away and off he came . . .

The piton held.

Once again we saw the same reaction as before. A rebuff as thorough-going as a fall rouses Heckmair to a cold fury. He immediately tackled the bulge again. This time he didn't trust to the icicles with which the Architect of our mighty prison had decorated it. Was it really a prison? Was this where we were going to have to give in and turn back?

No, our Andreas climbed up and out of our prison, having found an "ice-handle". An icicle hanging down had coagulated with an ice-stump pushing upwards – a stalagmite and a stalactite, both of ice, had grown into one. And this object, carpentered by some freak of nature, proved to be the key to our prison door. Heckmair threaded another sling through the handle, leaned outwards almost horizontally, banged some notches with his ice-hammer in the ice above the bulge, felt around with one hand, took a firm hold.

I had never seen a pitch that looked so hazardous, dangerous and utterly extraordinary. Fritz, who knows many of the famous key-pitches in the Alps, thought that the famous overhanging roof on the Pillar of the Marmolata looked child's play in comparison with this bulge. We were all pretty tense. Vorg had a tight hold on the rope, ready at any moment to hold Heckmair if he came off again.

But he didn't come off. We couldn't imagine how, but in some masterly fashion or other he had managed to drive an ice-piton deep into the ice above the bulge and thread the rope through a snap-link. Then he gave the order: "Pull!"

Vorg pulled him up on the rope, over the bulge, up to the piton.

Heckmair used his axe a few more times. Then "Let her go!" he said.

Vorg let the rope go loose, so that Heckmair could stand up; at the same time he was still keeping a careful watch in case of another fall. But Heckmair was soon in firm holds; he hurried a few feet up on to the ice-slope above the bulge, cut a roomy stance in the ice and drove a belaying-piton deep into firm ice. Then as the curtain-cue to an unusually dramatic scene we heard the welcome words: "Up you come!"

Our prison gate was open. Vorg followed through it. The North Face of the Eiger is so vast, so difficult and so serious that any display of human vanity would be out of place. No doubt Fritz and I could have climbed the bulge without any assistance from above, but it would have taken precious hours we would later have begrudged. So Fritz didn't hesitate a moment to take the rope Vorg let down to us. We who followed were robbed of the thrill and the adventure of this, the hardest pitch till now on the Face; we only tasted the toil it involves. And I, as last on the rope, had to knock out and retrieve all the pitons. I was decorated with them like a Christmas tree and the clank of the iron-mongery drowned my gasps as I struggled up over the bulge.

The ice-slope above was easy compared with what we had just done. We went straight up the ice for a short way only, then traversed out to the right at once.

It is of course easy enough for anyone who has made a successful first ascent to shake his head about the mistakes of those who follow. I do not propose to do it. But I am surprised that so many parties which climbed the Face after us went straight on up the ice-slope towards the Mittellegi Ridge and only tried to traverse across to the "Spider" much too high up. This was the cause of many delays and also brought about the disaster of 1957. It was perfectly clear to the four of us that the right-hand traverse must be attempted as soon as possible.

So we were traversing out to the right from the ice-slope, all four roped together, along a brittle belt of rock below an overhanging cliff. It was midday by now, and we could hear the hissing of the avalanches and the tattoo of the stones, but we were protected from both by the overhang.

While we were traversing these broken rocks – Heckmair was about 200 ft ahead of me at the time – we suddenly heard a fearful humming and whining sound. It was neither a stone-fall nor an avalanche, but an aeroplane flying past quite close to us. We could see the faces of its passengers quite plainly. They waved and we waved back. Hans Steiner, the Bernese photographer managed to take some photographs of unique documentary value at that moment. His pictures showed three of us on the traverse while Heckmair has already started up a crack beyond it.

That crack is the only possible line of ascent from where the brittle belt peters out to a level on which the traverse to the "Spider" can be completed. Heckmair thought he could climb it by the usual methods; but every pitch on the Eiger's Face is harder than it looks and tricky with ledges on which the snow is only pressed against the rocks, with hand- and foot-holds that let you down. So he had to leave his rucksack behind to have a second go at the pitch, unencumbered. For this he kept his crampons on, in view of the icing one continually meets on the Face. It was an entirely new type of rock-climbing, this ascent of severe, often super-severe rock, overhanging in places – on crampons. Heckmair frequently stood in imminent danger of a fall, but somchow his fingers held him when he thought his strength was used up. The scrape of his climbing irons on the hard rock sounded like a furious gritting of teeth, which only stopped when he disappeared from sight overhead.

We three followed without crampons.

It took ages before we had all got up that 100 ft vertical rock-pitch. But surely not so long that it was dusk already? It had suddenly grown very dark; but a glance at the watch showed that, in spite of the darkness, it was still early afternoon. Heavy clouds bulked up into the sky; and this time the thundering roar caught up by the rocks and thrown back in a hundred reverberations was not the sound of an aeroplane, flying past dangerously near. This was genuine thunder.

By the time I reached Fritz's stance, the other two had gone ahead. They had untied from the communal rope again, so as to reach the "Spider" before the storm broke.

The thunderstorm provided a gloomy, menacing, but magnificent setting. A few minutes before, the sun had been shining, at least for the people down in Grindelwald. This sudden change was typical of the North Face; but we were already so familiar with its caprices that the oncoming storm caused us no alarm. Indeed, I was even sorry that there was no time to linger on the stance where Fritz had been waiting for me. That stance had all the elements of the miraculous; it was the first place, indeed the only one in the whole 6,000-ft Face where you could make yourself comfortable. It would have been grand to sit and rest there, looking down the great wall, into the valley, out over the surrounding hills. But the weather was hunting us on, and we followed the others.

The rock-traverse to the "Spider" is no promenade. But at least the rocks at this point are horizontal and the stratification consequently favourable. And the patches of ice which link them were firm enough to allow us to bite deeply into them with our ice-pitons. Not only is the traverse indescribably fine from the scenic angle, but it is so exciting and technically safe that we almost forgot the approaching storm. I cannot remember who first gave it the name of "the Traverse of the Gods", but it is comprehensively descriptive.

We reached the "Spider", the great sheet of ice set in the Face, quickly and without encountering any great difficulties. We hadn't time to examine the scene and the terrain more closely, and now even the possibility of so doing was withdrawn, for the sky had meanwhile taken on a blue-black tinge; then it disappeared altogether, as tattered mists chased across the Face, closing in on us, then lifting again to give a glimpse of things, then settling into a thick blanket of cloud. As the storm set in it began to sleet, mixed with snow; lightning began to flash and thunder to grumble and roar.

We could still see Heckmair and Vorg, already on the way up the ice-slope of the "Spider", about a rope's length and a half ahead of us; so we followed them up.

As I have already explained, the name "Spider" has been given to this steep patch of neve or ice high up in the almost vertical Face because of the white streaks spreading out from it in every direction like legs and clutching arms. These run more especially upwards – in cracks and gullies up towards the summit snow-cap – and down towards the "Death Bivouac". But nobody had discovered how apt the appellation was before we got there; nor had we, as yet, while we went up the first rope's length. We hadn't yet discovered that this "Spider" of snow, ice and rock can become a fearful trap; that when hail or snow falls, ice particles and snow, coming sliding down from the steep summit-neve, get canalised in the cracks and gullies, shoot out on to the "Spider" under pressure, there join up in a flood of annihilating fury and then sweep across the "Spider's" body, finally to fling themselves outwards and downwards, obliterating and taking with them everything which isn't part of the living rock. Nor is there any escape from the "Spider" for anyone caught on it by bad weather and avalanches.

We didn't know it then, but we very soon found out. Very soon. Immediately . . .

I was already on the "Spider's" ice and had hacked out a reasonable stance in which I was able to stand quite well without crampons. I felt very safe on account of a deeply-embedded ice-piton. The rope ran through a snap-link hung on the piton-ring to Fritz, working his way up about sixty feet above me. I could see him vaguely through the mist and the driven snow.

Presently he disappeared from my sight, swallowed up in the mist. The screaming of the storm, the rattle of the hail, were alarming. I tried to penetrate the grey veils to catch a glimpse of him, but in vain. Only a greyness within a greyness . . .

The howling of the wind increased, gathering a very strange note – a banging and swishing, a whistling hiss. This wasn't the voice of the storm any more coming down out of wild dance of ice-particles and snowflakes, but something quite different. It was an avalanche and as its harbingers, rocks and fragmented ice!

I snatched my rucksack up over my head, holding it firmly with one hand, while the other gripped the rope which ran up to my companion. I jammed myself against the ice-cliff, just as the whole weight of the avalanche struck me. The rattle and hammering of stones on my pack was swallowed up by the clatter and roar of the avalanche. It snatched and clutched at me with fearful strength. Could I possibly survive such pressure? Hardly . . . I was fighting for air, trying above all to prevent my rucksack being torn away and also to stop the endless stream of rushing snow from building up between me and the ice-slope and forcing me out of my foot-holds.

I hardly knew whether I was still standing, or was sliding down with it. Had the ice-piton come adrift? No, I was still standing, and the peg was still firm; but the pressure was growing unbearable. And Fritz must be coming off any moment. Standing out there in the open he couldn't possibly withstand the fury of the avalanche . . . it must sweep him away . . .

My thoughts were quite clear and logical, although I felt certain that this avalanche must hurl us all off the "Spider" and down to the bottom of the mighty wall. I was only resisting because one tries to resist so long as there is life in one. I was still gripping the rope with one hand, determined to do all I could to hold Fritz. At the same time I began to wonder whether we were already so high on the "Spider" that he wouldn't hit the rocks below, but would remain hanging on the ice-slope if he came off, slid past me and fetched up on the full run of the rope sixty feet below? And could I stand the shock if he hit me in passing?

All these thoughts were calm, without any sense of fear or desperation. I had no time for things like that. When would Fritz come off? I seemed to have been standing in this crushing, sliding Hell for endless ages. Had stones cut the rope and Fritz fallen alone, deprived of its protection? No, if that had happened the loose rope would have come sliding down to me. It was still stretching upwards, so Fritz must somehow or other still be holding on . . .

The pressure decreased, but I got no time to draw new breath or to shout before the next avalanche arrived. Its fury exceeded that of the first; it must bring the end for us. Even that realization was almost objective. It was odd that no important thoughts moved me, such as one might expect on reaching the very frontier of existence itself. Nor did scenes from my whole life go chasing past in front of my eyes. My thoughts were almost banal, ridiculous, unimportant. I felt a little cross that the critics and wiseacres, and also the Grindelwald gravedigger, who had already numbered us, like all those who try the North Face, as belonging to his parish had been justified. Then I remembered my accident on the West Face of the Sturzhahn in the Totengebirge, years ago. I was trying to climb that difficult wall in the winter and fell 150 ft. On that occasion, too, I hadn't lived all my life over again, nor had I felt any great sense of despair, much as I loved life. Is everything different when one really crosses that border, then?

And now, I was still alive; my rucksack was still protecting my head; the rope was still threaded through the snap-link; and Fritz had still not fallen.

Then a new, unbelievable, and this time shattering realization came over me. The pressure of the avalanche had ceased. The snow and the ice-granules were tinkling away into the gulf. Even the raging of the storm seemed gentle to me, now that the crashing of the avalanche was stilled.

Then, tremulously, through the grey mists, came the first shouts, to be caught up by the cliffs framing the "Spider" and thrown back to the human beings, scarcely able to grasp the incredible truth. Names were being called, voices were answering: "Fritz! Heini! Anderl! Wiggerl!" I told myself that we were all alive. The others were all alive, and so was I. The greatest Eiger-miracle had happened. The "White Spider" had not claimed a victim.

But was it really a miracle? Had the mountain been kind? Would it be true to say that the "Spider" had spared the lives of her victims?

Climbers are not only men of action, they are also matter-of-fact people. Such reflections are only to be explained by the first upsurge of joy at one's recaptured life; they won't stand up to sober judgment. The miracle and the mercy were none of nature's fashioning nor the mountain's, but were the result of man's will to do the right thing even in moments of direst peril. Who can say we were merely lucky?

A famous man once said: "In the long run only the efficient man has luck." I am not so presumptuous as to claim that we mountaineers are always efficient. It seems to me that one of Alfred Wegener's remarks fits our situation on the Eiger's "Spider" better. He said: "Luck is the output of one's last reserves."

We had put out our last reserves.

Kasparek was standing sixty feet above me on the ice-slope.

When he heard the avalanche coming, he tried, with an instantaneous reaction, to drive in an ice-piton. He had no time to be frightened even for a split second. The piton was only a few centimetres into the ice, and quite loose, when the first avalanche arrived. In spite of the danger, even while the avalanche was roaring down on him in all its fury, he thought of the loose piton. It would have to stay firm, it simply mustn't be torn out by the shock of the cascading masses of snow and ice, nor by a falling stone; so Kasparek kept one protecting arm over the piton. Stones hit him on the hand, tearing the skin away. He was in great pain, but his will to keep the piton firm was greater. And during the short respite between the first and second avalanche, he drove the piton into the ice up to its ring, hooked a snap-link in and attached himself to it. And that is why Fritz didn't come off . . .

It was only afterwards, when the tension of the moment had passed, that I remembered having fastened myself by a rope-sling to my own piton for greater protection during that same interval.

The avalanche took Heckmair and Vorg by surprise, on a projection about sixty feet below the rock-rim above the "Spider". Owing to the configuration of the Face, it divided close above them into two separate streams; but the snow and ice-granules pouring down over each of them were quite strong enough to sweep even men of their build away. Neither of them could obtain protection by driving in a piton, not only because there was no time, but because they hadn't one between them. I had the whole collection by then: owing to being last on the rope, I was carrying about 20 lb of ironmongery which I had retrieved.

Heckmair only had his axe to hold him. The river of ice came up to his hips and threatened to whirl him away like a dead leaf; but he managed to resist the apparently irresistible pressure. At the same time he proved himself as an outstanding climbing partner as well as an outstanding leader of a climb. In spite of his own terrible distress, he had time to think of his number two, standing below him and still more exposed on the top of the knob. Holding his axe with one hand as an anchorage, he grabbed Vorg by the collar and held him tight. And so they both survived the assaults of the avalanches.

It was only now, when the danger was over, that Fritz felt the burning pain in his "scalped" hand. Only then did he shout up to Heckmair and Vorg. "Send a rope down, I'm hurt."

It took a long time to splice the ropes and send them down towards where Fritz was standing. And then they were still thirty feet short, so that Kasparek had to climb that distance unprotected.

How right Wegener is! Luck is certainly the output of one's last reserves.

This is how Heckmair described the end of the avalanche and his joy at finding that we were all still alive:

> Slowly it grew lighter and the pressure eased. We knew then, but still could hardly believe, that we had come through safely. And how had the others fared? The mists were thinning now – and there –
>
> "Wiggerl," I cried. "They're still on!"
>
> It seemed impossible, an outright miracle. We started to shout, and there they were, actually answering. An indescribable joy swept over us. One only discovers how strong a thing team-spirit can be when one sees the friends again whom one has counted for dead . . .

We all joined up again at the upper rim of the "Spider". Our feeling of delight at seeing the faces of our comrades again was overwhelming. As the outward sign of our friendship we decided to tie up again in a single rope of four – all the way to the top. And our leader should be Anderl. The "Spider's" avalanches hadn't been able to wipe us off the Face, but they had succeeded in sweeping away with them the last petty remnants of personal niggardliness and selfish ambition. The only answer to this mighty wall was the enduring bond of friendship, the will and the knowledge that each of us would give of his very best. Each of us was responsible for the lives of the others, and we refused to be separated any more. We were all filled with a great joy. From it stemmed the certainty that we would climb out of the Face on to the summit and find our way back to the valley where men live. It was in a mood of almost cheerful relaxation that we resumed the climb.

Our climb was in the full glare of public interest, though we neither knew nor cared about that; but it is interesting to note how the doings on the North Face were being interpreted by the watching eyes below. This is how Ulrich Link, the well-known Munich journalist, reported it from his observation post on the Kleine Scheidegg:

On Saturday at about 12.30 p.m., a break in the weather announced itself on the Eiger. A slate-grey menacingly dark cloud covered the Lauterbrunnen Valley. At that time the four climbers had, after five hours of tremendous labour, scaled the "Diagonal Gully", perhaps the hardest sector on the whole Face . . . At one o'clock all four were one behind the other at the left-hand edge of the snow field. Heckmair, himself a guide and probably the hardest-trained and most proficient on ice, was leading.

For half an hour a cloud hid the climbers from our view. At about 1.30 the Face was clear again. By then they had traversed the snow-ledge and the leader had already reached the crossing to the snow-field called the "Spider". Heckmair led in splendid style – he had been in the lead all day – across to the "Spider". Kasparek and Harrer had meanwhile rested at the end of the snow-ledge. From 3 to 3.30 p.m. the Face was once again enveloped in cloud. Then it cleared again and everyone rushed to the telescopes. The leader of the second rope was just traversing from the rocks on to the "Spider". At the same moment Heckmair reached the rock outcrop in the upper snow-couloir. The second party was moving more slowly, but with the same steadiness and caution as the first. Heckmair and Vorg had now reached a height of 11,800 ft and it was ten minutes past four. Mist came down on the Face again, and we were left cut-off with our fears and our hopes. The summit was still more than a thousand feet above the four men.

And now the weather was looking very bad again. Hour by hour it was impossible to tell whether it was going to finish up better or worse. The Lauterbrunnen Valley lay under a dirty grey pall; the Jungfrau and the Monch were wrapped in cloud. The ice-falls glimmered pale blue and bluish green in the lurid light. There was a patch of blue sky between the rain clouds. The Grosse Scheidegg over yonder was still quite clear, but the weather was making up relentlessly. Meanwhile the second party must be in the Funnel on the "Spider".

At 4.25 it began to rain gently, and exactly five minutes later a violent, noisy downpour set in, as if the clouds had been torn apart. It must be hitting the Face and the four climbers on it like a tidal wave. One could hear many voices raised in a confused gasp of alarm. The whole breadth of the North Face had become one fearsome waterfall. Water was pouring down the cliffs in ten, twelve, fifteen wide columns of white foam. A marvellous rainbow stood arched widely over Alpiglen; but who had any eyes for its miraculous play of colour? Up there, two of the men must be on the snow-slope, exposed to the full force of the flood pouring down on them. Would they be able to hang on?

At last the cloud lifted. The telescope was clear at last. There lay the great snow-slope . . . and there were the climbers, both moving up quietly and calmly. They had survived the deluge, then. Vorg and Heckmair had probably had a much easier passage, for they had managed to escape into the rocks at the edge of the couloir. Then the clouds closed down again . . .

At 6.45 all four men were re-united and moving towards the upper end of the belt of snow. At 7 o'clock they reached it; at 8 they were still moving on up, either because they had not yet found a bivouac-site or else having decided to go ahead as long as daylight allowed, to get as near the summit as possible. They had now reached 12,150 ft, high above the "Spider", a wonderful performance in fourteen hours. At 8.20 it began to rain again. During short intervals when the clouds permitted, we could see them climbing on and on. At 9 o'clock they were still moving, probably preparing their perch for the night; Kasparek and Harrer's third, Vorg and Heckmair's second bivouac. It will certainly be an ordeal, in wet clothes on an inadequate resting place most likely. But all four are tough as steel . . .

Ten o'clock and pitch dark now. From now on the four

men have to endure the long hours of darkness; they have enough food for six days. They will probably find little sleep during the night and will probably crouch over their cooker making hot tea and warming food. There can be no retreat now . . .

That report from a knowledgeable and experienced journalist makes pleasant reading even for a climber; for it is written in a manner which would also grip a layman, but without any uncalled-for dramatisation, and without cheap sensations thought up at a writer's desk. The mere facts, the keen observation of nature, the bare description of the Face are quite sensational enough by themselves.

But Ulrich Link was wrong about one thing. We couldn't crouch over our cooker. There was no room for that, though cooking still played its important part.

As to our bivouac-site, with the exception of the site above the crack leading to the "Traverse of the Gods", there is no single tiny spot where one can sit or where one can bivouac without thorough preparation.

After we had climbed an ice-bulge, we came upon a rock-ledge protected by overhangs from falling stones and avalanches. When I say a ledge, I do not mean a smooth comfortable feature on which it is possible to sit; it was far too narrow and precipitous for that. Heckmair found a place where he could drive in a rock-piton firmly, and with great patience fixed enough hooks on which to hang all the stuff, as well as securing himself and Vorg. There was no room there for us. Fritz and I arranged our overnight abode about ten feet away. The ledge was scarcely as broad as a boot, and only just allowed us to stand erect, pressed close against the rock; but we contrived to knock in a piton to which we could tie ourselves. Even then we still couldn't sit, not even on the outer rim of the ledge.

However, we found a solution. We emptied our rucksacks and tried fastening them too to the piton, in such a way that we could put our feet in them and so find a hold. We were sure it would work all right, and so it did.

Between us and our friends we had fixed a traversing rope, along which a cookery-pot went shuttling back and forth

hanging from a snaplink. Vorg had taken on the important post
of expedition-cook. So, even if we couldn't crouch over it, as
Link had imagined us doing, the bubbling of Vorg's cookery-
pot produced a comfortable feeling. None of us wanted any
solid food; all we needed was drink. So Ludwig brewed coffee,
for hours on end. As soon as a bowl was ready, he would have a
taste and then pass it to us others in turn. Fritz, being Viennese,
is a coffee connoisseur, and praised Ludwig's concoction.

But good coffee calls for a cigarette, if one is a smoker; and
Fritz was the only real addict amongst us four. Unfortunately,
his cigarettes hadn't stood the deluge of rain, hail, snow and
avalanches at all well; they were soaked and pulpy. Fritz, who
hadn't uttered a word or complaint about the considerable pain
in his damaged hand, grew feeble at the thought of his cigarettes: "If only I could light a dry cigarette with a dry match . . ."

I don't know what I would not have given to be able to fulfil
Fritz's wish, but I hadn't any cigarettes.

Then I remembered how I had come to know Fritz Kasparek
in the first place. It was at the beginning of the thirties, when I
was a young student with a great enthusiasm for climbing but
precious little money. Those were the days when one somehow
contrived the miracle of spending weeks on end in the Dolomites with but thirty shillings in one's pocket. A bicycle was
one's only means of transport and as one needed a licence for it
in Italy at that time, and since that cost money, we used to
tramp the roads for endless hours on foot, in order to reach one
mountain group from another.

One day I left my bike at the frontier at Sillian and walked
across into Italy, on my way to Innichen in the South Tyrol.
There is an old wayfarers' song of Hermann Lons' which goes:
"I never, never get my fill of dust." I was hungry, and thirstier
still, but I was compelled by the thought of my slender purse to
pass by inns and shops displaying the most glorious fruit and
delicacies.

Then I saw another wayfarer coming towards me. He too had
a huge pack, a typical climber's rucksack; he also had a mop of
fair hair, two amused-looking eyes and a sun-tanned face. We
summed each other up, mutually recognized a kindred soul in
one another, nodded. Then the fair-haired one, marching to-

wards the Austrian frontier, called out: "Hi, who are you? Where from? Where to?"

"I'm Heini Harrer from Graz," I told him, "on my way to the Sexten Dolomites."

"I'm Fritz Kasparek from Vienna."

Fritz Kasparek . . . I knew that name already. He was one of Vienna's most daring and experienced climbers. This young Viennese had done the Pillar of the Marmolata, the North Face of the Western Zinne, the North Buttress of the Admonter Reichenstein, innumerable other superseveres and new routes. He was only a year or two older than I was, but I addressed him as "Sir" out of respect for his great reputation. "Nonsense," said he, shaking his head. "I'm Fritzl and you're Heini and that's that." And then straight out: "Hungry? Thirsty? No money, eh?"

I nodded.

Kasparek disencumbered his shoulders of his rucksack, waved invitingly towards the bank of grass at the edge of the road, sat down and produced a huge bag of glorious pears and peaches out of his pack.

"Eat!" he commanded.

I didn't wait for a second order. We ate all the fruit, lock, stock and barrel, and I must admit that Fritz only consumed half the amount I did. He laughed, got up, shook my hand. "So long," he said. "I'll be seeing you."

Then he strolled off towards the Austrian frontier, and I stood watching him for a long time. I didn't know then – it wouldn't have been Fritz Kasparek if he had breathed a word of it – that he had bought that fruit as his provisions for the journey to Vienna with his last penny. As a result he had to pedal his pushbike 300 miles from Sillian to Vienna without a coin in his pocket and no food to eat. Maybe he used his unblushing Viennese charm to cadge an invitation from one or two farmers to a glass of milk; I couldn't say. But the reader will understand how sorry I was up there on the North Face not to be able to hand Fritz a dry packet of fags and say: "Smoke!" – just as he had once held out a bag of fruit to me on a red-hot high-road and said: "Eat!"

It was now 11 p.m. Ludwig had given over cookery and

"retired to rest". Even here, on this tiny perch 12,300 ft up, and 5,000 ft sheer above the nearest level ground, he hadn't foregone the comfort of those bivouac-slippers. Andreas had to keep his crampons on, so as to get some kind of a stance in the ice for him to maintain a hold; but his head rested on Vorg's broad back. Next morning we discovered that Vorg had sat motionless, without a single movement of a muscle, so that Heckmair's sleep might be undisturbed. Fritz and I had pulled the Zdarsky-sack over us; our rucksack architecture served splendidly as support for our legs, and very soon I could hear the deep, regular breathing of my friend as he slept by my side. Through the little window in the tent sack I could see that there were no stars in the sky and the weather was still bad; it looked as if it were snowing. There was an occasional small snow-slide from above, but they only slid over the skin of the tent, with a gentle swishing sound, like a hand stroking it . . . I wasn't worried about the weather. I was possessed by a great feeling of peace; not the resignation to our fate, but a certainty that, whatever the weather might be, we would reach the summit tomorrow and after that regain the safety of the valley. This sense of peace increased to a conscious glow of happiness. We humans often experience happiness without recognizing it; later we realize that at such and such a moment we were happy. But here, in that bivouac of ours, I was not only genuinely happy; I knew I was.

This, the third bivouac for Fritz and me on the North Face, was the smallest in terms of room; in spite of that it was the best. And if you ask why, the reason was the rest, the peace, the joy, the great satisfaction we all four enjoyed there.

If, during the hours just past, while we were being tried to the utmost, one of us had given in or lost his nerve for a second; if driven by the instinct of self-preservation, one of us had thought of trying to save his own life by leaving the party – no one would have blamed him. His companions would not have cut him, even if they might perhaps have greeted him a little less warmly ever after. If, down in the valley, people had honoured and cheered him, his friends would not have said a word. But that particular happiness which is born of absorption in a common endeavour would have passed him by and he would not have tasted its joy. We four in that bivouac on the

Face of the Eiger were all happy. It might snow, and the little slides might come swishing over our covering tent-sack; but our sense of happiness was deeply rooted in us. It allowed us to think pleasant thoughts; and we were able to sleep . . .

Putting oneself to the supreme test – the expression is in itself an exaggerated description of a healthy, honest experience, and a contradiction of the quiet account one renders to oneself. But a far greater mistake is to suggest that this extreme testing of oneself is the mainspring of mountaineering. It is a suggestion initiated by the incurable complex-fiends, because no better explanation of what was to them inexplicable has occurred to them. I really cannot help smiling when I imagine Fritz Kasparek's face if one of these know-it-alls asked him whether he climbed in order to prove himself. The questioner would no doubt retire discomfited, routed by a caustic reply couched in those well-known Viennese terms which are so hard to translate into good classical German.

Of course no climber embarks on a difficult climb in order to test himself. If during moments of extreme danger on the mountain he thinks first of his rope-mates, if he subordinates personal well-being to the common weal, then he has automatically passed the test; and so he probably would in any of the everyday disasters, flood or fire. Nor would such a man go whizzing past injured people on the Autobahn; but he would bring aid where he could. For him the knowledge that he has done his best is enough. A passion to prove his mettle can never be the mainspring which makes him tick.

It makes me very angry to think of the many critics who categorize climbers of the "extreme" school as mentally abnormal. I can think of no more normal men than my three Eiger companions. True, the position in which we were situated was quite out of the ordinary; but my friends' reaction to that element of extraordinariness was perfectly normal. Fritz longed for dry cigarettes; Ludwig changed into cosy, lined boots for the bivouac; and Andreas, anchored upright in the ice by his crampons, protected by Ludwig's broad back, slept the sleep of the just.

The peace and harmony of that night in the open allowed me to drift off into a twilight state between waking and sleeping.

My body, almost bereft of being, was at rest. The cold did not plague; it only served to remind me that I was on a great mountain-face, as indeed did the somewhat cramped posture imposed by our rucksack bivouac. But that didn't plague me either. Here, as elsewhere in life, bliss was born of contrast. For, after the drubbing we had gone through a few hours before at the hands of the avalanches on the "Spider", our bivouac-perch seemed a very Heaven.

I was awakened by a considerable snow-slide over our tent. Dawn was glimmering through the little window; a new morning was at hand. Unfortunately it was not heralded by the gorgeous play of colour of sunrise, nor by a clear pale-blue sky in which the stars were being dimmed by the new light of day; its approach was a greyness coming out of a grey fog. When we pulled the tent-sack away, we looked out on a winter landscape. It was still snowing; everything sharp or edgy had been fined away by the snow. Even our ledge had disappeared. Our friends, a few yards from us, appeared to be stuck on to the vertical rocks. The very idea that in this landscape, savage beyond the wildest dreams of imagination, people were alive, and actually planning to escape, this very day, from this prison of perpendicular rock, glassy with ice and plastered with snow, was ludicrous. But we were indeed alive; and we were not only planning to climb up out of it, we felt certain that we would manage to do so.

We could hear the gale shrieking across the ridges overhead. Where we were not a breath was stirring. Only the avalanches coming down and sweeping out over us generated a wind. We studied their timetable and planned how to use the knowledge. It was sombre to reflect in what poor case we would have been, had we been further down the Face, with the ice-slope of the "Spider" still to be climbed. The little slides which came down upon us from the gully were only a fraction of the great avalanches which get fed by the many diverse channels above to sweep over the slope of the "Spider". We were lucky indeed to be as high up as we were. But we soon realized that our cramped bivouac would seem a light trial compared with what we would still have to cope with today.

We were in good shape. The pain in Kasparek's hand seemed

to have diminished. Thanks to Vorg's broad back, Heckmair had enjoyed a splendid sleep. Vorg was already busy in his capacity as chef. He brewed pots-full of coffee, melted chocolate in condensed milk, and altogether prepared a fine and plentiful breakfast. And while we consumed it, we held a council of war. The weather had done all the changing it was likely to do – for the worse. It was as bad as it always was when men had to stay on the Face for days on end. We had enough food and fuel to bivouac there for several more days. What good would that do us? Even if it cleared up tomorrow or the day after or in three days' time, the conditions on the Face could not improve, nor the rocks be fit to climb, for several days after that. Were we to let ourselves be worn down by sitting and waiting?

"It is better to fall off than to freeze." This remark came from Michel Innerkofler, the oldest of a famous dynasty of Dolomite guides. We were not thinking of falling off, but still less of surrendering just because the Face had put on its winter raiment. We decided to move on.

As soon as the decision had been taken, I lightened our rucksacks, by throwing down the precipice that part of the equipment and provisions which had become superfluous. Among it was a whole loaf of bread, which disappeared at a great pace in the mists below us. I had grown up in hard circumstances and had never before thrown away a piece of bread; but now the act almost seemed symbolic to me – we were moving on. "Forward" was the only way now; no more turning back. The past was wiped out, all that mattered was the future; and the future lay over the snow-plastered, ice-glazed summit-wall. I believe no man can be completely able to summon all his strength, all his will, all his energy, for the last desperate move, till he is convinced that the last bridge is down behind him and that there is nowhere to go but on.

We moved on. Anderl would lead us out at the top of the Face; this was to be Heckmair's great day.

It is my considered opinion today, as I sit writing these lines, that we would all have escaped safely from the Face, even without his protection from in front; Fritz too would have done it solo, in spite of his injured hand. But we would never have done it so well, without Anderl's leadership; and we might in all probability have had to bivouac again. That probably wouldn't have killed us either; I think we were all good enough, strong enough and in high enough spirits to survive even that. But are we one whit the worse, do we lose one jewel out of our crown, by recognizing with all due admiration that one of us was the best of us all?

We roped up again as a single, united rope of four. The order was now: Heckmair, Vorg, myself and Kasparek, who was coming up last today so as not to have to haul on the rope with his damaged hand.

Heckmair ran into problems from the very start. The first decision to be made was which of two routes to take? The icy overhanging, crack-like chimney which looked damnably difficult, but seemed safe from snow-slides; or up the steep, icy gully to its left, down which little avalanches seemed to descend from time to time? He chose the chimney and Vorg belayed him; but it proved necessary to drive a piton straight away. The chimney proved so difficult that even Heckmair's skill was of no avail.

So back he had to come and try the gully, having first studied the time-table of the avalanches. It kept on snowing, and now that day had come, it was damp snow, the kind that slides and adds to the fury of avalanches. But even without an avalanche the couloir was so difficult that even Heckmair slipped down it twice and it was only at the third attempt that his well-known powers of attack succeeded in taking him up to a small rock-crest to the left of the gully. There he knocked the snow and ice away with his axe and so managed to fashion usable foot-holds.

"Up you come," he said.

Vorg went up, and we two followed. Then Heckmair went on climbing on stuff that made the utmost demands on us all. He could not afford to waste time, for he had to reach the next safe stance in the pauses between avalanches, before the next snow-slide arrived. Not that there were any safe stances; a step in the ice, a piton, on to which to belay oneself, were the best we could hope for up here. But the higher we got, the thinner grew the film of ice in the gully; so thin that it would not bear the strokes of an axe, nor offer a reliable hold for a piton. The steel shafts went clean through the ice, impinged on the rock beneath and simply bent over.

We were all on a single rope. If the leader came off and number two couldn't hold him, it would be up to me to try to arrest the fall. And if I should be pulled off, the whole force would come on Fritz. We knew that one man could not hold three on this terrain. No one knew it better than Heckmair, who was often moving, and was forced to move, at the very limit of safety, if he was to force a way up to freedom for us. And once we were very close to annihilation. I was standing on a small knob, seeing Fritz up to me. One hundred feet above me stood Vorg, safeguarding Heckmair, as he grappled with icy rock, treacherous ice gullies and snow-slides high above us in the mists and driving snow. We couldn't see either of them.

Fritz joined me on my stance.

Still no order from Vorg to come up. We could hear voices and short, muffled cries. What could have gone wrong up there?

Then we could only hear a murmur of voices. At the same time a snow-slide came down on us. That was nothing unusual and we were quite used to it by now; but this wasn't white snow. It was stained red with blood. Definitely blood, because the next thing to come down was an empty bandage cover and this was followed by a small empty medicine bottle.

"Hallo!" we yelled. "What's happened?"

No reply. We waited for what seemed an age, racked with doubt and anxiety. Then, according to schedule, another avalanche came down with savage force. Not till it had passed did we obtain relief in the shape of an invitation to move on up.

Vorg was hauling on the rope so hard that it took my breath away. But I understood what this man-handling meant. No longer was there time to climb pitches neatly according to the rules. Time was now the watchword, if we were to escape from the Face. And evidently something had happened up there to cause great delay. What could it be?

When I reached Vorg's stance, a great weight fell from me. They were both alive and not even seriously hurt. Vorg had a blood-soaked bandage on one hand, but Heckmair was already a whole rope higher up, on a tiny, exposed, rickety stance.

Later on, he reported in his dry but lively way how Vorg came by his injury:

Wet snow was coming down heavily. There hadn't been an avalanche for a long time. So – quick, up the overhang! Curse it . . . the ice on the rock had thinned out, and the pitons wouldn't hold any more. At the second stroke they went clean through and bent themselves on the rock. On the overhang itself I could only cross my crampons, because there was only a narrow strip of old ice in the gully and the new ice overlaying the rock was too hard, smooth and thin. The point of the ice-piton on to which I was clinging for dear life only went a little way in and so did the pick of my ice-axe. Suddenly the piton came out, and at the same moment my axe gave way. If I could only have straddled, I could have kept my balance. But with my legs crossed, there wasn't a hope.

I shouted, "Look out, Wiggerl!"

Then I came off.

Wiggerl was looking out all right. He took in as much rope as he could, but I bore straight down on him – not through thin air, for the gully was inclined, but in a light-ning-swift slide. Just as I fell, I turned face outwards so as not to go head over heels.

Wiggerl let the rope drop and caught me with his hands, and one of the points of my crampons went through his palm. I did turn head over heels, but in a split second I grabbed the rope-piton, which gave me such a jerk that I came up feet first again. I dug all twelve points of my irons into the ice – and found myself standing.

The force with which I had come down on Wiggerl had knocked him out of his holds but he, too, had been able to save himself and there we were, standing about four feet below our stance on steep ice without any footholds. One stride and we were back on it again. Naturally, the pitons had come out and I immediately knocked new ones in.

All this took only a matter of seconds. It was a purely reflex action which saved us; our friends, standing a rope's length below and linked to us by the same rope, hadn't even noticed that anything had happened. If we hadn't checked our fall we would have hurled them out from the face with us in a wide arc.

Meanwhile Wiggerl had taken his gauntlet off. Though blood spurted out, it was quite dark in colour, so it couldn't be a severed artery.

I looked quickly up the wall; thank goodness, there was as yet no avalanche on its way down. Off with my pack, out with the bandage, and I had Wiggerl's hand tied up. He was very pale; in fact if he had any colour at all, it was green.

"Do you feel bad?" I asked.

"I'm not very sure," he answered.

I placed myself in such a way that he could in no circumstances fall, and urged him to pull himself together, because it was now or never.

Just then a little phial of heart drops came to hand in the first-aid bag. That devoted woman Dr Belart of Grindelwald had made me take it along in case of emergency, remarking: "If Toni Kurz had only had them along, he might even have survived *his* ordeal."

We were only supposed to use them in the direst need, though.

On the bottle it said . . . "ten drops". I simply poured half of it into Wiggerl's mouth and drank the rest, as I happened to be thirsty. We followed it up with a couple of glucose lozenges, and were soon in proper order again.

An avalanche was due, but I couldn't see any signs of it.

"Look, I'm going to have another whack at the overhang," I told him.

"All right," he said, "but please" – and his voice was still quite weak – "no more using me as a mattress."

I braced myself, and managed the difficult pitch absolutely safely this time, doing entirely without pitons so as to get as quickly as I possibly could across the really tricky bit it turned out to be. I went up nearly 100 ft – almost the whole run of the rope – without finding a stance; but I was at least able to put in one of the small rock-pitons up there.

And just at that spot and at that moment, when Heckmair had anchored himself to that kindly little piton, down came the avalanche which shook us so severely down below, as already described.

It failed to carry away Heckmair or Vorg, or either of us; but it was many hours after our start before I was up alongside Vorg and in a position to see Fritz safely up. Vorg, freely assisted by the rope, hurried on to join Heckmair. I too hauled Fritz up. In fact we all pulled on the rope, for time was racing away and the sector still to be climbed was high, steep and difficult; nor had we any idea what it would be like. I had never been on a face-climb where there was so much chasing and racing with time as on this Eiger thing. And yet this final cliff, in its ice-armoured snowed-up state, called for an inch by inch struggle on the leader's part.

On we went. It snowed without respite. Visibility was hardly more than a rope's length upwards or sideways. Then through the cloud and the whirling flakes we heard shouts coming down to us, though we couldn't say exactly where from. They might come from the summit, or again from the West Ridge. Anyway they were reaching us. We agreed, on the spot, not to answer. Whoever was calling to us was too far from us to understand exactly what we might say in reply. Our answer might well launch a rescue operation which, once in motion, could not be called off; there might be a long descent for someone from the summit to the valley, a drumming up of the rescuers, a renewed ascent . . . one shout from us might well precipitate all that, if they misunderstood us . . . even if we only yodelled up a greeting . . .

So we climbed on with Anderl in the lead. Minutes passed into hours. Up we went, yard by yard, rope by rope.

Then we heard more shouts, this time clearer and nearer. We could even recognize that these were different voices from the earlier ones. Once again we refused to answer. We learned later that the first voices were those of Fraissl and Brankowsky, shouting down the Face, deep in their concern for our fate. The second time it was Hans Schlunegger, that great Oberland guide, shouting down to ask if we wanted help. True, he and the two Vienna boys were equally convinced that at the moment the foul conditions on the snow-laden Face made it quite impossible to lend us any aid; but he and our friends were equally ready to help us, or rescue us, as soon as the weather improved. At this point I must stress again the self-sacrificing readiness of the local guides. The two parties had reached the summit independently by the relatively easy normal route up the North-West Face, but had turned back immediately on receiving no answer from us. Obviously, after the hopeless reports brought back by those who had climbed to the summit to search for us, nobody rated the value of our lives very highly.

All the same, we were still alive, and still climbing. The steepness of the gully eased off. The avalanches were harmless now, too; up here they had as yet no strength. And then we emerged from the gully on to an ice-slope.

It was the Summit Ice-field. If we hadn't just come off the Eiger's Face we would have said it was steep; now it seemed flat. The final gully was behind us; we had escaped from the clutch of the "Spider's" last arm. It was noon when Heckmair reached the lower rim of the ice-slope. An hour later the last of us four was safely up.

Only the ice-slope now separated us from the summit ridge. We didn't traverse to the left towards the Mittellegi Ridge, but climbed diagonally to the right, somewhere in the direction of the summit.

Only the summit ice-slope. Only . . .

Even this last rampart of the Eiger is no joke. The wet snow had not cohered firmly with the neve and ice beneath; it kept on sliding away. This is the very source of the Eiger's avalanches. We couldn't hasten our assault. We all had it firmly anchored in our minds that the Face had not yet given us leave to feel indifferent and stroll away in a carefree manner. Anderl was still leading, as coolly and carefully as ever. He knew that a change of the lead would mean manoeuvring with the rope and the loss of time; added to which he could get his breath back while seeing us up on the rope, while we arrived completely out of breath. These explanations, too, sprang from the modesty of his nature.

At this point I was particularly conscious of the absence of my crampons. Even though Heckmair was cutting huge steps for me where necessary, even though Vorg was carefully watching the rope which ran down to me, I couldn't and wouldn't risk any sign of weakness. I dared not slip; but it called for a great output of strength to hang on with nothing but the claw-nails in my boots.

It was snowing harder than ever now. Nor were the flakes falling vertically any more but almost horizontally, whipped by the wind. The ice-slope seemed interminable. Two more hours had slipped away.

Then something happened which would have been amusing, if it had not meant a moment of extreme danger. Heckmair was climbing up the slope in the mist and the wild pother of snow. The slope was less steep now but, fighting his way against the wind and unable to see anything, he had not noticed it. Vorg, following him, suddenly saw dark patches in front of him. No – not in front – *below* him. Far, far below him . . .

They were the rocks on the South Side of the Eiger, which was not so thickly veiled in cloud and driven snow. The first two men ever to climb out of the North Face had almost fallen straight over the summit cornice down the South Face. If they had, I doubt whether we would have been able to hold them. As it was, they stepped back from the cornice in the nick of time.

We followed, gained a lodging on the wind-battered ridge, plodded our way over it to the summit of the Eiger. It was 3.30 p.m. on July 24th 1938. We were the first people to climb the North Face of the Eiger from its base to its top.

Joy, relief, tumultuous triumph? Not a bit of it. Our release had come too suddenly, our minds and nerves were too dulled, our bodies too utterly weary to permit of any violent emotion. Fritz and I had been on the Face eighty-five hours, Heckmair and Vorg sixty-one. We had not had a hair's-breadth escape from disaster; on the contrary, our bond of friendship had throughout given us a firm sense of mutual reliance. And hard as the climb had been, we had never doubted its successful outcome.

The storm was raging so fiercely on the summit that we had to bend double. Thick crusts of ice had formed around our eyes, noses and mouths; we had to scratch them away before we could see each other, speak or even breathe. We probably looked like legendary monsters of the Arctic, but we felt in no mood for the humour of such a reflection. Indeed, this was no place in which to turn handsprings or shriek with joy and happiness. We just shook hands without a word.

Then we started down at once. I remember another remark of

Innerkofler's: "Downhill's easy! You've got all the little angels with you . . ."

But it wasn't easy. The descent was full of spite and malice. The wind hadn't blown the snow away here; it had fallen wet and heavy on the western slope, covering the icy slabs to a depth of nearly three feet. We kept on slipping and recovering ourselves. We suddenly felt tired, terribly tired. I had been given the job of finding and leading the way down because I already knew the route; but when I had traversed the Eiger on that previous occasion, visibility had been good. Now I didn't always find the correct route immediately; then, my companions hauled me over the coals. I didn't argue, for they were quite right. Particularly Anderl, who had led like an absolute hero all the way up the climb – a real hero, quietly doing the job and serving his friends. He wasn't the sort who needed drums and bugles or the cheers of the crowd to spur him on to a great performance. The urge sprang from within him, from his nature, from his true character as a man.

But now we could see how he was collapsing, not in a physical but in a spiritual sense. Uncomplainingly, mechanically, he moved forward; but by now he had given up the leadership. The fantastic nervous tension under which he had lived for days and nights on that mighty Face just had to induce a reaction. During those endless hours of danger he had excelled himself; now he could afford to be an ordinary man again, with all an ordinary man's weakness, susceptible and exposed to all the caprices of normal life.

For instance, take the matter of Anderl's trousers. The elastic band of his overalls had broken. Anderl kept on pulling his trousers up and they kept on falling down again. This man, who had reacted with the speed of lightning when he fell in the icy gully and so saved us all from disaster, the man who had so often withstood the pressure of the deadly avalanches, who had climbed ice-bulges in a blizzard and, with unexampled endurance, fought a way to freedom for himself and his three teammates – this same man was almost driven to desperation by a broken elastic.

So Andreas had given up the lead. He had every right to expect to be led down on the descent just as surely and safely as he had led up that appalling Face; and he had every right to swear now when, racked by the exhaustion of a body exerted to the uttermost, he was asked to climb up a few hundred feet again because, in the mirk and the blown snow, I had led the wrong way down. I could see nothing amusing in this internal collapse of Anderl's. On the contrary, the very human nature of his reaction endeared him all the more to me.

We found the right route again and climbed on down it. We slipped, slid, stumbled, all securing one another. Gradually we lost height, and at last we were below the clouds. The snow turned into rain. But close down there now was the safe world of people.

For that multitude of dark dots down there, moving about on the glacier, were people. They were coming slowly up to meet us. We wondered what they were looking for on the glacier. Once we had seen people, we suddenly craved for the comforts of human civilization, about which we had not even dared to think during our bivouac nights. You mustn't long for a bed when you are hanging from a piton on a snowed-up precipice.

But now as we saw people coming up towards us we were gripped by an overwhelming desire for a hot bath, for a bed, for comfort. True, down there at the bottom of the wall stood our tent, a luxury home compared with our bivouac above the "Spider"; but we hadn't a dry stitch of clothing on us, and oh how we wanted to sleep in a bed! Would a hotel on the Kleine Scheidegg give us credit? How much money had we got left? Anderl was the richest; he still had a franc and a half, but that wouldn't go very far. Yet we still hankered after a bath and a bed.

Suddenly there was a young boy in front of us, staring at us as if we were ghosts. His face expressed embarrassed, incredulous astonishment. Then he summoned up his courage to ask:

"Have you come off the Face?"

"Yes," we admitted. "Off the Face."

Then the lad turned downhill again and ran away, screeching in a high treble: "They're coming! Here they are! They are coming!"

Soon we were encircled by people. Guides, our Viennese friends, the men from Munich, members of the Rescue Service, journalists, rubbernecks – all united in their great joy at seeing alive four men they had believed dead.

They took our rucksacks off for us, they wanted to carry us, and they would have, if we hadn't suddenly felt as fresh and gay as if we were back from a walk and not from the North Face of the Eiger. Someone gave Fritz his first dry cigarette. Rudi Fraissl held out a small flask of cognac to Andreas.

"Drink some," he said. "It'll warm you up."

Anderl emptied the flask at one pull. It didn't make him drunk. We were all drunk with the general joy around us. And then, for the first time, we felt the intense satisfaction, the relaxation, the relief from every care, and the indescribable delight at having climbed the North Face. Suddenly, too, all our problems were solved. Beds, baths? Everyone was showering invitations on us, simply everyone, just because they were human beings and we had come back safely to humanity.

Yes, we had made an excursion into another world and we had come back, but we had brought the joy of life and of humanity back with us. In the rush and whirl of everyday things, we so often live alongside one another without making any mutual contact. We had learned on the North Face of the Eiger that men are good and the earth on which we were born is good.

And now that earth was welcoming us home . . .

Mischabel

Geoffrey Winthrop Young

Born in 1876, the son of a mountaineer, Young began his climbing career on the spires of Trinity College, Oxford. One of the great mountaineers of the Edwardian era, particularly when teamed with the guide Josef Knubel, Winthrop Young lost a leg in action during the First World War but, undeterred he invented an artificial limb and carried on climbing. He died in 1958. Below he recounts the first ascent of the South-West face of the Taschhorn in the Alps, made in 1906 with V. J. E. Ryan and the guides Franz and Josef Lochmatter, Little J, and Josef Knubel.

The day was still bright and young, and the men obviously in fine climbing form. It was, therefore, no effort to telephone hearty remarks up and down the rope, or to emerge at Franz' feet after each struggle with a breathless but honest grin. But still the cliffs leaned out at us; still the unchancy upward and sideways traversing was forced upon us. A little cloud of anxiety crept upon the edge of my mind. My eye glanced unwillingly up or down: it was beginning to dodge, instinctively, the questions that the sight suggested. Our hands and feet grew gradually numb with the uninterrupted clinging to rounded, cold and slippery ledges.

At last – and how vividly the scene starts to mind – I stood on such a shelf, looking up at Franz' head and shoulders as he poised over a sheer wall above me, his prehensile feet balancing him erect upon a gutter-slope whose gracelessness I was yet to discover. The wall up to him bothered me a little; and as I got one arm over the coping and felt only the comfortless incline of the narrow band, I called out in joking patois, "Watch out, Franz, for my rope!" He looked down at me and out beyond me thoughtfully, almost abstractedly, without the customary flash of big brown eyes and big white teeth: "You must do what you can; here we can no longer help one another!" And then he turned away, dropping my rope symbolically from his hand and watching his brother, whose struggles, invisible to me, were audible far up round a black repulsive corner.

From such a man the words had the effect of an icy douche. The detachment of mind which a leader may never lose whatever his occupation with his own struggles returned upon the instant. I looked down over my arm: to see the deadly continuity of descending precipice with its narrow snowy eavelets leaning out one above another, and still one above another, dizzily; and seeming to shrug even the glance of my eye off into space. And I realized in a flash what a return down them must mean. I looked up: to discover that worse lay before us, if we failed to force a way up the chimney into which we were traversing for an escape. For hours already, deceived by our spacing from each other up a seeming ladder of terraces that were no terraces, we must have been climbing in reality at our several risks: each of us unprotected by the man above: the slip of any one imperilling the rest. For how many more hours would this, or could we, continue?

A slight, pricking snow began to drift across us. From the exposed height of our great pyramidal wall, surging above other ranges, we looked out across a frozen and unheeding stillness of white peak and glacier, disappearing under the darker clouds to the south. We seemed very much removed from the earth, and very much alone. As I turned back to the rock I could see nothing but antagonism in the ice-wrinkled face of the crags upon which we were venturing; and I had the feeling – it was too formless at the time to take the definite shape I must now give to it – as if somewhere low down beyond the horizon behind me a great grey bird was just lifting on its wings into heavy flight. As the hours wore on, this shadow at our backs seemed to be approaching soundlessly and covering more and more of the sky. Gradually it was enclosing us within its spread of cold wings, and isolating us from all the world of life and movement in our contest with the frigid wall of grey precipice.

Precariously we crawled up to and along, and up to and along, the sloping ribbons, silky with chill snow, and leading interruptedly upward towards the projecting corner which shut us off from the big couloir. On the decrepit mantelpiece by which we turned the corner itself, we could use a rock "hitch" for the rope, one of the only three we found on all this upper face! We edged round into the couloir, a forbidding chasm; and found ourselves on a slim, shattered ledge, that continued inwards at a high level across the sheer wall of rock forming our side of the rift.

We were more or less together now; and no one could any longer pretend that some one above saw a gleam of hope denied to himself. Forty feet below, the slabby back of the chasm slanted steeply outward, and down into space. Past us, the same backing of slabs mounted precipitously, to splay out in an amphitheatre of over-leaning walls far above. And every hopeless curve of slab was glassy with ice and glitter-film. The couloir, as an upward escape, needed no second glance. Josef was already clinging down our wall into the chasm below. His object was plain. The same belt or flaw by which we had entered the rift appeared again, at a lower level, upon the wall opposite to us, and disappeared round the profile of the further containing buttress. What could be seen of its re-start was no more than a sloping shelf, that wound steeply upwards and out of sight round the all but vertical corner. But Josef had evidently made up his mind that our only chance, now the couloir had failed, was to resume our perilous ribbon-traverses along the bands; in the hope – if they continued far enough – of finding the second, smaller chimney, the branch which forked out on to the southeast ridge, accessible; and if accessible, less icy-hearted. It appeared to me, and probably to him, a very faint and rather fearsome chance. Even the slabs below us, which gave difficult access to the crazy re-start of the traverse, looked villainous enough.

Josef moved tentatively about on the smooth shoot of the slabs, steadied by Ryan with the rope from our ledge. He never looked like crossing them; and I think that the nearer view of the re-start of the traverse was weakening his resolution. The dark chilly depths of the chasm gave muffled answer to his agitated comments. Franz, beside me on the ledge, watched him, hissing a gay little French song between his teeth, the only sign of excitement I have ever known him show. Then – "It won't go!" came in a hollow shout from below; and – "But it must go!" echoed from Franz, who at once leaped into action. I untied my rope to him. He was down and out on to the slabs in a breath, still singing to himself. He caterpillared his way across the ice-bosses above Josef. Josef, and other great guides, on slabs moved with the free poise of an athlete and the footcling of a chamois. Franz, in such case, had the habit and something of the appearance of a spider or crustacean. His curled head disappeared altogether. His body and square shoulders split and elongated into four steely tentacles, radiating from a small central core or hub of intelligence, which transmitted the messages between his tiny hands and boots as they clung attached and writhing at phenomenal angles and distances.

At the far side of the slabs he crawled on to and up the sloping shelf of the disappearing traverse, only keeping himself on it, so far as could be seen, by thrusting one foot firmly out against the aether. Presently Ryan followed, out of sight; and then Josef. Even with little J playing my rope from high up on the wall behind me, I found the crossing of the iced slabs of the couloir upon a descending diagonal nasty enough. More especially towards the farther side, when the rope, sagging across from above, began to pull me back with a heavy draw. But the start of the traverse looked unspeakable. A downward and outward leaning shelf, with nothing below and an over-hanging wall above it, screwed steeply upward out of sight round the but-tress. From far up along it came Josef's voice, thinly crying caution. How was I to keep on the shelf – and, much more, wriggle up it?

Little J joined me on the ice-nicks in the slabs; and after many attempts the end of Josef's rope, slung from above and weighted with a stone, was lassoed back and round to a point on the slabs from which we could recover it. I tied on, and started. Once up on the shelf, I found that there was nothing to keep me on it against the urgency of the slant into space. A hailing match between little J and Josef only produced the information that while he was "good" to hold – but not to pull – along the diagonal upward line of the shelf, he would be helpless against any direct downward strain, such as must result if I fell off the shelf. There was nothing for it but to thrust myself desperately upward, relying only upon the friction of my outer knee on the hem of the sloping ribbon to resist an outward drag to which the weight of the world seemed to be added. Of service, also, were two or three painful finger-tip pinches on the down-sloping prickles of the wall above my head.

When I reached Josef, I found him sprawled over rugosities on the buttress. His "hitch" – the second of our dauntless three – was no more than a prong of rock sticking downward like a tusk from the overhang above him, and of course useless against a pull from any but the one, sideways, direction. Little J, who had by now begun his assorted collection of all our sacks and axes, followed up magnificently.

The next clear memory is of finding ourselves inside the second, smaller, chimney, a precipitous narrow cleft up the face, of worn, skull-smooth rock. It was all dirty white and boneblue in the gloomy afternoon light, with blurred ice-nubbles bulking through the adhesive snow. But at least there was the singular rest for eye and nerves which the feeling of enclosing walls gives us after long hours on an exposed cliff. We even found a nominal stance or two, in ice-pockets on chockstones, where we could *almost* hold on without help from the hands. Franz, who was back again above me resting from the lead, could spare me a few partial hoists with the rope. I began to feel my muscles slackening with the relief, and I became conscious of the cold. I had time to notice that I was climbing less precisely, a symptom of relaxed tension: time, too, to admit ungrudgingly that nothing in the universe but Franz' rope could have got me up to and over some of the expulsive ice bulges in the chimney. Ignorant in my remote position of what the front men saw awaiting us above, I even thawed into a congratulatory remark or so: but I drew no response.

And then, it all ended! The chimney simply petered out: not under the south-east ridge, as we might have hoped, but in the very hard heart of the diamond precipice some 600 ft below the final and still invisible summit. The vague exit from the chimney faded out against the base of a blank cliff. One of its side walls led on for a little, and up to the left. There it too vanished, under the lower rim of a big snowy slab, sloping up, and slightly conical, like a dish-cover. I have reason to remember that slab. It formed the repellent floor of a lofty, triangular recess. On its left side, and in front, there was space and ourselves. On its right, and at the back, a smooth leap of colossal cliff towered up for a hundred feet of crystallized shadow, and then arched out above our heads in a curve like the dark underside of a cathedral dome. A more appalling-looking finish to our grim battle of ascent could hardly have been dreamed in a "falling" nightmare; and we had not even standing room to appreciate it worthily! As I looked up and down, I had an overpowering sense of the great grey wings behind us, shadowing suddenly close across the whole breadth of precipice, and folding us off finally from the world.

But our long apprenticeship to discouragement stood us in good stead. Muscles braced anew obstinately; determination quickened resentfully. The recess on whose lip we hung had been formed by the sliding of a great wedge of rock off the inclined, dish-cover slab, once its bed. But on our right the cliff continued the original line. My impression of this, therefore, was as of a high building viewed from under one corner. Its sheer front wall stretched away to the right, flush with the sill of our slab. The end wall of the building formed the right side of our recess, and overhung the slab. The rectangular house-corner, where the two walls joined, rose immediately above us, vertical and iced, but a little chipped by the rending out of the wedge. Again, the front wall of this projecting house did not rise to the same height as the cliff that backed our recess. Forty feet up – my measures are merely impressions – the wall slanted steeply back in a roof, receding out of sight. Presumably another huge wedge had here slid from its bed, on a higher plane. Above and beyond this roof the precipices rose again into sight, in the same line and of the same height as the cliffs which backed our recess. Only, the cliff vertically above us was crowned by the great dome or overhang. There must be, therefore, invisible above, some rough junction or flaw where the line of cliffs above the receding house-roof linked on to the forward jut of our dome. Four vital questions suggested themselves: Could the house-corner be climbed? Was the roof, if attainable, too steep to crawl up? Might there be a flawed connection where the precipice upon which the roof abutted joined on to the side of the dome? If there was such a flaw, would this yield us a passage out on to the face of the convex dome above its circle of largest dimension, on its retreating upper curve, or below it, under its hopeless arch? These details are tiresome, perhaps unintelligible. But they may help other climbers to a better understanding of Franz' remarkable feat.

Right up in the angle of the recess there was a rotund blister of rock modelled in low relief on the face of the slab; and round this a man, hunched on small nicks in the steep surface, could just belay the rope. Josef and Franz were crouching at this blister up in the recess. The rest of us were dispersed over freezing clingholds along the lower rim of the slab. And the debate proceeded, broken by gusts of snow. The man to lead had clearly to run out 100 to a 150 ft of rope. He could be given no protection. His most doubtful link would come some eighty feet up above the roof. If he found a flaw there, and it served him favourably, he would be out on the convex of the dome fully a hundred feet above us, and outside us in a direct line above our heads. If, at this point, he could not proceed – well, it was equally unlikely that he could return!

Franz showed no hesitation. The hampered preparations for the attempt went on hurriedly. We had all to unrope as best we could, so as to arrange for the 200 ft of possible run-out, and we hooked on to our holds with difficulty, while the snow-frozen rope kinked and banged venomously about us. In the end little J and I had to remain off the rope, to leave enough free.

Franz started up the corner, climbing with extraordinary nerve but advancing almost imperceptibly. It was much like swarming up the angle of a tower, rough-cast with ice. Ryan and little J crept up near the blister; but as there was no more room I remained hanging on to the fractured sill of the slab. In this position I was farther out; and I could just see Franz' two feet scratting desperately for hold to propel him up the tilt of the roof above the corner. The rest of him was now out of sight. The minutes crawled like hours, and the rope hanging down to us over the gable-end hardly seemed to stir upwards. The snow gusts distracted us cruelly. A precipice in sunshine seems at least interested in our microscopic efforts. Its tranquillity even helps our movement by giving to it a conspicuous importance. But when the stable and unstable forces of nature join in one of their ferocious, inconclusive conflicts, the little human struggle is carelessly swallowed up in uproar, and tosses unregarded and morally deflated, like a wet straw on a volcanic wave.

Suddenly I heard that unmistakable scrape and grit of sliding boot-nails and clothes. Above my head, over the edge of the roof to the right, I saw Franz' legs shoot out into space. Time stopped. A shiver, like expectancy, trembled across the feeling of unseen grey wings behind me from end to end of the cliff. I realized impassively that the swirl of the rope must sweep me from my holds before it tightened on the doubtful belay of the blister. But fate was playing out the game in regions curiously remote. My mind watched the moves, itself absorbed into the same remote, dispassionate atmosphere. It seemed unwilling to disturb the issue by formulating a thought, or even a fear. The fact of the body seemed negligible; it had no part in the observant aloofness into which all consciousness had withdrawn. Something of the same feeling of separation between the body and the watching mind is the experience of men actually falling or drowning, when action is at an end and there is not even pain to reunite bodily and mental sensation. But during the crises of this day the condition lasted, with me certainly, for spaces that could only be measured by hours.

Franz' boots again disappeared above the edge. No one in the recess had known of the slip, out of their sight and lost in the gusts. He had stopped himself miraculously on the rim by crushing his hands on to ice-dimples in the slab. The hanging rope began again to travel up along the slanting gable-end of the roof. There was a long interval, and now and then the sound of a scratting boot or the scrabble of loose surface. Then the rope began, jerkily, to work out and across far above our heads.

Franz had found a flaw in the join of the cliffs above the roof, and he was creeping out on to the projection of the dome. The lengthening rope now hung down well outside the men in the recess, and it might have hung outside me on the lower rim, had they not held in its end. Its weight upon Franz, as it swayed down through the snow, must have added to his immense difficulties. He was well out of sight, clinging somewhere above on the upper curve of the overhang.

An indistinct exchange of shouts began, half swallowed by echo, wind, and snow. Franz, it appeared, was still quite uncertain if he could get up any further. For the time he could hold on well enough to help one man with the rope; but he had not two hands free to pull. I could hear his little spurt of laughter at the question – "Could he return?" He suggested that Josef should join him, and the rest wait until they two might return with a rescue-party. Wait, there! – for at best fifteen hours, hanging on to the icy holds, in a snow wind!

At that hour of the day and upon those treacherous cliffs, now doubly dangerous under accumulating snow, all the odds were against any of us who turned back getting down alive. Franz in any case could not get back to us, and he might not be able to advance. We were committed, therefore, to the attempt to join him, however gloomy its outlook. As many as possible must be got up to him – and the rest must be left to chance.

Josef started his attempts on the corner. This left room for me to move up to Ryan on the slab. He asked me, I remember, what I thought were the chances of our escape. I remember, too, considering it seriously, and I can hear myself answering – "About one in five."

The end of the long rope hooted down past me. It hung outside the recess, dangling in air; and I could only recover it by climbing down again over the rim of the slab and reaching out for it one-handed with my axe. I passed it up; and then I stayed there, hanging on, because I could no longer trust my hands or feet to get me up the slope again. Ryan began the corner; but if I have described the position at all intelligibly, it will be seen that while the corner rose vertically on our right, the long rope hung down on a parallel line from the dome directly above our heads. So it came that the higher we climbed up the corner the more horizontal became the slanting pull of the rope, and the more it tended to drag us sideways off the corner and back under the overhang. Very coolly, Ryan shouted a warning before he started of the insufficient power left in frozen hands. Some twenty feet up, the rope tore him from his inadequate, snowy holds. He swung across above our heads and hung suspended in mid-air. The rope was fixed round his chest. In a minute it began to suffocate him. He shouted once or twice to the men above to hurry. Then a fainter call, "I'm done," and he dangled to all appearance unconscious on the rope. Franz and Josef could only lift him half-inch by half-inch. For all this hour – probably it was longer – they were clamped one above the other on to the steep face of the dome, their feet on shallow but sound nicks, one hand clinging on, and only the other free to pull in. Any inch the one lifted, the other held. The rough curve of the rock, over which the higher portion of the rope descended, diminished by friction the effectiveness of each tug. The more one considers their situation, the more superhuman do the cooperation and power the two men displayed during this time, at the end of all those hours of effort, appear. Little J and I had only the deadly anxiety of watching helplessly, staring upward into the dizzy snow and shadow: and that was enough. J had followed silently and unselfishly the whole day; and even now he said nothing: crouching in unquestioning endurance beside the freezing blister on the slab.

Ryan was up at last, somehow, to the overhang; and being dragged up the rough curve above. A few small splinters were loosened, and fell, piping, past me and on to me. I remember calculating apathetically whether it was a greater risk to try and climb up again into the recess, unroped and without any feel in fingers and toes, or to stay where I was, hanging on to the sill, and chance being knocked off by a stone. It is significant of the condition of body and mind that I decided to stay where I was, where at least stiffened muscles and joints still availed to hold me mechanically fixed on to my group of rounded nicks.

Ryan was now out of sight and with the others. When the constriction of the rope was removed he must have recovered amazingly toughly, and at once; for down once more, after a short but anxious pause, whistled the snow-stiffened rope, so

narrowly missing me that little J cried out in alarm. I could not
for a time hook it in with the axe; and while I stretched, frigidly
and nervously, Josef hailed me from seemingly infinite height,
his shouts travelling out on the snow eddies. They could not
possibly pull up my greater weight. Unless I felt sure I could
stick on to the corner and manage to climb round to them by
Franz' route, it was useless my trying! At last I had fished in the
rope, with a thrill of relief, and I set mental teeth. With those
two tied on to the rope above, and myself tied on – in the way I
meant to tie myself on – to the rope below, there were going to
be no more single options. We were all in it together; and if I
had still some faith in myself I had yet more in that margin of
desperation strength which extends the possible indefinitely for
such men as I knew to be linked on to me above. And if I were
once up, well there would be no question after that about little J
coming up too!

I gave hands and feet a last blue-beating against the rock to
restore some feeling to them. Then I knotted the rope round my
chest, made the loose end into a triple-bowline "chair" round
my thighs, and began scratching rather futilely up the icy
rectangular corner. For the first twenty-five feet – or was it
much less? – I could just force upward. Then the rope began to
drag me off inexorably. I clutched furiously up a few feet more;
and then I felt I must let go, the drag was too strong for frozen
fingers. As I had already resolved, at the last second I kicked off
from the rock with all my strength. This sent me flying out on
the rope, and across under the overhang, as if attached to a crazy
pendulum. I could see J crouching in the recess far below,
instinctively protecting his head. The impetus jumped the
upper part of the rope off its cling to the rock face of the dome
above, and enabled the men to snatch in a foot or two. The
return-swing brought me back, as I had half hoped, against the
corner, a little higher up. I gripped it with fingers and teeth, and
scrambled up another few feet. But the draw was now irresistible. I kicked off again; gained a foot or so, and spun back.

I was now up the corner proper, and I should have been by
rights scrambling up the roof on the far side of my gable edge.
But the rope, if nothing else, prevented any chance of my
forcing myself over it and farther to the right. Another cling

and scratch up the gable end, and I was not far below the level of the dome overhanging above and to my left. For the last time I fell off. This time the free length of the rope, below its hold upon the curve of the dome, was too short to allow of any return swing. So I shot out passively, to hang, revolving slowly, under the dome, with the feeling that my part was at an end. When I spun round inward, I looked up at the reddish, scarred wall freckled with snow, and at the tense rope, looking thin as a grey cobweb and disappearing fraily over the forespring of rock that arched greedily over my head. When I spun outward, I looked down – no matter how many thousand feet – to the dim, shifting lines of the glacier at the foot of the peak, hazy through the snowfall; and I could see, well inside my feet, upon the dark face of the precipice the little blanched triangle of the recess and the duller white dot of J's face as he crouched by the blister. It flashed across me, absurdly, that he ought to be more anxious about the effect of my gymnastics upon the fragile thread of alpine rope, his one link with hope, than about me!

I was quite comfortable in the chair; but the spinning had to be stopped. I reached out the axe at full stretch, and succeeded in touching the cliff, back under the overhang. This stopped me, face inward. I heard inarticulate shouting above, and guessed its meaning, although I was now too close under the dome to catch the words: "They could not lift my dead weight!" I bethought me, and stretched out the axe again; got its point against a wrinkle of the wall, and pushed out. This started me swinging straight out and in below the dome. After two pokes I swung in near enough to be able to give a violent, short-armed thrust against the cliff. It carried me out far enough to jump quite a number of feet of rope clear of its cling down the rock above. The guides took advantage of the easing to haul in, and I pendulum'd back a good foot higher. The cliff facing me was now beginning to spring out in the Gothic arch of the overhang; so it could be reached more easily. I repeated the shove-out more desperately. Again they hauled in on the released rope. This time I came back close under the arch; and choosing a spot as I swung in, I lifted both feet, struck them at the wall, and gave a convulsive upward and outward spring. The rope shortened up; and as I banged back the cornice of the arch loomed

very near above my head. But the free length of rope below it
was now too short to let me again reach to the back of the arch
with leg or axe. I hung, trying in vain to touch the lowest
moulding of the cornice above with my hands. I heard gasps and
grunts above quite distinctly now. The rope strained and
creaked, gritting over the edge of the rock above me. I felt
the tremor of the sinews heaving on it. But for all that, I did not
move up. I reached up with the axe in both hands, just hooked
the pick into a lucky chink of the under-moulding, and pulled,
with a frantic wriggle of the whole body. It was a feeble lift, but
enough for the sons of Anak above to convert into a valuable
gain. The axe slipped down on to my shoulder, held there by its
sling. I reached up and back with both arms, got hold of a
finger-grip and gained another inch. Infinitesimal inches they
seemed, each a supreme effort, until my nose and chin scratched
up against a fillet of the cornice. Then the arms gave out
completely, so much at the end of their strength that they
dropped lifeless. But the teeth of the upper jaw held on a
broken spillikin and, with the stronger succour of the rope,
supported me for the seconds while the blood was running back
into my arms.

Wrestle by wrestle it went on. Every reserve of force seemed
exhausted, but the impulse was now supplied by a flicker of
hope. Until, at last, I felt my knee catch over a moulding on the
edge, and I could sink for an instant's rest, with rucked clothes
clinging over the rough, steep, upward but *backward* curving of
the dome. It is impossible to suggest the relief of that feeling,
the proof that the only solid surface which still kept me in touch
with existence had ceased to thrust itself out for ever as a barrier
overhead, and was actually giving back below me in semi-
support.

But there was no time, or inclination, to indulge panting
humanity with a rest or a realization. I crept up a few feet, on to
small, brittle, but sufficient crinkles. The dark figures of the
three men above were visible now, clinging crab-like and
exhausted on to similar nicks, indistinct in the snow dusk,
but still human company. I had to stay where I was, and untie
my rope, knotting up a coil at the end of the heavy length so that
I could swing it inward to little J back and out of sight beneath

me in the recess. The second cast was true: I felt him handle it, and then I let it go for those in the more direct line above to hold. Presently I saw it writhing away from me across the few visible feet of stooping crag, as J below moved away to start the icy corner. He had, I think, two sacks beside his own and at least three extra axes slung on to him; but he grappled up the corner masterfully and forced his way out on to the roof. Hopeless of lifting him as they had lifted us, the men above had learned, from pure fatigue, to leave him more free upon the rope. But he was naturally a very long time; and there was all too much leisure in which to realize how irrevocably our descent was now cut off, and how improbably our ascent could be continued.

The first flare of blinding relief died down. The obscure future settled round again like a fog. The precipice receding into murky uncertainty above looked more than ever dark with discouragement for a vitality ebbing on the tide of reaction. The shadowy, humping figures above were silent; there was none of that heartening talk which greets us over a difficult edge, giving us assurance that the worst is past. With no longer even the rope about me as a reminder of companionship, the sense that others were near me and in like case passed out of mind. My thoughts wandered drowsily, and all life in the limbs seemed suspended, as we feel it to be sometimes in the moments just preceding sleep.

The snow began to fall in large, soft flakes; not the tingling darts that assail us with the crisp hostility of intruders upon our alien earth, but flakes like wings, instinct with life, surrounding and welcoming a visitor to their own region of air with vague but insistent friendliness. A few of them settled inquisitively, to gleam and fade for a second like fallen starlight, on the short arc of brown crag racing into shadow between my feet. The rest drifted lightly and recklessly down past my heels, to disappear over the rim of void: suggesting how easy and restful might be my own descent could tired muscles but be persuaded to relax their tenacious hold upon the few remaining feet of inhospitable rock. Far below and to the right, a brow of bending and frosted precipice frowned into sight; and against and round its more familiar obstruction, lit by a pale glare diffused through the low clouds, the white flakes twirled and circled intimately, already forgetful of their more timid flight past the stranger above. When they sank from it, it was into an immensity of grey haze, featureless but for the black ribbons of moraine which floated high and distinct above their unseen glaciers, as reeds seem to sway and float high over the reflecting depths of a transparent stream. Into these immeasurably grey depths everything seemed to be descending, unresistingly and as of choice – the long lines of ice-fast crag, the shifting eddies of snow, the rays of darkness under the storm-clouds, even the eye and the tired mind. Some rebellious instinct of hand and foot alone appeared to defy a universal law.

The appearance of little J as he clambered, a clattering brown goblin of sack-humps and axe-points, over a boss on the shadowy dome beside me brought me back to the world of human company, and struggle. The day was darkening steadily – or is my memory of darkness only the shadow of our circumstance? for it was not yet four o'clock: but the snow stopped, having done its worst where it could most impede us. We roped up patiently, and began again our age-long crawl and halt up icy slabs as little kindly as before; and every fifty feet above us loomed still the threat of a total interruption. If it came now – it must just come! We had none of us, I think, any apprehension left: or for that matter, any comprehension of much more than hanging on and forcing up. In my own case – and a truthful record of sensation limits me to thinking only of myself – the capacity to feel or to remark was exhausted. Franz must have been more nervously alert, for he ground out a devious upward line through the upheaving of giant slabs without a halt or a false attempt. I can recall nothing but obscurity, steepness, and an endless driving of the muscles to their task. Still no message of hope reached us from above; and yet we must have left another 400 ft of rib and crack, snow-ice and equivocal holds below us. Even fancy dared not whisper to itself of the summit: the next five feet, and still the next five feet were the end of all effort and expectation.

And then, something was happening! There came a mutter of talk from the dusk above. Surely two shadows were actually moving at one time? I was at the foot of a long icy shelf, slanting up to the right. It was overhung by cliff on the left, as usual; and it had the usual absence of any holds to keep me on it. I began the eternal knee-friction crawl. The rope tightened on my waist. "Shall I pull?" – called Josef's voice, sounding strange after the hours of silence, and subdued to an undertone as if he feared that the peak might still hear and wake up to contrive some new devilment. "Why not? – if you really can!" – I echoed, full of surprise and hope; and I skimmered up the trough, to find Josef yoked to a royal rock hitch, the third and the best of the day! And, surely, we were standing on the crest of a great ridge, materialized as if by magic out of the continuous darkness of cliff and sky? And the big, sullen shadow just above must be the summit! It was indeed the mounting edge of the south-east ridge upon which we had arrived; and sixty feet above us it curled over against the top of the final pyramid. Josef unroped from me, while I brought up little J; and as we started to finish the ascent together in our old-time partnership, I saw the silhouettes of the other three pass in succession over the pointed skyline of the peak.

We found them, relaxed in spent attitudes on the summit-slabs, swallowing sardines and snow, our first food since half-past seven in the morning. It was now close upon six o'clock. Franz came across to meet me, and we shook hands. "You will never do anything harder than that, Franz!" "No," he said reflectively, "man could not do much more."

Avalanche

George Leigh Mallory

Born in Cheshire, England, in 1886, Mallory was the golden boy of early-twentieth century mountaineering. Originator of the cliche "Because it's there", he was a member of the first three Everest expeditions (the episode below is taken from the 1922 attempt). The mountain took his life on 8 June 1924 when he, and the very inexperienced Andrew Irvine, departed Camp VI to climb the last 600 m (1,900 ft) to the summit. They were briefly spotted below the peak but never seen alive again. Almost a decade later an ice-axe belonging to Irvine was found at 8,400 m (27,500 ft), suggesting that an accident happened at that height and that they did not reach the summit still more than 400 m (1,300 ft) above them. Mallory's body was discovered in 1999, perfectly preserved. See "We Had Found George Mallory" (p. 393) by Conrad Anker.

The project of making a third attempt this season was mooted immediately on the return of Finch and Geoffrey Bruce to the Base Camp. There in hours of idleness we had discussed their prospects and wondered what they would be doing as we gazed at the mountain to make out the weather on the great ridge. We were not surprised to learn when they came down that the summit was still unconquered, and we were not yet prepared to accept defeat. The difficulty was to find a party.

Of the six who had been already engaged only one was obviously fit for another great effort. Somervell had shown a recuperative capacity beyond the rest of us. After one day at the Base he had insisted on going up again to Camp III in case he might be of use to the others. The rest were more or less knocked out. Morshead's frost-bitten fingers and toes, from which he was now suffering constant pain, caused grave anxiety of most serious consequences, and the only plan for him was to go down to a lower elevation as soon as possible. Norton's feet had also been affected; he complained at first only of bruises, but the cold had come through the soles of his boots; his trouble too was frost-bite. In any case he could not have come up again, for the strain had told on his heart and he now found himself left without energy or strength.

Geoffrey Bruce's feet also were so badly frost-bitten that he could not walk. Finch, however, was not yet to be counted out. He was evidently very much exhausted, but an examination of his heart revealed no disorder; it was hoped that in five or six days he would be able to start again. My own case was doubtful. Of my frost-bitten finger-tips only one was giving trouble; the extremity above the first joint was black, but the injury was not very deep. Longstaff, who took an interest which we all appreciated in preventing us from doing ourselves permanent injury, pointed out the probability that fingers already touched and highly susceptible to cold would be much more severely injured next time, and was inclined to turn me down, from his medical point of view, on account of my fingers alone. A much more serious matter was the condition of my heart. I felt weak and lazy when it was a question of the least physical exertion, and the heart was found to have a "thrill". Though I was prepared to take risks with my fingers I was prepared to take none with my heart, even had General Bruce allowed me. However, I did not abandon hope. My heart was examined again on June 3rd, no thrill was heard, and though my pulse was rapid and accelerated quickly with exertion it was capable of satisfactory recovery. We at once arranged that Somervell, Finch and I, together with Wakefield and Crawford, should set forth the same day.

It was already evident that whatever we were to do would

now have to wait for the weather. Though the Lama at the Rongbuk Monastery had told us that the monsoon was usually to be expected about June 10th, and we knew that it was late last year, the signs of its approach were gathering every day. Mount Everest could rarely be seen after 9 or 10 a.m. until the clouds cleared away in the evening; and a storm approaching from the West Rongbuk Glacier would generally sweep down the valley in the afternoon. Though we came to despise this blustering phenomenon – for nothing worse came of it than light hail or snow, either at our camp or higher – we should want much fairer days for climbing, and each storm threatened to be the beginning of something far more serious. However, we planned to be on the spot to take any chance that offered. The signs were even more ominous than usual as Finch and I walked up to Camp I on the afternoon of June 3rd; we could hardly feel optimistic; and it was soon apparent that, far from having recovered his strength, my companion was quite unfit for another big expedition. We walked slowly and frequently halted; it was painful to see what efforts it cost him to make any progress. However, he persisted in coming on.

We had not long disposed ourselves comfortably within the four square walls of our "sangar", always a pleasant change from the sloping sides of a tent, when snow began to fall. Released at last by the west wind which had held it back, the monsoon was free to work its will, and we soon understood that the great change of weather had now come. Fine, glistening particles were driven by the wind through the chinks in our walls, to be drifted on the floor or on our coverings where we lay during the night; and as morning grew the snow still fell as thickly as ever. Finch wisely decided to go back, and we charged him with a message to General Bruce, saying that we saw no reason at present to alter our plans. With the whole day to spend confined and inactive we had plenty of time to consider what we ought to do under these conditions. We went over well-worn arguments once more. It would have been an obvious and easy course, for which no one could reproach us, to have said simply: The monsoon has come; this is the end of the climbing season; it is time to go home. But the case, we felt, was not yet hopeless. The monsoon is too variable and uncertain to be so easily admitted as the final arbiter. There might yet be good prospects ahead of us. It was not unreasonable to expect an interval of fine weather after the first heavy snow, and with eight or ten fair days a third attempt might still be made. In any case, to retire now if the smallest chance remained to us would be an unworthy end to the expedition. We need not run our heads into obvious danger; but rather than be stopped by a general estimate of conditions we would prefer to retire before some definite risk that we were not prepared to take or simply failed to overcome the difficulties.

After a second night of unremitting snowfall the weather on the morning of June 5th improved and we decided to go on. Low and heavy clouds were still flowing down the East Rongbuk Glacier, but precipitation ceased at an early hour and the sky brightened to the west. It was surprising, after all we had seen of the flakes passing our door, that no great amount of snow was lying on the stones about our camp. But the snow had come on a warm current and melted or evaporated, so that after all the depth was no more than 6 inches at this elevation (17,500 ft). Even on the glacier we went up a long way before noticing a perceptible increase of depth. We passed Camp II, not requiring to halt at this stage, and were well up towards Camp III before the fresh snow became a serious impediment. It was still snowing up here, though not very heavily; there was nothing to cheer the grey scene; the clinging snow about our feet was so wet that even the best of our boots were soaked through, and the last two hours up to Camp III were tiresome enough. Nor was it a cheering camp when we reached it. The tents had been struck for the safety of the poles, but not packed up. We found them now half-full of snow and ice. The stores were all buried; everything that we wanted had first to be dug out.

The snow up here was so much deeper that we anxiously discussed the possibility of going farther. With 15 to 18 inches of snow to contend with, not counting drifts, the labour would be excessive, and until the snow solidified there would be considerable danger at several points. But the next morning broke fine; we had soon a clear sky and glorious sunshine; it was the warmest day that any of us remembered at Camp III; and as we watched the amazing rapidity with which the snow solidified and the rocks began to appear about our camp, our spirits rose. The side of Everest facing us looked white and cold; but we observed a cloud of snow blown from the North Ridge; it would not be long at this rate before it was fit to climb. We had already resolved to use oxygen on the third attempt. It was improbable that we should beat our own record without it, for the strain of previous efforts would count against us, and we had not the time to improve on our organization by putting a second camp above the North Col. Somervell, after Finch's explanation of the mechanical details, felt perfectly confident that he could manage the oxygen apparatus, and all those who had used oxygen were convinced that they went up more easily with its help than they could expect to go without it. Somervell and I intended to profit by the experience. They had discovered that the increased combustion in the body required a larger supply of food; we must arrange for a bountiful provision. Their camp at 25,000 ft had been too low; we would try to establish one now, as we had intended before, at 26,000 ft. And we hoped for a further advantage in going higher than Finch and Bruce had done before using oxygen; whereas they had started using it at 21,000 ft, we intended to go up to our old camp at 25,000 ft without it, perhaps use a cylinder each up to 26,000 ft, and at all events start from that height for the summit with a full supply of four cylinders. If this was not the correct policy as laid down by Professor Dryer, it would at least be a valuable experiment.

Our chief anxiety under these new conditions was to provide for the safety of our porters. We hoped that after fixing our fifth camp at 26,000 ft, at the earliest three days hence, on the fourth day of fine weather the porters might be able to go down by themselves to the North Col in easy conditions; to guard against the danger of concealed crevasses there Crawford would meet them at the foot of the North Ridge to conduct them properly roped to Camp IV. As the supply officer at this camp he would also be able to superintend the descent over the first steep slope of certain porters who would go down from Camp IV without sleeping after carrying up their loads.

But the North Col had first to be reached. With so much new snow to contend with we should hardly get there in one day. If we were to make the most of our chance in the interval of fair weather, we should lose no time in carrying up the loads for some part of the distance. It was decided therefore to begin this work on the following day, June 7th.

In the ascent to the North Col after the recent snowfall we considered that an avalanche was to be feared only in one place, the steep final slope below the shelf. There we could afford to run no risk; we must test the snow and be certain that it was safe before we could cross this slope. Probably we should be obliged to leave our loads below it, having gained, as a result of our day's work, the great advantage of a track. An avalanche might also come down, we thought, on the first steep slope where the ascent began. Here it could do us no harm, and the behaviour of the snow on this slope would be a test of its condition.

The party, Somervell, Crawford and I, with fourteen porters (Wakefield was to be supply officer at Camp III), set out at 8 a.m. In spite of the hard frost of the previous night, the crust was far from bearing our weight; we sank up to our knees in almost every step, and two hours were taken in traversing the snowfield. At 10.15 a.m. Somervell, I, a porter, and Crawford, roped up in that order, began to work up the steep ice-slope, now covered with snow. It was clear that the three of us without loads must take the lead in turns stamping out the tracks for our porters. These men, after their immense efforts on the first and second attempts, had all volunteered to "go high", as they said once more, and everything must be done to ease the terrible work of carrying the loads over the soft snow. No trace was found of our previous tracks, and we were soon arguing as to where exactly they might be as we slanted across the slope. It was remarkable that the snow adhered so well to the ice that we were able to get up without cutting steps. Everything was done by trenching the snow to induce it to come down if it would; every test gave a satisfactory result. Once this crucial place was passed, we plodded on without hesitation. If the snow would not come down where we had formerly encountered steep bare ice, *a fortiori*, above, on the gentler slopes, we had nothing to fear. The thought of an avalanche was dismissed from our minds.

It was necessarily slow work forging our way through the deep snow, but the party was going extraordinarily well, and the porters were evidently determined to get on. Somervell gave us a long lead, and Crawford next, in spite of the handicap of shorter legs, struggled upwards in some of the worst snow we met until I relieved him. I found the effort at each step so great that no method of breathing I had formerly employed was adequate; it was necessary to pause after each lifting movement for a whole series of breaths, rapid at first and gradually slower, before the weight was transferred again to the other foot. About 1.30 p.m. I halted, and the porters, following on three separate ropes, soon came up with the leading party. We should have been glad to stay where we were for a long rest. But the hour was already late, and as Somervell was ready to take the lead again, we decided to push on. We were now about 400 ft below a conspicuous block of ice and 600 ft below Camp IV, still on the gentle slopes of the corridor. Somervell had advanced only 100 ft, rather up the slope than across it, and the last party of porters had barely begun to move up in the steps. The scene was peculiarly bright and windless, and as we rarely spoke, nothing was to be heard but the laboured panting of our lungs. This stillness was suddenly disturbed. We were startled by an ominous sound, sharp, arresting, violent, and yet somehow soft like an explosion of untamped gunpowder. I had never before on a mountainside heard such a sound; but all of us, I imagine, knew instinctively what it meant, as though we had been accustomed to hear it every day of our lives. In a moment I observed the surface of the snow broken and puckered where it had been even for a few yards to the right of me. I took two steps convulsively in this direction with some quick thought of getting nearer to the edge of the danger that threatened us. And then I began to move slowly downwards, inevitably carried on the whole moving surface by a force I was utterly powerless to resist. Somehow I managed to turn out from the slope so as to avoid being pushed headlong and backwards down it. For a second or two I seemed hardly to be in danger as I went quietly sliding down with the snow. Then the rope at my waist tightened and held me back. A wave of snow came over me and I was buried. I supposed that the matter was settled. However, I called to mind experiences related by other parties; and it had been suggested that the best chance of escape in this situation lay in swimming. I thrust out my arms above my head and actually went through some sort of motions of swimming on my back. Beneath the surface of the snow, with nothing to inform the senses of the world outside it, I had no impression of speed after the first acceleration – I struggled in the tumbling snow, unconscious of everything else – until, perhaps only a few seconds later, I knew the pace was easing up. I felt an increasing pressure about my body. I wondered how tightly I should be squeezed, and then the avalanche came to rest.

My arms were free; my legs were near the surface. After a brief struggle, I was standing again, surprised and breathless, in the motionless snow. But the rope was tight at my waist; the porter tied on next me, I supposed, must be deeply buried. To my further surprise, he quickly emerged, unharmed as myself. Somervell and Crawford too, though they had been above me by the rope's length, were now quite close, and soon extricated themselves. We subsequently made out that their experiences had been very similar to mine. But where were the rest? Looking down over the foam of snow, we saw one group of porters some little distance, perhaps 150 ft, below us. Presumably the others must be buried somewhere between us and them, and though no sign of these missing men appeared, we at once prepared to find and dig them out. The porters we saw still stood their ground instead of coming up to help. We soon made out that they were the party who had been immediately behind us, and they were pointing below them. They had travelled farther than us in the avalanche, presumably because they were nearer the centre, where it was moving more rapidly. The other two parties, one of four and one of five men roped together, must have been carried even farther. We could still hope that they were safe. But as we hurried down we soon saw that beneath the place where the four porters were standing was a formidable drop; it was only too plain that the missing men had been swept over it. We had no difficulty in finding a way round this obstacle; in a very short time we were standing under its shadow. The ice-cliff was from forty to sixty feet high in different places; the crevasse at its foot was more or less filled up with avalanche snow. Our fears were soon confirmed. One man was quickly uncovered and found to be still breathing;

before long we were certain that he would live. Another whom we dug out near him had been killed by the fall. He and his party appeared to have struck the hard lower lip of the crevasse, and were lying under the snow on or near the edge of it. The four porters who had escaped soon pulled themselves together after the first shock of the accident, and now worked here with Crawford and did everything they could to extricate the other bodies, while Somervell and I went down into the crevasse. A loop of rope which we pulled up convinced us that the other party must be here. It was slow work loosening the snow with the pick or adze of an ice-axe and shovelling it with the hands. But we were able to follow the rope to the bodies. One was dug up lifeless; another was found upside down, and when we uncovered his face Somervell thought he was still breathing. We had the greatest difficulty in extricating this man, so tightly was the snow packed about his limbs; his load, four oxygen cylinders on a steel frame, had to be cut from his back, and eventually he was dragged out. Though buried for about forty minutes, he had survived the fall and the suffocation, and suffered no serious harm. Of the two others in this party of four, we found only one. We had at length to give up a hopeless search with the certain knowledge that the first of them to be swept over the cliff, and the most deeply buried, must long ago be dead. Of the other five, all the bodies were recovered, but only one was alive. The two who had so marvellously escaped were able to walk down to Camp III, and were almost perfectly well next day. The other seven were killed.

We Had Found George Mallory

Conrad Anker

When George Mallory and Andrew Irvine left their tent on 8 June 1924 for Everest's summit they climbed into myth. No mystery has possessed mountaineering more than the question of whether Mallory and Irvine did or did not reach Everest's summit. In 1999 a Mallory and Irvine Research Expedition went to Everest to discover the two climbers' fate. Their primary search area was high on the North Face where in 1975 a Chinese climber, Wang Hong-bao, had seen what he thought was the body of an Englishman. The American high altitude climber Conrad Anker was one of the searchers for Mallory and Irvine.

I had just sat down to take off my crampons, because the traverse across the rock band ahead would be easier without them. I drank some fluid – a carbohydrate drink I keep in my water bottle – and sucked a cough drop. At that altitude, it's essential to keep your throat lubricated.

I looked out over this vast expanse. To the south and west, I could see into Nepal, with jagged peaks ranging toward the horizon. In front of me on the north stretched the great Tibetan plateau, brown and corrugated as it dwindled into the distance. The wind was picking up, and small clouds were forming below, on the lee side of some of the smaller peaks.

All of a sudden, a strong feeling came over me that something was going to happen. Something good. I usually feel content when the climb I'm on is going well, but this was different. I felt positive, happy. I was in a good place.

It was 11:45 a.m. on 1 May. We were just below 27,000 feet on the north face of Mount Everest. The other four guys were fanned out above me and to the east. They were in sight, but too far away to holler to. We had to use our radios to communicate.

I attached my crampons to my pack, stood up, put the pack on, and started hiking up a small corner. Then, to my left, out of the corner of my eye, I caught a glimpse of a piece of blue and yellow fabric flapping in the wind, tucked behind a boulder. I thought, I'd better go look at this. Anything that wasn't part of the natural landscape was worth looking at.

When I got to the site, I could see that the fabric was probably a piece of tent that had been ripped loose by the wind and blown down here, where it came to rest in the hollow behind the boulder. It was modern stuff, nylon. I wasn't surprised – there are a lot of abandoned tents on Everest, and the wind just shreds them.

But as I stood there, I carefully scanned the mountain right and left. I was wearing my prescription dark glasses, so I could see really well. As I scanned right, I saw a patch of white, about a hundred feet away. I knew at once there was something unusual about it, because of the colour. It wasn't the gleaming white of snow reflecting the sun. It wasn't the white of the chunks of quartzite and calcite that crop up here and there on the north side of Everest. It had a kind of matte look – a light-absorbing quality, like marble.

I walked closer. I immediately saw a bare foot, sticking into the air, heel up, toes pointed downward. At that moment, I knew I had found a human body.

Then, when I got even closer, I could see from the tattered clothing that this wasn't the body of a modern climber. This was somebody very old.

It didn't really sink in at first. It was as if everything was in slow motion. *Is this a dream?* I wondered. *Am I really here?* But I also thought, *This is what we came here to do. This is who we're looking for. This is Sandy Irvine.*

We'd agreed beforehand on a series of coded messages for the search. Everybody on the mountain could listen in on our radio conversations. If we found something, we didn't want some other expedition breaking the news to the world.

"Boulder" was the code word for "body". So I sat down on my pack, got out my radio, and broadcast a message: "Last time I went bouldering in my hobnails, I fell off." It was the first thing that came to mind. I just threw in "hobnails", because an old hobnailed boot – the kind that went out of style way back in the 1940s – was still laced onto the man's right foot. That was another reason I knew he was very old.

We all had our radios stuffed inside our down suits, so it wasn't easy to hear them. Of the other four guys out searching, only Jake Norton caught any part of my message, and all he heard was "hobnails". I could see him, some fifty yards above me and a ways to the east. Jake sat down, ripped out his radio, and broadcast back, "What was that, Conrad?"

"Come on down," I answered. He was looking at me now, so I started waving the ski stick I always carry at altitude. "Let's get together for Snickers and tea."

Jake knew I'd found something important, but the other three were still oblivious. He tried to wave and yell and get their attention, but it wasn't working. At 27,000 feet, because of oxygen deprivation, you retreat into a kind of personal shell; the rest of the world doesn't seem quite real. So I got back on the radio and put some urgency into my third message: "I'm calling a mandatory group meeting right now!"

Where we were searching was fairly tricky terrain, down-sloping shale slabs, some of them covered with a dusting of snow. If you fell in the wrong place, you'd go all the way, 7,000 feet to the Rongbuk Glacier. So it took the other guys a little while to work their way down and over to me.

I rooted through my pack to get out my camera. That morning, at Camp V, I thought I'd stuck it in my pack, but I had two nearly identical stuff sacks, and it turns out I'd grabbed my radio batteries instead. I realized I'd forgotten my camera. I thought, Oh, well, if I had had the camera, I might not have found the body. That's just the way things work.

When I told a friend about this, he asked if I'd read Faulkner's novella *The Bear*. I hadn't. On reading that story, I saw the analogy. The best hunters in the deep Mississippi woods can't even catch a glimpse of Old Ben, the huge, half-mythic bear that has ravaged their livestock for years. It's only when Ike McCaslin gives up everything he's relied on – lays down not only his rifle, but his compass and watch – that, lost in the forest, he's graced with the sudden presence of Old Ben in a clearing: "It did not emerge, appear: it was just there, immobile, fixed in the green and windless noon's hot dappling."

As I sat on my pack waiting for the others, a feeling of awe and respect for the dead man sprawled in front of me started to fill me. He lay face down, head uphill, frozen into the slope. A tuft of hair stuck out from the leather pilot's cap he had on his head. His arms were raised, and his fingers were planted in the scree, as if he'd tried to self-arrest with them. It seemed likely that he was still alive when he had come to rest in this position. There were no gloves on his hands; later I'd think long and hard about the implications of that fact. I took off my own gloves to compare my hands to his. I've got short, thick fingers; his were long and thin, and deeply tanned, probably from the weeks of having walked the track all the way from Darjeeling over the crest of the Himalaya to the north face of Everest.

The winds of the decades had torn most of the clothing away from his back and lower torso. He was naturally mummified – that patch of alabaster I'd spotted from a hundred feet away was the bare, perfectly preserved skin of his back. What was incredible was that I could still see the powerful, well-defined muscles in his shoulders and back, and the blue discoloration of bruises.

Around his shoulders and upper arms, the remnants of seven or eight layers of clothing still covered him – shirts and sweaters and jackets made of wool, cotton, and silk. There was a white, braided cotton rope tied to his waist, about three eighths of an inch in diameter – many times weaker than any rope we'd use today. The rope was tangled around his left shoulder. About ten feet from his waist, I could see the frayed end where the rope had broken. So I knew at once that he'd been tied to his partner, and that he'd taken a long fall. The rope had either broken in the fall, or when his partner tried to belay him over a rock edge.

The right elbow looked as if it was dislocated or broken. It lay imbedded in the scree, bent in an unnatural position. The right scapula was a little disfigured. And above his waist on a right rib, I could see the blue contusion from an upward pull of the rope as it took the shock of the fall.

His right leg was badly broken, both tibia and fibula. With the boot still on, the leg lay at a grotesque angle. They weren't compound fractures – the bones hadn't broken the skin – but they were very bad breaks. My conclusion was that in the fall, the right side of the man's body had taken the worst of the impact. It looked as though perhaps in his last moments, the man had laid his good left leg over his broken right, as if to protect it from further harm. The left boot may have been whipped off in the fall, or it may have eroded and fallen apart. Only the tongue of the boot was present, pinched between the bare toes of his left foot and the heel of his right boot.

Goraks – the big black ravens that haunt the high Himalaya – had pecked away at the right buttock and gouged out a pretty extensive hole, big enough for a gorak to enter. From that orifice, they had eaten out most of the internal organs, simply hollowed out the body.

The muscles of the left lower leg and the thighs had become stringy and desiccated. It's what happens, apparently, to muscles exposed for seventy-five years. The skin had split and opened up, but for some reason the goraks hadn't eaten it.

After fifteen or twenty minutes, Jake Norton arrived. Then the others, one by one: first Tap Richards, then Andy Politz, then Dave Hahn. They didn't say much: just, "Wow, good job, Conrad," or, "This has to be Sandy Irvine." Later Dave said, "I started blinking in awe," and Tap remembered, "I was pretty blown away. It was obviously a body, but it looked like a Greek or Roman marble statue."

The guys took photos, shot some video, and discussed the nuances of the scene. There seemed to be a kind of taboo about touching him. Probably half an hour passed before we got up the nerve to touch him. But we had agreed that if we found Mallory or Irvine, we would perform as professional an excavation as we could under the circumstances, to see if what we found might cast any light on the mystery of their fate. We had even received permission from John Mallory (George's son) to take a small DNA sample.

Tap and Jake did most of the excavating work. We'd planned to cut small squares out of the clothing to take down to Base Camp and analyze. Almost at once, on the collar of one of the shirts, Jake found a name tag. It read, "G. Mallory." Jake looked at us and said, "That's weird. Why would Irvine be wearing Mallory's shirt?"

We didn't have all that much time to work. We'd agreed on a tentative turnaround hour of 2:00 p.m., to get back to Camp V while it was still daylight, and by the time we started excavating, it was past noon. There were clouds below us, but only a slight wind. As one can imagine, this was hard work at 26,700 feet (the altitude of the body, as I later calculated it). We had taken off our oxygen gear, because it was just too cumbersome to dig with it on.

Because the body was frozen into the scree, we had to chip away at the surrounding ice and rock with our ice axes. It took some vigorous swings even to dislodge little chunks, the ice was so dense. We were all experienced climbers, we were used to swinging tools, so we did the chipping pretty efficiently; only once did a pick glance off a rock and impale the man's arm. As we got closer to the body, we put down our axes and started chipping with our pocketknives.

We were so sure this was Sandy Irvine that Jake actually sat down, took a smooth piece of shale in his lap, and started to scratch out a tombstone with Irvine's name and dates, 1902–1924. But then we found the "G. Mallory" tag on the collar, and shortly after, Tap found another one on a seam under the arm. It read, "G. Leigh Mallory." We just stared at each other, stunned, as we realized this wasn't Irvine. We had found George Mallory.

As we excavated, Tap chipped away on his left side, Jake on his right. I did mostly lifting and prying. Dave and Andy took pictures and shot video.

It was good fortune that George was lying on his stomach, because most of the stuff you carry when you climb is in the front pockets, so it had been protected by his body for seventy-five years. It may seem funny, or even pretentious, but we referred to him as "George", not as "Mallory". All through the weeks before, we'd talked about Mallory and Irvine so much that it was as if we knew them, like old friends; they had become George and Sandy.

We left George's face where it was, frozen into the scree, but once I could lift the lower part of his body, Tap and Jake could reach underneath him and go through the pockets. The body was like a frozen log. When I lifted it, it made that same creaky noise as when you pull up a log that's been on the ground for years.

It was disconcerting to look into the hole in the right buttock that the goraks had chewed. His body had been hollowed out, almost like a pumpkin. You could see the remains of seeds and some other food – very possibly Mallory's last meal.

We didn't go near George's head. We moved the loose rock away from it, but we didn't try to dig it out. I think that was a sort of unspoken agreement, and at the time, none of us wanted to look at his face.

Of course we were most excited about the possibility of finding the camera. Jake even thought for a minute he'd found it. George had a small bag that was lodged under his right biceps. Jake reached in there, squeezed the bag, and felt a small, square object, just about the right size. We finally had to cut the bag to get the object out, and when we did, we found it wasn't the camera after all, it was a tin of beef lozenges!

The clincher that it was Mallory came when Jake pulled out a neatly folded, new-looking silk handkerchief in which several letters had been carefully wrapped. They were addressed to Mallory. On the envelope of one of them, for instance, we read, "George Leigh Mallory Esq., c/o British Trade Agent, Yalung Tibet."

Besides the letters, we found a few penciled notes in other pockets. As we found out later, they were all about logistics, about bringing so many loads to Camp VI, and so on. We read them carefully, hoping Mallory might have jotted down a note about reaching the summit or turning back, but there was nothing of the sort.

One by one, Jake and Tap produced what we started calling

"the artifacts". It seemed an odd collection of items to carry to the summit of Everest. There was a small penknife; a tiny pencil, about two and a half inches long, onto which some kind of mint cake had congealed (we could still smell the mint); a needle and thread; a small pair of scissors with a file built into one blade; a second handkerchief, well used (the one he blew his nose on), woven in a red and yellow floral pattern on a blue background, with the monogram G.L.M. in yellow; a box of special matches, Swan Vestas, with extra phosphorus on the tips; a little piece of leather with a hose clamp on it that might have been a mouthpiece for the oxygen apparatus; a tube of zinc oxide, rolled partway up; a spare pair of fingerless mittens that looked like they hadn't been used.

Two other artifacts seemed particularly intriguing. Jake found a smashed altimeter in one pocket. The hand was missing from the dial, but you could see that the instrument had been specially calibrated for Everest, with a range from 20,000 feet to 30,000 feet. Inscribed on the back, in fine script, was "M.E.E. II" – for Mount Everest Expedition II. And in the vest pocket, we found a pair of goggles. The frames were bent, but the green glass was unbroken. It was Andy who came up with the possible significance of the goggles being in the pocket. To him, it argued that George had fallen after dusk. If it had been in the daytime, he would have been wearing the goggles, even on rock. He'd just had a vivid lesson in the consequences of taking them off during the day, when Teddy Norton got a terrible attack of snow blindness the night after his summit push on 4 June.

As we removed each artifact, we put it carefully in a Ziploc bag. Andy volunteered to carry the objects down to Camp V. To some people, it may seem that taking George's belongings with us was a violation. We even had a certain sense that we were disturbing the dead – I think that's why we had hesitated to begin the excavation. But this was the explicit purpose of the expedition: to find Mallory and Irvine and to retrieve the artifacts and try to solve the mystery of what had happened on 8 June, 1924. I think we did the right thing.

As interesting as what we found was what we didn't find. George had no backpack on, nor any trace of the frame that held the twin oxygen bottles. His only carrying sack was the little bag we found under his right biceps. He didn't have any water bottle, or Thermos flask, which was what they used in '24. He didn't have a flashlight, because he'd forgotten to take it with him. We know this not from Odell, but from the 1933 party, who found the flashlight in the tent at the 1924 Camp VI.

And we didn't find the camera. That was the great disappointment.

It was getting late – we'd already well overstayed our 2:00 p.m. turnaround. The last thing we gathered was a DNA sample, to analyse for absolute proof of the identity of the man we'd found. Simonson had received approval for this procedure beforehand from John Mallory, George's only son, who's seventy-nine and living in South Africa. I had agreed to do this job.

I cut an inch-and-a-half-square patch of skin off the right forearm. It wasn't easy. I had to use the serrated blade on Dave's utility knife. Cutting George's skin was like cutting saddle leather, cured and hard.

Since the expedition, I've often wondered whether taking the tissue was a sacrilegious act. In Base Camp, I had volunteered for the task. On the mountain, I had no time to reflect whether or not this was the right thing to do.

We wanted to bury George, or at least to cover him up. There were rocks lying around, but not a lot that weren't frozen in place. We formed a kind of bucket brigade, passing rocks down to the site.

Then Andy read, as a prayer of committal, Psalm 103: "As for man, his days are as grass: as a flower of the field, so he flourisheth. /For the wind passeth over it, and it is gone . . ."

We finally left at 4:00 p.m. I lingered a bit after the other four. The last thing I did was to leave a small Butterfinger candy bar in the rocks nearby, like a Buddhist offering. I said a sort of prayer for him, several times over.

The Void

Kees Egeler

A Dutch mountaineer and professor of geology, Egeler, accompanied by Tom De Booy and the French guide Lionel Terray (a member of Herzog's Annapurna expedition) sought, in 1950, the untrodden summit of Nevada Huantsan, 6,395 m (20,981 ft) in the Andes. Although the expedition met with eventual success, the first assault involved a catastrophic accident.

At long last, all was ready. A few curt final instructions, and Terray slid down. About 200 ft below, at the end of the rope, he cut out a broad step in the ice-wall. Then I followed – first over a bulge, then a short distance dangling through the air, and finally down the steep ice-pitch of which the lower portion of the flank consisted. By the time I arrived, Terray had already hammered in a long ice-piton for the next rappel. We waited side by side, with our faces to the wall, until De Booy could join us. He had a most ticklish job. Whilst Terray during his descent had been secured by me at the end of the rope, and I, in turn, had been safeguarded by De Booy, the latter now had to lower himself down by the double rope unsecured. He naturally went to work with the utmost caution, particularly when tackling the first stage over the bulge.

Terray and I looked at each other. Up above, when it looked as though we were caught like rats in a trap, he had been definitely apprehensive. Now he was back again to true form. He grinned at me and said:

"What a game! Ever been up against anything like this, Kees? Who would have guessed, this morning . . .?"

I smiled back. His magnificent self-assurance was infectious. I no longer doubted that, under his skilful guidance, we should extricate ourselves from this ugly situation. Nevertheless, we were not happy about the next rappel. The steep ice-wall (about sixty degrees) on which we were poised went down another 100 ft or so and then abruptly ended in a void. Apparently the wall over-hung at that point, but how far it projected and what came underneath were imponderables. We could only assume that it would be exceptionally steep. We were, we thought, about 300 ft above the glacier at the moment. But the foot of the wall was not visible.

To our great relief De Booy joined us safe and sound on our little artificial shelf. We could now restart roping down from the lower piton. But would the rope be long enough to reach over the bulging overhang and enable us to gain a foothold lower down? Again Lionel went first so that he could make preparations as quickly as possible for the succeeding stage. About 100 ft down, he reached the edge of the bulge and could see what lay below.

"Ca touche nettement!" he called up. This was great news, for visibility was fading fast and we had not a moment to spare. A second later he disappeared from view, whilst De Booy and I waited in suspense. Then a vague reverberating shout came from below. To us above, it was completely incomprehensible. The words were lost under the overhang. Yet it was essential for me to know what awaited me down below, so I bellowed out to Terray that I could not catch what he was shouting. De Booy and I waited anxiously, debating what to do next. Then we felt the tension on the rope slacken, indicating that Terray had found a foothold somewhere and had released the rope. Once again several precious minutes were lost. Then, further hesitation being out of the question, I let myself down the rope as quickly as possible until I reached the edge of the overhang. Peering warily over, I saw Terray about eighty feet directly below, clinging to the rock face.

The situation was unpleasant. The overhang projected so far out that the whole of the next eighty feet down had to be descended through space. Never before had I been faced with such a manoeuvre. Thank goodness I was being secured from above by my companion. There was not much time to dally. De Booy had asked me to give him a shout as to the position so I called out that the rappel went fairly deep and that everything seemed all right. Then cautiously turning over on my stomach, I let my legs dangle into nothing, slid over the edge, and in the failing light began to descend the thin rope. This swaying through space made an unforgettable impression on my mind. The upper crust of the overhang was fringed with enormous icicles, one of which broke off as I accidentally came in contact with it and went tinkling past me down into the void. It was eerie.

If it had not been for the pressing time factor this would have been a thrilling adventure; but, suspended there, I was all too conscious that the occasion was not just another interesting descent. It was grim reality. A desperate race against time.

Farther down, the wall receded sharply away. I lowered myself, feeling very much like a spider on its thread, until my foot touched the ice-wall below. What a relief! As always, after a long descent by rope, it was wonderful to find one's feet again. Actually I had quite a job to get a footing, for the flank on which I landed was pitched at a gradient of at least sixty-five degrees and I was almost at the end of the rope. There was little scope for manoeuvring. Luckily Terray came to my assistance and cut out a few steps for me. He himself had had the greatest difficulty in arriving safely. What was worse, he found himself suddenly hampered by stubborn cramp in the arm.

I simply could not manage to get any more favourable stance than one with holds for one foot and one hand. I waited quietly for the next move, hoping that it would not take too long. It was De Booy's turn to come down. As experience had shown that it was useless to call out from below, I untied myself and gave three hard tugs at the rope, that being the agreed signal for him to follow down. He understood, for immediately there was a movement in the rope. Two minutes later his dim shadow appeared above on the edge of the overhang. In the meantime darkness had descended apace. A last spark of light seemed to linger on the spot where De Booy stood, but below the bulge, where we were, everything was shrouded in dusk. We exchanged a few words. De Booy asked what the position was like, and I shouted to him to try and land as high up the slope as possible because the rope was too short to allow of much playing about for position. I implored him to take the utmost care. One end of the rope was longer than the other, I bawled, but he ought to be able to manage.

Like some dim ghost De Booy slid down the thin nylon rope. Everything was going so swimmingly that I jocularly complimented him on his style. But, as he tried to get a foothold on the ice just above me, the treacherous light misled him. The slope was far steeper than he thought. His feet slid away. His hands found no hold on the slippery rock, covered with verglas. The heavy weight of his rucksack pulled him down and over backwards, and . . .

He fell.

To my horror he fell past me. Several yards lower, however, he was brought up with a jerk, hanging head downward, his feet tangled in the rope. I frantically concentrated on ways and means of rescuing him. My own delicate position prevented me from getting nearer. The wall, where I was precariously poised, was terribly steep, and the rocks at my side were covered with ice. Somehow or other I managed to grasp the looped end of the longer rope which was hanging loosely down and gave it a turn round my hand. Then, by grabbing the other rope, I formed, as it were, a continuous ring of rope, from a part of which De Booy hung upside-down. This action, I thought, would at least reduce the possibility of his slipping away. My brain worked feverishly, taking in every detail, trying to straighten out things, wondering whether De Booy's hands were also still clinging to the rope. If his feet did not untangle, he might be able to hold out until Terray came to his aid. I saw the latter some ten yards to our right on the slope, busily unearthing his torch from his ruck-sack. It had all happened in a matter of seconds, and as yet he had noticed nothing amiss. Only when I lustily yelled for help did he realise what was up. Then,

without even giving himself time to grasp his axe, he sped
across the wall towards us. And once again my heart stood
still! He, too, missed his footing.

Some forty feet or so farther down he managed, in his own
inimitable way, to save himself. Thank God! For a moment he
was completely dazed: he had wrenched his arm. I cried out to
him to do his utmost, for De Booy's life was in peril. He could
not possibly hang on the rope much longer.

De Booy was aware of this, too, for he said in a remarkably
quiet voice:

"This is it, Kees! It's all over with us."

But I still had hope. I called out that it wasn't all over! He
must do everything to hang on! Then, I focused my attention
again on Terray who, on my other side, was laboriously climbing up the steep slope. It was slow, agonisingly slow. I spurred
him on: "Quicker, Lionel, much quicker!"

Then I heard a rending noise. I turned instantly to the other
side, only to see De Booy plunging down towards the glacier.
For a dramatic second or two I followed his fall as his crampons
scraped the rock and sent up showers of sparks. Then he
vanished in the void. A terrible silence followed.

Terray and I clung, petrified, to the face. Black despair for
our comrade choked us. I saw no reason to call out. De Booy
could hardly have escaped being killed.

Staring into the darkness below, I thought I could distinguish
a vague dark blob against the white snow. From his greater
distance Lionel had secured a rather better view. He had the
feeling that, if De Booy had not bashed his head against
projecting rocks and had avoided falling into the bergschrund,
he might possibly be alive. He called at the top of his voice:
"Tom! Tom!" The dead silence seemed to confirm our worst
fears; but Terray kept on calling and suddenly there came an
answer – an unmistakable answer!

What a wonderful moment that was! To hear a voice, as it
were, from the dead! For a time we were almost too astounded
to react. Then we realized that the incredible had happened. An
excited babble of Dutch and French went up. Anxiously we
yelled to ask what he had broken. From the depths came the
laconic reply: "Nothing!"

A few moments later we saw a tiny light appear some hundreds of feet below. We had brought out with us special "forehead" lamps in case we ever had to climb in the dark. The light was fastened on an elastic band which went round the forehead, thus enabling one to have the hands free. De Booy had obviously put his on to show us where he was. Seeing his light was our signal to get into action. Terray climbed up towards me and pulled at the end of the rope, but it wouldn't budge. This was the worst that could possibly happen at such a critical time. The nightmare thought of a jammed rope after a rappel over an overhang is always enough to give any climber grey hairs. Terray pulled with increasing force. He raged and swore – and, curiously enough, it seemed as though this helped, for suddenly the rope freed itself and was easily pulled through. Terray worked with might and main to prepare a new rappel. Once it had been rigged up, I was able to leave my awkward position and slide downwards, feeling my way in the dark. The rope reached to about sixty-five feet above the bergschrund. I cut a big step with my axe and then waited for Terray to join me.

Meanwhile I could talk more easily with De Booy. My disquiet lessened considerably when he called out: "Why the devil are you two taking so long? I showed you the quick way down, didn't I?" This was an encouraging sign. That he could still wise-crack cheered me up no end. I saw his light going to and fro and assumed that he was moving about to keep warm. He even climbed a little way up the slope to give me some light when, a little later, I came, via the bergschrund, on to the glacier. Terray followed closely behind. The three of us stood united again at the foot of the slope.

In the dark it was naturally impossible to trace the line of De Booy's fall. Not until next day were we able to assess its length and direction. But even in the dark one could tell that he had fallen at least 300 ft. He had been hanging upside down when he started falling and must have turned a somersault. His feet had struck the rock face some yards lower down and had taken the first brunt of his fall.

This probably saved his life. The steep ice-wall down which he had slithered with ever-increasing velocity was actually fraught with much less danger. We reckoned that he cleared the gaping mouth of the bergschrund which, at this point, was several yards wide, by sailing right over it. Landing on the sloping glacier, he had gradually lost speed because it was thickly covered with snow.

At that time all this did not interest us so much as finding out if he really were uninjured. It was almost unbelievable. He was examined in the light of our torches and prodded all over. A first glance only revealed a skinned nose. He complained of pains in the back. How could it be otherwise after a fall of some 300 ft? He was also chilled to the marrow, a poor condition to be in with the prospect of an ice-cold bivouac at a height of 18,000 ft without tent or sleeping-bag. It was clear now that we should have to spend the night on the glacier, for De Booy was in no fit state to cope with a descent lasting several hours.

As soon as we found a more or less suitable spot we levelled it off as far as possible and laid down the ropes to insulate us a little from the rising glacial cold and to keep us as dry as possible. We then put on everything that we could find in the shape of clothing. We took off our boots and put on dry socks. Then we got into our nylon bivouac-sets, consisting of a long anorak and a narrow bag in which to place the legs, the so-called *pied d'éléphant*. Both parts fastened together with press studs.

We also drew our rucksacks over our feet to help keep them warm, and thus installed ourselves for the night. For extra security we belayed ourselves with ropes attached by a turn or two to axes rammed in the ice – a necessary precaution, as several yards away down the slope an enormous crevasse gaped open and we had no desire to slide into this in our sleep.

Actually we hardly snatched any sleep. The air was crystal clear and the pitiless cold cut us to the bone. Terray and I had De Booy between us, and were continually rubbing and massaging him, but we found it difficult to keep him at all warm. We ourselves had to keep on piano-playing with our fingers and toes. Blood circulation had to be maintained at all costs to prevent frost-bite. If we dozed off, it was only to wake a moment later, disturbed by some movement of the others or tormented by the terrible thirst from which we now all suffered.

I unearthed a lemon from my rucksack and squeezed some of

its juice on lumps of sugar, which I tried to get to De Booy. But it was no good. The acid lemon-juice caused him acute agony, owing to split lips. Then I tried to obtain some water to drink by filling my field-flask with snow and putting it under my clothes against the bare flesh. Apparently I, too, must have been near freezing-point, because the snow did not melt.

There is no comparison between a bivouac in the Cordillera Blanca and one in the Alps. In Europe a bivouac lasts only about seven hours and one can get going again towards four in the morning. In the Andes it gets dark about six and the night lasts a full twelve hours. Even when dawn breaks, no start is possible because it is still too freezingly cold and the risk of frost-bite is too great.

It seemed that the wretched night would never end. We tried to divert our thoughts. Amongst other titbits, Terray told us of the many bivouacs he had endured in his career. He spoke of that terrible night on the Annapurna when, at an altitude of 23,000 ft, he had huddled in a crevasse with his companions, two of whom, Lachenal and Herzog, were suffering horribly from frost-bitten extremities. His last bivouac had occurred the previous winter on the vertical face of the Fitz Roy in Patagonia.

None of us had much heart for talk. Our thoughts were too taken up by our recent nerve-racking experiences and by the miraculous turn of events. What would have happened if De Booy had broken an arm or a leg? He could not possibly have survived this bleak icy bivouac. Yet there he was between us, apparently unscathed. We wondered if and when we should ever to able to renew the attack.

Thinking of the past eventful hours, I realized that it was not only De Booy who had enjoyed fantastic luck. Terray, too, might have hurtled precipitously down that face. And, if both of them had been seriously injured, what chance should I have had, without a light, to grope my way down that wall in the dark? Yes, we were all lucky to be still alive and kicking.

Between a Rock and a Hard Place

Aron Ralston

In April 2003 a boulder fall in a remote Utah canyon pinned down the right arm of climber Aron Ralston. After five days of dehydration, pain and deprivation Ralston realized that he could save himself only by amputating his own arm.

I thrash myself forward and back, side to side, up and down, down and up. I scream out in pure hate, shrieking as I batter my body to and fro against the canyon walls, losing every bit of composure that I've struggled so intensely to maintain. Then I feel my arm bend unnaturally in the unbudging grip of the chockstone. An epiphany strikes me with the magnificent glory of a holy intervention and instantly brings my seizure to a halt:

If I torque my arm far enough, I can break my forearm bones.

Like bending a two-by-four held in a table vise, I can bow my entire goddamn arm until it snaps in two!

Holy Christ, Aron, that's it, that's it. THAT'S FUCKING IT!

I scramble to clear my stuff off the rock, trying to keep my head on straight. There is no hesitation. Under the power of this divine interaction, I barely realize what I'm about to do. I slip into some kind of autopilot; I'm not at the controls anymore. Within a minute, I orient my body in a crouch under the boulder, but I can't get low enough to bend my arm before I feel a tugging at my waist. I unclip my daisy chain from the anchor webbing and drop my weight as far down as I can, almost making my buttocks reach the stones on the canyon floor. I put my left hand under the boulder and push hard, harder, HARDER!, to exert a maximum downward force on my radius bone. As I slowly bend my arm down and to the left, a Pow! reverberates like a muted cap-gun shot up and down Blue John Canyon. I don't say a word, but I reach to feel my forearm. There is an abnormal lump on top of my wrist. I pull my body away from the chockstone and down again, simulating the position I was just in, and feel a gap between the serrated edges of my cleanly broken arm bone.

Without further pause and again in silence, I hump my body up over the chockstone, with a single clear purpose in my mind. Smearing my shoes against the canyon walls, I push with my legs and grab the back of the chockstone with my left hand, pulling with every bit of ferocity I can muster, hard, harder, HARDER!, and a second capgun shot ends my ulna's anticipation. Sweating and euphoric, I again touch my right arm two inches below my wrist, and pull my right shoulder away from the boulder. Both bones have splintered in the same place, the ulna perhaps a half inch closer to my elbow than my radius. Rotating my forearm like a shaft inside its housing, I have an axis of motion freshly independent of my wrist's servitude to the rock vise.

I am overcome with the excitement of having solved the riddle of my imprisonment. Hustling to deploy the shorter and sharper of my multi-tool's two blades, I skip the tourniquet procedure I have rehearsed and place the cutting tip between two blue veins. I push the knife into my wrist, watching my skin stretch inwardly, until the point pierces and sinks to its hilt. In a blaze of pain, I know the job is just starting. With a glance at my watch – it is 10:32 a.m. – I motivate myself: "OK, Aron, here we go. You're in it now."

I leave behind my prior declarations that severing my arm is nothing but a slow act of suicide and move forward on a cresting wave of emotion. Knowing the alternative is to wait for a progressively more certain but assuredly slow demise, I choose to meet the risk of death in action. As surreal as it looks for my arm to disappear into a glove of sandstone, it feels gloriously perfect to have figured out how to amputate it.

My first act is to sever, with a downward sawing motion, as much of the skin on the inside surface of my forearm as I can, without tearing any of the noodle-like veins so close to the skin. Once I've opened a large enough hole in my arm, about four inches below my wrist, I momentarily stow the knife, holding its handle in my teeth, and poke first my left forefinger and then my left thumb inside my arm and feel around. Sorting through the bizarre and unfamiliar textures, I make a mental map of my arm's inner features. I feel bundles of muscle fibers and, working my fingers behind them, find two pairs of cleanly fractured but jagged bone ends. Twisting my right forearm as if to turn my trapped palm down, I feel the proximal bone ends rotate freely around their fixed partners. It's a painful movement, but at the same time, it's motion I haven't made since Saturday, and it excites me to know that soon I will be free of the rest of my crushed dead hand. It's just a matter of time.

Prodding and pinching, I can distinguish between the hard tendons and ligaments, and the soft, rubbery feel of the more pliable arteries. I should avoid cutting the arteries until the end if I can help it at all, I decide.

Withdrawing my bloody fingers to the edge of my incision point, I isolate a strand of muscle between the knife and my thumb, and using the blade like a paring knife, I slice through a pinky-finger-sized filament. I repeat the action a dozen times, slipping the knife through string after string of muscle without hesitation or sound.

Sort, pinch, rotate, slice.

Sort, pinch, rotate, slice.

Patterns; process.

Whatever blood-slimy mass I fit between the cutting edge and my left thumb falls victim to the rocking motion of the multi-tool, back and forth. I'm like a pipe cutter scoring through the outer circumference of a piece of soft tubing. As each muscle bundle yields to the metal, I probe for any of the pencil-thick arteries. When I find one, I tug it a little and remove it from the strand about to be severed. Finally, about a third of the way through the assorted soft tissues of my forearm, I cut a vein. I haven't put on my tourniquet yet, but I'm like a five-year-old unleashed on his Christmas presents – now that

I've started, there's no putting the brakes on. The desire to keep cutting, to get myself free, is so powerful that I rationalize I haven't lost that much blood yet, only a few drops, because my crushed hand has been acting like an isolation valve on my circulation.

Another ten, fifteen, or maybe twenty minutes slip past me. I am engrossed in making the surgical work go as fast as possible. Stymied by the half-inch-wide yellowish tendon in the middle of my forearm, I stop the operation to don my improvised tourniquet. By this time, I've cut a second artery, and several ounces of blood, maybe a third of a cup, have dripped onto the canyon wall below my arm. Perhaps because I've removed most of the connecting tissues in the medial half of my forearm, and allowed the vessels to open up, the blood loss has accelerated in the last few minutes. The surgery is slowing down now that I've come to the stubbornly durable tendon, and I don't want to lose blood unnecessarily while I'm still trapped. I'll need every bit of it for the hike to my truck and the drive to Hanksville or Green River.

I still haven't decided which will be the fastest way to medical attention. The closest phone is at Hanksville, an hour's drive to the west, if I'm fast on the left-handed reach-across shifting. But I can't remember if there's a medical clinic there; all that comes to my mind is a gas station and a hamburger place. Green River is two hours of driving to the north, but there is a medical clinic. I'm hoping to find someone at the trailhead who will drive for me, but I think back to when I left there on Saturday – there were only two other vehicles in the three-acre lot. That was a weekend, this is midweek. I have to accept the risk that when I get to the trailhead, there won't be anyone there. I have to pace myself for a six-to-seven-hour effort before I get to definitive medical care.

Setting the knife down on the chockstone, I pick up the neoprene tubing of my CamelBak, which has been sitting off to the top left of the chockstone, unused, for the past two days. I cinch the black insulation tube in a double loop around my forearm, three inches below my elbow. Tying the black stretchy fabric into a doubled overhand knot with one end in my teeth, I tug the other end with my free left hand. Next, I quickly attach a carabiner into the tourniquet and twist it six times, as I did when I first experimented with the tourniquet an eon ago, on Tuesday, or was it Monday?

"Why didn't I figure out how to break my bones then?" I wonder. "Why did I have to suffer all this extra time?" God, I must be the dumbest guy to ever have his hand trapped by a boulder. It took me six days to figure out how I could cut off my arm. Self-disgust catches in my throat until I can clear my head.

Aron, that's all just distraction. It doesn't matter. Get back to work.

I clip the tightly wound carabiner to a second loop of webbing around my biceps to keep the neoprene from untwisting, and reach for my bloody knife again.

Continuing with the surgery, I clear out the last muscles surrounding the tendon and cut a third artery. I still haven't uttered even an "Ow!" I don't think to verbalize the pain; it's a part of this experience, no more important to the procedure than the color of my tourniquet.

I now have relatively open access to the tendon. Sawing aggressively with the blade, as before, I can't put a dent in the amazingly strong fiber. I pull at it with my fingers and realize it has the durability of a flat-wound cable; it's like a double-thick strip of fiber-reinforced box-packaging tape, creased over itself in quarter-inch folds. I can't cut it, so I decide to reconfigure my multi-tool for the pliers. Unfolding the blood-slippery implement, I shove the backside of the blade against my stomach to push the knife back into its storage slot and then expose the pliers. Using them to bite into the edge of the tendon, I squeeze and twist, tearing away a fragment. Yes, this will work just fine. I tackle the most brutish task.

Grip, squeeze, twist, tear.

Grip, squeeze, twist, tear.

Patterns; process.

"This is gonna make one hell of a story to tell my friends," I think. "They'll never believe how I had to cut off my arm. Hell, I can barely believe it, and I'm watching myself do it."

Little by little, I rip through the tendon until I totally sever the twine-like filament, then switch the tool back to the knife, using my teeth to extract the blade. It's 11:16 a.m.; I've been cutting for over forty minutes. With my fingers, I take an inventory of what I have left: two small clusters of muscle, another artery, and a quarter circumference of skin nearest the wall. There is also a pale white nerve strand, as thick as a swollen piece of angel-hair pasta. Getting through that is going to be unavoidably painful. I purposefully don't get anywhere close to the main nerve with my fingers; I think it's best not to know fully what I'm in for. The smaller elastic nerve branches are so sensitive that even nudging them sends Taser shocks up to my shoulder, momentarily stunning me. All these have to be severed. I put the knife's edge under the nerve and pluck it, like lifting a guitar string two inches off its frets, until it snaps, releasing a flood of pain. It recalibrates my personal scale of what it feels like to be hurt – it's as though I thrust my entire arm into a cauldron of magma.

Minutes later, I recover enough to continue. The last step is stretching the skin of my outer wrist right and sawing the blade into the wall, as if I'm slicing a piece of gristle on a cutting board. As I approach that precise moment of liberation, the adrenaline surges through me, as though it is not blood coursing in my arteries but the raw potential of my future. I am drawing power from every memory of my life, and all the possibilities for the future that those memories represent.

It is 11:32 a.m., Thursday, 1 May 2003. For the second time in my life, I am being born. This time I am being delivered from the canyon's pink womb, where I have been incubating. This time I am a grown adult, and I understand the significance and power of this birth as none of us can when it happens the first time. The value of my family, my friends, and my passions well up a heaving rush of energy that is like the burst I get approaching a hard-earned summit, multiplied by ten thousand. Pulling tight the remaining connective tissues of my arm, I rock the knife against the wall, and the final thin strand of flesh tears loose; tensile force rips the skin apart more than the blade cuts it.

A crystalline moment shatters, and the world is a different place. Where there was confinement, now there is release. Recoiling from my sudden liberation, my left arm flings down-canyon, opening my shoulders to the south, and I fall back against the northern wall of the canyon, my mind surfing on euphoria. As I stare at the wall where not twelve hours ago I etched "RIP OCT 75 ARON APR 03", a voice shouts in my head:

I AM FREE!

This is the most intense feeling of my life. I fear I might explode from the exhilarating shock and ecstasy that paralyze my body for a long moment as I lean against the wall. No longer confined to the physical space that I occupied for nearly a week, I feel drugged and off balance but buoyed by my freedom.

The Top of the World

Tenzing Norgay

*Tenzing Norgay was a sherpa on the British 1953 Everest
Expedition, led by John Hunt. On 28 May Norgay and the
New Zealand climber Edmund Hillary made their bid for the
mountain's summit. It was Norgay's second attempt at the
top; only the year before he had tried for the prize with the
Swiss climber Raymond Lambert.*

May the 28th . . . It had been on the 28th that Lambert and
I had made our final effort, struggling up as far as we
could above our high camp on the ridge. Now we were a day's
climb lower; a day later. A year later.

When it first grew light it was still blowing, but by eight
o'clock the wind had dropped. We looked at each other and
nodded. We would make our try.

But a bad thing had happened during the night: Pemba had
been ill. And it was clear that he could not go higher. The day
before we had lost Ang Tempa, who had been one of those
supposed to go up to Camp Nine, and now, with Pemba out of
it, only Ang Nyima was left of the original Sherpa team of three.
This meant that the rest of us would all have to carry heavier
loads, which would make our going slower and harder; but there
was nothing we could do about it. A little before nine Lowe,
Gregory, and Ang Nyima started off, each of them carrying
more than forty pounds and breathing oxygen, and about an

hour later Hillary and I followed, with fifty pounds apiece. The idea of this was that our support party would do the slow, hard work of cutting steps in the ice, and then we would be able to follow at our own pace, without tiring ourselves . . . Or perhaps I should say without tiring ourselves *too much*.

We crossed the frozen rocks of the col. Then we went up the snow-slope beyond, and up a long couloir, or gully, leading towards the south-east ridge. As had been planned, the fine steps cut by the others made the going easier for us, and by the time they reached the foot of the ridge – about noon – we had caught up with them. A little above us here, and off to one side, were some bare poles and a few shreds of canvas that had once been the highest camp for Lambert and me; and they brought back many memories. Then slowly we passed by and went on up the ridge. It was quite steep, but not too narrow, with rock that sloped upward and gave a good foothold, if you were careful about the loose snow that lay over it. About 150 feet above the old Swiss tent we came to the highest point that Colonel Hunt and Da Namgyal had reached two days before, and there in the snow were the tent, food, and oxygen-tanks which they had left for us. These now we had to add to our own loads, and from there on we were carrying weights of up to sixty pounds.

The ridge grew steeper, and our pace was now very slow. Then the snow became thicker, covering the rocks deeply, and it was necessary to cut steps again. Most of the time Lowe did this, leading the way with his swinging axe, while the rest of us followed. But by two in the afternoon all of us, with our great loads, were beginning to get tired, and it was agreed that we must soon find a camping-place. I remembered a spot that Lambert and I had noticed the year before – in fact, that we had decided would be our highest camp-site if we had another chance at the top – but it was still hidden above us, and on the stretch between there was no place that could possibly have held a tent. So on we went, with myself now leading – first still along the ridge, then off to the left, across steep snow, towards the place I was looking for.

"Hey, where are you leading us to?" asked Lowe and Gregory. "We have to go down."

"It can't be far now," I said. "Only five minutes."

But still we climbed: still we didn't get there. And I kept saying, "Only five minutes. . . . Only five minutes."

"Yes, but how many five minutes are there?" Ang Nyima asked in disgust.

Then at last we got there. It was a partly level spot in the snow, down a little from the exposed ridge and in the shelter of a rocky cliff, and there we dropped our loads. With a quick "Good-bye – good luck" Lowe, Gregory, and Ang Nyima started down the col and Hillary and I were left alone. It was then the middle of the afternoon, and we were at a height of about 27,900 feet. The summit of Lhotse, the fourth highest peak in the world, at which we had looked up every day during the long expedition, was now below us. Over to the south-east Makalu was below us. Everything we could see for hundreds of miles was below us, except only the top of Kangchenjunga, far to the east – and the white ridge climbing on above us into the sky.

We started pitching the highest camp that has ever been made. And it took us almost until it was dark. First we chopped away at the ice to try to make our sleeping-place a little more level. Then we struggled with frozen ropes and canvas, and tied the ropes round oxygen-cylinders to hold them down. Everything took five times as long as it would have in a place where there was enough air to breathe; but at last we got the tent up, and when we crawled in it it was not too bad. There was only a light wind, and inside it was not too cold to take off our gloves. Hillary checked the oxygen-sets, while I got our little stove going and made warm coffee and lemon-juice. Our thirst was terrible, and we drank them down like two camels. Later we had some soup, sardines, biscuits, and tinned fruit, but the fruit was frozen so hard we had first to thaw it out over the stove.

We had managed to flatten out the rocks and ice under the tent, but not all at one level. Half the floor was about a foot higher than the other half, and now Hillary spread his sleeping-bag on the upper half, and I put mine on the lower. When we were in them each of us rolled over close against the canvas, so that the weight of our bodies would help hold it in place. Mostly the wind was still not too bad, but sometimes great gusts would

come out of nowhere, and the tent would seem ready to fly
away. Lying in the dark, we talked of our plans for the next day.
Then, breathing the "night-oxygen", we tried to sleep. Even in
our eiderdown bags we both wore all our clothes and I kept on
my Swiss reindeer-boots. At night most climbers take off their
boots, because they believe this helps the circulation in the feet;
but at high altitudes I myself prefer to keep them on. Hillary, on
the other hand, took his off and laid them next to his sleeping-
bag.

The hours passed. I dozed and woke, dozed and woke. And
each time I woke I listened. By midnight there was no wind at
all. God is good to us, I thought. Chomolungma is good to us.
The only sound was that of our own breathing as we sucked at
our oxygen.

May the 29th . . . On the 29th Lambert and I had descended in
defeat from the col to the cwm. Down – down – down . . .

At about three-thirty in the morning we began to stir. I got
the stove going and boiled snow for lemon-juice and coffee, and
we ate a little of the food left over from the night before. There
was still no wind. When, a little while later, we opened the tent-
flap everything was clear and quiet in the early-morning light.
It was then that I pointed down and showed Hillary the tiny dot
that was the Thyangboche Monastery, 16,000 feet below. "God
of my father and mother," I prayed in my heart, "be good to me
now – today."

But the first thing that happened was a bad thing. Hillary's
boots, lying all night outside his sleeping-bag, had frozen, and
now they were like two lumps of black iron. For a whole hour
we had to hold them over the stove, pulling and kneading them,
until the tent was full of the smell of scorched leather and we
were both panting as if we were already climbing the peak.
Hillary was very upset, both at the delay and at the danger to his
feet. "I'm afraid I may get frostbitten, like Lambert," he said.
But at last the boots were soft enough for him to put on, and
then we prepared the rest of our gear. For this last day's
climbing I was dressed in all sorts of clothes that came from
many places. My boots, as I have said, were Swiss; my wind-
jacket and various other items had been issued by the British.

But the socks I was wearing had been knitted by Ang Lahmu. My sweater had been given me by Mrs Henderson, of the Himalayan Club. My woollen helmet was the old one that had been left to me by Earl Denman. And, most important of all, the red scarf round my neck was Raymond Lambert's. At the end of the autumn expedition he had given it to me and smiled and said, "Here, perhaps you can use it some time." And ever since I had known exactly what that use must be.

At six-thirty, when we crawled from the tent, it was still clear and windless. We had pulled three pairs of gloves on to our hands – silk, wool, and windproof – and now we fastened our crampons to our boots, and on to our backs slung the forty pounds of oxygen apparatus that would be the whole load for each of us during the climb. Round my axe were still the four flags, tightly wrapped. And in the pocket of my jacket was a small red-and-blue pencil.

"All ready?"

"*Ah chah*. Ready."

And off we went.

Hillary's boots were still stiff, and his feet cold, so he asked me to take the lead. And for a while that is how we went on the rope – up from the camp-site to the south-east ridge, and then on along the ridge towards the south summit. Sometimes we found the footprints of Bourdillon and Evans and were able to use them; but mostly they had been wiped away by the winds of the two days before, and I had to kick or chop our own steps. After a while we came to a place I recognized – the point where Lambert and I had stopped and turned back. I pointed it out to Hillary, and tried to explain through my oxygen-mask, and as we moved on I thought of how different it was these two times – of the wind and the cold then and the bright sunshine now – and how lucky we were on this day of our great effort. By now Hillary's feet were feeling better, so we changed places on the rope; and we kept doing this from then on, with first one of us leading the way and then the other, in order to share the work of kicking and chopping. As we drew near the south summit we came upon something we had been looking for – two bottles of oxygen that had been left for us by Bourdillon and Evans. We scraped the ice off the dials, and were happy to see that they were still quite full. For this meant that they could be used later for our downward trip to the col, and meanwhile we could breathe in a bigger amount of what we were carrying with us.

We left the two bottles where they were and climbed on. Until now the climbing – if not the weather – had been much the same as I remembered from the year before – along the steep, broken ridge, with a rock precipice on the left and snow cornices hiding another precipice on the right. But now, just below the south summit, the ridge broadened out into a sort of snow-face, so that the steepness was not so much to the sides as straight behind us, and we were climbing up an almost vertical white wall. The worst part of it was that the snow was not firm, but kept sliding down, sliding down – and we with it – until I thought, next time it will keep sliding, and we will go all the way to the bottom of the mountain. For me this was the one really bad place on the whole climb, because it was not only a matter of what you yourself did, but what the snow under you did, and this you could not control. It was one of the most dangerous places I had ever been on a mountain. Even now, when I think of it, I can still feel as I felt then, and the hair almost stands up on the back of my hands.

At last we got up it, though, and at nine o'clock we were on the south summit. This was the highest point that Bourdillon and Evans had reached, and for ten minutes we rested there, looking up at what was still ahead. There was not much farther to go – only about 300 feet of ridge – but it was narrower and steeper than it had been below, and, though not impossible-looking, would certainly not be easy. On the left, as before, was the precipice falling away to the Western Cwm, 8,000 feet below, where we could now see the tiny dots that were the tents of Camp Four. And on the right were still the snow cornices, hanging out over a 10,000-foot drop to the Kangshung Glacier. If we were to get to the top it would have to be along a narrow, twisting line between precipice and cornices – never too far to the left, never too far to the right, or it would be the end of us.

One thing we had eagerly been waiting for happened on the south summit. Almost at the same moment we each came to the end of the first of our two bottles of oxygen, and now we were able to dump them here, which reduced the weight we were carrying from forty to only twenty pounds. Also, as we left the south summit, another good thing happened. We found that the snow beyond it was firm and sound. This could make all the difference on the stretch that we still had to go.

"Everything all right?"

"*Ah chah*. All right."

From the south summit we first had to go down a little. Then up, up, up. All the time the danger was that the snow would slip, or that we would get too far out on a cornice that would then break away; so we moved just one at a time, taking turns at going ahead, while the second one wrapped the rope round his axe and fixed the axe in the snow as an anchor. The weather was still fine. We were not too tired. But every so often, as had happened all the way, we would have trouble breathing, and have to stop and clear away the ice that kept forming in the tubes of our oxygen-sets. In regard to this, I must say in all honesty that I do not think Hillary is quite fair in the story he later told, indicating that I had more trouble than he with breathing, and that without his help I might have suffocated. In my opinion our difficulties were about the same – and luckily never too great – and we each helped and were helped by the other in equal measure.

Anyhow, after each short stop we kept going, twisting always higher along the ridge between the cornices and the precipices. And at last we came to what might be the last big obstacle below the top. This was a cliff of rock rising straight up out of the ridge and blocking it off, and we had already known about it from aerial photographs and from seeing it through binoculars from Thyangboche. Now it was a question of how to get over or round it, and we could find only one possible way. This was along a steep, narrow gap between one side of the rock and the inner side of an adjoining cornice, and Hillary, now going first, worked his way up it, slowly and carefully, to a sort of platform above. While climbing he had to press backward with his feet against the cornice, and I belayed him from below as strongly as I could, for there was great danger of the ice giving way. Luckily, however, it did not. Hillary got up safely to the top of the rock, and then held the rope while I came after.

Here, again, I must be honest and say that I do not feel his account, as told in *The Ascent of Everest*, is wholly accurate. For one thing, he has written that this gap up the rock-wall was about forty feet high, but in my judgment it was little more than fifteen. Also, he gives the impression that it was only he who really climbed it on his own, and that he then practically pulled me, so that I "finally collapsed exhausted at the top, like a giant fish when it has just been hauled from the sea after a terrible struggle". Since then I have heard plenty about that "fish", and I admit I do not like it. For it is the plain truth that no one pulled or hauled me up the gap. I climbed it myself, just as Hillary had done; and if he was protecting me with the rope while I was doing it, this was no more than I had done for him. In speaking of this I must make one thing very clear. Hillary is my friend. He is a fine climber and a fine man, and I am proud to have gone with him to the top of Everest. But I do feel that in his story of our final climb he is not quite fair to me: that all the way through he indicates that when things went well it was his doing, and when things went badly it was mine. For this is simply not true. Nowhere do I make the suggestion that I could have climbed Everest by myself; and I do not think Hillary should suggest that he could have, or that I could not have done it without his help. All the way up and down we helped, and were helped by, each other – and that was the way it should be. But we were not leader and led. We were partners.

On top of the rock-cliff we rest again. Certainly, after the climb up the gap, we are both a bit breathless, but after some slow pulls at the oxygen I am feeling fine. I look up; the top is very close now; and my heart thumps with excitement and joy. Then we are on our way again. Climbing again. There are still the cornices on our right and the precipice on our left, but the ridge is now less steep. It is only a row of snowy humps, one beyond the other, one higher than the other. But we are still afraid of the cornices, and, instead of following the ridge all the way, cut over to the left, where there is now a long snow-slope above the precipice. About a hundred feet below the top we come to the highest bare rocks. There is enough almost level space here for two tents, and I wonder if men will ever camp in this place, so near the summit of the earth. I pick up two small stones and put them in my pocket to bring back to the world below. Then the rocks too are beneath us. We are back among the snowy humps. They are curving off to the right, and each time we pass one I wonder, Is the next the last one? Is the next the last? Finally we reach a place where we can see past the humps, and beyond them is the great open sky and brown plains. We are looking down the far side of the mountain upon Tibet. Ahead of us now is only one more hump – the last hump. It is not a pinnacle. The way to it is an easy snow-slope, wide enough for two men to go side by side. About thirty feet away we stop for a minute and look up. Then we go on . . .

I have thought much about what I will say now – of how Hillary and I reached the summit of Everest. Later, when we came down from the mountain, there was much foolish talk about who got there first. Some said it was I, some Hillary. Some that only one of us got there – or neither. Still others, that one of us had to drag the other up. All this was nonsense. And in Kathmandu, to put a stop to such talk, Hillary and I signed a statement in which we said "we reached the summit almost together". We hoped this would be the end of it. But it was not the end. People kept on asking questions and making up stories. They pointed to the "almost" and said, "What does that mean?" Mountaineers understand that there is no sense to such a question; that when two men are on the same rope they are *together*, and that is all there is to it. But other people did not understand. In India and Nepal, I am sorry to say, there has been great pressure on me to say that I reached the summit before Hillary. And all over the world I am asked, "Who got there first? Who got there first?"

Again I say, "It is a foolish question. The answer means nothing." And yet it is a question that has been asked so often – that has caused so much talk and doubt and misunderstanding – that I feel, after long thought, that the answer should be given. As will be clear, it is not for my own sake that I give it. Nor is it for Hillary's. It is for the sake of Everest – the prestige of Everest – and for the generations who will come after us. "Why," they will say, "should there be a mystery to this thing?

Is there something to be ashamed of? To be hidden? Why can we not know the truth?" . . . Very well: now they will know the truth. Everest is too great, too precious, for anything but the truth.

A little below the summit Hillary and I stopped. We looked up. Then we went on. The rope that joined us was thirty feet long, but I held most of it in loops in my hand, so that there was only six feet between us. I was not thinking of "first" and "second". I did not say to myself, "There is a golden apple up there. I will push Hillary aside and run for it." We went on slowly, steadily. And then we were there. Hillary stepped on top first. And I stepped up after him.

So there it is – the answer to the "great mystery". And if, after all the talk and argument, the answer seems quiet and simple I can only say that that is as it should be. Many of my own people, I know, will be disappointed at it. They have given a great and false importance to the idea that it must be I who was "first". These people have been good and wonderful to me, and I owe them much. But I owe more to Everest – and to the truth. If it is a discredit to me that I was a step behind Hillary, then I must live with that discredit. But I do not think it was that. Nor do I think that, in the end, it will bring discredit on me that I tell the story. Over and over again I have asked myself, "What will future generations think of us if we allow the facts of our achievement to stay shrouded in mystery? Will they not feel ashamed of us – two comrades in life and death – who have something to hide from the world?" And each time I asked it the answer was the same: "Only the truth is good enough for the future. Only the truth is good enough for Everest."

Now the truth is told. And I am ready to be judged by it.

We stepped up. We were there. The dream had come true . . .

What we did first was what all climbers do when they reach the top of their mountain. We shook hands. But this was not enough for Everest. I waved my arms in the air, and then threw them round Hillary, and we thumped each other on the back until, even with the oxygen, we were almost breathless. Then we looked round. It was eleven-thirty in the morning, the sun was shining, and the sky was the deepest blue I have ever seen. Only a gentle breeze was blowing, coming from the direction of

Tibet, and the plume of snow that always blows from Everest's summit was very small. Looking down the far side of the mountain, I could see all the familiar landmarks from the earlier expeditions – the Rongbuk Monastery, the town of Shekar Dzong, the Kharta Valley, the Rongbuk and East Rongbuk Glaciers, the North Col, the place near the north-east ridge where we had made Camp Six in 1938. Then, turning, I looked down the long way we ourselves had come – past the south summit, the long ridge, the South Col; on to the Western Cwm, the icefall, the Khumbu Glacier; all the way down to Thyangboche, and on to the valleys and hills of my homeland.

Beyond them, and around us on every side, were the great Himalayas, stretching away through Nepal and Tibet. For the closer peaks – giants like Lhotse, Nuptse, and Makalu – you now had to look sharply downward to see their summits. And, farther away, the whole sweep of the greatest range on earth – even Kangchenjunga itself – seemed only like little bumps under the spreading sky. It was such a sight as I had never seen before and would never see again – wild, wonderful, and terrible. But terror was not what I felt. I loved the mountains too well for that. I loved Everest too well. At that great moment for which I had waited all my life my mountain did not seem to me a lifeless thing of rock and ice, but warm and friendly and living. She was a mother hen, and the other mountains were chicks under her wings. I too, I felt, had only to spread my own wings to cover and shelter the brood that I loved.

We turned off our oxygen. Even there on top of the world it was possible to live without it, so long as we were not exerting ourselves. We cleared away the ice that had formed on our masks, and I popped a bit of sweet into my mouth. Then we replaced the masks. But we did not turn on the oxygen again until we were ready to leave the top. Hillary took out his camera, which he had been carrying under his clothing to keep it from freezing, and I unwound the four flags from around my axe. They were tied together on a string, which was fastened to the blade of the axe, and now I held the axe up, and Hilary took my picture. Actually he took three, and I think it was lucky, in those difficult conditions, that one came out so well. The order of the flags from top to bottom was United Nations, British, Nepalese,

Indian; and the same sort of people who have made trouble in other ways have tried to find political meaning in this too. All I can say is that on Everest I was not thinking about politics. If I had been, I suppose I would have put the Indian or Nepalese flag highest, though that in itself would have been a bad problem for me. As it is, I am glad that the U.N. flag was on top. For I like to think that our victory was not only for ourselves – not only for our own nations – but for all men everywhere.

I motioned to Hillary that I would now take his picture. But for some reason he shook his head; he did not want it. Instead he began taking more pictures himself, around and down on all sides of the peak, and meanwhile I did another thing that had to be done on the top of our mountain. From my pocket I took the package of sweets I had been carrying. I took the little red-and-blue pencil that my daughter, Nima, had given me. And, scraping a hollow in the snow, I laid them there. Seeing what I was doing, Hillary handed me a small cloth cat, black and with white eyes, that Hunt had given him as a mascot, and I put this beside them. In his story of our climb Hillary says it was a crucifix that Hunt gave him, and that he left on top: but if this was so I did not see it. He gave me only the cloth cat. All I laid in the snow was the cat, the pencil, and the sweets. "At home," I thought, "we offer sweets to those who are near and dear to us. Everest has always been dear to me, and now it is near too." As I covered up the offerings I said a silent prayer. And I gave my thanks. Seven times I had come to the mountain of my dream, and on this, the seventh, with God's help, the dream had come true.

"*Thuji chey, Chomolungma*. I am grateful . . ."

The Death of Harsh Bahuguna

Murray Sayle

The Indian climber Harsh Bahuguna was a member of the 1971 International Expedition to Everest. During a descent of Everest's West Ridge, Bahuguna suffered an accident, which prompted a scratch team of fellow expeditionaries to set out to rescue him. That they failed ultimately does not detract from their courage and altruism. Murray Sayle reported the expedition for the Sunday Times *of London.*

Since we set off on this expedition, I considered Harsh Bahuguna one of my closest friends among the climbers. We often walked together on the march in, and talked about all sorts of things: his wife and two small daughters, his obsession with Mount Everest, and his career in the Indian Army.

Harsh – which in Sanskrit means "happiness" – came from an Indian tribal group, the Garhwali, who are famous as soldiers and hill climbers (they are first cousins of the Gurkhas of Nepal). His uncle, Major Nandu Jayal, died in 1958 while attempting another Himalayan giant, Cho Oyu.

Harsh himself came within 800 feet of the summit of Everest as a member of the successful Indian Army expedition of 1965. His own attempt was delayed to the last of the Indian groups because of stomach trouble, and then a sudden break in the weather robbed him of his chance of the summit.

I was not alone in thinking that Harsh was a special friend –

after his death, I found that at least two-thirds of the climbers were sure they were particularly close to him. But, if he had a special companion on the expedition, it was undoubtedly the Austrian Wolfgang Axt. They ate together, shared a tent on the march in and another at Base Camp, shared much of the dangerous work of forcing a passage up the Icefall (where they were outstanding) and they spent the last five days of Harsh's life together in a tiny tent perched high on the West Ridge of Everest.

They made odd, but clearly close friends. Axt is six feet three inches, beautifully built, and his approach to people, to life itself, is in terms of physical strength and endurance. He is married to the former Austrian women's sixty-metre sprint champion; and no one has ever heard him discuss any other subjects but health diets, fitness, climbing mountains and related topics. He often told us how much he enjoyed climbing with Harsh.

The sequence of events which ended with Bahuguna's death and the subsequent dissensions began on the evening of 17 April, when a deputation called on Norman Dyhrenfurth, our Swiss-American joint leader, in his tent at the Advance Base Camp in the Western Cwm (Camp II, 21,700 feet), and presented something like an ultimatum. The visitors were Carlo Mauri, the Italian mountaineer and adventurer (he was a member of the Ra voyage), Pierre Mazeaud, the member of the French National Assembly who hopes one day to be Minister for Youth and Sport, and other members of the ridge team.

They said what everyone knew: that, largely because of the weather, the face route was looking hopeful and the ridge route, for which the deputation had opted, was lagging behind. Unless more Sherpa porters were switched to ferrying supplies to the ridge they said, then the whole ridge group should turn their efforts to the classical, "easy" route – up the South Col.

Dyhrenfurth is a genial man who prefers discussion and consensus to giving orders. He was severely hampered by a bad case of high-altitude laryngitis, which he was trying to treat by inhaling steam from a pan of melted snow; but he did his best to explain that both he and the British joint leader, Colonel

Jimmy Roberts (directing the Sherpa lift of supplies up the Icefall from Base Camp), were also disturbed about the supply situation. The Icefall, much trickier than usual, was absorbing a lot of Sherpa labour, and a log-jam of supplies was building up at Camp I, perched on an ice-cliff at the top of the fall. The answer, said Dyhrenfurth tactfully, was for the sahibs themselves to start carrying up some supplies.

The deputation had touched on a sore spot which, sooner or later, was bound to disturb an expedition like ours. No one enjoys the dull work of carrying supplies in support – climbing thousands of feet with a reel of rope, a couple of oxygen cylinders and a box of food, then dumping it and climbing down again. And at those altitudes, everyone seems to have a definite stock of energy, no more and no less, although the amount varies with individuals. Ambitious people who conserve their energies for the glamorous summit push are being no more than human.

Still, a story going around the expedition is that one eminent climber by mistake picked up the rucksack of another during a "support" climb and found he could easily lift it with his little finger. And, when our chapter of calamities began, there were only two oxygen bottles in the high camps on the face, only one on the ridge.

Not that all work on the two routes up Everest had ceased for lack of supplies. The same day as the deputation, Odd Eliassen of Norway and Michel Vaucher of Switzerland (Yvette's husband) completed a fixed-rope traverse across a steep ice-slope near the foot of the ridge, cutting out an unnecessary 300-foot descent before the final crossing of the glacier to Advance Base Camp. And, far up the ridge, Bahuguna and Axt had spent four days together moving Camp III, the first on the ridge, 1,000 feet nearer the summit.

That night the All-India Radio forecast bad weather for the Everest area. As we supply some of the data for this forecast, we assumed that the Indian broadcast was telling us about the unsettled weather we already had. In fact, the forecast well understated what was coming.

Next morning, 18 April, Norman Dyhrenfurth, reasoning that one good example is worth any amount of ordering or exhortation, set off alone to walk down the Western Cwm from Camp II to Camp I and collect a symbolic load of two cylinders of oxygen, and walk back.

I enter the story, very peripherally, at this point. About the same time, I set out from Base Camp to ascend the Icefall and examine the supply situation in the Western Cwm for myself. We were three on a rope: our Sirdar (boss) of the Sherpas, Sonam Girme, obligingly guiding two duffers, Dr Harka Gurung, the eminent Nepalese geographer, determined to do a bit of field work on his subject, and my clumsy self.

It started to snow as we strapped on our crampons. By halfway up, at a piece of ice we call "The Dump", it was snowing hard, and by good luck I declined a suggestion that I should stay there overnight without food, fuel or a sleeping-bag.

We passed the final maze of ladders, ropes and log bridges in a freshening blizzard. The racing clouds descended until we could no longer see the tops of the icecliffs we were climbing; once, an avalanche of stones as big as barrels crashed out of the clouds 100 yards to our right. Snow smothered the trail a foot deep in an hour; towards the end, even our Sirdar started to lose his way. I got one leg up to the hip in a crevasse; the other two pulled me out.

After a six-hour ascent we arrived, not a moment too soon, in the middle of a ring of red tents – Camp I (20,500 feet), set on a 1,000-ton ice-block entirely surrounded by crevasses 50 feet deep. As it happened we were the last people through the Icefall for more than a week. We found the two Americans, doctors David Isles and Dave Peterson, in charge of the camp, and they treated my frost-nipped toes. We were told that Norman Dyhrenfurth had just left for Camp II with his two symbolic bottles of oxygen.

We sat down in our madly flapping tents, powdery snow driving in through every crack, to wait out the blizzard. Only later did we learn something of the tragic events taking place a mile and a half up the cwm.

Dyhrenfurth's route took him close under the 5,000-foot face of Nuptse on his right, and already the mountain was beginning to growl with incipient avalanches as the blizzard plastered thick snow on the face. A small avalanche clipped his heels as he hurried towards Advance Base (Camp II), the snow obliterating the trail before his eyes (there are small but nasty crevasses all the way up the cwm). Then, away on his left, he heard a man shouting. The wind whipped the words away, but to Dyhrenfurth it sounded like a cry for help. He redoubled speed to Advance Base.

About the same time, Wolfgang Axt plodded exhausted and alone into Advance Base. His blond hair and beard were stiff with ice. The first person he met was Antony Thomas, a BBC director who is making a documentary on the climb. Axt's first words were, "Harsh is in difficulties up there."

A concerned knot quickly gathered – Odd Eliassen of Norway, Michel Vaucher of Switzerland, Carlo Mauri of Italy, Pierre Mazeaud of France, Don Whillans and Dr Peter Steele of Britain. While Axt related, as well as his tired condition permitted, what had happened, they began preparations for a rescue attempt. Through the swirling snow, they could occasionally hear the same muffled shouts Dyhrenfurth had heard.

Both men were very tired. Bahuguna especially, said Axt, so at about 3.30 p.m. when the weather began to deteriorate seriously, they had decided to come down to Advance Base from Camp III.

All had gone well with the descent, Axt leading, until they reached the horizontal fixed rope traverse. Neither of them had seen it before, as Vaucher and Eliassen had installed it only the previous day.

These rope traverses are common in the Alps, where Axt has done most of his climbing, but less so in the Himalayas, where Bahuguna had gained most of his experience. A rope, slung horizontally between a series of ice pitons, enables a climber to cross an ice-wall, going sideways. The climber clips a carabiner (a sort of snap link) over the rope; this is in turn fastened to a harness round his body. He then propels himself along by using his hands on the rope, and digging the front points of his crampons into the ice at his feet.

The tricky part is where the rope, which is not completely taut, passes a piton: the last bit of rope is uphill and the climber must unclip, pass the piton without support, and clip on again.

Axt said that he had gone first along the rope traverse and

round a corner where his companion was out of sight, then across an easier second section of the rope. At the end of the traverse he waited about twenty minutes; but then, feeling his feet beginning to freeze and the storm getting worse, he returned to Advance Base to get help.

As this was being told, Dr Steele called for a Sherpa volunteer to come with him and bring his resuscitation gear, and Ang Parba at once stepped forward, while Don Whillans collected as many ski sticks as he could lay hands on to mark a new path over the glacier moraine. The forlorn rescue effort set out through the blizzard at 5.15 p.m., Michel Vaucher and Odd Eliassen in the lead, Whillans, Dr Steele, Ang Parba, Carlo Mauri and Pierre Mazeaud close behind.

Vaucher and Eliassen found the dying man still clipped to the traverse rope, at a point where he should have unclipped to pass a piton. He had lost a glove, his hands were frozen, his face was coated with ice and his protective clothing had been pulled up by his harness to expose his mid-section to the driving storm.

Asked by Eliassen, "Are you okay?" he appeared to mumble an affirmative. The Swiss and the Norwegian were unable to move Bahuguna sideways, so they tried to lower him on a 130-foot rope, which Eliassen had brought for the purpose. Meanwhile, at the foot of the ice-slope, Dr Steele, Mazeaud and the Sherpa were trying to find a level and sheltered spot for a resuscitation attempt. But the rope was 35 feet too short, as near as they could judge in the snow and darkness.

Whillans, who had been following the unsuccessful lowering operation, decided to try a last forlorn hope. Without an ice-axe or a protective rope, he clawed his way on the front points of his crampons across the steep ice-slope to where Bahuguna hung upside down by his harness from the end of the rescuers' rope. Whillans managed to right him. His face was blue; he was unconscious, with wide staring eyes. He was barely alive, and could not have lasted more than half an hour.

Whillans, clinging by his crampon points to the ice-cliff, had no way of getting the dying man up or down, and in a blizzard at night at 22,000 feet, had only one decision to make – although he said later it was probably the hardest of his life.

"Sorry, Harsh old son, you've had it," he muttered, in a

north-countryman's gruff farewell, and scrambled back over the ice.

Next morning, the climbers struggled through the storm to a breakfast of sorts in the "Indian" tent – ironically, an Indian Army bell tent very like the ones used on the Everest expeditions in the 1920s. Major Bahuguna had borrowed it for our expedition. Rations were short and everyone deeply depressed. Axt came in, refreshed from his sleep. "How is Harsh?" he asked cheerily. "*Ist tod*," someone said in German – "He is dead." Axt was thunder-struck, a pitiable spectacle. Grimfaced, Dyhrenfurth announced there would be an inquiry in the Indian tent, and directed Bill Kurban of the BBC to tape-record the brief proceedings.

Those concerned related what they knew in their own languages, except Odd Eliassen, who spoke English. Axt, normally bursting with self-reliance, had difficulty in enunciating his statement. Dyhrenfurth asked Axt only two questions, both in a hoarse whisper, difficult to hear against the raging storm.

"Why were you not roped together?"

"We had run out of rope in establishing the way to Camp III."

"Why did you not go back along the traverse to look for Harsh after you had waited twenty minutes for him?"

"I was getting cold, I thought I had better fetch help."

The blizzard raged a full week after that, and by the time it ended it was apparent to most of us that even the South Col route was no longer possible. If the supply lines can be re-established, if the weather holds, if morale can be restored then there is just a chance that something can be saved from the disasters we have faced.

Direttissima

Chris Bonington

Born in 1934 in London, Christian Bonington was an officer in the Royal Tank Regiment, an instructor with the Army Outward Bound School and a sales executive with Unilever before becoming a professional mountaineer and explorer. He was knighted in 1996 for his services to climbing. Here, Bonington recounts one of his early climbs, his ascent of the North Face of the Cima Grande in the Italian Dolomites, in 1959.

"That's where they usually come off," murmured the German climber lying beside us.

We could just discern the arms and legs of the man spread-eagled on the yellow rock 1,000 feet above. He was like a tiny black ant on the wall of a huge windowless warehouse. About fifty feet below him, stationary, was another minute figure. The rope joining them looked like gossamer thread, and the wall stretched above, below and to either side: grey, compact, yellow, featureless.

Suddenly the leading dot shot downwards. It was all over before the impact of the fall registered on my mind. The climber was dangling twenty feet from his original position, presumably held by a piton. He rested for a few minutes and then started up again, soon reaching the point from which he had fallen. A long pause, the faint thudding of a piton hammer and he was up.

I was sitting with a group of Austrian and German climbers on a boulder at the foot of the North Face of the Cima Grande in the Italian Dolomites. The two performers, far above, were on the "Direttissima", a route that had only been opened the previous year and which was reputed to be the hardest in the Dolomites.

A year had passed since my holiday in Chamonix and my ascent of the South-west Pillar of the Dru. I was climbing with Gunn Clark who was still a student, slightly younger than I, but with very similar mountaineering experience.

"It must be a good peg, anyway. What do you think, Gunn? Shall we have a crack at it?" I asked.

"Let's see how they get on at the traverse. It looks bloody terrifying to me," he replied.

We had been camped below the Tre Cime for a week and had done several of the easier climbs in the area, but from the start, the Direttissima had fascinated us. Four young Germans had made the first ascent, taking five days to complete it. They had used several special techniques. The wall was so continuously over-hanging that it would have been impossible to retreat from it in the normal way, by abseiling: at the end of the rope they would have been swinging in mid-air several feet out from the rock. They therefore had to leave in place all their pitons, several hundred of them, so that if they had to turn back owing to a change in the weather, they would be able to climb down. This of course meant carrying heavy loads for they also had to carry water and food. To overcome the problem, they took with them a 1,000-foot length of line* so that they could haul loads up from the bottom of the cliff. This was only possible because the face was so steep that the bundles nowhere touched rock on the way up.

It was much easier, of course, for the parties that followed, since all the pitons had been left in place, but even so the face maintained its reputation for difficulty. When we arrived that summer there had been a dozen ascents, mainly by German and Austrian parties. I was both attracted and frightened by the climb for I had done comparatively little artificial climbing and certainly nothing of the length or standard of the Direttissima.

* Thin rope – not used for climbing.

No other British party had done it and this made it seem even more formidable – there was no one with whom we could compare our own capabilities.

We heard any number of stories about the climb; there were plenty of other candidates camped around the Tre Cime waiting to go on it. They told us of the huge overhangs in the middle of the face and showed us various pieces of specialised equipment: drills for making holes in the rock where there were no cracks, expansion bolts to hammer into them, and even a hook for pulling up on pitons that were out of reach. But, more alarming, we heard that a member of the party that had last attempted the climb, had had a fall and had pulled out two expansion bolts. No one had been hurt but they had been unable to get up without the bolts in place and did not have any of their own. Since we did not have any either, we had decided to wait until another party did the climb. I think everyone was playing the same waiting game for no one went on to it for several days, until at last two Germans plucked up courage. We were watching their efforts that afternoon.

An hour went by and the two little dots slowly, almost imperceptibly, edged their way across the wall.

"They're on the traverse now," said the German who had already done the climb. "This is where the bolts came out." We watched with double interest. The leader stayed in the same place for a long time, went back, crept forward. We could hear faint shouts as he talked to his second. He moved again and there was a whoop of triumph: he was across.

We decided to go on to the climb the next morning and spent the rest of the day preparing our equipment, but that evening clouds began to build up and there was even a little rain in the air. That evening we drank late into the night in the Rifugio Laveredo, confident that the weather would be bad the following-day, before tottering, very drunk, back to the tent.

Someone was shaking me; I kept my eyes closed and pretended to be asleep.

"Wake up, Chris. There's not a cloud in the sky. The Germans next door are getting ready. I think they must be going for the Direttissima," said the voice. I peered out of my sleeping-bag, hating to leave its pleasant warmth, and resenting Gunn's enthusiasm; but then I saw the thin blue of the sky and the two Germans bustling round their tent with last-minute preparations. The sight of them roused my competitive instinct.

We quickly cooked our breakfast, finished packing our sacks and set out for the face. It was only half an hour's walk from our campsite and along a good path all the way. It was eight in the morning when we reached the foot of the climb. There was no introduction to it, no glacier or snow couloir, not even the easy broken rocks that are found at the foot of most Dolomite walls.

It rose, sheer and uncompromising, straight from the path. Our way lay up a thin crack that was adorned with a solitary piton about thirty feet up. I have always hated climbs with difficult first pitches for there is no time to warm up, to find any kind of climbing rhythm. At the first step from the path I was hanging on my arms, thrust backwards by the steepness of the rock. I muttered to myself, cursed my rucksack which I had been too proud to leave at the bottom, fought the crack, clinging to it fearfully, until I reached the piton, clipped in and rested a moment. I was now more relaxed and felt my way up the rock, realising that it was not too difficult, just steep, and reached the stance. Gunn followed up quickly and I then set out on the next pitch, for we had decided that I should do all the leading. I was very happy with this arrangement – I love being out in front. (When second on the rope, I lose concentration, am aware of the danger of falling off, even though it would not matter if I did, and climb too quickly, without thinking out each move before making it.)

The first 300 feet gave straightforward climbing to the top of a buttress that flanked the great, blank, yellow wall. The two Germans who had set out before us, were already 100 feet ahead. It was reassuring to see them. The wall was so smooth and sheer that it was difficult to believe that anyone could climb it without pitons, and yet there were very few in sight, just one every 20 feet or so.

"What the hell do you do in between the pegs," I asked plaintively.

"You'll soon find out," the German replied.

Our route lay diagonally across the wall, so we were soon

above unclimbable rock that dropped away to the path far below. The climbing was all-absorbing, the most airy and spectacular I had ever undertaken. Miraculously, the holds appeared: tiny, square-cut ledges that the toes of one's boots just rested on, that fingertips could curl over. There was no rest for the arms as nowhere did the angle relent. We were heading for a roof that jutted horizontally from the face. This gave me my first taste of A_3 – almost the top grade of artificial climbing. The pegs were anything but reassuring, hammered into tiny holes and blind cracks, at the most an inch of steel biting into the rock. I handled each peg with loving care, eased my weight on to the etrier step, pulled delicately on the next one, and tried to avoid swinging too much as I heaved over the lip of the roof.

I had hardly noticed that we had nearly caught up the Germans. Suddenly there was a yell from above. I glanced up to see a body, all arms and legs, rush down towards me. Instinctively I ducked, clung to the rock, but he never reached me. I looked up and saw him dangling on the end of the rope, about ten feet below the peg that had held his fall. He also had come off in the "usual" place. With hardly a pause he climbed back up, stepped cautiously into the top rung of his etrier and, precariously balanced, hammered in a piton above his head. The dull thud of the hammer inspired little confidence, but he clipped in his etrier and was soon standing on the ledge above. His second followed up quickly and all too soon it was my turn to start.

The rock was even more smooth and compact than it had been before. There were no cracks for pitons and, from the stance, I could see no holds. About fifty feet above, at the foot of a shallow groove, I could just see a tiny black ring protruding from the blank wall, obviously an expansion bolt. I slowly edged my way up towards it. There were just sufficient holds but I had to weave my way from side to side, sometimes coming back a few moves when I had taken a blind alley. On reaching the groove I found some more pitons and a couple of expansion bolts. They were all at extreme reach: climbing on pegs might be compared to going up an iron ladder with rungs six feet apart and rotting away with rust.

Another twenty feet and I reached the point where the German and many of his predecessors had fallen off. There was an expansion bolt and then, a good eight feet above, the piton he had hammered in, a minute Cassin peg protruding downwards from a hole. I cautiously climbed the etrier until I was standing in the top rung, my left foot bridged out on a crease in the surface of the rock, my arms spreadeagled to keep me in balance for there was nothing to hold on to. My fingers crept up the rock towards the peg but they were still a couple of inches too low. I tried to stand on tiptoe on the etrier rung, it slipped and I was off.

Before I had had time to think, I found myself hanging a few feet below the expansion bolt which had bent over in a graceful curve. I felt no sensation of shock or fear for my entire concentration was devoted to that piton only a few feet above but seemingly out of reach. I went up again and this time placed my foot more carefully on the rung, stretched as far as I could but was losing my balance. My finger tips brushed the ring of the piton; another effort – the top joints of my fingers curled round it. My foot on the etrier scuffed round and I was hanging with all my weight on the two fingers. I now had to clip in a karabiner with my left hand and somehow extract the fingers of my right, which were trapped and extremely painful. My hands were tiring. All that existed in the world was a piton, a karabiner and a few inches of rock. A last struggle and my fingers were free: I was able to clip in my etrier and rest, panting, on it. Then a difficult move enabled me to pull up on to a narrow ledge.

Another pitch of free climbing, which was easy compared to the groove we had just climbed, led to the traverse where the expansion bolts had been pulled out. A line of pegs ran across a horizontal fault.

"It doesn't look too bad, Gunn," I shouted, for ever optimistic as I started out. But after twenty feet the pegs came to an end – the last one was a long channel peg, resting loosely in a crumbling hole, that held when pulled sideways but could be plucked straight out with a direct pull. A few feet farther to the left, and at a lower level, was a small peg jammed by a piece of paper into the hole left by the missing bolt. Farther still to the left a ring piton dropped from another hole. I did not feel like trusting my weight to any of them but there was no other way, for the wall was gently impending and completely holdless.

I am not often aware of the drop below me, and certainly am not worried by it, but here I was unpleasantly reminded of it as I leant down, hanging on the long channel peg, to place an etrier on the paper-plugged bolt – my eyes inevitably strayed down the giddy drop of the wall to the screes 600 feet below. Stepping on the top rung of the etrier, held in balance only by the tension of my rope running back to Gunn, I breathlessly reached across to the next peg, clipped in my other etrier and stood on the rung, fully expecting the peg to plop out as I put my weight on it. Another tensed move and I was across on good rock holds that I could grasp and pull on. I felt a surge of relief and the rich satisfaction gained from completing a particularly thin piece of climbing.

I could hear voices just round the corner and a few minutes later we reached the bivouac ledge, the only one for eleven hundred feet. The two Germans had already settled down but there was plenty of room. There were two ledges each only two foot wide but to us they seemed as big as railway-station platforms. For the first time that day we were able to relax, to sit down. It was only four o'clock in the afternoon and there were still several hours of daylight, but the wall now reared over our heads in a series of jutting roofs and it was obvious we should never be able to get up through them before dark. It was pleasant anyway to sit in the afternoon sun and to eat for the first time that day – we had had no thought of anything but the climbing earlier on. We had two pints of water with us, and brewed tea, greatest luxury of all, over a solid fuel tablet. We spent the rest of the afternoon making our ledge more comfortable, shifting loose blocks and dropping them to the screes seven hundred feet below. A group of spectators, sitting near the foot of the cliff, quickly scattered as our bombardment crept towards them.

This was undoubtedly a four-star bivouac ledge: we could actually lie down, moored to the rock by a complicated system of belays. For the first time on a bivouac I slept really well, only waking with the dawn. There was no hurry, anyway, as we had to allow the two Germans to get away. We sat on the ledge watching them at work above us. Most of the time they were swinging clear of the rock in their etriers. Below we could see two tiny figures at the start of the climb. The German leader ran out 100 feet of rope, and took a stance hanging in etriers immediately below the huge roof. His second followed up with surprising speed and, passing the stance, soon disappeared over the roof. We could hear him calling down from somewhere out of sight but the rope moved slowly and the pitch was obviously difficult.

Three hours went by and we were still sitting on the ledge. I was restless, wanting to get to grips with the problem, so finally started up the pitch. The previous day most of the climbing had been on vertical rock but now it was all overhanging and one relied entirely on the pitons that were already in place. I arrived below the German and made myself a cradle of rope to sit in. I had to stay there for a further hour, immediately above me the German's backside, below – space. I pulled loose a stone. Without touching anything, it dropped to the ground 800 feet below.

At last the German moved on and I was able to bring Gunn up to my belay. Changing stances was a nightmare of dangling bodies and tangled ropes that tried my patience to breaking point. This type of artificial climbing was something that neither of us had ever met before: it demanded a machine-like methodical approach. The ropes were threaded through anything up to forty karabiners and it meant concentrating the whole time on which rope to use, how to thread it, whether it was likely to cross the other or get jammed in a crack. I was for ever haunted by the fear of the rope jamming immovably when I was half-way up a pitch so that I could move neither up nor down.

After traversing a few feet to the right, away from Gunn, I had to pull up over the first roof. My view was immediately constricted to a few feet of rock. Below I could only see the scree, the entire face being cut off by the overhang, and above, the rock jutted out once again, hiding the sky. I felt utterly alone, frightened by the immensity of the face. Swinging in my etriers, feet well clear of the rock, I pulled into an overhanging chimney whose back was lined with loose blocks. I was already running short of karabiners, and the rope was beginning to drag – tugging remorselessly at my waist – but there was still no sign of a stance or even a piton on which I would dare to belay.

It never seemed to end; then at last, when I had used up all my karabincrs and most of my strength, I reached a foothold and three expansion bolts* which were obviously used for belaying. Gunn now had to come up. It was just as hard for him as it had been for me: the rope passed through so many karabiners that he got little help from it. There were long periods when there was no movement at all and I boiled with impatience, though in fact he was taking no longer than I had done.

The change-over on the stance was even more awkward than on the previous one, and the pitch above every bit as long and tiring, but it did lead to a ledge of sorts, about nine inches wide, on which I could just stand in balance. By the time I had brought Gunn up, it was nearly dark and it was obvious that we would be able to get no further that night. It had taken us an entire day to climb three hundred feet. There was just room for both of us to sit on the ledge with legs dangling over the void. It was impossible to lean back for the wall behind us was gently impending. But our worst trial was thirst: we had only half a pint of water left and this did not begin to satisfy us. There were some drips falling from the overhangs above and we spent much of the night trying to catch them in a mess tin. It was a frustrating game for no drip fell in the same place twice, and the chances of one landing in the waiting pan were slight. Still, it helped to pass the time and we knew that we were now nearly up the steep section of the cliff, that we should be able to get out thc following morning.

We started as soon as it was light – there was no temptation to linger. It was surprising how refreshed we felt after our uncomfortable night, especially since both of us had been exhausted at the end of the previous day. The overhangs above were not as severe as the ones we had already climbed and we soon reached a large ledge where we could have spent the night in luxury. Resting on it was a small lead case holding a book in which everyone who had climbed the "Direct" had signed their

---

* Where there are no cracks for pitons, a hole may be drilled into the rock, and a bolt tapped in.

names. We could not help feeling some pride as we added ours to the list.

The angle now relented – it was merely vertical – and our way lay up a deep-cut chimney that cleaved the face. The rock was grey and firm to the touch, offering cracks in which to jam our hands, and ledges and pockets. It was a delight to put away the etriers, to climb on rock, once more obeying the natural instincts of our muscles instead of the complex rope engineering of the previous day. Pitch followed pitch, through deep chimneys and over great boulders jammed in the bed of the gully. We were now climbing with real enjoyment, carefree in our confidence that we would soon be at the top.

Another 100 feet and we were there, lying in the sun below the great cross that marks the summit of the Cima Grande, but we did not linger long. The pile of empty tins that littered the summit rock reminded us of our own hunger. We coiled our ropes, packed away all the ironmongery and raced down the broken rocks of the descent, our mouths watering at the thought of spaghetti bolognese and bottles of Chianti.

Hope Lost

Anatoli Boukreev

In the late afternoon of 10 May 1996 a blizzard swept up the Himalaya valleys and engulfed Everest. Wind speed hit 100 kilometres per hour, the temperature dropped by as much as fifteen degrees in as many seconds. There were no less than ten expeditions on Everest that day. Soon eight climbers would be dead, in the worst-ever Everest tragedy.

Anatoli Boukreev was the Russian high altitude guide for the commercial Mountain Madness Expedition. On 10 May 1996 Boukreev, who had summited Everest without oxygen earlier in the day, went into the storm and rescued expedition members Charlotte Fox, Tim Madsen and Sandy Hall Pitman from certain death. Meanwhile, the Mountain Madness leader Scott Fischer had collapsed, apparently close to death, on a ledge 3,657 m (12,000 ft) above South Col. Boukreev was determined to make a last attempt to save Fischer's life:

I slept like two hours and after seven-thirty that morning Pemba came with tea. And I heard some Sherpas pass by our tent, and I ask Pemba, "What is the situation now? Somebody go to Scott or no?" And he gave some tea and he was just quiet. No answer. I said, "Scott needs help. Please send some Sherpas up." So, he went to the Sherpas' tent and he began to talk. And now I have no power. It would be for me a stupid idea to go again. I needed some recovery time.

At probably eight-thirty I took a look at our climbing route from yesterday, and I can see the storm has lost power. I see some Sherpas going up, and he says, "Okay, father of Lopsang started together with Tashi Sherpa," and I ask, "They carry oxygen?" and he tells me, "Yes."

And then I speak with Neal. "Okay, this is my position. I would like to stay here," and he says "Okay" and he worked for the clients and took them down.

A strong wind had come up, and I kept myself inside the tent, but around one or two I went out, and I spoke with Todd Burleson and Pete Athans with Alpine Ascents (guides for a commercial expedition), who had come to Camp IV to help with getting climbers down from the trouble we had had. I asked them, "Do you know what is happening?" and they said some Sherpas had returned with Makalu Gao, [the leader of the Taiwanese expedition] so I went to the Taiwanese tents.

When I went into the tent, I saw this Makalu Gau, his face and hands all frostbitten, but he was talking a little bit, and I asked him, "Did you see Scott?" and he says, "Yes, we were together last night." And I had hopes that Scott could survive, but with this news I thought, "Scott is finished, dead already," and I got upset about this, but this news is only from the Taiwanese, so I want to talk with our Sherpas who went up.

'I go inside the Sherpas' tent, and the father of Lopsang is crying with great sadness, and he says, "We cannot help." And he speak very small, very little bit of English. I don't understand. "What is happening?" And they said to me, "He died." And then I said, "Was he still breathing?" and they told me. "Yes, he's still breathing, but no more signs of life."

I asked, "Did you give him oxygen?" and they said, "Yes, we give oxygen," and I asked, "Did you give him some medicine?" and they said, "No." And now I understood, so I went outside the tent and talked with Todd Burleson and Pete Athans, and I asked, "Can you help me go up to help with Scott? People say he is still alive, like 8,350 metres."

Pete Athans, who spoke Nepali, understood the situation, and he said to me, "Actually I spoke with the Sherpas, and they said it's impossible to help Scott." And I said, "Why? Maybe we will try." He says, "But it is bad weather coming. Storm didn't finish. And people try to give him oxygen, but oxygen didn't help him." Todd Burleson was quiet, but Pete Athans talked with me. And he said, "Scott was, yes, able to breathe, but he wasn't able to drink tea, people just put his tea inside of his mouth, but he couldn't swallow."

And Pete Athans said, "Impossible. For this situation, impossible for him." I said, "But maybe, maybe some breathing, if he has some breathing, maybe oxygen will improve, and I go out again."

I went inside the tent again with Lopsang's father and asked im, "Can you say little more information? Did you give him no medicine? When you gave him new oxygen?" He said, "Oh, we gave him one bottle oxygen, put mask, and open oxygen."

And I said okay and got a radio from the Sherpas and radioed to Base Camp, and I spoke with Ingrid and asked her, "This is the situation, what do you advise?" And she is upset also and says to me, "Anatoli, try to help everything that is possible for you; please try to find some possibility." I said, "Okay, I will try everything that is possible, but what is your advice?" She said, "Okay, about medicine, do you have this small packet with the injections?" And I told her, "Yes, I have the injection." And she said for me to try it with Scott, and I promised her I would try everything.

Then, I go to the Sherpas' tent, and see that Lopsang is using oxygen and some other Sherpas are using oxygen. And I said, "Okay, I need some oxygen. I need three bottles of oxygen and a thermal bottle of tea. Can you make it for me?" And people said, "Why you need?" I said, "I will go up." People say, "It is stupid idea."

So, I left the tent and then Lopsang's father came and began to speak with Pete Athans in Nepali, and Pete Athans came and said, "Anatoli, what do you want to do?" I said, "I will go up; I need oxygen; I need thermal bottles of tea." And Pete Athans tried to explain to me that it was a bad idea. He said, "Now the storm has gone down a little bit, and if you go now, you will get this storm again." I said to him, "This is what I need to do."

I knew from my experience; I explained to him my position. This situation with Scott was a slow process; maybe Scott, if he had oxygen, would possibly revive. Scott is just before the

Balcony, and he has enough oxygen maybe until seven o'clock. I need some oxygen.

Pete is like the Sherpas, and I understand he thinks it is a stupid idea, but I get some oxygen. I ask for three, but get only two. I think maybe it came from David Breashear's expedition, but I don't know for sure. I began to hurry; I began to prepare myself, but as I prepared, the wind began to come higher. It is just around four o'clock, maybe four-fifteen.

I took my pack and was leaving, and I saw Pete Athans outside of the tent, and I asked Pete Athans, "Maybe you will go up?" He said just, "No." And I said, "How many will try to help?" And just – he got sad, he just cried a little bit. He thinks there is no chance.

I just started from the tents and maybe 150 metres ahead, I saw a small moving point, somebody coming down to me, and I was very wondered. I thought it was like a phantom, a miracle, and I began to hurry. And in a short time I came up on this man, who was carrying his hands without gloves up in front of his body like a surrendering soldier. And I did not know then who this was, but now I understand it was Beck Weathers.

I said, "Who are you?" He didn't speak or answer, and I asked him, "Did you see Scott?" And he said to me, "No one I saw. No one I saw. It is my last time in the mountains. I don't want to come back to these mountains. Never, never . . ." It was like crazy talk.

Just I think my head is broken, and I am thinking, "Anatoli, you need to be able to think if you go up again." And I yell back, "Burleson! Pete! Please help me!" And I asked them, "Can you help with this man? I will go. I will keep my time." And they tell me, "Don't worry, we will take care of him."

Everyone said it was stupid to go for Scott, but I saw this man survived, and this was a push for me. And I took a mask, everything, and I began to move with oxygen, without resting, and I climbed steadily, but darkness started to come, nightfall just began. And also a strong wind began with a blizzard and a difficult time.

And just around seven o'clock, five minutes past probably, I found Scott. Dark also, with a serious storm, and I saw him through the snow, again like a mirage. I saw the zipper of his down suit open, one hand without a mitten, frozen. I opened his face mask, and around the face mask it is frozen, but a different temperature, and under the mask it is like a blue color, like a big bruise. It is like not life in the face. I saw no breathing, just a clenched jaw.

I lose my last hope. I can do nothing. I can do nothing. I cannot stay with him.

It began to storm again, seven o'clock. Oxygen – I lose my last hope, because I thought when I started, "Oxygen will improve his life." If by now oxygen does not improve, no signs of life, no pulse or breathing . . .

Very strong wind began, I am without power, without power. And for me, just what do I need to do? Actually, I understood this. If I found him like Beck Weathers, it would be possible to help him. He was revived. Like Beck Weathers revived, he would need help and possibly giving him this help, like oxygen, everything would be possible. It would be possible to help Scott. I understand there is no way for me. No way for him. What do I need to do?

And I saw his pack and I roped it around his face to keep away the birds. And with maybe four or five empty oxygen bottles around, I put them on his body to help cover. And just maybe at seven-fifteen I started to go down fast. And I understand I lose power, I lose emotion. I can't say how it was. I was very sad.

Storm began, very strong, new blow of fresh snow with strong wind. And I began to use the ropes, and when I finish at like 8,200 metres, visibility is gone. Began just darkness, probably seven-forty, impossible to see. I have my headlamp. I used oxygen a little bit. Then I stopped oxygen because it is not helping my visibility, like two metres, three metres probably, impossible to see. And I found again Kangshung Face, same place, I think, near Yasuko Namba probably. I can see just two metres, but I understood. And then I go some more in a changed direction, and the snow on the ground is finished and I began to see some oxygen bottles. I turn back a little and go up a little, and I saw some tents.

I know these are not our tents, but next will be ours. When I found this place, I began to hear some voices. And I go without visibility, by the noise. And I come to the noise in a tent. I open.

I see this man just alone by himself. I saw Beck Weathers, and I don't understand why he is alone, but I lose power, go for my tent, because I cannot help. Some sleeping bag I have. Just I crawl inside of my tent and go to sleep.

For his heroic actions on Everest that day, the American Alpine Club awarded him its highest honour for bravery, the David A. Sowles Memorial Award.

Boukreev died in 1997 while attempting a winter assault on Annapurna.

Only the Air That We Breathe

Peter Habeler

The Austrian Peter Habeler was one of the new breed of climbers in the 1970s who eschewed the aid of oxygen at high altitude on "sport-ethical" grounds. After an oxygenless ascent of Gasherbrun I (8,068 m/26,470 ft) in 1975 Habeler and his then climbing partner, Reinhold Messner, decided to try to reach the highest place on Earth without bottled air. Their summit push on Everest came on 28 May 1978.

After four hours, towards half past nine, we stood in front of the tents of Camp V at an altitude of 8,500 metres. Mallory and Irvine, too, had managed to get this far. From now on we would be entering completely new territory. We were left totally to our own resources. If anything happened to us now, no rescue team would be able to come up to help us, no helicopter – nothing. The smallest accident would mean certain death.

Reinhold and I had often spoken together about the fact that, in this last phase, it would be impossible to help each other should anything untoward occur. Although we were incredibly close to each other, and formed an indivisible unit, we were agreed on one thing. If one of us should get into difficulty, the other would have to try at all costs to find safety for himself alone. The small amount of strength which remained to each of us was hardly enough for one; any attempt to rescue, or even to recover the other, would be doomed to failure.

I sat in front of the small tent which was half-covered by snow, while inside Reinhold tried desperately to get a cooker going to brew up tea. I snuggled up to the side of the tent in order to rest in the lee side, and stared out into the fog. Occasionally the wall of fog would lift for a moment, and I could see deep below me the Valley of Silence. I could see Lhotse, and again and again I looked up to the South Summit where an enormous trail of snow signified that up there a far more violent storm was raging than down here in Camp V. The weather would undoubtedly worsen. The fine weather period was over.

Perhaps our attempt on the summit was finally over too, our Everest expedition wrecked once and for all. Of one thing I was convinced: I would never come up here a second time. Already the desire to turn back was almost overpowering. To bivouac here in Camp V, and perhaps to wait for the weather to improve, was also completely out of the question. We would probably never have got out of the tent at all again, and in no event would we have had the physical or mental strength to climb any further. Our energy would have lasted at the most for the descent and no more. Yet climbing on was, under these circumstances, also a "way of no return".

In 1956, two Japanese had mastered the route from the South Col to the summit in one go. This had taken them a whole day, and having therefore reached the main summit late in the afternoon, they were forced to bivouac on the way back. Consequently, in spite of carrying oxygen, they had suffered terrible injuries through frost-bite. But neither Reinhold nor I had time to think of these dangers. The will to push on blotted out everything else, even the wish to turn back or at least to sleep. We wanted in any case to go on up, even if we could only reach the South Summit which is 8,760 metres high. After all, to conquer even the South Summit without oxygen would have been a tremendous success. It would have proved that one day it would be possible to reach the main summit by human strength alone.

It took exactly half an hour for Reinhold to prepare the tea. My deliberations were also shared by him; we exchanged them wordlessly. We were completely united in our determination to continue the assault on the summit.

Once again we set off. The tracks of our predecessors, which could still be seen in the snow, served as an excellent orientation guide. The clouds were moving over from the south-west, from the bad weather corner of the Himalayas. We had to push ourselves even more because that promised bad news. We found ourselves in the lower area of the jet stream, those raging winds of speeds up to 200 kilometres per hour, upon which the enormous passenger planes are carried from continent to continent. We had traversed the troposphere and were approaching the frontier of the stratosphere. Here cosmic radiation was already noticeable and the intensity of the ultra-violet radiation had multiplied. Only a few minutes without our snow-goggles sufficed, even in the fog, to diminish our powers of vision. In a very short space of time direct insolation would lead to snow-blindness and painful conjunctivitis.

Reinhold and I photographed and filmed as often as we had the opportunity. To do this, we had to take off our snow-goggles and we also had to remove our overgloves. Each time it became more difficult for us to put the gloves back on again. But losing them would have led to the very rapid paralysis and frost-bite of our hands.

Since it was no longer possible to go on in this deep snow, we had made a detour towards the South-East Ridge. Here the wall dropped 2,000 metres down to the south-west. One false step and we would have plunged down into the Valley of Silence. The exposed and airy climb on brittle rock without any rope demanded extreme concentration. Reinhold was right behind me. I took the lead to the South Summit. Completely without warning, we suddenly found we had passed through the clouds and now stood on the last stage before our goal.

At this point the storm attacked us with all its might. However, in spite of the storm and the fatigue, my fear of the mountain had dissipated with the clouds. I was quite sure of myself. Over there lay the main summit, almost near enough to touch, and at this precise moment I was sure we were going to do it. Reinhold, too, told me later: "This was the moment in which I was convinced of the success of our adventure."

A sort of joyful intoxication overcame the two of us. We looked at each other – and shrank back. From Reinhold's appearance I could only conclude that my own was very similar. His face was contorted in a grimace, his mouth wide open while he gasped panting for air. Icicles hung in his beard. His face was almost without human traits. Our physical reserves were exhausted. We were so utterly spent that we scarcely had the strength to go ten paces in one go. Again and again we had to stop, but nothing in the world could have held us back now.

We had roped ourselves together because the Summit Ridge, as Hillary has already described it, was densely covered in cornices. It is true, however, that in an emergency a rope would not have helped us.

We crawled forwards at a snail's pace, trusting to instinct alone. The sun glistened on the snow, and the sky above the summit was of such an intense blue that it seemed almost black. We were very close to the sky, and it was with our own strength alone that we had arrived up here at the seat of the gods. Reinhold signified to me with a movement of his hand that he wanted to go on ahead. He wanted to film me climbing up over the ridge, with the bubbling sea of clouds below.

To do this he had to take off his snow-goggles in order to focus the camera better. It occurred to me that his eyes looked inflamed, but I thought nothing more of it, no more than he did. Our altitude was now 8,700 metres, and we had obviously reached a point in which normal brain functions had broken down, or at least were severely limited. Our attentiveness and concentration declined; our instinct no longer reacted as reliably as before; the capacity for clear logical thinking had also apparently been lost. I only thought in sensations and loose associations, and slowly I was overcome by the feeling that this threatening fearful mountain could be a friend.

Today I am certain that it is in these positive and friendly sensations that the real danger on Everest lies. When one approaches the summit, one no longer perceives the hostile, the absolutely deadly atmosphere. I have probably never been so close to death as I was during that last hour before reaching the summit. The urgent compulsion to descend again, to give in to fatigue, which had overcome me already in Camp V, had disappeared. I was now feeling the complete opposite. I had been seized by a sense of euphoria. I felt somehow light and relaxed, and believed that nothing could happen to me. At this altitude the boundaries between life and death are fluid. I wandered along this narrow ridge and perhaps for a few seconds I had gone beyond the frontier which divides life from death. By a piece of good fortune I was allowed to return. I would not risk it a second time, my reason forbids me to gamble with my life in such a way again.

In spite of all my euphoria, I was physically completely finished. I was no longer walking of my own free will, but mechanically, like an automaton. I seemed to step outside myself, and had the illusion that another person was walking in my place. This other person arrived at the Hillary Step, that perilous 25-metre-high ridge gradient, and then climbed and pulled himself up in the footsteps of his predecessors. He had one foot in Tibet and the other in Nepal. On the left side there was a 2,000-metre descent to Nepal; on the right the wall dropped 4,000 metres down towards China. We were alone, this other person and myself. Although he was connected to me by the short piece of rope, Reinhold no longer existed.

This feeling of being outside myself was interrupted for only a few moments. Cramp in my right hand bent my fingers together, and tore me violently back to reality. I was attacked by a suffocating fear of death. "Now I've had it." This thought went through my head, "Now the lack of oxygen is beginning its deadly work." I massaged my right forearm and bent my fingers back, and then the cramp eased.

From then on I prayed, "Lord God, let me go up right to the top. Give me the power to remain alive, don't let me die up here." I crawled on my elbows and knees and prayed more fervently than I have ever done in my life before. It was like a dialogue with a higher being. Again I saw myself crawling up, below me, beside me, higher and higher. I was being pushed up to the heights, and then suddenly I was up again on my own two feet: I was standing on the summit. It was 1.15 on the afternoon of 8 May 1978.

And then suddenly Reinhold was with me too, still carrying his camera and the three-legged Chinese surveying instrument. We had arrived. We embraced each other. We sobbed and stammered and could not keep calm. The tears poured from under my goggles into my beard, frozen on my cheeks. We embraced each other again and again. We pressed each other close. We stepped back at arm's length and again fell round each other's necks, laughing and crying at the same time. We were redeemed and liberated, freed at last from the inhuman compulsion to climb on.

After the crying and the sense of redemption, came the emptiness and sadness, the disappointment. Something had been taken from me; something that had been very important to me. Something which had suffused my whole being had evaporated, and I now felt exhausted and hollow. There was no feeling of triumph or victory. I saw the surrounding summits, Lhotse, Cho Oyu. The view towards Tibet was obscured by clouds. I knew that I was standing now on the highest point in the whole world. But, somehow, it was all a matter of indifference to me. I just wanted to get home now, back to that world from which I had come, and as fast as possible.

Solo

Reinhold Messner

Messner was born in the Austrian Tyrol in 1944. One of the greatest mountaineers of all time Messner was, with Peter Habeler (see "Only the Air That We Breathe" p. 452), the first to summit Everest without oxygen. In 1980 Messner came back to Everest, this time to attempt the summit solo. Again, he disdained the use of oxygen.

Half an hour later I am again in the tent with Nena. Already absent in spirit I prepared my body for the days of utmost exertion. I drink and eat, and sleep in between. In the tent the temperature is pleasant. The ventilation flap and entrance are open.

This time I have myself under control. I give fear no chance from the outset. The most dangerous part of the route, the ascent to the North Col, I know already, and as far as that is concerned I could only get stuck in the snow or lose myself in the mist, but not perish. The weather is fine, there will be no mist! My self-control costs energy. I sense how keyed-up my whole body is. Even during the night I have to force myself to lie quietly. Only twice do I look out at the weather. It is fine but the air is too warm. In the blue of the night Mount Everest stands over me like a magic mountain. No pondering, no asking why, I prepare myself with every fibre of my being for the big effort.

When it is time to get up I pick up socks, boots, breeches and top clothes like a sleep-walker. Each movement is quick and sure as if I had practised them a hundred times. No wasted movement.

In front of the tent I stretch myself, sniff the night air. Then I continue my ascent of the previous day. I am soon well up. Nena has remained down below. I reach the ice hollow and pick up the rucksack.

[*Nena:*] 18 August 1980. Yes, he has gone! A tender kiss on the lips was all. Just once. When Reinhold kisses me it is full of meaning. I call after him: "I shall be thinking of you!" He didn't hear me properly or didn't want to hear me. His voice sounded absent-minded, as he asked back: "What?" He was a bit disturbed because the night had been warmer than usual. He was much afraid that the snow would have become too soft. So what I called after him in the still morning must for him have been irrelevant. So as not to hold him up any more I said simply: "Bye, bye". And back comes his answer: "Bye, bye!" Empty words hanging in the air. What experiences will he have? What sort of change will take place in him, in me?

[*1,300 metres higher*] The snow suddenly gives way under me and my headlamp goes out. Despairingly I try to cling on in the snow, but in vain. The initial reaction passes. Although it is pitch-dark I believe I can see everything: at first snow crystals, then blue-green ice. It occurs to me that I am not wearing crampons. I know what is happening but nevertheless remain quite calm. I am falling into the depths and experience the fall in slow-motion, strike the walls of the widening crevasse once with my chest, once with the rucksack. My sense of time is interrupted, also my perception of the depth of the drop. Have I been falling only split seconds or is it minutes? I am completely weightless, a torrent of warmth surges through my body.

Suddenly I have support under my feet again. At the same time I know that I am caught, perhaps trapped for ever in this crevasse. Cold sweat beads my forehead. Now I am frightened. "If only I had a radio with me" is my first thought. I could call Nena. Perhaps she would hear me. But whether she could climb the 500 metres up to me and let a rope down to me in the crevasse is more than questionable. I have consciously committed myself to this solo ascent without a radio, and discussed it many times before starting.

I finger my headlamp and suddenly everything is bright. It's working! I breathe deeply, trying not to move at all. Also, the snow surface on which I am standing is not firm. Like a thin, transparent bridge it hangs fragile between both walls of the crevasse. I put my head back and see some eight metres above the tree trunk-sized hole through which I have fallen. From the bit of black sky above a few far, far distant stars twinkle down at me. The sweat of fear breaks from all my pores, covers my body with a touch which is as icy as the iridescent blue-green ice walls between which I am imprisoned. Because they converge obliquely above me I have no chance of climbing up them. With my headlamp I try to light up the bottom of the crevasse; but there is no end to be seen. Just a black hole to the left and right of me. The snow bridge which has stopped my fall is only one square metre large.

I have goose-pimples and shiver all over. The reactions of my body, however, are in stark contrast to the calm in my mind: there is no fear at the prospect of a new plunge into the bottomless depths, only a presentiment of dissolving, of evaporation. At the same time my mind says, that was lucky! For the first time I experience fear as a bodily reflex without psychological pain in the chest. My only problem is how to get out again. Mount Everest has become irrelevant. I seem to myself like an innocent prisoner. I don't reproach myself, don't swear. This pure, innocent feeling is inexplicable. What determines my life at this moment I do not know. I promise to myself I will descend, I will give up, if I come out of this unhurt. No more solo eight-thousanders!

My sweaty fear freezes in my hair and beard. The anxiety in my bones disappears the moment I set my body in motion, as I try to get my crampons out of the rucksack. But at each movement the feeling of falling again comes over me, a feeling of plunging into the abyss, as if the ground were slowly giving way.

Then I discover a ramp running along the crevasse wall on

the valley side, a ledge the width of two feet in the ice which leads obliquely upwards and is full of snow. That is the way out! Carefully I let myself fall forward, arms outstretched, to the adjoining crevasse wall. For a long moment my body makes an arch between the wedged snow block and the slightly over-hanging wall above me. Carefully I straddle across with the right foot, make a foothold in the snow which has frozen on the ledge on this crevasse wall on the downhill side. I transfer weight to the step. It holds. The insecure spot I am standing on is thus relieved. Each of these movements I instinctively make as exactly as in a rehearsed ballet. I try to make myself lighter. Breathing deeply my whole body identifies itself with the new position, I am for a moment, a long, life-determining moment, weightless. I have pushed myself off from the snow bridge with the left foot, my arms keep me in balance, my right leg supports my body. The left foot can get a grip. Relieved deep-breathing. Very carefully I move – face to the wall – to the right. The right foot gropes for a new hold in the snow, the left boot is placed precisely in the footstep which the right has vacated a few seconds before. The ledge becomes broader, leads obliquely upwards to the outside. I am saved!

In a few minutes I am on the surface – still on the valley side to be sure – but safe. I am a different person, standing there rucksack on my shoulders, ice axe in my hand as if nothing had happened. I hesitate for a moment longer, consider what I did wrong. How did this fall happen? Perhaps my left foot, placed two centimetres above the underlying edge of the crevasse, broke through as I tried to find a hold with the right on the opposite wall.

Down below in the crevasse I had decided to turn round, give up, if I got out unharmed. Now that I am standing on top I continue my ascent without thinking, unconsciously, as if I were computer-programmed . . .

Higher up above, I know from experience, it will be only willpower that forces the body from complete lethargy for another step. This sort of snail's pace compels me to rest now for some minutes every thirty paces, with longer rests sitting down every two hours. As the air up here contains only a third of the usual quantity of oxygen I climb as the Sherpas do.

I climb and rest, rest and climb. I know that I shall feel comparatively well as soon as I sit down but put off this compelling feeling minute by minute. I must be careful to avoid any harsh irritation of the respiratory tracts. The bronchial tubes and throat are my weakest points. I know it. And already I sense some hoarseness. So I am doubly glad that on this windy mountain hardly a breeze is blowing today. A steep rise now costs me more energy than I thought. From below, going over it by eye, I supposed it would require five rest stops. Meanwhile it has become eight or nine and I am still not on top. There, where it becomes flatter, something like deliverance awaits me. I don't want to sit down until I am over the rounded top . . .

While climbing I watch only the foot making the step. Otherwise there is nothing. The air tastes empty, not stale, just empty and rough. My throat hurts. While resting I let myself droop, ski sticks and legs take the weight of my upper body. Lungs heave. For a time I forget everything. Breathing is so strenuous that no power to think remains. Noises from within me drown out all external sounds. Slowly with the throbbing in my throat will power returns.

Onwards. Another thirty paces. How this ridge fools me! Or is it my eyes? Everything seems so close, and is then so far. After a standing rest stop I am over the top. I turn round, let myself drop on the snow. From up here I gaze again and again at the scenery, at the almost endless distance. In the pastel shades of the ranges lies something mystical. It strengthens the impression of distance, the unattainable, as if I had only dreamed of this Tibet, as if I had never been here. But where I am now, I have been already, that much I know . . .

The forward-thrusting impulse in climbing is often referred to as aggression; I prefer to call it curiosity or passion. Now all that has gone. My advance has its own dynamic force, fifteen paces, breathe, propped on the ski sticks which are inwardly and upwardly adjusted. With the knowledge that God is the solution. I confess that in moments of real danger something acts as a defense mechanism; it aids survival, but evaporates as soon as the threat is past. I am not at this moment under threat. It is all so peaceful here around me. I am not in any hurry. I cannot go any faster. I submit to this realization as to a law of Nature . . .

What disquiets me is the weather. No wind. The sun burns. Clouds press in from the south. Like wedges they push their grey white masses northwards. Yes, there is no doubt; the monsoon storms are sending out their scouts . . .

I am on the best route to the summit. The going is at times tiring, at times agony, it all depends on the snow conditions. The downward-sloping slabs luckily lie buried beneath a layer of neve and up to now I have been able to go round all the rock outcrops. I can see the North-East Ridge above me, but know that at the moment nothing of the pioneers can be found there. Mallory and Irvine climbed along this ridge, exactly on its edge. That is no guess. I am convinced that Odell saw them on the "first step", on that knob which rises out of the line of the ridge. I know now that they failed on the "second step". In the deep trough above me Mallory and Irvine lie buried in the monsoon snow. This hunch absorbs me like an old fairytale and I can think about it without dread . . . "First" and "second step" now lie above me. There Mallory and Irvine live on. The fate of the pair is now free from all speculation and hopes. It is alive in me. I cannot tell whether I see it as on a stage or in my mind's eye. At all events it is happening in my life – as if it belonged to it . . .

I am there. The ridge is flat. Where is the summit? Groaning I stand up again, stamp the snow down. With ice axe, arms and upper body burrowing in the snow, I creep on, keeping to the right. Ever upwards.

When I rest I feel utterly lifeless except that my throat burns when I draw breath. Suddenly it becomes brighter. I turn round and can see down into the valley. Right to the bottom where the glacier flows. Breathtaking! Automatically I take a few photographs. Then everything is all grey again. Completely windless.

Once more I must pull myself together. I can scarcely go on. No despair, no happiness, no anxiety. I have not lost the mastery of my feelings, there are actually no more feelings. I consist only of will. After each few metres this too fizzles out in an unending tiredness. Then I think nothing, feel nothing. I let myself fall, just lie there. For an indefinite time I remain completely irresolute. Then I make a few steps again.

At most it can only be another ten metres up to the top! To the left below me project enormous cornices. For a few moments I spy through a hole in the clouds the North Peak far below me. Then the sky opens out above me too. Oncoming shreds of cloud float past nearby in the light wind. I see the grey of the clouds, the black of the sky and the shining white of the snow surface as one. They belong together like the stripes of a flag. I must be there!

Above me nothing but sky. I sense it, although in the mist I see as little of it as the world beneath me. To the right the ridge still goes on up. But perhaps that only seems so, perhaps I deceive myself. No sign of my predecessors.

It is odd that I cannot see the Chinese aluminium survey tripod that has stood on the summit since 1975. Suddenly I am standing in front of it. I take hold of it, grasp it like a friend. It is as if I embrace my opposing force, something that absolves and electrifies at the same time. At this moment I breathe deeply . . .

Like a zombie, obeying an inner command, I take some photographs. A piece of blue sky flies past in the background. Away to the south snow cornices pile up, which seem to me to be higher than my position. I squat down, feeling hard as stone. I want only to rest a while, forget everything. At first there is no relief. I am leached, completely empty. In this emptiness nevertheless something like energy accumulates. I am charging myself up.

Touching the Void

Joe Simpson

In June 1985 two British climbers, Joe Simpson and Simon Yates, set out to ascend the unclimbed West Face of the 6,400-m (21,000-ft) Siula Grande in the Peruvian Andes. Simpson and Yates achieved the summit but then disaster struck; first Simpson broke his leg, then fell off an overhang while being lowered on a rope by Yates.

T he wind swung me in a gentle circle. I looked at the crevasse beneath me, waiting for me. It was big. Twenty feet wide at least. I guessed that I was hanging fifty feet above it. It stretched along the base of the ice cliff. Below me it was covered with a roof of snow, but to the right it opened out and a dark space yawned there. Bottomless, I thought idly. No. They're never bottomless. I wonder how deep I will go? To the bottom . . . to the water at the bottom? God! I hope not!

Another jerk. Above me the rope sawed through the cliff edge, dislodging chunks of crusty ice. I stared at it stretching into the darkness above. Cold had long since won its battle. There was no feeling in my arms and legs. Everything slowed and softened. Thoughts became idle questions, never answered. I accepted that I was to die. There was no alternative. It caused me no dreadful fear. I was numb with cold and felt no pain; so senselessly cold that I craved sleep and cared nothing for the consequences. It would be a dreamless sleep. Reality had become a nightmare, and sleep beckoned insistently; a black hole calling me, pain-free, lost in time, like death.

My torch beam died. The cold had killed the batteries. I saw stars in a dark gap above me. Stars, or lights in my head. The storm was over. The stars were good to see. I was glad to see them again. Old friends come back. They seemed far away; further than I'd ever seen them before. And bright: you'd think them gemstones hanging there, floating in the air above. Some moved, little winking moves, on and off, on and off, floating the brightest sparks of light down to me.

Then, what I had waited for pounced on me. The stars went out, and I fell. Like something come alive, the rope lashed violently against my face and I fell silently, endlessly into nothingness, as if dreaming of falling. I fell fast, faster than thought, and my stomach protested at the swooping speed of it. I swept down, and from far above I saw myself falling and felt nothing. No thoughts, and all fears gone away. So this is it!

A whoomphing impact on my back broke the dream, and the snow engulfed me. I felt cold wetness on my cheeks. I wasn't stopping, and for an instant blinding moment I was frightened. Now, the crevasse! Ahhh . . . NO!!

The acceleration took me again, mercifully fast, too fast for the scream which died above me . . .

The whitest flashes burst in my eyes as a terrible impact whipped me into stillness. The flashes continued, bursting electric flashes in my eyes as I heard, but never felt, the air rush from my body. Snow followed down on to me, and I registered its soft blows from far away, hearing it scrape over me in a distant disembodied way. Something in my head seemed to pulse and fade, and the flashes came less frequently. The shock had stunned me so that for an immeasurable time I lay numb, hardly conscious of what had happened. As in dreams, time had slowed, and I seemed motionless in the air, unsupported, without mass. I lay still, with open mouth, open eyes staring into blackness, thinking they were closed, and noting every sensation, all the pulsing messages in my body, and did nothing.

I couldn't breathe. I retched. Nothing. Pressure pain in my chest. Retching, and gagging, trying hard for the air. Nothing. I felt a familiar dull roaring sound of shingles on a beach, and relaxed. I shut my eyes, and gave in to grey fading shadows. My chest spasmed, then heaved out, and the roaring in my head suddenly cleared as cold air flowed in.

I was alive.

A burning, searing agony reached up from my leg. It was bent beneath me. As the burning increased so the sense of living became fact. Heck! I couldn't be dead and feel that! It kept burning, and I laughed – Alive! Well, fuck me! – and laughed again, a real happy laugh. I laughed through the burning, and kept laughing hard, feeling tears rolling down my face. I couldn't see what was so damned funny, but I laughed anyway. Crying and laughing at high pitch as something uncurled within me, something tight and twisted in my guts that laughed itself apart and left me.

I stopped laughing abruptly. My chest tightened, and the tension took hold again.

What stopped me?

I could see nothing. I lay on my side, crumpled strangely. I moved an arm cautiously in an arc. I touched a hard wall. Ice! It was the wall of the crevasse. I continued the search, and suddenly felt my arm drop into space. There was a drop close by me. I stifled the urge to move away from it. Behind me I felt my legs lying against a slope of snow. It also sloped steeply beneath me. I was on a ledge, or a bridge. I wasn't slipping, but I didn't know which way to move to make myself safe. Face down in the snow I tried to gather my confused ideas into a plan. What should I do now?

Just keep still. That's it . . . *don't move* . . . Ah!

I couldn't stop myself. Pain in my knee jolted through me, demanding movement. I had to get my weight off it. I moved, and slipped. Every muscle gripped down at the snow – *DON'T MOVE*.

The movement slowed, then stopped. I gasped, having held my breath for too long. Reaching out again I felt my hand touch the hard ice wall. Then I groped for the ice hammer attached to a lanyard of thin cord clipped to my harness. Fumbling in the dark, I found the cord running tightly away from me and pulled it, bringing the hammer up out of the drop in front of me. I had to hammer an ice screw into the wall without pushing myself off the ledge I was perched on.

It proved harder than I expected. Once I had found the last remaining screw attached to my harness I had to twist round and face the wall. My eyes had adjusted to the darkness. Starlight and the moon glimmering through my entry hole in the roof above gave enough light for me to see the abysses on either side of me. I could see grey-shadowed ice walls and the stark blackness of the drops, too deep for the light to penetrate. As I began to hammer the screw into the ice I tried to ignore the black space beyond my shoulder. The hammer blows echoed around the ice walls, and from deep below me, from the depths of blackness at my shoulder, I heard second and third echoes drift up. I shuddered. The black space held untold horrors. I hit the screw, and felt my body slide sideways with each blow. When it was driven in to its hilt I clipped a karabiner through the eye and hurriedly searched for the rope at my waist. The black spaces menaced and my stomach knotted in empty squeezing clenches.

I hauled myself into a half-sitting position close to the wall, facing the drop on my left. My legs kept slipping on the snow so that I had constantly to shuffle back to the wall. I dared not let go of the ice screw for more than a few seconds, but my fingers needed a lot longer to tie the knot. I swore bitterly each time I made a mess of the knot and feverishly tried again. I couldn't see the rope, and although normally I could tie the knot blindfold, I was now hampered by frozen hands. I couldn't feel the rope well enough to thread it back on itself and form the knot. After six attempts I was at the point of tears. I dropped the rope. Reaching for it I slipped forward towards the drop and lunged back scrabbling at the wall for the screw. My mitt slipped across the wall, and I began to fall backwards. I clawed at the ice trying to get my fingers to grip through the mitts, and then felt the screw hit my hand. My fingers locked round it, and the fall stopped. I stayed motionless, staring at the black hole in front of me.

After several abortive attempts suddenly I found that I had tied a knot of sorts. I held it close to my face and looked up through it at the dim light shining through the entry hole in the roof above. I could see the bulge of the knot, and above it the loop I had been struggling to tie. I chuckled excitedly, feeling ridiculously pleased with myself, and clipped it to the ice screw, smiling foolishly into the darkness. I was safe from the black spaces.

I relaxed against the comforting tightness of the rope and looked up at the small hole in the roof, where the sky was cloudless, packed with stars, and moonlight was adding its glow to their bright sparkle. The screwed-up tension in my stomach flowed away, and for the first time in many hours I began to order my mind into normal thoughts. I'm only, what . . . fifty feet down this crevasse. It's sheltered. I can get out in the morning if I wait for Simon . . .

"SIMON!?"

I spoke his name aloud in a startled voice. The word echoed softly back. It hadn't occurred to me that he might be dead, and as I thought about what had happened the enormity of it struck me. Dead? I couldn't conceive of him dead, *not now, not after I've survived*. The chill silence of the crevasse came over me; the feel of tombs, of space for the lifeless, coldly impersonal. No one had ever been here. Simon, dead? Can't be! I'd have heard him, seen him come over the cliff. He would have come on to the rope, or down here.

I began to giggle again. Despite my efforts I couldn't prevent it, and the echoes bounced back at me from the ice walls, sounding cracked and manic. It became so that I couldn't work out whether I was laughing or sobbing. The noises that returned from the darkness were distorted and inhuman, cackling echoes rolling up and around me. I giggled more, listened and giggled again, and for a moment forgot Simon, and the crevasse, and even my leg. I sat, hunched against the ice wall, laughing convulsively, and shivering. It was the cold. Part of me recognized this; a calm rational voice in my head told me it was the cold and the shock. The rest of me went quietly mad while this calm voice told me what was happening and left me feeling as if I were split in two – one half laughing, and the other looking on with unemotional objectivity. After a time I realized it had all stopped, and I was whole again. I had shivered some warmth back, and the adrenalin from the fall had gone.

I searched in my rucksack for the spare torch battery I knew was there. When I had fitted it, I switched on the beam and looked into the black space by my side. The bright new beam cut down through the blackness and lit ice walls that danced away down into depths my torch couldn't reach. The ice caught the light, so that it gleamed in blue, silver and green reflections, and I could see small rocks frozen into the surface dotted the walls at regular intervals. They glistened wetly as I swept the beam down the smooth scalloped dimples. I swallowed nervously. By the light I could see down into 100 feet of space. The walls, twenty feet apart, showed no sign of narrowing. I could only guess at how many hundreds of feet the blackness beyond my torch was hiding. In front of me the opposite wall of the crevasse reared up in a tangle of broken ice blocks and fifty feet above me they arched over to form a roof. The slope to my right fell away steeply for about thirty feet, after which it disappeared. Beyond it lay a drop into darkness.

The darkness beyond the light gripped my attention. I could guess what it hid, and I was filled with dread. I felt trapped, and looked quickly around me for some break in the walls. There was none. Ice flashed light back from hard blank walls, or else the beam was swallowed by the impenetrable blackness of the holes on either side. The roof covered the crevasse to my right and fell down in frozen chaos to my left, blocking the open end of the crevasse from my view. I was in a huge cavern of snow and ice. Only the small black hole above, winking starlights at me, gave any view of another world, and unless I climbed the blocks it was as unreachable as the stars.

I turned the torch off to save the batteries. The darkness seemed more oppressive than ever. Discovering what I had fallen into hadn't cleared my mind. I was alone. The silent emptiness, and the dark, and the star-filled hole above, mocked my thoughts of escape. I could only think of Simon. He was the only chance of escape, but somehow I was convinced that if he was not dead, then he would think that I was. I shouted his name as loud as I could, and the sound jumped back at me, and then faded in dying echoes in the holes below me. The sound would never be heard through the walls of snow and ice. The roof was fifty feet above me. On the rope I had hung at least fifty feet above the roof. Simon would see the huge open side of the crevasse, and the cliff, and he would know at once that I was dead. You can't fall that far and survive. That's what he would think. I knew it. I would think the same if I were in his place. He would see the endless black hole and know that I had died in it. The irony of falling 100 feet and surviving unscathed was almost unbearable.

I swore bitterly, and the echoes from the darkness made it a futile gesture. I swore again, and kept swearing, filling the chamber with angry obscenities which cursed me back in echoes. I screamed frustration and anger until my throat dried, and I could shout no more. When I was silent I tried to think of what would happen. If he looks in he will see me. He might even hear me. Maybe he heard me just then? He won't leave unless he's sure. How do you know he's not dead already? Did he fall with me? Find out . . . pull the rope!

I tugged on the loose rope. It moved easily. When I turned my torch on I noticed it hanging down from the hole in the roof. It hung in a slack curve. I pulled again and soft snow flurried on to me. I pulled steadily, and as I did so I became excited. This was a chance to escape. I waited for the rope to come tight. I wanted it to come tight. It kept moving easily. It was strange to want the weight of Simon's body to come on to the rope. I had instantly found a way to get out, and it meant only that. When Simon had fallen he would have swept out and clear of the crevasse. So he must have hit the slope and stopped. He would be dead. He must be after that fall. When the rope comes tight I can Prussik up it. His body will anchor it solidly. Yes. That's it . . .

I saw the rope flick down, and my hopes sank. I drew the slack rope to me, and stared at the frayed end. Cut! I couldn't take my eyes from it. White and pink nylon filaments sprayed out from the end.

With Simpson's weight pulling him off and avalanching snow pushing him off the mountain, Yates had cut the rope to Simpson. It was that or die with him.

Yates made it back to base camp. So, against all the odds, did Simpson. With a sheer eighty-foot wall above him, Simpson took the terrifying decision of going further down into the crevasse to see if there was another way out. There was: a snow slope which led him back up to the surface. His ordeal was not yet over, however, for he then had to push himself, seated, over miles of glacier and through snow storms. Three days after falling, Simpson, delirious, reached base camp too.

Escape

Stephen Venables

Stephen Venables was the lone British climber on a 1988 American expedition that forced a new route up Everest's Kangshung Face. Only Venables – who climbed without oxygen – reached the summit. He did so behind schedule, resulting in an open bivouac at 8,500 m (27,900 ft) on the night of 12 May. The next morning he met up with team mates Robert Anderson and Ed Webster, but the descent took an ominous turn as the effects of altitude, frost-bite and exhaustion gripped.

I knew that this was all wrong. It was now the afternoon of 14 May and we had spent almost four days above 8,000 metres. We had broken the rules and we were asking for trouble. We should have left early that morning to descend all the way to Camp I, but now we would be pushed even to reach Camp II before dark.

It was nearly 4 p.m. when we eventually left. A combination of laziness and the intention of glissading most of the way down meant that we did not bother to rope up. We did not have the strength to take the tents we had carried up from Camp II and left them standing on the bleak plateau; we would have to manage without them when we got down to the Flying Wing. I left my Therma-Rest, my spare mittens, my down sleeping boots and the windsuit which had saved my life two days earlier.

I could manage without it now and I had to keep weight to a minimum. Before he left, Ed asked, "What shall we do with this?"

"Ah – the mail packet. Perhaps the Australians will wander over here and pick it up, if they're still on the mountain."

"I'll leave it here in the tent. You never know, even if no one picks it up now, the tent might still be standing in the autumn, when the next lot comes up here. Right, I'm going. Make sure you and Robert come soon." He left quickly, determined to escape to a safer altitude.

Robert was still nurturing his last few ounces of gas, making one final brew of tepid water. I concentrated on my crampons. When they were safely on my feet I sat drinking half a pan of water, watching Robert staggering over to the edge of the plateau to start down the East Face. About ten minutes later I managed to stand up, put on my rucksack, pick up my ice axe, fit its safety loop over my wrist, put one foot forward and start walking.

I did not get very far before sinking to my knees to rest. That was better than sitting down, because it required less effort to stand up again from a kneeling position.

The afternoon had closed in, it was snowing and the South Col seemed even more forlorn than usual. I knew that if I failed to follow the other two I would die, but still I dallied, stopping to rest every few steps. When I reached the brink of the plateau and looked down the East Face Robert was resting far below. I saw the furrow where he had slid down and yelled, "Is it all right?" I took his garbled shout to mean "Yes" and jumped over the edge, landing in a sitting position and glissading off down the slope.

It was steeper than I remembered and I accelerated rapidly. I leaned hard over to one side, braking with the ice axe, but it made little difference. I was sliding faster and faster, then suddenly I hit submerged rocks. The ice axe skidded on the rocks; then it was plucked up in the air. I felt a sharp crack on my hipbone, I bounced faster and faster and then I was flung up in a rag doll somersault, spinning over and landing on my back to accelerate again. I was shooting down the slope, but now I was on snow again and could dig in my heels, braking desperately and finally coming to a gasping halt, coughing and spluttering in a shower of powder snow.

I lay there, battered, bruised and helpless, almost succumbing to terror before finding the courage to stand up. Luckily I had broken no bones but my one ice axe had been wrenched off my wrist, almost taking the Rolex with it, and now I had no tool to safeguard my descent. I was blinded by snow and frantically took off mittens to wipe clear my glasses, irretrievably dropping one mitten in the process. Now I had to split the remaining double mitten, wearing the flimsy down mitt on one hand and the outer on the other.

Robert was still a long way below watching impassively and Ed was far ahead, out of sight. Again I felt weak and helpless and in a fit of terror I yelled down, "Robert, wait. Please wait! Don't go without me." Then I started to kick shaky steps down towards him, holding my useless penguin arms out to the side.

Robert waited patiently and when I reached him he explained that he had also slid out of control. "I never saw those rocks at all. Then the snow below avalanched, carrying me all the way down here."

"Can I borrow your spare tool?" I asked. "You had two tools · with you, didn't you?"

"Sorry, I've lost both of them. The ice axe was ripped off my wrist and the spare ice hammer fell out of my holster. Now I just have this ski stick. I could break it in half . . ."

"No, it's all right."

We carried on down, Robert leaning on his ski stick, I holding out my mittened hands for balance. Dusk was falling as I followed the others' tracks across the big slope above the Flying Wing. That traverse seemed an interminable purgatory. Robert and Ed were now out of sight and I was sitting down every few steps, finding it harder and harder each time to stand up again. Snow was still falling and everything was cold and grey.

I suddenly remembered a winter evening in 1976, in Italy, returning exhausted to the roadhead after an abortive climb above the Val Ferret. I longed to be back there, taking off snowshoes and walking into the little bar where I had sat on a high stool and made myself gloriously dizzy with a tumblerful of dark sweet Vermouth and a cigarette. Then I thought about skiing in bad weather, succumbing to temptation and ordering an overpriced Swiss gluhwein. Which took me back to the soft green twilight of an evening in January 1986, camping amongst the primeval tree heathers of Bigo Bog in the Ruwenzori Mountains of East Africa. It had been a long wet day and after changing into dry clothes we had lit a fire to make mulled wine. Soon the air had been infused with the hot steam of wine, lemons, Cointreau and spices, sweetened with heaped spoons of sugar.

Darkness fell and there was no restorative hot drink. I wanted help to remove my sunglasses and I shouted out to Ed and Robert; but they were too far ahead, so I had to manage on my own, fumbling with wooden fingers to take off sunglasses, open the zipped lid of my rucksack and take out clear glasses and headtorch. Now I could see where I was going but I still felt lonely and frightened that I would not make it to Camp II. I kept shouting "Robert! Ed!" as I trudged laboriously over the little crevasse, past the marker wand, down into the dip, then back right, following the shelf under the Flying Wing, longing for warmth and rest and the reassuring company of my friends.

At last I saw their lights at the site of our Camp II. They had already fitted one of the cached gas cylinders to the burner Robert had carried down and the first brew was on the way. The instant coffee and milk which they had found in the Asians' tent two nights earlier tasted disgusting but we drank it anyway, hoping that it would give us some strength. For an hour I just lay in the snow, too feeble to get into my sleeping bag. When I eventually made the effort I kept boots and overboots on my feet, deciding now that it would be best to disturb the frozen toes as little as possible. I had left my inflated Therma-Rest on the South Col but my down sleeping bag kept me warm enough in the snow. Robert produced one or two more brews before we all fell into a deep sleep.

Thirst and a croaking cough woke me at dawn on 15 May. For ages I lay inert, coughing up foul lumps of phlegm from my throat. Then I tried to rouse Robert and Ed, begging them to light the stove. I tried several times but there was no response. In the end I had to do it myself. It was a big effort, leaning up on one elbow, scooping snow into the pan, setting the stove upright and struggling with my slightly frostbitten right thumb to work the flint of the lighter. Fifteen minutes later I had to replenish the snow, then I dozed again. Eventually we had a full pan of dirty tepid water but the stove fell over and we lost it. I started the laborious process again, forcing myself to repeat the whole exhausting routine, but after about forty-five minutes the stove fell over again.

The day was now well advanced. The weather was fine again and the open cave under the Flying Wing was a blazing suntrap. The heat was appalling, pressing down on us and intensifying our thirst. I managed to haul myself out of my sleeping bag and unzip the legs of my down bibs but I could not find the energy actually to take them off.

The third attempt to make a drink was successful. Then Robert's slurred zombie voice suggested that we should eat some food. The bag we had left here five days earlier contained chocolate, freeze-dried shrimp and clam chowder and potato powder. "No – I couldn't," croaked Ed. "Not the chowder."

"Can you make some potato then, Stephen?" Robert asked.

He managed to eat a reasonable helping, and I forced down a few spoonfuls but Ed could not face it. He was more concerned about getting off the mountain and kept urging, "We must go down! Soon we won't be able to move." We knew that he was right, but each of us was lost in his own private world of dreams, sprawled helpless in the stultifying heat, powerless to face reality.

"We should signal to the others."

"Yes, we should stand up so that they can see us."

"Maybe they saw our lights last night. Anyway, they'll see us when we start moving."

"We should go soon."

"But I want to sleep."

"We'll go soon."

"We need another drink. It's so hot!"

The heat grew worse as the East Face was covered by a layer of cloud, thin enough to let the sun through, but also just dense enough to reflect the white heat back onto the snow. We were imprisoned in a merciless shimmering glasshouse and it was only in the afternoon, when the cloud thickened and snow started to fall, that we felt cool enough to move.

Ed urged us on as usual. His frostbitten fingers had now ballooned into large painful blisters, but he still managed to be ready first. Again we had wasted nearly a whole day and it was after 3 p.m. when Ed set off, wading through the deep heavy snow below the Flying Wing. I followed last, nearly an hour later. It was snowing and visibility was bad. After I had descended about 150 metres I heard Ed's voice further below, shouting up through the cloud to Robert.

"This is scary – I can't see a thing and I've just slipped over a cliff. We're not going to make it to Camp I tonight. If we try and continue we're just going to get lost. We'll have to go back up to Camp II, where we've got shelter and gas. We'll just have to spend another night there and make sure we leave early in the morning."

I knew that Ed was right but groaned with despair at the horror of having to force my body uphill. It was a slow painful battle to climb back up that slope and Ed quickly overtook me. He had our one remaining ice axe and moved alongside me as I balanced my way up a fifty-degree bulge of ice which we had slipped over on the way down, sweeping off the snow. Ed would drive his pick into the ice as high as possible, then I would use it as a handhold to step up higher, before letting go and balancing on my tiptoe crampon points, with the mittened palms of my hands just pressed to the ice, while Ed moved up alongside and placed the axe higher. Robert was approaching the bulge from below and shouted gloomily, "What am I supposed to do?"

"I'll leave it here – halfway up!" Ed shouted encouragingly.

"Thanks a lot. How am I meant to reach it?"

"Jump – I suppose."

It was dark by the time Robert eventually joined us under the Flying Wing. Ed and I were sprawled once again in our sleeping bags and I was starting to melt snow. We had no tea, coffee, Rehydrate or sugar – nothing to flavour our water except the remains of the potato powder. After the first cup of water I promised to produce another solid meal of potato, knowing how desperately our bodies needed fuel, but the meal never materialized for I fell too soon into an exhausted sleep.

When we woke at dawn on 16 May, we knew that this was our last chance. If we stayed another night at this altitude with virtually no food we would probably become too weak to move. It was now five days since Paul had left us on the South Col. We knew that he and the others would be worried, but once again we were too apathetic to take advantage of the cloudless morning and stand up to wave; instead we lay hidden under the Flying Wing, reasoning that the others would see our tracks of the previous evening and realize that we were on the way down.

Ed's blistered fingers were now agonizing and Robert's finger tips, though less badly damaged, were also painful, so I prepared the morning water. Everything smelled and tasted disgusting and the other two refused to eat the chocolate-coated granola bars that I had found. However I managed to sit up and eat two bars, concentrating stubbornly on the unpleasant task and swilling them down with sips of dirty melted snow. All this took time and we failed to leave before the sun hit us. This time I found it even harder to struggle out of the stifling oven of my sleeping bag and the down bibs. Beside me, Ed looked like an old man. His face was lean and haggard, his hair hung lankly and the light had gone out of his eyes as he stared in horror at his swollen blistered fingers. His voice too was the dry croak of an old, old man, repeating over and over again, "We've got to go down. We *must* go down. If we don't go down today we're going to die."

Robert, like me, was almost silent, fighting his own private battle against lassitude, building himself up for the great effort of departure. Ed, the most sensitive member of the team, seemed more deeply affected by the trauma of our descent and actually said that it was going to take him a long time to get over the psychological shock of this experience. However, because he was so sensitive to the danger threatening us and because he so urgently needed to reach Mimi's medical help, he had become our leader.

The only help Ed could give us was his insistent croaks of encouragement. We were powerless to help each other physically and I thought with detachment how our situation was starting to resemble the 1986 tragedy on K2, when the storm finally cleared, allowing the Austrian climbers, Willi Bauer and Kurt Diemberger, to bully their companions into fleeing the hell of Camp IV, after eight days at nearly 8,000 metres feet had reduced them all to emaciated wrecks. Julie Tullis had already died in the storm. Alan Rouse was only semiconscious, incapable of moving, pleading deliriously for water. Diemberger and Bauer could do nothing and had to leave him lying in his tent. The other two Austrians, Immitzer and Wieser, collapsed in the snow soon after leaving the camp. The Polish woman, "Mrufka" Wolf, managed to keep going but died later that day on the fixed ropes. Only Bauer and Diemberger, both large heavy men with enormous bodily reserves, crawled down alive.

Our experience had not approached the horror of K2: we had only spent four days, not eight, above 8,000 metres; we had been hindered slightly by poor weather, but we had experienced nothing to compare with the horrendous storm on K2; we had failed to make adequate brews but we had at least been drinking something, our gas at Camp II was still not finished and there were further stocks at Camp I; nevertheless we were now in danger of re-enacting the K2 tragedy and as I lay flat on my back, delaying feebly the moment of departure, I realized how easy and painless it would be just to lie there until I died.

"Come on, you guys, we've got to move! It's clouding over already." Ed was right: it was only 9 a.m. and the clouds had arrived earlier today with their crippling greenhouse effect. I reached out for the things I wanted to take – cameras, torch, down bibs and jacket. The sleeping bag would have to stay here, like Ed's and Robert's. It seemed monstrous to litter the mountain with $1,500 worth of sleeping bags, but they weighed two and a half kilos each and the less weight we carried the greater chance we would have of reaching safety.

At 10 a.m. Ed was ready. Again he urged me to move. "Don't wait long, Stephen. You've got to get up and move: if you don't get down alive you won't be able to enjoy being famous." Then he left.

Robert made his final preparations, and I fitted my crampons. Everything was now ready but I wanted another rest so, while Robert set off, I sat on my rucksack. I sat there for nearly an hour, bent over with my elbows on my knees and my head cupped in my hands. My eyes were shut and I swayed slightly, almost falling asleep as I dreamed of life after Everest. Ed was right: life would be fun when I returned to earth. People would be surprised and pleased by our success. I would be so happy and everything would be so easy. I would be able to eat delicious food and I would have that sweet red Vermouth, with great crystals of ice and the essential sharpness of lemon. And I would drink orange juice, cool tumblers full of it, sitting in the green shade of a tree. That life was so close, so easily attainable; all I had to do was reach Advance base – just one more day of effort and then the others would take over.

I tried to stand up and failed. It was a feeble attempt and I told myself that next time I would succeed. After all, I *wanted* to descend, didn't I? I was just being a little lazy. I would have to concentrate a little harder on the task: lean forward, go down on my knees, shoulder the rucksack, stand up and away! Easy. Let's try now.

Nothing happened.

I began to worry. It was nearly an hour since Robert and Ed had left and I knew that they would not have the strength to climb back up for me. It was 11 a.m. and I had to leave now and catch up with them. I just had to take that simple action to save my life but I was finding it so hard. I was also frightened now that when I stood up my legs might be too weak to remain standing.

There was only one way to find out and with a final concentrated effort I started to move. This time it worked. I went down on my knees, reached round behind me and pulled the rucksack onto my shoulders. Now came the hardest part. I pressed a mittened hand to one knee, pushed up with the other knee, held out both hands for balance and stood up. I managed to stay upright and took a few wobbly penguin steps to the edge of the shelf under the Wing. It was so tempting to sink back down onto the shelf and fall asleep, but I forced my mind to concentrate on directing all energy to those two withered legs. The effort succeeded and I managed six faltering steps down the slope, sat back for a rest, then took six steps more, then again six steps. It was going to be a long tedious struggle, but I knew now that I was going to make it.

AFTERWORD
The Pleasures and Penalties of Mountaineering

A. F. Mummery

The British climber Albert Mummery was arguably the founder of modern Alpinism. Certainly he was the foremost mountaineer of the late-nineteenth century, counting among his first ascents the West Face of the Plan and Col des Courtes, these achieved despite myopia and congenital physical deformity. His book My Climbs in the Alps and Caucasus *published in 1894 became an instant classic of mountaineering literature, its ultimate chapter: "The Pleasures and Penalties of Mountaineering" being the most eloquent "defence" of mountaineering ever penned. Mummery died on an 1895 expedition to Nanga Parbat in Kashmir.*

Well-known climbers, whose opinions necessarily carry the greatest weight, have recently declared their belief that the dangers of mountaineering no longer exist. Skill, knowledge and textbooks have hurled them to the limbo of exploded bogies. I would fain agree with this optimistic conclusion, but I cannot forget that the first guide to whom I was ever roped, and one who possessed – may I say it? – more knowledge of mountains than is to be found even in the Badminton library, was none the less killed on the Brouillard Mont Blanc, and his son, more recently, on Koshtantau. The memory of two rollicking parties, comprising seven men, who one day in 1879 were climbing on the west face of the Matterhorn, passes with ghost-like admonition before my mind and bids me remember that of these seven, Mr Penhall was killed on the Wetterhorn, Ferdinand Imseng on the Macugnaga Monte Rosa, and Johann Petrus on the Fresnay Mont Blanc. To say that any single one of these men was less careful and competent, or had less knowledge of all that pertains to the climber's craft, than we who yet survive, is obviously and patently absurd. Our best efforts must sometimes be seconded by the great goddess of Luck; to her should the Alpine Club offer its vows and thanksgivings.

Indeed, if we consider for a moment the essence of the sport of mountaineering, it is obvious that it consists, and consists exclusively, in pitting the climber's skill against the difficulties opposed by the mountain. Any increase in skill involves, *pari passu*, an increase in the difficulties grappled with. From the Breuil ridge of the Matterhorn we pass on to the Dru, and from the Dru to the Aiguille de Grepon: or to take a yet wider range, from the Chamonix Mont Blanc to the same mountain by way of the Brenva Glacier and the Aiguille Blanche de Peteret. It can scarcely be argued that Bennen and Walter were less fit to grapple with the cliff above the "Linceul" than we moderns to climb the Grepon "crack"; or that Jacques Balmat was less able to lead up the "Ancien passage" than Emile Rey to storm the ghastly precipices of the Brenva Peteret. But if it be admitted that the skill of the climber has not increased relatively to the difficulties grappled with, it would appear to follow necessarily that climbing is neither more nor less dangerous than formerly.

It is true that extraordinary progress has been made in the art of rock climbing, and that, consequently, any given rock climb is much easier now than thirty years since, but the essence of the sport lies, not in ascending a peak, but in struggling with and overcoming difficulties. The happy climber, like the aged Ulysses, is one who has "drunk delight of battle with his peers", and this delight is only attainable by assaulting cliffs which tax to their utmost limits the powers of the mountaineers engaged. This struggle involves the same risk, whether early climbers attacked what we now call easy rock, or whether we moderns attack formidable rock, or whether the ideal climber of the future assaults cliffs which we now regard as hopelessly inaccessible. Doubtless my difference with the great authorities referred to above is, in the main, due to a totally different view of the *raison d'être* of mountaineering. Regarded as a sport, some danger is, and always must be, inherent in it; regarded as a means of exercise amongst noble scenery, for quasi-scientific pursuits, as the raw material for interesting papers, or for the purposes of brag and bounce, it has become as safe as the ascent of the Rigi or Pilatus was to the climbers of thirty years since. But these pursuits are not mountaineering in the sense in which the founders of the Alpine Club used the term, and they are not mountaineering in the sense in which the elect – a small, perchance even a dwindling body – use it now. To set one's utmost faculties, physical and mental, to fight some grim precipice, or force some gaunt, ice-clad gully, is work worthy of men; to toil up long slopes of screes behind a guide who can "lie in bed and picture every step of the way up with all the places for hand and foot", is work worthy of the fibreless contents of fashionable clothes, dumped with all their scents and ointments, starched linen and shiny boots, at Zermatt by the railway.

The true mountaineer is a wanderer, and by a wanderer I do not mean a man who expends his whole time in travelling to and fro in the mountains on the exact tracks of his predecessors – much as a bicyclist rushes along the turnpike roads of England – but I mean a man who loves to be where no human being has been before, who delights in gripping rocks that have previously never felt the touch of human fingers, or in hewing his way up ice-filled gullies whose grim shadows have been sacred to the mists and avalanches since "earth rose out of chaos". In other words, the true mountaineer is the man who attempts new ascents. Equally, whether he succeeds or fails, he delights in the fun and jollity of the struggle. The gaunt, bare slabs, the square, precipitous steps in the ridge, and the black, bulging ice of the gully, are the very breath of life to his being. I do not pretend to be able to analyze this feeling, still less to be able to make it clear to unbelievers. It must be felt to be understood, but it is potent to happiness and sends the blood tingling through the veins, destroying every trace of cynicism and striking at the very roots of pessimistic philosophy.

Our critics, curiously enough, repeat in substance Mr Ruskin's original taunt that we regard the mountains as greased poles. I must confess that a natural and incurable denseness of understanding does not enable me to feel the sting of this taunt. Putting aside the question of grease, which is offensive and too horrible for contemplation in its effects on knickerbockers – worse even than the structure-destroying edges and splinters of the Grepon ridge – I do not perceive the enormity or sin of climbing poles. At one time, I will confess, I took great delight in the art, and, so far as my experience extends, the taste is still widespread amongst English youth. It is possible, nay even probable, that much of the pleasure of mountaineering is derived from the actual physical effort and from the perfect state of health to which this effort brings its votaries, and, to this extent, may plausibly be alleged to be the mere sequence and development of the pole and tree climbing of our youth. The sting of the taunt is presumably meant to lurk in the implication that the climber is incapable of enjoying noble scenery; that, in the jargon of certain modern writers, he is a *"mere* gymnast". But why should a man be assumed incapable of enjoying aesthetic pleasures because he is also capable of the physical and non-aesthetic pleasures of rock climbing?

A well-known mountaineer asserts that the fathers of the craft did not regard "the overcoming of physical obstacles by means of muscular exertion and skill" as "the chief pleasure of mountaineering". But is this so? Can anyone read the great classic of mountaineering literature, *The Playground of Europe*, without feeling that the overcoming of these obstacles was a main factor of its author's joy? Can anyone read *Peaks, Passes and Glaciers* and the earlier numbers of the *Alpine Journal* without feeling that the various writers gloried in the technique of their craft? Of course the skilful interpolation of "chief" gives an opening for much effective dialectic, but after all, what does it mean? How can a pleasure which is seated in health and jollity and the "spin of the blood" be measured and compared with a purely aesthetic feeling? It would appear difficult to argue that as a man cultivates and acquires muscular skill and knowledge of the mountains, he correspondingly dwarfs and impairs the aesthetic side of his nature. If so, we magnify the weak-kneed and the impotent, the lame, the halt, and the blind, and brand as false the Greek ideal of the perfect man. Doubtless a tendency in this direction may be detected in some modern thought, but, like much else similarly enshrined, it has no ring of true metal. Those who are so completely masters of their environment that they can laugh and rollick on the ridges, free from all constraint of ropes or fear of danger, are far more able to appreciate the glories of the "eternal hills" than those who can only move in constant terror of their lives, amidst the endless chatter and rank tobacco smoke of unwashed guides.

The fact that a man enjoys scrambling up a steep rock in no way makes him insensible of all that is beautiful in Nature. The two sets of feelings are indeed wholly unconnected. A man may love climbing and care naught for mountain scenery; he may love the scenery and hate climbing; or he may be equally devoted to both. The presumption obviously is that those who are most attracted by the mountains and most constantly return to their fastnesses, are those who to the fullest extent possess both these sources of enjoyment – those who can combine the fun and frolic of a splendid sport with that indefinable delight which is induced by the lovely form, tone and colouring of the great ranges.

I am free to confess that I myself should still climb, even though there were no scenery to look at, even if the only climbing attainable were the dark and gruesome pot-holes of the York-shire dales. On the other hand, I should still wander among the upper snows, lured by the silent mists and the red blaze of the setting sun, even though physical or other infirmity, even though in after aeons the sprouting of wings and other angelic appendages may have sunk all thought of climbing and cragsmanship in the whelming past.

It is frequently assumed, even by those who ought to know better, that if mountaineering involves danger of any sort, it should never be indulged in – at all events by such precious individuals as the members of the English Alpine Club. Before considering this most pernicious doctrine, it is well to remember, that though the perils of mountaineering may not have been wholly dissipated into space by the lightning-like flashes of the Badminton and All England series, yet, nevertheless, these perils are not very great. With a single exception, the foregoing pages contain an account of every difficulty I have experienced which has seemed to render disaster a possible contingency. As my devotion to the sport began in 1871, and has continued with unabated vigour ever since, it will be evident that the climber's perils – in so far as a modest individual may regard himself as typical of the class – are extremely few and very rarely encountered. Such, however, as they have been, I would on no account have missed them. There is an educative and purifying power in danger that is to be found in no other school, and it is worth much for a man to know that he is not "clean gone to flesh pots and effeminacy". It may be admitted that the mountains occasionally push things a trifle too far, and bring before their votaries a vision of the imminence of dissolution that the hangman himself with all his paraphernalia of scaffold, gallows and drop could hardly hope to excel. But grim and hopeless as the cliffs may sometimes look when ebbing twilight is chased by shrieking wind and snow and the furies are in mad hunt along the ridges, there is ever the feeling that brave companions and a constant spirit will cut the gathering web of peril, *forsan et hœc olim meminisse juvabit*.

The sense of independence and self-confidence induced by the great precipices and vast silent fields of snow is something wholly delightful. Every step is health, fun and frolic. The troubles and cares of life, together with the essential vulgarity of a plutocratic society, are left far below – foul miasmas that cling to the lowest bottoms of reeking valleys. Above, in the clear air and searching sunlight, we are afoot with the quiet gods, and men can know each other and themselves for what they are. No feeling can be more glorious than advancing to attack some gaunt precipitous wall with "comrades staunch as the founders of our race". Nothing is more exhilarating than to know that the fingers of one hand can still be trusted with the lives of a party, and that the lower limbs are free from all trace of "knee-dissolving fear", even though the friction of one hobnail on an outward shelving ledge alone checks the hurtling of the body through thin air, and of the soul (let us hope) to the realms above.

I am of course aware that it is an age which cares little for the more manly virtues, and which looks askance at any form of sport that can, by any stretch of extremest imagination, be regarded as dangerous: yet since we cannot all, for most obvious reasons, take our delight "wallowing in slimy spawn of lucre", something may surely be urged in favour of a sport that teaches, as no other teaches, endurance and mutual trust, and forces men occasionally to look death in its grimmest aspect frankly and squarely in the face. For though mountaineering is not, perhaps, more dangerous than other sports, it undoubtedly brings home to the mind a more stimulating sense of peril; a sense, indeed, that is out of all proportion to the actual risk. It is, for instance, quite impossible to look down the tremendous precipices of the Little Dru without feeling in each individual nerve the utter disintegration of everything human which a fall must involve; and the contingency of such a fall is frequently brought before the mind – indeed, throughout the ascent, constant and strenuous efforts are needed to avoid it. The love of wager, our religious teachers notwithstanding, is still inherent in the race, and one cannot find a higher stake – at all events in these materialistic days, when Old Nick will no longer lay sterling coin against the gamester's soul – than the continuity of the cervical vertebrae; and this is the stake that the mountaineer habitually and constantly wagers. It is true the odds are all on his side, but the off-chance excites honesty of thought and tests how far decay has penetrated the inner fibre. That mountaineering has a high educational value, few, who have the requisite knowledge to form a fair judgment, would deny. That it has its evil side I frankly admit. None can look down its gloomy death-roll without feeling that our sport demands a fearful price.

Acknowledgments & Sources

The editor has made every effort to locate all persons having any rights in the selections appearing in this anthology and to secure permission from the holders of such rights. The editor apologises in advance for any errors or omissions inadvertently made. Queries regarding the use of material should be addressed to the editor c/o the publishers.

"Ladder Down the Sky" is an extract from *K2: The Savage Mountain* by Charles S. Houston and Robert H. Bates, McGraw-Hill Book Company, Inc., 1954. Copyright © 1954, 1979, 1997 by Charles S. Houston and Robert Bates.

"The Upper Tower" by Peter Boardman is an extract from *The Boardman Tasker Omnibus* by Peter Boardman and Joe Tasker, Hodder & Stoughton, 1995. Extract copyright © Peter Boardman 1978. Reprinted by permission of Hodder Headline.

"The Death Zone" is an extract from *On the Heights*, Walter Bonatti, Rupert Hart-Davis, 1964.

"The Loneliest Place on Earth" by Hermann Buhl is an extract from *Nanga Parbat*, Karl M. Herrligkoffer, Elek Books, 1954.

"Thin Air" is an extract from *Thin Air: Encounters in the Himalayas* by Greg Child, Patrick Stephens Ltd, 1988. Copyright © Greg Child 1988.

"The Climb" is an extract from *Total Alpinism* by Rene Desmaison, Granada Publishing, 1982. Copyright © 1973 Flammarion. Translation © 1982 Granada Publishing.

"The Gods Giveth, The Gods Take Away" is an extract from *Summits and Secrets* by Kurt Diemberger, George Allen & Unwin Ltd, 1971. English translation © 1971 George Allen & Unwin Ltd. Reprinted by permission of The Mountaineers, Seattle.

"Mirror, Mirror" by Ed Drummond is reprinted from *Ascent*, 1973. All rights reserved. Copyright © Ed Drummond and Sierra Club Books.

"The Void" is an extract from *The Untrodden Andes* by C. G. Egeler, Faber, 1955.

"White Spider" is an extract from *The White Spider* by Heinrich Harrer, Rupert Hart-Davis, 1959. Copyright © 1958 Ullstein AG Berlin. Translation copyright © 1959 Rupert Hart-Davis.

"Annapurna, Mon Amour" is an extract from *Annapurna* by Maurice Herzog, Jonathan Cape, 1952. Copyright © 1952, 1997 Maurice Herzog.

"The Ridge" is an extract from *Everest: The West Ridge*, Thomas F. Hornbein, Sierra Club, 1965. Copyright © 1965, 1980 Thomas F. Hornbein.

"The Devil's Thumb", is an extract from "The Devil's Thumb", *Eiger Dreams: Ventures Among Men and Mountains* by Jon Krakauer, Dell Publishing, 1990. Copyright © 1990 Jon Krakauer.

"Avalanche" by George Leigh Mallory is an extract from *The Assault on Mount Everest* by Brigadier-General Hon. C. G. Bruce CB, MVO, and other members of the expedition, Edward Arnold, 1923.

"The Pleasures and Principles of Mountaineering" is an extract from *My Climbs in the Alps and Caucasus*, A. F. Mummery, Basil Blackwell, 1936.

"The Storm" is an extract from *Cho Oyu* by Herbert Tichy, Methuen, 1957.

"The Hard Way" by Doug Scott and Dougal Haston is an extract from *Everest – The Hard Way*, Chris Bonnington, Hodder & Stoughton, 1976, Copyright © 1975, British Everest Expedition.

"Attack on Kangchenjunga" is an extract from *The Kanchenjunga Adventure* by F. S. Smythe, Gollancz, 1930.

"The Ascent of Nanda Devi" is an extract from *The Ascent of Nanda Devi* by H. W. Tilman, Cambridge University Press, 1937. Reprinted by permission of Bafon Wicks Publications, Joan A. Mullins and Pamela Davis.

"Aurora" by Jonathan Waterman is reprinted from *Ascent*, 1983.

"Triumph and Tragedy on The Matterhorn" is an extract from *The Ascent of the Matterhorn* by Edward Whymper, John Murray, 1880.

"Mischabel" is an extract from *On High Hills*, Geoffrey Winthrop Young, Methuen, 1927.

"We Had Found George Mallory" an extract from *The Lost Explorer* by Conrad Anker and David Roberts, Simon & Schuster (US), 1999. Copyright © 1999 Conrad Anker and David Roberts.

"Direttissima" is an extract from *I Chose to Climb* by Chris Bonington, Gollancz, 1966. Copyright © Chris Bonington 1966.

"Hope Lost" is an extract from *The Climb* by Anatoli Boukreev and G. Weston DeWalt, St Martin's Press, 1998. Copyright © Anatoli Boukreev and G. Weston.

DeWalt's "Only the Air That We Breathe" is an extract from *Impossible Victory* by Peter Habeler, Arlington, 1979. Copyright © 1979 Peter Habeler.

"Solo" is an extract from *Crystal Horizon: Everest the First Solo Ascent*, The Crowood Press, 1989. Copyright © 1989 Reinhold Messner.

"The Top of the World" is an extract from *Man of Everest* by Tenzing Norgay and James Ramsey Ullmann, G Harrap & Co. Ltd, 1958. Copyright © 1958 Tenzing Norgay and James Ramsey Ullmann.

"Between a Rock and a Hard Place" is an extract from *Between a Rock and a Hard Place* by Aron Ralston, Simon & Schuster UK Ltd/Atria Books, 2004. Copyright © 2004 Aron Ralston.

"The Death of Harsh Bahuguna" by Murray Sayle is from the *Sunday Times*, 2 May 1971. (Originally printed as "Sorry, Harsh, you've had it"). Reprinted by permission of News International Syndication.

"Touching the Void" is an extract from *Touching the Void* by Joe Simpson, Vintage, 2004. Copyright © 1988, 2004 Joe Simpson.

"Escape" is an extract from *Everest: Kangshung Face* by Stephen Venables, Hodder & Stoughton, 1989. Copyright © 1989 Stephen Venables.